AQUINAS & MARITAIN ON EVIL

AQUINAS & MARITAIN ON EVIL

Mystery and Metaphysics

EDITED BY JAMES G. HANINK

AMERICAN MARITAIN ASSOCIATION

Distributed by

THE CATHOLIC UNIVERSITY
OF AMERICA PRESS
Washington, D.C.

Manufactured in the United States of America

Distributed by the Catholic Univesity of America Press
620 Michigan Avenue, N.E., 240 Leahy Hall
Washington, D.C. 20064

Library of Congress Cataloging-in-Publication Data
Aquinas & Maritain on evil : mystery and metaphysics /
edited By James G. Hanink.
pages cm
Includes bibliographical references and index.
ISBN 978-0-9827119-4-1 (alk. paper)
1. Maritain, Jacques, 1882–1973.
2. Good and evil—Religious aspects—Christianity.
3. Thomas, Aquinas, Saint, 1225?–1274
I. Hanink, James G., editor of compilation.
II. Title: Aquinas and Maritain on evil.
B2430.M34A74 2013
231'.8—dc23
2013030295

CONTENTS

IV. EVIDENCE, PROBABILITY, AND PRUDENCE

V. TRUTH, FALSEHOOD, AND THE FUTURE OF MAN

Acknowledgements

I owe a debt of gratitude to Michael D. Torre, the longtime general editor of the American Maritain Association Publications. His expert assistance has been unflagging. To Robert J. Rose, Bishop Emeritus of the Diocese of Grand Rapids, Michigan, I owe a different kind of debt. It was he who introduced me to both Jacques and Raïssa Maritain when as young student I became interested in philosophy.

And to Elizabeth, as always, for whom *mil gracias* is only a start.

JAMES G. HANINK

Introduction

To Renew the Theory of Evil

While creatively drawing on St. Thomas Aquinas, Jacques Maritain made the problem of evil a life-long philosophical inquiry. Indeed, Maritain tells us in his *God and the Permission of Evil* that "If philosophers lived up to their calling in the new age into which we have entered, the crucial work for them would be to renew the theory of evil ... by examining it more profoundly."[1]

And why not? Exploring the problem of evil, indeed its profound mystery, comes near the heart of the Christian philosopher's vocation to seek a fuller understanding of the faith. If we join in that endeavor, we will struggle within a constricting web of near paradoxes. That struggle is, in part, to free ourselves. It will soon enough put us in mind of Job. With Job we will come to reflect on God's providence and the folly of conventional "wisdom." Our reflections will lead us to probe our experience of both good and evil and to try to understand something of their nature. In doing so, we will be searching out the origin of the evil that we ourselves bring about and from which we all suffer.

What dynamic, for example, could account for the savagery that Turner's *The Slave Ship*, an image of slaves jettisoned as cargo, so hauntingly portrays? And in response to what malignity did John Paul II beg the Mother of God to intercede for "the vast numbers of babies not allowed to be born" and for "the elderly and sick killed by indifference or out of misguided

1. Jacques Maritain, *God and the Permission of Evil,* translated by Joseph W. Evans (Milwaukee, Wisconsin: Bruce Publishing Co., 1966), 4.

mercy"?[2] In the end, might we come to see that evil reflects the collapse of the person, with an attendant denial of reason and freedom and responsibility? From this negation, this descent into nothingness, the believer realizes that only grace can restore us.

The several contributors to this volume, despite their differences, understand pure evil as a privation. It is a de-privation, a distortion of the good. From this perspective, it follows that in attempting to explain evil we must begin with that which is not evil. For is there not always some apparent good that leads to the free choice of evil? But the free choice of privation puts the evildoer into a kind of nothingness. And in this place, as Robert Spaemann tells it, on his own "no man can awaken."[3] The slaves who survived crossing the seas to be sold to masters in America inspired a slave trader to hymn to us all that neither slave nor master win their salvation. Rather, each of us must say "'Twas grace that saved a wretch like me."

I. Setting an Expansive Stage

Federico Tedesco's elegant discussion, "The Paradoxes of Evil as the *Rationis Exodus in Deum*," helps us to initiate our reflections on the multifaceted problem of evil. Yet even to initiate these reflections might give us pause. For does not the sometimes almost overwhelming presence of evil give rise to a scandal to human intelligence? Even to a paralyzing scandal? It might well seem that it does. But Tedesco tells us that this scandal could prove to be salutary. For the scandal is so provocative that it might well lead us to confront, once more, the metaphysics of being. If it does, and we grasp the theological significance of that confrontation, we might even be able to speak of a baptism in evil. Here, we might pause to ask if it is just such a baptism that can prepare us for life in these extraordinary times, a time of established *dis*order. But scandal there will be, for the problem of evil throws common sense into disarray, compels us to dare to do metaphysics, and—in the moral sphere—reminds us that Jesus the Christ invites us *not* to resist evil!

In his sobering "Job, our Contemporary," John Conley, SJ, gives us fresh evidence of his intellectual range. Conley is a playwright as well as a philos-

2. John Paul II, *Evangelium Vitae,* 106.

3. Robert Spaemann, *Persons: The Difference between 'Someone' and 'Something,'* translated by Oliver O'Donovan (Oxford: Oxford University Press, 2006), 218.

opher. (He notes that in 1940 Karol Wojtyla penned a play titled *Job*.) With a dramatist's verbal economy, Conley sketches a Job that we recognize as one who lives in our midst. How is it, then, that Job is among us? His treatment at Satan's hands plunges Job into depression and leads him to the edge of nihilism. And what of his friends? Their accusations force him into isolation. Job experiences the scandal of an evil that would altogether crush him and decisively obscure the reality of God. But in a time in which so many live *etsi Deus non daretur*, we have come to share Job's lot. We find sleep elusive; we fear isolation; we experience the temptation of nihilism. So did Job. And yet, with Job, we look for a nobility in suffering that only the Lord of History can promise. With Job as our contemporary, we can find our deepest identity, despite the false morality of friends who fail us and the secular culture that dismisses us. But, if we are to stand fast in the storm and scandal of evil, we must be willing to join in Job's embrace of the sometimes harsh mystery of God's love. Such is the lesson of Conley's self-described "projective eisegesis" of the Book of Job.

In recent decades, St. Thomas Aquinas's scriptural studies have finally come to receive something of the recognition they merit. This rich legacy of both Old Testament and New Testament exegesis is finding a new and appreciative audience. In this vein, Mary Catherine Sommers explores, with exquisite care, Thomas's work on Job. In her erudite study, "Topsy-Turvy: The Problem of Providence in Aquinas's *Commentary of Job*," Sommers leads us in a trenchant analysis of Thomas's exegesis of the Book of Job. It begins with the acknowledgement of scandal. The problem of evil, especially the suffering of the innocent, is a constant provocation for those who accept the God of Love. Yet Thomas argues, at length, that there are reasonable grounds for the belief that God's providence makes even Job's suffering intelligible. For a start, divine rule need not limit itself to the "best practices" of human organizations. God's ordinances, after all, reach through the whole of Creation, and we should hardly expect to see their ultimate coordination. Sommers sets out to follow Thomas's explication of the disanalogy between the *regimen divinum* and the *regimen humanum*. To do so, she first highlights the distinction between providence and predestination. Predestination, which looks to results, is beyond our grasp. But providence we experience in the very lives we live. Sommers likens it to "performance art" in its immediacy and tells us that for Aquinas providence is God's leading us to himself as our final end. In his discussion of Job's miseries, Thomas contrasts God's providence with our limited prudence and God's Kingdom with our temporal regimes. Paradoxically, God is completely transparent, and yet we can only see through a glass and darkly.

God alone knows our history. Our philosophy of history, Jacques Maritain argues, like our study of ethics, must take into account the whole of the human condition, and that we can discern only through Revelation. Thomas would concur: in our limited experience, we must turn to the testimony of the ancients and their testimony of God's self-disclosure. Job, for his part, and as Thomas comments, knew both that his own conscience was clear and that he could not fault God, since the divine will is incomprehensible. Yet Aquinas offers us an apt analogy. Consider the case of gold: it does not become gold by being subjected to fire; yet through the process of firing it becomes visible to others, and only then do we appreciate its preciousness.

Next we turn from the role of providence to the character of evil and to the nature of the good. James V. Schall, SJ, in a customarily engaging essay, "How Evil Is Evil? How Good Is Good?" is our guide. He aims to help us fathom, insofar as we can, the force and range of evil. For a start, he says, knowledge alone is no match for evil. Nietzsche was right: the devil is the best friend of knowledge. Yet the range of evil suggests how we might overcome it. For evil is parasitic on the good; it is a privation of the good. But everything that is, in its integrity, is good. We can overcome evil in the choosing of the good. Here, though, we blunder badly if we suppose that evil is simply suffering. Socrates is right: it is better to suffer evil than do evil; that is, it is better that we suffer from the wrong that others do than that we ourselves sin.

In the end, Schall affirms, good is as good as God—and *Deus est caritas*. God allows evil only to make space for our freely choosing to share in his life. While Schall dismisses Manichean accounts of evil, he celebrates the wisdom of Charles Schulz's Peanuts. Do we remember, Schall asks, that Lucy knows that Charlie Brown will be happy if she tells him that she likes him, that she knows it is a little thing to ask, and yet that she cannot bring herself to do it? Weep for the banality of evil! Ultimately, for Schall, the power of the good begins with God's super-abounding love, a love that respects human freedom. We can reject the invitation to share in this superabundance. But, even then, evil cannot overcome God's forgiveness, if we but open ourselves to it.

Yet it is emblematic of our "interesting times" that the loss of a Christian vision leads to confusion about even the most fundamental concepts that Christian thought brings into play. Siobhan Nash-Marshall, in her provocative essay, "Evil, Pain, and the Problem of Properties," challenges representatives of secular analytic philosophy to come to terms with their convenient assumptions about what evil is and their facile conclusions about its incompatibility with God's existence. They exhibit a peculiar reluctance, she argues, to come to terms with just what evil is and cannot begin to see it as a mystery. Too often, she contends, they are content with telling us that evil is a primitive concept; as such, it is not to be explained in terms of other concepts. Or, alternatively, we are simply told that evil is suffering. And yet neither strategy is plausible. To treat a concept as primitive too easily proves to be a refusal to engage in analysis and argument. Moreover, if we once take time to investigate the relation between evil, on the one hand, and pain and suffering pain, on the other hand, it is clear that they are not equivalent—however much accounts of suffering emotionally affect us. We lose sight of this non-equivalence to our own peril. Murder, after all, need not cause pain, and remorse for wrongdoing, surely a good thing, might well be painful.

Jonathan J. Sanford adroitly steers us away from the mistaken identification of suffering and evil. His clarifying essay, "On Vice and Free Choice," notes that if we are not clear about just what evil is, we will surely be confused about what acts we ought to judge to be evil. Indeed, we will also be hard pressed to understand how evil comes to distort our freedom and corrupt our characters. There follows, too, an intellectual perplexity about the structure of the vices and the role of malice. In the manner of St. Thomas, Sanford distinguishes between metaphysical and moral accounts of evil, between the will directly or indirectly bringing about evil, and between the will *prior to choice* ignoring the moral rule that should guide it and the will *proceeding to act* while overriding the rule that should be its guide. (At this point, Sanford gives textual support in St. Thomas for Maritain's analysis of moral evil.) Sanford clearly distinguishes between the incontinent man and the vicious man; the former suffers from a weakness of will, while the latter acts in accord with a corrupted will. The vicious man becomes prey to his own chosen self-deception, and only grace can release him from the malice that makes his life a mockery of the constancy that a good man exemplifies.

II. Jacques Maritain on Moral Evil: Some Disputed Questions

John F. X. Knasas, in his challenging essay, "Maritain and the Cry of Rachel," contends that Jacques Maritain succeeds in responding to the problem of evil only to the extent that he allows himself to draw on Revelation in working out his professedly philosophical analysis of the problem of moral evil. If this complaint is correct, a pair of critical questions emerges. First, to what extent does Maritain part company from Thomas Aquinas? Second, to what extent is Maritain's analysis helpful to the philosopher? Yet suppose that Maritain's strategy depends on an ambiguity. What consolation might a more stringent Thomist offer to those who suffer from great wrongs at the hands of others? Knasas urges us to answer this last question by opening ourselves to the whole range of being rather than reducing it to some existentially pressing but nonetheless limited experience. The source of human dignity, he writes, is "the intimate relation of the rational soul to the *ratio entis*." From this it follows that the person is, as Thomas argues, not a whole but rather "a principle part" of the whole.

Laura L. Garcia, in her searching analysis, "Does Maritain Solve the Problem of Evil?" contends that the problem of evil remains, in large part, a mystery. Borrowing a metaphor from Maritain, she argues that the efforts of any Christian philosopher to resolve the problem succeed only in "running smack into insurmountable difficulties" on which one will "break one's teeth." Thus, although Maritain's criticisms of both Dominic Bañez and Luis de Molina (and the Molinists of today) are telling, his own solution is also flawed. For, according to Maritain, God's knowledge of future contingent propositions, including propositions about the sinful acts that we will perform, depends on a "science of vision." Thus, Maritain thinks that "[God] is capable in his eternal instant of shaping, forming, and ordaining everything in a single glance by taking account of all that which happens at each moment of time in created wills." But Garcia counters that God's vision of free acts logically depends on what will actually happen. Indeed, such a knowledge, in that it is passive, would bring about a change in God. Yet Maritain is by no means willing to surrender divine immutability. Garcia concludes that we will not, on our own, be able to resolve the tension between God's knowledge and man's freedom. So be it. She reminds us of John Paul II's words: "Faith asks that its object be understood with the help of reason, and at the summit of its searching, reason acknowledges that it cannot do without what faiths presents" (*Fides et Ratio*, 42).

In his vigorously argued "God, Freedom, and the Permission of Evil," we find Steven A. Long first setting forth St. Thomas's view of God's simplicity and its import for God's permission of evil. Turning next to the nature of human freedom, Long observes that for Thomas when we act freely we nonetheless do so within the context of God's providential causality; both the necessary and the contingent, for Thomas, are modes of the universal being of which God is the source. (Libertarians take heed!) Finally, he urges us to consider whether Jacques Maritain did not misread Thomas's view that the negation of a negation, in a real subject, is yet an instance of God's causality. Does the point seem overly technical? Maritain's analysis of our non-negation of the moral rule in the lead-up to moral evil depends on this point, and Maritain muddles what is at stake. (Nor, Long argues, does Bernard Lonergan improve on Thomas's account of the permission of evil.)

Long well knows that his critics argue that he himself misreads Aquinas—and thus fails to do justice to human freedom. He answers, nonetheless, that "the teaching that evil is only permitted for the sake of … the common good of the universe, and for the sake of a higher good that finally resolves into the Beatific Vision … is a profoundly consoling doctrine." Doubtless all Thomists affirm this much. But now it is time that we turn to contributors who stoutly affirm Jacques Maritain's contribution to the multi-faceted debate before us.

III. On Jacques Maritain's Enduring Contribution

Bernadette E. O'Connor, in her judiciously presented "Insufficient Ado about the Human Capacity for Nothing, Too Much Ado about the Human Capacity for Being, and Maritain's Dissymmetry Solution" highlights Jacques Maritain's focus on the critical moments in an existential whole that "consists of acting-without-consideration of that rule-which-ought-to-guide human action." Her interest here is chiefly ontological in that she directs us to the causality of moral evil. Prior to this moment, there is a voluntary defect not in the sense of a fault, she notes, but rather in the sense of an absence. Neither a fault nor a punishment, rather it is a pure negation. This non-considering of the moral rule, which is ontologically primary, becomes privation in a second ontological moment. As such, it is the cause of moral evil. However, the initial negation, through the initiative of the will, is not itself an action. Here, O'Connor observes that recognizing the will's *mera negatio* as ontologically prior to an evil act reflects Thomas's axiom that what comes from nothingness tends toward nothingness (*De Veritate*, q. 5, a. 2). In retrospect, misunderstanding this relation, and Thomas's appreciation of it, led some Thomists to suggest that indirectly God is the cause of moral evil. This same misunderstanding led Molinists to allow a true act of the will to exist independently of God's causality. Maritain, to his credit, points a way between the Scylla and Charybdis of their protracted and confused debate.

Michael D. Torre, in his deeply informed study, "The Grace of God and the Sin of Man: The Drama of Man Before God" develops a thorough defense of Jacques Maritain's contribution to an understanding of moral evil. Maritain's analysis is historically informed by the work of Francisco Marín-Sola, OP, who retrieves the central Dominican reading of Thomas on the source of moral evil. In this vein, Torre voices the perplexing question: how do we fail to act in accord with the measure of morality? There is, he contends, no other explanation than the creature's own will. As Thomas observes "of something of this sort, that is the … non-use of the [moral] rule, it is not necessary to search for a cause, because the will itself, by which one can act or not act, suffices for this" (*De Malo*, 1, 3). Here, Thomas is in accord with Augustine's teaching. "Since the causes of the [will's] defections are not efficient but deficient causes, to wish to trace them is as if someone were to set his heart on seeing darkness or hearing silence" (*The City of God*, Book XII, Chapter VII).

The interplay between God's will and human freedom, Torre contends, however perplexing, is such that God is indeed the first cause of the human activity in sin. But God only wills to cause what *we* have defectively disposed ourselves towards. And He uses our defect and failure to achieve a surpassing good. Moreover, that God knows of our sin is not due to his knowing himself or to charting a *scientia media* of future possibles. Rather, Torre argues that for Thomas God sees sin as it deforms the sinner who is physically present to His eternity. In this matter, Thomas follows Boethius.

In his "The Measure of Morality," Nicolaj Zunic helps us appreciate Maritain's distinctive analysis by charting the worsening loss of the role of measure in moral reasoning. Nowhere has it been more evident than in the Holocaust, a paradigmatic blasphemy of our time. Distinguishing between ontological good and evil, on the one hand, and moral good and evil, on the other, Zunic develops the role of the measure in reference to both objective and subjective dimensions of morality. He does so by a bold historical tracing of the collapse of the moral measure, initiating his discussion with a reference to Friedrich Hölderlin's "In Lovely Blue" ("*In lieblicher Bläue*"). For Hölderlin, God, manifest as the sky, is our measure. But Hölderlin continues:

> Well deserving, yet poetically
> Man dwells on this earth. But the shadow
> Of the starry night is no more pure, if I may say so,
> Than man, said to be the image of God.
> Is there measure on earth? There is
> None.

The distorting lineage of Nietzsche, Heidegger, and Foucault leads us to our familiar contemporary nihilism.

In sharp contrast, Zunic develops Jacques Maritain's insight into the origin of evil in the agent's non-consideration of the moral rule. In doing so, he introduces Maritain's own doctrine of moral philosophy adequately considered and its insistence on God's guiding role in the moral life. In this context, he reflects on Maritain's deep regard for the Jews. In his *Anti-Semitism* (London: Geoffrey Bles, 1939), Maritain writes: "Israel, which is not of the world, is to be found at the very heart of the world's structure, stimulating it, exasperating it, moving it." In Zunic's judgment, any purely naturalistic measure of morality fails.

Perhaps now, though, we should turn from an exploration of the great absolutes, which always constitute our horizon, to a consideration of how evidence, probability, and prudence emerge in light of these absolutes.

IV. Evidence, Probability, and Prudence

Eric Manchester, in his original and searching "Creation and the Probability (But Not Necessity) of Evil," submits current atheological probabilistic arguments from evil to his own independent probabilistic analysis. His conclusions are significant—and decidedly challenging for the atheologian. Manchester develops his critique from the starting point of Jacques Maritain's thesis that moral evil begins with a failure to consider the proper rule for action. This failure stems from the non-sinful result of our natural limitations. But this failure to consider the moral measure is not logically necessitated. Indeed, Maritain's position is entirely compatible with the claim that evil can be avoided in any free world. To be sure, and Maritain would agree, evil is practically certain to occur in such a world. Indeed, the greater the creaturely variety in a world becomes, the more likely it is that sin occurs. In the final analysis, and as a matter of probability, it is practically certain that evil occurs in any free world that God creates. But what follows from this? Is it that God, therefore, should not create any world at all? By no means, contends Manchester. For evil is always genuinely avoidable, however statistically probable it may be. Furthermore, there is no actual being for whom it would be better that God create no world at all. God is *not* in the dock!

Bryan R. Cross in "Aquinas on the Original Harmonies and the Problem of Evil," strategically focuses our attention on the evidentialist or inductive version of the problem of evil. According to this popular line of argument, the sheer amount of natural, as distinct from moral, evil is so great that it is highly improbable that an omnipotent, omniscient, and perfectly good being could coexist with it. But this sort of skeptical analysis depends on a key claim that does not bear up under examination. The claim is that we have no reason to think that there might be goods of surpassing worth that outweigh all the multiform natural evils that so painfully perplex us. Cross observes, though, that an intellectual poverty leads this kind of atheological argument to preclude there being any reason that could justify the natural evil we experience. As Cross points out, the inductive version of the problem of evil largely ignores the metaphysical context in which evil occurs. Yet for Aquinas this context reveals, first, that the good has primacy over evil and, second, that God makes use of evil in effecting the harmony of Creation and the perfection of free and responsible creatures. Indeed, if the evils we endure serve to restore us to right order, there is a suggestion of the diabolical in the charge that those evils (so poorly understood) can only advance the cause of atheism.

In his helpful essay, "Why Must We Not Do Evil? Avoiding vs. Allowing Evil and the Principle of Double Effect," John F. Morris explores the understanding of moral evil and human agency that is implicit in the principle of double effect. (In doing so, he also shows how proportionalists have misused that principle.) One must not do evil, not even the lesser of two evils, so that good might come. For to do evil amounts to the wounding of oneself and of others, an assault that we might even come to accept as somehow tolerable. Nonetheless, one may act to bring about the good even when one foresees that some evil, as a side-effect of one's action, will also come about. (Indeed, in an analogous fashion, God allows both physical and moral evil.) Morris points out that while we are to strive for the good, there are limits in pursuing the good that are permanent features of life: we are limited both by our own capacities and by the boundless needs of others. But we are not so limited in our efforts to avoid evil. The principle of double effect, if rightly understood, offers us practical direction in how to avoid evil, even as we recognize that often some evil is an indirect result of our good actions.

Denis A. Scrandis, in his perceptive "How Maritainian Choice of Evil Forms the Moral Object," argues that a close examination of Aristotle and Aquinas on voluntary action sets out an interchange between intellect and will. Together they give rise to 12 steps: four establish the action's end; four establish the means to achieve it; four execute the means and monitor the attainment of the end. Reflecting on this process, some might think that it is a disorder in the will that originates evil. Does not the will reject good means to an end and instead favor bad means to that end? But the will, Scrandis points out, neither designs nor considers the evil it chooses. And were the will defective in itself, the choice of evil could not be free. Whence then comes evil? Maritain rightly insists that we look to a non-evil cause in the non-act of non-consideration of the moral rule. Thus, Scrandis further contextualizes Maritain's distinctive focus.

Our authorial reflections on evil, taken together, help us better to understand the truth about man. And this self-knowledge, in turn, illuminates the everyday importance of truth telling. It underscores, as well, the "futurist" peril of distorting the human nature that only flourishes in truth. It is time, then, to turn to the final pair of contributions to this volume.

V. Truth, Falsehood, and the Future of Man

Andrew Jaspers, in his "The Evil of Lying: a Case in Thomistic Realism," reminds us that, as philosophers (of whatever bent), we aim to produce sound arguments. Such arguments require formal validity and true premises. If both are realized, the truth of the conclusion follows. In seeking sound arguments, philosophers see truth as a *sine qua non* of right reason. In contrast, deliberately to affirm what is false with the intent to deceive, that is, to lie, undercuts both reason and one's personal integrity. And yet deception, in so many forms, is now endemic. Can we really imagine how contemporary society might function without it? But what precisely is the evil of lying? Are we, perhaps, left with only Pilate's self-exculpatory question: "What is Truth?"

Andrew Jaspers contends that a careful investigation of Thomas Aquinas's analysis of the wrongness of the lie can be a powerful antidote to endemic deceit and self-serving euphemism. Aquinas, and Maritain follows his lead, identifies a metaphysical moment in which the will moves away from the right order of being. In telling a lie, moreover, we reject the right order of the triadic structure of word-*ratio-res*. When we act against the right order of being, we would refashion the world in our own image; when we deceive ourselves and one another, we seek to refashion reality in speech. But in the end we fashion only idols.

Robert Vigliotti in "The Anti-Humanism of Technological Humanism," critically reviews the increasingly rapid development of what he terms technological humanism and the disturbing agenda of what now presents itself, in Promethean terms, as "transhumanism." His thoughtful discussion underscores that both the good and the evil of the human person are increasingly ours to choose and, in a new way, to bring into existence.

To lie is to betray the nature that one lies about, and in doing so one betrays one's own nature. Of course, one might develop one's nature without betraying it, and such development might be deep and wide-ranging. It might approach a kind of *transformation*. But should it? To what extent might we rightly transform our own nature? When is transformation, in contrast to integral development, for the good? When is it for the evil? And what are we to say and do when a proposed transformation of our nature threatens its very *telos*? Vigliotti observes that, for Maritain—indeed, for any Christian—insofar as transhumanism limits itself to the material realm, it remains closed to the full meaning of the human person that only an openness to the transcendent offers.

VI. An Envoi: On the Construction of Character

Our authors have done much to explore the problem of evil in light of St. Thomas and Jacques Maritain. They highlight both the mystery of so enduring a problem and the metaphysics that rightly understanding it requires. But there is always more to say, and there is the further and inescapable question of the praxis that should flow from whatever intellectual advance we secure.

I turn then to the construction of character in light of the problem of evil.[4] Here we might begin with Greek myth: the folly and fate of Icarus. His father had fashioned wings of feathers, a pair for each of them, to escape from Crete. "My son," Daedalus warned, "neither soar too high, lest the sun melt the wax; nor swoop too low, lest the feathers be wetted by the sea." Again, as they began their flight, he anxiously cried "Follow me closely; do not set your own course!"[5] But Icarus chose instead to exult in his new power and thus became thoroughly distracted. So it was that he flew upward without regard to measure—and quickly fell to his death.

But what of us? How might *we* attend to reason's measure in our "interesting times" and thus come to know ourselves as never before? Indeed, in fixing our attention, might we not gain a deeper sense of substantival self and its agency?[6] Simone Weil, with such questions in mind, offers an intriguing distinction between will and attention.[7] Will alone is, as it were, strenuous.[8] Attention, in contrast, is intuitive, and solitude fosters its creativity. Such attention is a "non-acting action of prayer in the soul."[9] If we are resolutely receptive in such attention, we cannot go wrong. With attention, as with love, we become open to what is real. Weil tells us that "attention consists in suspending thought, in leaving it available...." She adds

4. Here I borrow from my "The Metaphysics of Moral Evil: Context, Truth and Character," *Ètudes Maritainiennes/Maritain Studies*, Vol. XXVI (2010), 106–09.

5. Robert Graves, *The Greek Myths*, Volume I, introduced by Kenneth McLeish, illustrations by Grahame Baker (London: The Folio Society: 1996), 291.

6. On this point, see Tim Bayne, "The Phenomenology of Agency," in *Philosophy Compass* 3/1 (2008): 182–202.

7. For a searching analysis of Weil's dark and even damaged side, see Sharon Cameron's "The Practice of Attention: Simone Weil's Performance of Impersonality," in her *Impersonality* (Chicago: The University of Chicago Press, 2007), 108–43.

8. Here we might consider Joseph Ratzinger's words: "Heroic virtue does not mean that the saint performs a type of 'gymnastics' of holiness, something that normal people do not dare to do [but] rather that in the life of a person God's presence is revealed—something man could not do by himself and through himself" ("Letting God Work," *L'Osservatore Romano*, Oct. 6, 2002). Contrast this view with Aristotle's call to "go to all lengths to live a life in accord with our supreme element ..." (*Nicomachean Ethics*, second edition, translated by Terence Irwin [Indianapolis: Hackett Publishing Company, 1999], Bk. 10, Ch. 7, §8, 165).

9. See her "Attention and the Will," in *Simone Weil: An Anthology*, edited and introduced by Siân Miles (New York: Grove Press, 1986), 214.

that “The most precious goods should not be sought out, but waited for”; in contrast, he who tries for himself to find these goods finds counterfeits “whose falsehood he will not be able to discern.”[10]

For Weil, then, the will is not enough; it exhausts itself. No better is the inattention of one who is distracted. Rather, the good comes as a gift to one who waits upon the grace of the real. Jacques Maritain makes room for this waiting. Yet he does so in his own language. For him, the will is never stripped of reason; and reason itself has an intuitive dimension. Nonetheless, he writes that when the creature, under grace, “does not take the initiative of nothingness, then divine motion or grace merely sufficient or breakable fructifies of itself into *unbreakable* divine motion or grace efficacious by itself.”[11] To be sure, the faith of one who waits, if it has not works, is dead. So we return to Icarus.

Listen to W. H. Auden’s “*Musée de Beaux Arts*” a poem in which he says that the Old Masters were never wrong about suffering.

> In Brueghel’s Icarus, for instance: how everything turns away
> Quite leisurely from the disaster; the ploughman may
> Have heard the splash, the forsaken cry,
> But for him it was not an important failure; the sun shone
> As it had on the white legs disappearing into the green
> Water; and the expensive delicate ship that must have seen
> Something amazing, a boy falling out of the sky,
> Had somewhere to get to and sailed calmly on.

How might the ploughman have turned his attention to the falling Icarus? How might the delicate ship have turned around? And how might we see the many that perish, almost in plain sight, as *we* hurry on?

Solidarity is one measure of reason. We cannot have it always in mind. Still, we can ask how to bring it to mind in carrying out the acts that constitute our character. We can learn to consider, in times of reflection, the field of deliberation that the pressing moment must narrow. Nor is it enough to know the measure of reason. When argument is spent, the will must make that measure its own. Now comes a point of convergence at once perilous and sublime. Here, as Jacques Maritain would have it, one waits on an un-

10. Simone Weil, *Waiting on God,* introduction by Leslie Fiedler (New York: Harper Colophon Books, 1951), 105–16.

11. Jacques Maritain, *St. Thomas and the Problem of Evil* (Milwaukee, Wisconsin: Marquette University Press, 1942), 38.

breakable grace.[12] Yet this grace can come through human hands. But how? Bl. John Henry Newman prefaces his *Grammar of Assent* with St. Ambrose's remark, "*Non in dialectica complacuit Deo salvum facere populum suum.*"[13] If not then in argument, how then does it please God to save his people?

Once again, let us return to Icarus. His father had urged that he follow him, rather than set his own course. It is a lesson that takes many forms. Aristotle teaches that citizens must look to the man of practical wisdom if the city is to flourish. St. Thomas teaches us that we must look to the saints. Jacques Maritain, in these "interesting times," calls our attention to "prophetic shock-minorities."[14] In this vein, we might look to the Austrian farmer and martyr, Bl. Franz Jägerstätter. In 1943, the Nazi regime executed this husband and father for refusing as a Catholic to take the military oath of allegiance.

In his last meditation before death, Bl. Franz affirms both the freedom of the will and the role of grace in achieving the good. (Thus, he illustrates what Maritain terms acting "in the line of good.")[15] He begins "I'll write down a few words as they come to me from my heart. Although I am writing them with my hands in chains, this is still much better than if my will were in chains."[16] Noting his struggle of conscience, he continues "If God had not bestowed on me the grace and power to die for my faith—if this is demanded of me—then I would be doing the same as the majority of people are doing. God can give someone as much grace as God wants."[17] So much grace, Maritain would say, is "unbreakable."[18] (Such a grace is one form of "the problem of good," a dilemma for the *a*theist.)

Blessed Franz shows us that we can say more about the interplay of our own minds and wills and the fixing of our attention. The measure of reason, for him, is clear. "I set before you life or death, blessing or curse.

12. Ibid., 38.

13. John Henry Newman, *An Essay in Aid of a Grammar of Assent* (South Bend, Indiana: University of Notre Dame Press, 1979).

14. Jacques Maritain, *Man and the State* (Washington, D.C.: The Catholic University of America Press, 1998), 139.

15. Jacques Maritain, *St. Thomas and the Problem of Evil,* 38. Maritain takes both this term and "the line of evil," from Marín-Sola. See Michael D. Torre, "Francisco Marín-Sola, O.P., and The Origin of Jacques Maritain's Doctrine on God's Permission of Evil," *Nova et Vetera,* vol. 4, No. 1 (Winter 2006): 55–93, 94.

16. Franz Jägerstätter, *Franz Jägersätter: Letters and Writings from Prison,* edited by Erna Putz, translated with commentary by Robert A. Krieg, introduction by Jim Forest (Maryknoll, New York: Orbis Books, 2009), 243–44.

17. Ibid.

18. Jacques Maritain, *St. Thomas and the Problem of Evil,* 38.

Choose life" (Dt. 30: 19). Now even this is a measure to which one cannot always attend.[19] But neither may one act nor fail to act without its guide. One need not always scan its moral horizon; but when one is in the presence of life, one must measure that life against this horizon. Earlier on, Jägerstätter called attention to what others sought to obscure:

> Professor Hermann Muckermann has given data that the total number of deaths of German soldiers during World War I was less than the total number of deaths of children in Germany each year as a result of murders and abortion. According to this data, there are two million children in Germany every year who lose their lives because of acts similar to Herod's.[20]

The measure of reason, Jägerstätter understood, is a coherent ethics of life.[21]

I close with a contrast. Hannah Arendt argues that *thinking* is the antidote for genocide. Thinking is a Socratic but "solitary dialogue," and anyone might show an "inability to think" and so become an agent of "*infinite* evil."[22] Yet, for Arendt, thinking undermines all "measurements for good and evil" and leads to perplexities that we cannot resolve.[23] Such thinking is scarcely enough for the moral life. Nor, as she claims, is thinking together with the judgment of particulars enough.[24] Rather, an attentive waiting must make a space for our thinking; and our thinking is fruitless without the will's engagement. Judgment, too, is empty unless our will bridges the gap between non-being and being. This it can do only at the call, and with the measure, of its Creator. In his thinking and acting, Franz Jägerstätter heroically answered such a call and its measure.

19. Ordinary language, in this regard, recognizes the difference between "not saving" and "letting die." The former, but not the latter, is inescapable.

20. Franz Jägerstätter, *Franz Jägerstätter: Letters and Writings from Prison*, 181. Hermann Muckermann, a former Jesuit, broke with the Nazis over eugenics policy.

21. Joan Andrews, the American pro-life leader, cites Blessed Franz as a source of inspiration; see her *You Reject them, You Reject Me: The Prison Letters of Joan Andrews*, edited by Richard Cowden-Guido (Manassas, Virginia: Trinity Publications, 1988), 109.

22. Hannah Arendt, "Thinking and Moral Considerations," in *Responsibility and Judgment*, edited with an introduction by Jerome Kohn (New York: Schocken, 2003). Peter Schotten ably critiques Arendt in his "Hannah Arendt's Eichmann Reconsidered," in *Modern Age*, Volume 49, Number 2 (Spring 2007): 139–47.

23. Hannah Arendt, "Thinking and Moral Considerations," in *Responsibility and Judgment*, 176.

24. Ibid., 188–89.

≈I≈

SETTING AN EXPANSIVE STAGE

FEDERICO TEDESCO

The Paradoxes of Evil as the *Rationis Exodus in Deum**

A world with evil may be incomparably better than other worlds without evil.[1]

I. The Concept of Paradox

It is necessary to recognize that the presence of evil in being is a fact so baffling that it provokes a true scandal for intelligence. This means that when reason comes up against evil, it receives such a violent shock that it is reduced to silence.[2] This mortifying impact with evil shows reason just how insufficient is its understanding of being itself. Now, Maritain intended to describe just this scandal of reason when in *St. Thomas and the Problem of Evil* he spoke of evil as a "metaphysical monstrosity," an "utter anomaly,"

*I would like to thank Maurizio Malaguti, Kay Heathcote, Rev. Gregorio De Francesco, Samuel Kimbriel, and James Hanink for their valuable suggestions.

1. Charles Journet, *The Meaning of Evil*, translated by Michael Barry (London: Geoffrey Chapman, 1963), 123.

2. In this regard, it is interesting to observe that the Greek word *mystērion* is related to the verb *myo*, which is made up by the onomatopoeic expression *my*, that refers to the suffering produced by the closing of the mouth. In this light, the following statement of Christ seems to assume a new meaning: "I bless you, Father ... for hiding these things from the learned and the clever and revealing them to little children" (Mt 11, 25). The expression "little children" is the English translation of the Greek word *nēpioi*, which basically refers to somebody who does not have the capacity to use words (*epos*). If the *nēpios* does not have the *epos yet*, he or she is just a little child; but if the *nepios* does not have the *epos anymore* he or she is, properly speaking, a metaphysician, that is to say a human being who, facing the very mystery of being, deals with something which is beyond what Aquinas would call *enarratio* (propositional knowledge).

and when he wrote that "the existence of evil in things injects into being an incongruity from which nothing can console us."[3]

Having said that, the first thesis that I would like to affirm is that the scandal of reason—that is, the fact that evil appears as a monstrosity, an anomaly and an incongruity to reason—arises from the fact that, for reason, evil is a wholly paradoxical dimension. The theories that philosophers and theologians have formulated about evil are, consequently, all paradoxes. For instance, Étienne Gilson, having said that the presence of evil in the universe is rendered intelligible only by the existence of a real subject to support it, defines this fact as "somewhat paradoxical."[4]

By paradox (*paradoxon* in Greek) I mean a thesis that abruptly removes the evidence from the beliefs that until that moment were accepted by all, demonstrating at the same time the truth of the contrary point of view. This radical overthrow of common sense, of that which the ancients called *doxa*, causes such an intense disorientation for intelligence that we can call it a scandal (*skandalon*).

In order to understand how the theories about evil formulated by philosophers from Plato to Maritain are all paradoxes, it is enough to affirm them, confronting them with that which is commonly considered to be true. What is more opposed to common sense than the theory that evil, properly speaking, does not exist, that is, that it does not belong to the luminous sphere of being?[5] A scandal no less significant arises with the theory that evil is, properly speaking, *sine causa per se*, in so far as it is caused accidentally by good.[6] In the end, while the presence of evil in the world is commonly used as an incontrovertible argument to prove that God does not exist,[7] St. Thomas in

3. Jacques Maritain, *Saint Thomas and the Problem of Evil*, translated by Gordon Andison (Milwaukee, Wisconsin: Marquette University Press, 1942), 12.

4. Étienne Gilson, *The Christian Philosophy of St. Thomas Aquinas*, translated by L. K. Shook, CSB (Notre Dame, Indiana: University of Notre Dame Press, 1994), 156. "If there is a paradox in the definition of evil—it exists but as a privation—there will be a paradox also in the origin of evil: however terrible its ravages may be, evil is caused as a privation" (Journet, *The Meaning of Evil*, 71). See also Maritain, *The Problem of Evil*, 33–34; Maritain, *Existence and the Existent*, translated by Lewis Galantiere and Gerald Phelan (New York: Pantheon, 1948), 91; Maritain, *God and the Permission of Evil*, translated by Joseph W. Evans (Milwaukee, Wisconsin: Bruce Publishing Co., 1966), 11.

5. See the *Summa Theologiae* (hereafter cited as *ST*) I, q. 48, a. 1; *Questiones Disputatae de Malo* (hereafter cited as *QDM*), q. 1, a. 1.

6. See the *Summa Contra Gentiles* (hereafter cited as *SCG*) III, 4; *QDM*, q. 1, a. 3.

7. See, e.g., *ST* I, q. 2, a. 3, obj. 1.

the *Summa Contra Gentiles* draws the precise opposite conclusion from the same premise, affirming that "*si malum est, Deus est.*"[8]

II. The Concept of the Exodus of Reason

It is also necessary to recognize that there is an admirable and secret unity among the paradoxes of evil, as if they were the various steps of a single path. This is owing to the fact that, if the theories about evil are all paradoxes, it is not for this that they are without sense. On the contrary, in the very moment in which they scandalize common sense, the paradoxes of evil liberate it from a wholly partial perception of things, to raise itself to a higher degree of rationality.[9] Therefore, the very notion of paradox, as it is meant here, necessarily implies a movement of intelligence from a lower to a higher degree of understanding of being. From paradox to paradox, across painful scandals, intelligence achieves possession of its own good, and at the same time it is liberated from an erroneous perception of things. Now, biblical wisdom teaches us to think of the exodus as a passage that leads, from a state of slavery, across the desert, to a state of freedom. If therefore the paradoxes of evil constitute the steps of a narrow path that liberates intelligence and will, then it seems legitimate to consider such paradoxes to be responsible for the exodus of reason.

III. The First Paradox: the Scandal of Common Sense

I now propose to describe the essential steps of the exodus that reason carries out at the moment in which it asks itself, as does St. Augustine in his *Confessions, unde malum*?

The first paradox, which we can also call the scandal of common sense, consists undoubtedly in the theory that evil, strictly speaking, does not belong in any way to the luminous sphere of being. To prove that good and being are the same in reality (*idem secundum rem*), but differ only conceptually (*rationem tantum*), St. Thomas begins from the Aristotelian defini-

8. *SCG* III, 71.

9. "An ordinary, superficial knowledge of God will not perhaps be affected to any startling degree by an ordinary, superficial knowledge of evil. But once evil suddenly reveals the horror of its features, this insufficient knowledge of God will be troubled and falter; it must either give in to atheism ... or, on the other hand, it must shake off its torpor, gain more height and grow in awareness of a mystery which it had not before suspected" (Journet, *The Meaning of Evil*, 22).

tion of good as *perfectio quod omnia appetunt,* and shows that the origin of every perfection is precisely the act-of-being: "*unde manifestum est quod in tantum est aliquid bonum, inquantum est ens.*"[10] Even matter, as far as it is itself directed to receive the act-of-being, must be considered to be good, contrary to the neoplatonic conception.[11]

It is interesting to observe at this point that Greek, Jewish, and Latin traditions preserve the memory of identity between being and good in their respective languages. To indicate the totality of that which exists, that is, the world, the ancient Greeks used the word *kosmos,* a word that is associated with the ideas of order and good, obviously eminently desirable things. In Latin, the same is meant by the word *mundus,* which evokes something pure and as such is positive. In Hebrew, moreover, the concept of being, *hāyâ,* calls to mind in fact the very name of God, Yehwâ, Who, in the book of Exodus, seems to identify Himself with being.[12]

However, if it is an element completely extraneous to the sphere of being, how should we think about evil? St. Thomas, developing the Aristotelian concept of privation (*sterēsis*),[13] observes that, if good is perfection and the fullness of being, evil is necessarily the lack that destroys this ontological integrity.[14] It is necessary to recognize the presence of evil in a thing every time it lacks even a single one of the properties that it should have according to its essence. For this reason, the ancients affirmed that *bonum ex integra causa, malum ex quocumque defectu,* which means: good requires the completeness of a being, whereas evil is generated by any defects or lacks.[15]

However, placed before the philosophical theory that identifies good and being and defines evil as "*privatio perfectionis debitae,*"[16] common sense objects that, if in fact evil is truly a dimension wholly extraneous to the luminous sphere of being, it should not overshadow being almost complete-

10. *ST* I, q. 5, a. 1; see also Jacques Maritain, *An Introduction to The Basic Problems Of Moral Philosophy,* translated by Cornelia N. Borgerhoff (Albany, New York: Magi Books, 1990), 28–33.

11. See Plotinus, *The Enneads,* I, 8; on Plotinus's conception of evil, see Journet, *The Meaning of Evil,* 28–29.

12. See Ex 3, 14.

13. See, e.g., his commentray on the *Physics,* I, 9, 192 a 3–25; his commentrary on *Metaphysics,* V, 22; and also his *De principiis naturae,* ch. 2.

14. *ST* I, q. 48, a. 1.

15. See, e.g., his commentary on *Nicomachean Ethics* II, 6, 1106 b 29–31: "... bonum procedit ex una et perfecta causa, malum autem procedit ex multis particularibus defectibus. Et hoc apparet tam in naturalibus, quam in moralibus." See also *In Dionysius Divinae Nominibus,* chapter 4.

16. *Compendium Theologiae,* chapter 117, n. 229.

ly as in effect it does. The first paradox is able truly to scandalize common sense only at the moment in which it is able to provide a suitable response to the question about the origin of evil in being itself, in this way permitting common sense to rise to a higher degree of rationality.

Responding to the question *utrum malum invenitur in rebus,* St. Thomas observes that the First Cause of being, in drawing up the world *ex nihilo sui et subiecti,* gave the world the unique destiny of representing His perfection in space and time.[17] This means that the end towards which all things tend, and in a superior manner all intelligent beings, is participation in that infinite good that is *Esse ipsum.* Since it is impossible for a single being, no matter how perfect, to represent the First Mover *sufficienter,* it is necessary that the world be made of a multiplicity of beings that are distinguishable one from the other according to that which St. Thomas calls *distinctio formalis.* It is necessary, however, to note that the *rerum distinctio* necessarily implies *inequalitas rerum,* that is, different degrees of metaphysical perfection: "But formal diversity always requires inequality, since, as *Metaphysics* 8 says, the forms of things are like numbers, in which the species are differentiated by the addition or subtraction of a unit."[18] In order for the universe to achieve its destiny of participating in the metaphysical fullness of the first Cause, it is necessary that it also contain *entia corruptibilia.* Paradoxically, the death of living beings, and more generally the endless destruction of material substances, is a fatality that derives from the destiny given to the world of representing in the dispersion of space and time the perfection that the first Cause of being possesses in the unity of *nunc stans*: "And so in causing the good of the universe among things, God consequently and, as it were, *per accidens,* causes the corruption of things."[19]

In order correctly to evaluate the presence of evil in nature and understand how even in this order there is a perfect identity between being and good, it is necessary to consider not only the fact that the corruption of things is a collateral effect of the participation of the universe in the First Cause, but also the fact that every single natural agent causes evil simply

17. *ST* I, q. 48, a. 2.

18. "Distinctio autem formalis semper requirit inaequalitatem: quia, ut dicitur in VIII Metaphysica, formae rerum sunt sicut numeri, in quibus species variantur per additionem vel subtractionem unitatis" (*ST* I, q. 47, a. 2).

19. "Et sic Deus, in rebus causando bonum ordinis universi, ex consequenti, et quasi per accidens, causat corruptiones rerum" (*ST* I, q. 49, a. 2).

per accidens. In *De principiis naturae* when St. Thomas defines "*generatio*" as "*motus ad formam*," he means to express precisely this fact that the destruction that is produced in conjunction with this action is a completely accidental event, and as such without a real and true cause.[20]

The evil *secundum quid* that is produced in nature is at any rate always *praeter intentionem agentis* and is owing to the expansion of a natural being towards its own good and towards that of the universe. To the eye of the metaphysician, nature appears—in its ceaseless processes of generation and degeneration—to be a dimension completely permeated with good and, in itself, uncontaminated by the stains of evil. It is for this reason that we cannot completely agree with Maritain when he defines St. Thomas's conception of nature as "rather pessimistic indeed."[21] To better understand the innocence of the *corruptibilia*, one can note that in the *Quaestiones disputatae de malo*, St. Thomas—having observed that good is the accidental cause of evil in nature both *ex parte effectus* and *ex parte causae*—makes the point that the causality *per accidens* of a perfect good is always to be found at the origin of evil caused by a *bonum deficiens*, that is, by a deficient efficient cause.[22]

Having proven, however, that the identity between being and good holds true just as much for *corruptibilia* as for *incorruptibilia*, common sense is compelled to recognize on the one hand the innocence of nature and of the Cause from which nature originates, and on the other hand the fact that only the defections of will are evil in a true sense. In fact, if evil is *privatio perfectionis debitae*, then the existence of the corruptible perfection that it destroys has a certain necessity, in such a way that its absence cannot be required in any way. Indeed, we have seen that the defections of nature are in fact necessary in order to produce the perfection of the universe (both visible and invisible). The defections of will, on the other hand, are not only not necessary in any way to the perfection of the universe, but rather impede its realization, so that these defections are never transformed into good in the bosom of All.[23]

20. See *De principiis naturae*, chapter 1.

21. Maritain, *The Problem of Evil*, 11. See also Gilson, *Christian Philosophy*, 189; Jude P. Dougherty, *Jacques Maritain: An Intellectual Profile* (Washington, D.C: The Catholic University of America Press, 2003), 44–59.

22. *QDM*, q. 1, a. 3; *ST* I, q. 49, a. 1.

23. "Moral evil will never, under any circumstances, be a good with respect to a superior order of any kind; it will remain eternally an evil (though it may be reordered to a greater good—that's another matter)" (Maritain, *Basic Problems*, 78).

IV. The Second Paradox: the Scandal of Metaphysics

At the moment in which the identity between being and good is discovered, metaphysical investigation identifies the first cause of evil in the defection of will.[24] Now, the moral quality of a man, that which Aristotle called his *ēthos*, depends entirely on the ultimate end a man proposes to achieve with his actions.[25] The ultimate purpose is nothing other than the good through the attainment of which man achieves the fullness of life that the ancients called *eudaimonia*. The moral quality of a man depends therefore entirely on his beliefs about happiness.[26] Yet Aquinas, in the *Quaestiones disputatae de veritate*, observes that a specific tendency towards happiness does not exist in man: "Every rational mind naturally desires happiness in an undetermined and general way [*indeterminate et in universali*], and in this regard it cannot fail. But the motion of the will of a creature is not determined in particular to seek happiness in this or that."[27] If happiness is the possession of good in which man recognizes the perfection of his essence, happiness evidently depends on the understanding that he has of himself, that is of his own individual essence and destiny. It is for this reason that Aquinas says that "the first thing that occurs to a person to think about at that time [*scilicet*: when he or she begins to have the use of reason] is to deliberate about himself."[28] The scandal of metaphysics resides in the discovery that man, being unable ever to achieve a radical understanding of himself, is never able—even if that were his wish—to free himself completely from evil.[29] In the final analysis, this is owing to the fact

24. "That is the metaphysical grandeur of the universe of freedom: there, and only there can the creature do something by itself alone, but that something consists in non-being, and that 'doing' is an absence of action" (Maritain, *The Problem of Evil*, 34–35). See also the first chapter of *God and the Permission of Evil.*

25. "Unde voluntas naturaliter tendit in suum finem ultimun ... Et ex hac naturali voluntate causantur omnes aliae voluntates: cum quidquid homo vult, velit propter finem" (*ST* I, q. 60, a. 2). See also Maritain, *Basic Problems*, 86–87.

26. See Ralph McInerny, "Ethics," in *The Cambridge Companion to Aquinas*, edited by Norman Kretzmann and Eleonore Stump (Cambridge University Press: New York, 2009), 198–202.

27. *Questiones Disputatae de Veritate* (hereafter cited as *QDV*) q. 24, a. 7 ad 6; see also Maritain, *Basic Problems*, 89–91.

28. "... primum quod tunc homini cogitandum occurit, est deliberare de seipso" (*ST* I-II, q. 89, a. 6).

29. See *QDV*, q. 10, a. 8. "It is important, I believe, to note well that my experimental knowledge of my soul ... belongs to the purely existential order and implies the presentation to the mind of no other *quid* than my operations reflexively perceived in their emanation from their

that the *ratio cognoscendi* of anything resides precisely in its *ratio essendi*, which is to say that it resides in the cause on which its *positio extra nihil* depends.[30] Since the *ratio essendi* of man is God Himself, and since God is a reality that transcends the order of creation without proportion, one sees how impossible it is for man, with only the power of his intellect, to raise himself up to such a Cause, to contemplate in His essence his own reason of being.[31] With the traumatic experience of not being able to know himself all the way through, man is compelled to adopt a radical change of perspective. His intelligence, which until that moment has taken as its fundamental task the explanation of things, discovers that it must itself be explained. If intelligence pondered the nature of things before it was struck by the second paradox of evil, now it seeks its own reason of being and says of itself, as St. Augustine wrote of himself in his *Confessions*, "*Factus eram ipse mihi magna quaestio*."[32] When, struck by the paradox of evil, intelligence shifts its gaze from things to itself, to turn at last to the darkened sky of the First Cause of being, it carries out a movement that the ancients called *conversio*, that Plotinus named *epistrophe*, and that The New Testament calls *metanoia*. It is necessary therefore to recognize that evil shifts the gaze of man, and, insofar as man's intelligence no longer seeks only the science of things but also the wisdom of the Beginning, we must admit that evil produces an authentic metaphysical aptitude.[33]

V. The Third Paradox: the Scandal of the Righteous Man

If, from the point of view of simple nature, the pursuit of happiness cannot but remain unfinished, drawing near to its completion in an asymptotic way, one must note that there exists a supernatural pathway that leads man to the radical understanding of himself and thereby to a total freedom from

---

principle. Whence it follows that I cannot during this life experience my soul or my substance in its essence" (*The Degrees of Knowledge*, translated by Gerald B. Phelan [Notre Dame: University of Notre Dame Press, 2002], 471); see also Maritain, *Existence and the Existent*, 68–80.

30. See Maurizio Malaguti, *In humanitatem spiritus* (Bologna, Italia: Inchiostri Associati Editore, 2005), 41–44.

31. See Maritain, *The Problem of Evil*, 12–13.

32. Augustine, *Confessiones* IV, 4.9.

33. It is for this reason that "Maritain ... has made the problem of evil one of the constant preoccupations of his philosophical enquiries" (Journet, *Meaning of Evil*, 14); see also Maritain, *The Problem of Evil*, 39; Maritain, *The Permission of Evil*, viii.

evil. In fact, if no man is able to cross the sacred Abyss of the Deity and see the inaccessible light in which He dwells, it is nonetheless possible—and this is achieved in Christ—that the light descend from His sky to illumine men. It is for this reason that Christ says of Himself: "I came into the world as light."[34] If the *scientia Christi* has the power to reveal to man the features of his own face, it is because Christ, being united with *Logos "per unitatem hypostasis seu personae,"*[35] has the beautifying knowledge of God's very essence, where the reason of being of all that is past, present and future is preserved. In that man is initiated into the *scientia Christi,* he discovers in it the features of his own face, and, together with the understanding of his own reason of being, he can acquire a radical freedom from evil: "if you hold to my teaching, you are really my disciples. Then you will know the truth, and the truth will set you free."[36] Therefore, it is no accident that Jesus heals by means of his teaching, or that the author of *The Letter of James* compares the *logos* of Christ to a mirror in which man contemplates his own face (*prosōpon*), that is, the individual essence of his person.[37]

But it is necessary to observe that the *logos* of Christ on evil has an eminently paradoxical character. In *The Gospel of Luke,* in fact, it is written that the witnesses of the healing of the paralyzed man say fearfully that "*Eidomen paradoxa semeron.*"[38] The paradoxical character of Christ's *logos* on evil consists in his command to not resist it: "I say to you, offer no resistance to one who is evil."[39] Now, we can see that the natural order takes more care of more valuable things, so that everyone would consider someone who did not protect a valuable possession, or who even went so far as voluntarily to cause its destruction, to be foolish. Therefore, from the point of view of common sense, God is foolish in exactly this way, given that the logic underlying the teachings of Christ on evil is exactly the opposite of the logic of common sense and metaphysics.[40] God asks the righteous man to abandon himself—just as Christ has himself been the first to do—to the

34. Jn 12, 46.

35. *Compendium Theologiae,* chapter 214, n. 426.

36. Jn 8, 31–32.

37. Jn 1, 23; concerning Maritain's notion of the person, see Jacques Maritain, *The Person and the Common Good,* translated by John J. Fitzgerald (Notre Dame: University of Notre Dame, 2009); Maritain, *Scholasticism and Politics* (New York: Image Books, 1960), 61–89; Pedro Descoqs, SJ, "Individu et personne," *Archives de philosophie* 14, No. 2 (1938): 18–33.

38. Lk 5, 26.

39. Mt 5, 39.

40. 1 Cor 1, 18–25.

will of those who, rejecting divine motion, cause grievous wounds to beings.[41] The Bible uses the word *agapē* to refer to this abandon with which the righteous man immerses himself in the death caused by evil, and teaches that God Himself is *agape*.[42] Therefore, in the very moment in which the righteous man plunges into the abyss of evil, he is paradoxically brought into the intimate life of God.

Yet is it possible, on the basis of Revelation, to recognize a meaning of "abandon" in which the righteous man, removed from the divine *agapē*, immerses himself in evil? From the book of Wisdom we know that "God did not make death ... To exist—for this he created all things,"[43] and that "Death came into the world only through the Devil's envy."[44] Immersing himself in the death of evil, the righteous man carries the divine *agapē* into a dimension that is wholly separate from God, in that it was generated by the rebellion of the fallen angel (and it may be for this reason that Psalm 88 says: "Do you work wonders for the dead, can shadows rise up to praise you? ... Are your wonders known in the darkness, your saving justice in the land of oblivion?")[45] The baptism in evil to which Christ invites his disciples seems therefore to have the purpose of restoring that admirable unity of being that was torn by the fallen angel. Since it is performed *ex obedientia et caritate*, the free baptism in evil is able to transfigure the meaning of evil, suffering and death, making them God-like.[46]

The righteous man, already partaking of the intimate life of God at the moment in which he immersed himself in evil, is introduced to God's very essence with the resurrection from death; and, in God's essence, the righteous man can finally contemplate *facie ad faciem* his own reason of being. Thus it is no accident that Job, at the completion of his painful exodus in God, says: "I had heard of you by word of mouth, but now my eye has seen you."[47]

41. Maritain, *The Problem of Evil*, 37–38; see also Journet, *The Meaning of Evil*, 155–59. A paradigmatic example of the abandon of the righteous man is that provided by Saint Stephen, who causes with his luminous teaching the violent reaction of the Sanhedrin: see Acts 6, 8–7, 59.

42. 1 Jn 4, 8.

43. Ws 1, 13–14.

44. Ibid., 2, 24.

45. Ps 88, 11–13; see also Is 38, 18. Concerning the fallen angels see *ST* I, q. 63, a. 1 ad 4; *Compendium Theologiae*, chapter 113; see also Jacques Maritain, *The Sin of the Angel*, translated by William L. Rossner, SJ (Westminster, Maryland: The Newman Press, 1959).

46. See Journet, *The Meaning of Evil*, 248. Concerning the role played by Christ's *obedientia* and *caritas* in human redemption, see *ST* III, qq. 46–49.

47. Jb 42, 5; see also Aquinas's *Super Iob*, chapter 42.

JOHN J. CONLEY, SJ

Job, Our Contemporary

The biblical Book of Job has long intrigued philosophers as a privileged locus to explore the problem of evil, especially the suffering of the innocent.[1] Jacques Maritain's discussion of Job in *God and the Permission of Evil* (1966) is only one of many contemporary philosophical discussions of the book.[2] More recently, John Wilcox, Robert Eisen, Eleonore Stump, François Chirpaz, Denise Leduc-Fayette, and Phillipe Nemo have published substantial philosophical commentaries on Job and the related problem of theodicy.[3] Not least in this concert of philosophical voices is Karol Wojtyla, whose 1940 play *Job*, as well as his apostolic exhortation *Salvifici Doloris* (1984), explore the mystery of morally inexplicable suffering in the figure of Job, counterpoised in both works to the suffering/redeeming figure of Jesus in Gethsemane and on the cross.[4]

1. Citations from the Book of Job are based on the *New American Bible* translation. This commentary on Job also relies on Mayer Gruber's introduction to the Book of Job in *The Jewish Study Bible*, edited by Adele Berlin and Marc Zvi Brettler (Oxford: Oxford University Press, 1985), 1499–1505.

2. See Jacques Maritain, *God and the Permission of Evil*, translated by Joseph Evans (Milwaukee, Wisconsin: Bruce Publishing Co., 1966).

3. See John T. Wilcox, *The Bitterness of Job: A Philosophical Reading* (Ann Arbor: University of Michigan Press, 1989); Robert Eisen, *The Book of Job in Medieval Jewish Philosophy* (Oxford: Oxford University Press, 2006); Eleonore Stump, "Aquinas on the Sufferings of Job," in *The Evidential Argument from Evil*, edited by Daniel Howard-Snyder (Bloomington, Indiana: Indiana University Press, 1966); François Chirpaz, *Job: La force de l'espérance* (Paris: Presses universitaires de France, 2001); Denise Leduc-Fayette, *Pascal et le mystère du mal: La clef de Job* (Paris: Cerf, 1996); Philippe Nemo, *Job et l'excès du mal*, 2nd ed. (Paris: Albin Michel, 2001).

4. For commentaries on Wojtyla's phenomenological and dramatic interpretations of Job, see John J. Conley, "On the Philosophical Foundations of the Thought of John Paul II," in *The Thought of John Paul II*, edited by John McDermott (Rome: Gregorian, 1993), 23–28, and "Karol

Not only can the Book of Job illuminate the generic problem of evil and the universal enigma of the suffering of the innocent; it can shed its opaque light on the unmerited suffering typical of our own time. In this paper, I shall attempt to sketch how the torment of Job can articulate and probe the evils proper to our own culture as it faces an often inscrutable God. In particular I will focus on the nihilism, the psychological depression, the persecution of moral minorities, and the political terror that characterize our increasingly secularized society.

After Job has lost his possessions, his family, and his bodily integrity, he often calls out to God and to his hapless interlocutors in the tones of nihilism. His personal torment reflects a universe that now appears without purpose or hope. In his anguish, he recognizes that it is better not to have been born. "Perish the day on which I was born,/ the night when they said, 'The child is a boy!'/ May that day be darkness:/ let God above not call for it, nor let light shine upon it!... Why did I not perish at birth,/ come forth from the womb and expire?/ O why was I not buried away like an untimely birth,/ like babes that have never seen the light?" (Jb 3: 3–4, 11) In the excess of suffering, life appears as a pointless burden, nature as a stony source of physical and mental pain. The perception of the universe as an ordered place, where suffering finds clear explanations and compensations, has collapsed. The efforts of Job's friends to discern a teleological pattern in Job's torment in an apparently indifferent cosmos are in vain. Job's suffering cannot be explained away as the effect of hidden faults in Job himself or in his ancestors.

Theological nihilism allies itself to metaphysical nihilism. The search for God's presence now yields to a disorienting absence. "But if I go to the east, [God] is not there; or to the west, I cannot perceive him./ Where the north enfolds him, I behold him not;/ by the south he is veiled, and I see him not." (Jb 23: 8–10) God remains veiled from all perception. If Job insists that he remains faithful to God through his earlier vowed promises, the divine being is now obscured from all positive affirmation. Job's enduring covenant appears to rest on a questionable memory.

Job's nihilistic experience of the cosmos and of an absent God illuminates contemporary society's experience of a similarly disenchanted uni-

---

Wojtyla Artist; John Paul II, Theologian of Art," in *Creed and Culture*, edited by Koterski and Conley (Philadelphia: Saint Joseph's University Press, 2004), 173–88.

verse. If suffering cannot be healed by technological means or compensated by a commensurate benefit in the future, it cannot find justification or purpose in a world that is strikingly mute. For the scientific elite, final purpose disappeared centuries ago; there is no larger metaphysical framework into which the suffering can be inscribed and display a certain worth. If God survives in such a cosmos, God is only a mute cosmic principle, not a personal being who can console those who cry out in the suffering of sudden and devastating loss.

Job's narrative of loss also illuminates a psychic suffering typical of our time: that of depression. As Julia Kristeva notes in her work on the subject, major depression manifests itself as the loss of all interest in one's work, relationships, and avocations: in short, in life itself.[5] The desire for death becomes so strong that even the articulation of one's desires becomes painful and borders on the inarticulate. Job evokes the weight of this interior depression. "If only my anguish could be measured and my calamity weighed with it in the scales,/ They would now outweigh the sands of the sea!/ Because of this I speak without restraint./ For the arrows of the Almighty pierce me, and my spirit drinks in their poison; the terrors of God are arrayed against me.... Oh, that I might have my request, and that God would grant what I long for:/ Even that God would decide to crush me, that he would put forth his hand and cut me off!" (Jb 6: 2–4, 8–9) Job's lament expresses what cannot by nature be expressed: a depressed spirit that cannot be measured, a depth of anguish that exceeds the greatest of imaginable quantities, a terror that eludes any measure of speech. On the verge of despair, to which he never finally surrenders, Job evokes the anguish without limit and without remedy.

Especially striking is the Book of Job's depiction of one of the typical symptoms of depression: namely, insomnia. On his sickbed, Job evokes the distortion of time provoked by his internal disarray. "Is not man's life on earth a drudgery?/ Are not his days those of a hireling? He is a slave who longs for the shade, a hireling who waits for his wages./ So I have been assigned months of misery, and troubled nights have been told off for me./ If in bed I say, 'When shall I arise? Then the night drags on;/ I am filled with restlessness until the dawn." (Jb 7: 1–4) The insomniac's vigil graphi-

5. See Julia Kristeva, *Black Sun: Depression and Melancholia,* translated by Leon Roudiez (New York: Columbia University Press, 1989).

cally describes a space of suffering where clock time has disappeared. Suppressed rest becomes akin to the perpetual work of the most miserable of slaves.

As Kristeva argues, the contemporary expression of depression, probably the most widespread of mental illnesses in the West, differs from the experience of depression in an earlier age.[6] Whereas depression was once triggered by an identifiable stressor, such as the loss of a spouse or legal difficulties or sudden unemployment, contemporary depression often seems to express a global sense of the futility of the cosmos itself and any futility of struggle against obstacles within it. The redemptive purposes ascribed to suffering by earlier religious communities have disappeared, especially for elite sectors of the academy and the professions. It is the very vagueness of Job's experience of depression, rendered through an insomniac's experience of the suppression of clear temporal and spatial boundaries, which successfully translates the bewildered *ennui* that seems so graphic a part of the contemporary experience of a fundamental emptiness clothed in the externals of mechanical matter and in the internals of repetitious, pointless, psychic struggle. No restoration of financial security or of social intercourse can ultimately remedy a depressive mental state rooted in the apprehension of space and time as a suspended, threatening blur.

The suffering of Job is not confined to the anguish of one sorely tried individual; it represents the suffering of those who find themselves members of a moral minority. Throughout his laments, Job recounts the rejection he experiences at the hands of former friends. It is this social humiliation that constitutes part of his unbearable suffering. "Yet now they sing of me in mockery;/ I am become a byword among them./ They abhor me, they stand aloof from me,/ they do not hesitate to spit in my face!/ Indeed, they have loosed their bonds; they lord it over me,/ and have thrown off restraint in my presence." (Jb 30: 9–11) Job's loss of face is not due to the psoriasis alone; it is the result of the loss of esteem in the eyes of the powerful who once honored him. His tragedy is that of the disgraced moral hero, who now experiences raw contempt, and not only rejection, from erstwhile admirers. His experience of humiliation and social isolation, deepened by the *schadenfreude* of his former colleagues, plunges Job into an anguish tied to one's status in the social hierarchy.

6. See Ibid., 3–30.

The social humiliation of Job is not the result of criminal or immoral activity on the part of Job himself; on the contrary, it is Job's religious fidelity and moral uprightness that constitute the brunt of the ostracism to which he is subjected. "I have become the sport of my neighbors:/ 'The one whom God answers when he calls upon him, the just, the perfect man,' is become a laughingstock./ The complacent esteem my downfall a disgrace such as awaits unsteady feet." (Jb 12: 4–5) Even the silent God appears to participate in this act of social ostracism and ridicule of the pious. "You [God] put my feet in the stocks; you watch all my paths and trace out all my footsteps." (Jb 13: 27) Job is exposed to public obloquy as he sits metaphorically immobilized in the stockyard because his moral righteousness and religious fidelity in the face of catastrophic suffering and a mute God have become an object of ridicule rather than of respect.

Job's experience of social humiliation in his torment can illuminate a very particular type of suffering we experience in the Church in the contemporary West. It is the suffering of experiencing contempt by those who find our religious loyalties and moral convictions quite literally incredible. The belief that the life of each human being should be respected from conception until natural death, the conviction that we shall face a judgment on our moral choices at the moment of death, and the trust that God remains providential despite or even perhaps through the unspeakable suffering of the innocent in an age of recidivist genocide—such positions are dismissed as ridiculous, and not only erroneous, by learned critics of the Church. The recent turn of stand-up comedy, one of the dramatic genres typical of our age, to bitter satire against such views and the institutions defending them is one of the signs of this intensified hostility to those who remain faithful to a set of moral and theological beliefs stigmatized as dangerously archaic. An earlier American code of civility on matters religious has vanished; the amused smile of Voltaire has returned. Nor is this assault confined to the comic space of Bill Maher and Penn and Teller. The current political efforts to reduce the borders of religious freedom, especially the rights of conscience of health care workers who refuse to acquiesce on our bourgeoning culture of death, indicate the increasing coercion employed to ostracize and remove from social influence the moral minorities whose beliefs have been tagged as absurd by the cultural elite.[7] In his laments over

7. For a discussion of the increasing coercion of conscience in religious health-care institutions, see Michael D. Place, "Health Care as an Essential Building Block for a Free Society:

social humiliation, Job the prophet still has much to teach us in our anguish as we suffer for the truth against a mocking majority.

This social suffering is further darkened by the regime of terror that characterizes the society where Job labors. The unjust society created by Job's gloating enemies has plunged all members of this society into terror concerning an uncertain future. "You have unjustly kept your kinsmen's goods in pawn,/ left them stripped naked of their clothing./ To the thirsty you have given no water to drink,/ and from the hungry you have withheld bread;/ As if the land belonged to the man of might,/ and only the privileged were to dwell in it./ You have sent widows away empty-handed, and the resources of orphans you have destroyed./ Therefore, snares lie round about you, and a sudden terror causes you dismay,/ Or darkness, in which you cannot see./ A deluge of waters covers you." (Jb 22: 6–11) The social order of theft and contempt engineered by the powerful is only an apparent one; in fact, it is an anarchy that exposes all, including the powerful themselves, to the terror of sudden violence capable of engulfing anyone and everyone. Stripped of metaphysical purpose and moral constraint, political action becomes the raw exercise of power that can as easily turn upon its architects as it currently does on its prey, the vulnerable of society.

The translation of Job's social disorder to our current political struggles is not a difficult one. As Hannah Arendt argues in her meditation on totalitarianism, totalitarian regimes distinguish themselves from traditional dictatorships by their capacity to annihilate members of their own ruling party as brutally as they attempt to eliminate the obvious opponents of the regime.[8] Job's portrait of an engulfing reign of terror is the emblem of many contemporary polities, where the erosion of religious and moral constraint has freed the political forum to descend into a simple arena of the play of brute force and pressure. In the absence of transcendent law, power alone remains.

As I have suggested in my philosophical exegesis, which is inevitably a projective eisegesis of our current preoccupations, Job is our contemporary not only because he invites us to probe more deeply the perennial scandal of the excessive suffering of the innocent and the relationship of an omniscient, omnipotent, and all-good deity to this scandal; he is our con-

---

The Convergence of the Catholic and Secular American Imperative," *Kennedy Institute of Ethics Journal* 9.3 (1999): 245–62.

8. See Hannah Arendt, *On the Origins of Totalitarianism* (New York: Harcourt, Brace, 1951).

temporary because he offers such a penetrating mirror up to the particular figure evil has taken in our own culture. He provides the rhetoric and the imagery to depict our own contemporary nihilism, depressive tendencies, and political anarchy disguised as order. More positively, he discloses the solitary nobility of suffering out of fidelity to the truth of a divine order that transcends and judges the secular order despite its apparent silence. As we meditate, we ultimately encounter a sovereign God who is other than the moralizing fantasies of Job's interlocutors. We also discover ourselves, caught in a personal anguish and a fractured social order that is shared by our suffering contemporary, Job.

MARY CATHERINE SOMMERS

Topsy-Turvy

The Problem of Providence in Aquinas's Commentary on Job

I. Introduction

The title of this paper could be taken to refer to the reversal of fortune suffered by Job or, in general, to the human condition where, contrary to the view of Job's friends, there is no simple correlation between the heart of a man as known to God and his worldly fortunes. Indeed, a world where a "man perfect in every virtue" is serially deprived of his possessions, his children, and his bodily health, and where experience tells us that the wicked can really prosper, is to all appearances a topsy-turvydom. Job's friends hold that to deny that the temporal fortunes of men are rewards and punishments is either to deny divine action in human affairs or to impute injustice to God. Faced with such alternatives, they must sacrifice Job to re-set the world right side up—for God to be just, Job must be a secret sinner, hypocritically maintaining his innocence in the face of overwhelming evidence. St. Thomas agrees with Job's friends that the "affliction of the just" is the strongest counter to the claim that God rules in human history, and he sets out to show, through "probable reasons," that there is an understanding of divine providence that makes Job's sufferings intelligible apart from claiming that they are a proportionate punishment of sin.

However, that the world is turned upside down for Job is not the immediate thrust of my Gilbertian image.[1] Nor is it Job's friends' attempts to skew

1. "Topsyturvydom" is a one-act operetta and political satire by W.S. Gilbert (1874) based on one of his *Bab Ballads*; more broadly, it refers to a reversal of the natural order: "For that which

the evidence of his life in order to sustain their understanding of divine providence. Rather, it is Thomas Aquinas's explanation of why human beings, Job and his friends included, fail to understand divine rule and divine judgments: not only are we always squinting through the veil of the visible trying to discern invisible realities, always on the outside looking in, but we are also lured into interpreting divine rule according to the structures we observe in human organizations: political, ecclesiastical, and others.

> It should be noted that we fall short of understanding divine things for two reasons: first because, since we are not able to know the invisible things of God except through the things which are made, while the things which are made fall very short of the power of their maker, it is necessary that there remain many things to be considered in the maker that are hidden from us, and these are called the secrets of the wisdom of God ... Secondly, in addition because we are not able to comprehend in full the very order in creatures insofar as it is dispensed by divine providence. For human regimes differ from the divine: for in human affairs, to the extent that someone is higher in government, to that degree does the scope of his ordinances extend only to the more universal matters; the particulars on the other hand he leaves to inferiors. And thus the law of the higher ruler is universal and simple. But God insofar as he is higher in government to that degree does the scope of his ordinances extend all the way to the smallest things: whence the law of his regime is not only hidden, if we consider the height of the ruler exceeding any proportion of the creature, but also multiple, dispensing under a given order all singulars even the smallest; and thus he adds that his law is multiple. And this certainly is not only to be noted in natural things, inasmuch as they are subordinated to the divine regime, but also in human affairs.[2]

---

we call folly here,/ Is wisdom in that favoured sphere;/ The wisdom we so highly prise/ Is blatant folly in their eyes."

2. Thomas Aquinas, *Expositio super Iob ad litteram Opera Omnia* V. 26, ed. Leon., 1965, c. 11, 50–77 (hereafter cited as *Super Iob*): "Considerandum autem quod ab intellectu divinorum duplici ratione deficimus: primo quidem quia cum invisibilia Dei cognoscere non possimus nisi per ea quae facta sunt, ea vero quae facta sunt multum deficiant a virtute factoris, oportet quod remaneant multa in factore consideranda quae nobis occultantur, et haec vocantur secreta sapientiae Dei, de quibus dicit *ut ostenderet tibi secreta sapientiae.* Secundo quia etiam ipsum creaturarum ordinem ad plenum comprehendere non possumus secundum quod a divina et aliter in divino: nam apud homines quanto aliquis est superior in regendo tanto eius ordinatio ad universaliora solum se extendit, particularia vero relinquit inferioribus rectoribus dispensanda, et sic lex regiminis superioris rectoris est universalis et simplex; sed Deus quanto est superior in regendo tanto eius ordinatio etiam usque ad minima se extendit: unde lex sui regiminis non solum est secreta, si respiciamus ad altitudinem rectoris excedentem universam proportionem creaturae, sed etiam est multiplex, universa etiam singularia et minima sub certo ordine, dispensans, et ideo addidit *et quod multiplex sit lex eius.* Et hoc quidem non solum in rebus naturalibus est considerare, prout divino subduntur regimini, sed etiam in rebus humanis." All translations, except for the *De regno,* are mine.

The universe, then, from a human point of view, is a topsy-turvydom, since its divine ruler does not disdain to handle the small things that in a human government would be the province of minor bureaucrats.

Now Thomas Aquinas famously explains the function of the king in the *De regno* through analogy with divine providence: *ut sit in regno sicut in corpore anima et sicut Deus in mundo*: "let him be in the kingdom like the soul in the body and as God in the world."[3] Further, Aquinas explains the natural law as the human being's participation in divine providence. In other words, the divine rule illuminates human beings' struggles to govern their own lives and set up government in the public realm. However, in the *Expositio* on Job, Aquinas gives us reason to think that, while holding human rule to the divine measure is helpful, even necessary, the reverse is not necessarily the case. It seems that the analogies need supplementation from a negative approach, where the understanding of divine rule is illuminated through differentiating it from human rule. It is this *dis*analogy between the *regimen divinum* and the *regimen humanum*, then, that I will try to explore in this paper.

First, I will attempt some definitions, before moving (secondly) to consider the language that Aquinas uses to articulate the analogy between divine and human governance, with the object of clarifying the source of *dis*analogy. Thirdly, I will turn to Maritain, to ask whether there exists some *remedium* for the deficiences of human and regnant prudence. Finally, I will conclude with some comments on Job's topsy-turvy world.

II. Providence Defined

"Providence," unlike "predestination," presents a problem to be unravelled by natural reason. "Providence," according to Aquinas, "refers universally to the ordination to the end, and so extends to everything that has been ordered to some end by God, rational or irrational, good or bad; but predestination refers only to that end which is possible for a rational creature, namely glory." Further, with respect to the rational creatures, providence regards only the *ordering* towards the end, "whence through the providence of God all human beings are ordered to beatitude." Predestina-

3. Thomas Aquinas, *De regno ad regem Cypri, Opera Omnia* V. 42, ed. Leon., 1979 (hereafter cited as *De regno*), Bk. 2, c. 1, 464, 34–35; *On Kingship: to the King of Cyprus* translated by Gerald B. Phelan and I. Th. Eschmann, OP (Toronto: Pontifical Institute of Mediaeval Studies, 1949).

tion, however, is about the results—not everyone reaches the pole—and, so while providence is an act of reason alone, as is prudence of which it is a part, predestination requires God's will, which singles out the elect through a love, which like Isaac's for Esau has no basis in rational differentiation.[4] Finally, while predestination and election are about individual human beings, providence is a *collatio*, a set of connections, a pattern—from the human point of view, it is a puzzle.[5]

'Providence,' when translated as 'foresight,' has a static quality about it, but, for Aquinas, of course, it is nothing of the kind. Providence is not simple sight, it is rule or governance, it is about the means to the end. As Aquinas puts it in the *De veritate* 5, 1:

> Providence differs from the divine art and from [divine] disposition, because we speak of 'divine art' with respect to the production of things, of 'disposition' with

4. Thomas Aquinas, *Quaestiones disputatae de veritate, Opera Omnia* V. 22, I, fasc. 2, 175–76, ed. Leon., 1975 (hereafter cited as *De veritate*), q. 6, a. 1, 163–214: "Sed tamen praedestinatio quantum ad duo a providentia differt. Providentia enim dicit universaliter ordinationem in finem, et ideo se extendit ad omnia quae a Deo in finem aliquem ordinantur, sive rationalia sive irrationalia, sive bona sive mala; sed praedestinatio respicit tantum illum finem qui est possibilis rationali creaturae, utpote gloriam, et ideo praedestinatio non est nisi hominum, et respectu horum quae pertinent ad salutem. Differt etiam alio modo: In qualibet enim ordinatione ad finem est duo considerare: scilicet ipsum ordinem, et exitum vel eventum ordinis; non enim omnia quae ad finem ordinantur, finem consequuntur. Providentia ergo ordinem in finem respicit tantum, unde per Dei providentiam homines omnes ad beatitudinem ordinantur; sed praedestinatio respicit etiam exitum vel eventum ordinis, unde non est nisi eorum qui gloriam consequentur. Sicut igitur se habet providentia ad impositionem ordinis, ita se habet praedestinatio ad ordinis exitum vel eventum: quod enim aliqui finem gloriae consequantur, non est principaliter ex propriis viribus, sed ex auxilio gratiae divinitus dato. Unde sicut de providentia supra dictum est quod consistit in actu rationis, sicut et prudentia cuius est pars, eo quod solius rationis est dirigere vel ordinare, ita etiam et praedestinatio in actu rationis consistit dirigentis vel ordinantis in finem. Sed ad directionem in finem praeexigitur voluntas finis: nullus enim aliquid in finem ordinat quem non vult. Unde etiam et perfecta prudentiae electio non potest esse nisi in eo qui habet virtutem moralem, secundum philosophum in VI Ethicorum: per virtutem enim moralem affectus alicuius in fine stabilitur ad quem prudentia ordinat. Finis autem in quem praedestinatio dirigit, non est universaliter consideratus, sed secundum comparationem eius ad illum qui finem ipsum consequitur, quem oportet esse distinctum apud dirigentem ab his qui finem illum non consequentur. Et ideo praedestinatio praesupponit dilectionem, per quam Deus vult salutem alicuius, ut sicut prudens non ordinat in finem nisi in quantum est temperatus vel iustus, ita Deus non praedestinat nisi in quantum est diligens; praeexigitur etiam et electio, per quam ille qui in finem infallibiliter dirigitur ab aliis separatur qui non hoc modo in finem ordinantur."

5. Thomas Aquinas, *Scriptum super libros Sententiarum* (http://www.corpusthomisticum.org), Bk. 1, d. 41, q. 1, a. 2 (hereafter cited as *Super Sent.*): "Ipsa enim divina ordinatio qua quidam aliis praeferuntur ad consequendam beatitudinem, electio dicitur. Providentia autem attenditur in collatione eorum per quae res attingunt finem; et in applicatione ad finem. Similiter praedestinatio attenditur in hoc quod electis praeparantur bona gratiae et bona gloriae, quibus applicantur ad finem." Cf. also *Super Sent.*, Bk. 1, d. 40, q. 4, a. 1.

respect to the order of the things produced; 'providence,' however, indicates the order to the end. But, because whatever is in the product of art is unified through its end, the order to the end is closer to the end than the order among the parts and in some way is its cause; therefore providence in some way is the cause of disposition and for this reason disposition is frequently attributed to providence.[6]

In the *Commentary on the Sentences*, the image of God as the artist frames this distinct meaning of providence:

... the artist in pre-conceiving his work of art first considers the end; and then he considers the ordering of the thing he intends to produce to that end and the ordering among the parts, for example, as the foundation is under the wall and the wall is under the roof. Thirdly, it is necessary that he consider those things by which [the work] is advanced step-by-step to the end and how he can remove those things which can impede the end; whence he thinks about the supports of the house through additions and windows and things of this kind, through which the house becomes habitable. This planning is called 'science,' when considered as knowledge alone, rather than operationally, both about the end and the means. But as the order of operation, it is called "disposition": because disposition signifies a certain order; whence it is called the order of production. And considered as moving things forward to the end it is called "providence."[7]

It is this distinction between "disposition" and "providence" that "separates Thomas from the definition crafted by Boethius," according to Denis Chardonnens in his fine book on the *Expositio* on Job, *L'Homme sous le Regard de la Providence.*[8] *"Providentia est ipsa divina ratio in summo om-*

6. *De Veritate*, V. 22, I, fasc. 2, 141 q. 5, a. 1 ad 9, 273–94: "Providentia differt ab arte divina et dispositione quia ars divina dicitur respectu productionis rerum, sed dispositio respectu ordinis productorum, providentia autem dicit ordinem in finem. Sed quia ex fine artificiati colligitur quicquid est in artificiato, ordo autem ad finem est fini propinquior quam ordo partium ad invicem et quodam modo causa ei, ideo providentia quodam modo est dispositionis causa, et propter hoc actus dispositionis frequenter providentiae attribuitur."

7. *Super Sent.*, Bk. 1, d. 39, q. 2, a.1: "... artifex praeconcipiendo artificiatum suum considerat finem primo; et deinde considerat ordinem rei quam facere intendit, ad finem illum, et ordinem etiam partium ad invicem, sicut quod fundamentum sit sub pariete, et paries sub tecto; et iste ordo partium ad invicem ordinatur ulterius ad finem domus. Tertio oportet quod consideret ea quibus promoveatur ad consecutionem finis, et ut tollantur ea quae possunt impedire finem; unde excogitat sustentamenta domus per aliquas appendicias et fenestras et hujusmodi, quibus domus sit apta ad habitationem. Ista ergo excogitatio nominatur nomine scientiae, ratione solius cognitionis et non ratione alicujus operationis. Unde est et finis, et eorum quae sunt ad finem. Sed ratione ordinis excogitati in re operanda, vocatur nomine dispositionis: quia dispositio ordinem quemdam significat; unde dispositio dicitur generationis ordinatio. Sed ratione eorum quae promovent in finem, dicitur providentia...."

8. Denis Chardonnens, *L'Homme sous le Regard de la Providence: Providence de Dieu et con-*

nium principe constitua, quae cuncta disponit" (IV, Pr. 6). "Dispositio," for Aquinas, "is named from the two-fold order which [God] places in things, namely of thing to thing, by which they provide mutual support in pursuit of the ultimate end; and again of the whole universe to God Himself." Disposition, then, refers to the pattern of relationships: mother to daughter, St. Peter to the Apostles, wolves to sheep, Greeks to Romans, Canada to the United States, all hierarchies, genealogies, successions, and proximities. Since, however, the great design, no matter how inclusive and intricate, is not simply the relationship of "thing to thing," but of all things to God, it is not museum art, but "performance art." Divine providence, then, for Aquinas, is the rule or governance of a creative God over the return of His creatures to Himself as to their final end.

III. The Analogy and the *Dis*analogy between Divine and Human Government

That there is an analogy between divine and human government is significant for Aquinas, who differentiates the author of the *De causis* from the Epicureans on this point. They argued that the gods did not "rule," i.e., they had no "cares," so that they could be completely leisurely instead of busy, completely uniform instead of "over extended." For how could they otherwise be thought happy? In the *De causis*, however, it is argued that the first cause can have both "universal rule over things" and "the highest unity." Nevertheless, the very possibility of divine rule also requires a *dis*analogy: "because in human government, we see this happening, that the one who has the responsibility of the rule of many necessarily is pulled in many directions on account of his rule; while the one who is free from ruling others is more able to preserve uniformity in himself."[9]

---

dition humaine selon l'Exposition littérale sur le Livre de Job de Thomas d'Aquin (Paris: Vrin, Bibliothèque Thomiste, 1997), 108: "C'est la signification que dégage Thomas de la définition forgée par Boèce au sujet de la providence—définition citée dans les oeuvres de jeunesse comme dans celles de la maturité. . . ."

9. Thomas Aquinas, *Sancti Thomae de Aquino super Librum De Causis*, ed. H.D. Saffrey (Fribourg 1954) (hereafter cited as *Super De Causis*), l. 20: "Circa primum ponit talem propositionem: causa prima regit omnes res creatas praeter quod commisceatur cum eis. Ad cuius evidentiam considerandum est quod in humano regimine hoc contingere videmus quod ille qui habet curam regiminis plurimorum, necesse est ut ex suo regimine ad plura distrahatur; qui vero a cura regiminis aliorum est liber, magis in seipso potest uniformitatem conservare, unde et epicurei Philosophi, ut quietem et uniformitatem divinam conservarent, posuerunt deos nullius

If it is allowed that God can rule without ceasing to be "a god," are there limits to his rule in order to preserve this "godliness"? We read, on the contrary, in the *Summa Contra Gentiles* III, that:

> In those things which are governed by human providence, it happens that any higher overseer plans out how certain important and universal things are to be ordered by himself, but he does not himself plan the ordering of the less important things, but leaves them to be thought through by others lower down [the chain of command]. And this happens by reason of his deficiencies: either insofar as he is ignorant of the conditions pertaining to the less important particulars; or because he is not capable of formulating a plan for everything, because of the labor or the amount of time that would be required. But this defect is far from being the case with God: for he himself knows all singulars; nor does he labor in understanding, or take time, since in understanding himself, he understands everything else, as was shown above. He, therefore, plans out the order of all things, even singulars. Therefore, his providence is immediately of all singulars.[10]

Though God, indeed, governs through mediating secondary causes in terms of the *execution* of providence, his disposition or ordination of providence "immediately extends to all things."[11] If the smallest thing escaped his understanding, it would also escape his providence. Indeed, "the more perfect the providence of a ruler, the greater will be the downward reach of his cognition and ordination to singular things."[12] "But God is able to know

---

regiminis curam habere, sed omnino otiosos et nihil curantes, ut sic videantur esse felices. Et ideo contra hoc in hac propositione inducitur quod haec duo in causa prima non sunt contraria nec se invicem impediunt universale regimen rerum et summa unitas, per quam Deus exaltatur supra omnia."

10. Thomas Aquinas, *Summa contra Gentiles* (http://www.corpusthomisticum.org) III, 76 (hereafter cited as *SCG*): "In his quae humana providentia reguntur, invenitur quod aliquis superior provisor circa quaedam magna et universalia per seipsum excogitat qualiter sint ordinanda, minimorum vero ordinem ipse non excogitat, sed aliis inferioribus excogitandum relinquit. Et hoc quidem contingit propter eius defectum: inquantum vel singularium minimorum conditiones ignorat; vel non sufficit ad omnium ordinem excogitandum, propter laborem et temporis prolixitatem quae requireretur. Huiusmodi autem defectus longe sunt a Deo: nam ipse omnia singularia cognoscit; nec in intelligendo laborat, aut tempus requirit, cum intelligendo seipsum, omnia alia cognoscat, sicut supra ostensum est. Ipse igitur omnium et singularium ordinem excogitat. Eius igitur providentia est omnium singularium immediate."

11. Thomas Aquinas, *Compendium theologiae, Opera Omnia* V. 42, ed. Leon., 1979, Bk. 1, c. 131, 131, ll. 1–5: "Secundum hoc igitur patet quod licet rerum gubernatio fiat a Deo mediantibus causis secundis, quantum pertinet ad prouidentie executionem, tamen ipsa dispositio seu ordinatio divine prouidentie immediate se extendit ad omnia."

12. Ibid., c. 130, 131, ll. 41–43: ". . . et tanto perfectior est providentia gubernantis, quanto eius cognitio et ordinatio magis descendit ad singularia. . . ."

many things at once," and so does not need to retreat from the big picture, while attending to the details.[13]

That Aquinas's understanding of divine providence is founded on both the analogy and *dis*analogy with human government is born out by an examination of his use of the terms *providentia, regnum,* and *regimen.* While the term *providentia* occurs in the works of Aquinas 1862 times in 947 places, 767 times and 504 places as *providentia divina,* only five times do we hear about *providentia humana,* which does not reach "necessary things," because humanity does not initiate nature,[14] but as synonomous to prudence, controls the contingent and operable.[15] As products of their own providence, human acts are more prone to defects and disorder than natural acts, but are, as self-directing, "nobler in rank."[16] Aquinas juxtaposes divine and human providence for a brief moment in the *Expositio,* which highlights the near inextricability of their joint operations. Job is prosperous; prosperity has a two-fold cause: sometimes it proceeds "from human providence, for example, when a person prudently and cautiously disposes individual things ... sometimes ... it proceeds from a superior cause, namely from divine providence." One is like light, borrowed from another; the other is the lamp. Similarly, the loss of prosperity can come about in two ways, when a person or his family "lack prudence in their counsels" or when the light of divine providence is snuffed out, if only in that person's world. When a human being lets go of the light of human providence, which is the light of practical reason, does he or she deserve the protec-

13. Ibid., 12–14: "Sed Deus simul multa potest cognoscere, ut supra ostensum est, unde non retrahitur ab ordinatione maximorum per hoc quod dispensat minima."

14. Thomas Aquinas, *Summa Theologiae* (http://www.corpusthomisticum.org) I, q. 22, a. 2 ad 3 (hereafter cited as *ST*): "Ad tertium dicendum quod homo non est institutor naturae, sed utitur in operibus artis et virtutis, ad suum usum, rebus naturalibus. Unde providentia humana non se extendit ad necessaria, quae ex natura proveniunt. Ad quae tamen se extendit providentia Dei, qui est auctor naturae."

15. *ST* II-II, q. 49, a. 6: "Et quamvis aliqua necessaria sint propter finem quae subiiciuntur divinae providentiae, humanae tamen prudentiae non subiiciuntur nisi contingentia operabilia quae per hominem possunt fieri propter finem."

16. *De veritate* V. 22, I, fasc. 2, 151, q. 5, a. 5 ad 2, 119–31: "Ad secundum dicendum, quod res naturales insensibiles providentur solum a Deo, et ideo non potest ibi accidere defectus ex parte providentis, sed solummodo ex parte provisorum; humani autem actus possunt habere defectum ex parte providentiae humanae, et ideo plures defectus et inordinationes inveniuntur in humanis actibus quam in actibus naturalibus. Et tamen hoc quod homo habet providentiam suorum actuum, ad nobilitatem eius pertinent, unde multiplicitas defectuum non impedit quin homo nobiliorem gradum sub providentia teneat."

tion of the light of divine providence? Does the obliteration of the divine light always accompany the darkening of prudence? When Job's prosperity ends, how are he and his friends to sort through these layers of causation?[17]

Aquinas, when explaining why we cannot understand Job's fortunes *ad plenum,* contrasts the state of things *in humano regimine* with that *in divino* [*regimine*] and the differences *in regendo* between the two. However, the astonishing analogy between God and kings from the treatise *On Kingship* employs the term *regnum* instead of *regimen*. Is there anything to be learned from the difference in terminology? Aquinas commonly uses the term *regnum* to mean "monarchy" or "kingdom," where it is a species of the genus *regimen* meaning "government" (*De regno* 1, 1). He also uses it not to denote a type of government, but a unit of government—*civitas vel regnum*, perhaps Italian cities and French or German kingdoms, although sometimes the civitas is said to be part of a *regnum*. It could be argued that, as *regimen* seems to be a genus of which *regnum* is a species, then Aquinas uses it because he wants to contrast divine rule with any type of human rule, whether it is "kingly", i.e., a *regnum,* or any other. However, it may be because it is the *dis*analogy between divine and human governance that is at issue.

Regnum is a term which has 2775 instances within the authentic works of St. Thomas. Over 1300 of these instances are combined with *deus, divinus, caelum or caelestis,* and *Christi*: in other words, are said with reference to the reward of the "peacemakers" or the analogue of the "mustard seed." When one adds to these the teleological uses of the terms, e.g., *ad regnum* and *in regnum,* it becomes clear that Thomas Aquinas cannot use the term *regnum* without recalling the antonomastic kingdom, i.e., the kingdom of God. In his sermon on the Lord's Prayer, commenting on *adveniat regnum tuum,* Aquinas says "For 'regnum' means nothing else but 'government' [*regimen*]. We find the best government, however, where there is nothing contrary to the will of the ruler. But the will of God is the salvation of hu-

17. *Super Iob,* c. 18, 71–89: "Est autem considerandum quod prosperitas successus humani ex duplici causa procedit: quandoque quidem ex humana providentia, puta cum homo prudenter et caute singula quaeque disponit, et quantum ad hoc de cessatione prosperitatis dicit *Lux obtenebrescet in tabernaculo illius,* quia scilicet tam ipse quam sui familiares prudentia in consiliis carebunt; quandoque vero prosperitas humani successus ex causa superiori procedit, scilicet ex divina providentia, et quantum ad hoc cessationem prosperitatis describens dicit *et lucerna quae super eum est extinguetur,* non quidem ut in se non luceat sed ut impium non illustret. Et bene providentiam hominis 'lucem' dixit quasi ab alio mutuatam, providentiam Dei 'lucernam' quasi per se lucentem. Praemisit autem de luce humanae providentiae, quia per hoc quod homo lucem rationis dimittit videtur mereri ut luce divinae providentiae non protegatur."

manity, because he wills human beings to be saved; and this will be at its most powerful in Paradise, where nothing will exist that is repugnant to human salvation."[18]

This, then is the basis for all the arguments in the *De regno* for the preference for the rule of the one, rather than the rule of the few or the many—that the rule of God over the world is tending towards "the kingdom," where there will be perfect congruence between the will of ruler and ruled. "King-dom," therefore, where human beings organize their political life under the rule of one, does not have a secular meaning for Aquinas, if by that we mean one where substituting "Caesar" for "king" would make it intelligible. The odd chapters in the *De regno* that discuss the king's office as founder of the city, analogous to God's creative activity, are explicable on this interpretation. Interestingly, in the first redactions of the *Summa Contra Gentiles* III, Aquinas differentiates divine and human rule on this point, saying that the "ruler of a human society makes uses of human beings already existing through nature and orders their operations to the end."[19] Here the term is *regimen humanum* and, indeed, Aquinas never uses the term *regnum humanum*. In sum, while having usages that are solidly political, *regnum* so clearly signals "the kingdom come," that Aquinas may not have found it suitable to express the dynamic nature of providence, which is, after all, about process, not results.

There are a few uses of *regnum* in the Expositio,[20] however, which are

18. Thomas Aquinas, *Collationes in orationem dominicam* (http://www.corpusthomisticum.org), a. 2: "Nec mirum: nam regnum nihil aliud dicitur nisi regimen. Ibi autem est optimum regimen ubi nihil invenitur contra voluntatem regentis. Voluntas autem Dei est salus hominum, quia vult homines salvos fieri; et hoc potissime erit in Paradiso, ubi nihil erit saluti hominum repugnans."

19. Thomas Aquinas, *Primae redactiones Summae contra Gentiles* (http://www.corpusthomisticum.org), Bk. 3: "Rector enim humanae societatis utitur hominibus iam praeexistentibus per naturam, et eorum operationes ordinat ad finem."

20. The few uses of *regnum hominum* are quotations from Daniel IV, 17: "*dominatur excelsus in regno hominum, et cuicumque voluerit dabit illud*" ("the most High ruleth in the kingdom of men and giveth it to whomsoever he will"). 1) This accounts for five of the eight instances, one of which is in the *Expositio* on Job, with all having a single purpose: establishing the absolute dependence of all kingly power on the will of God. With respect to Job, it is used to show that the spoils of predators are also the gifts of God, so that "the opinion of those who argue that riches are given by God as a reward for justice is refuted." 2) Two other instances, in *reportationes*, use the *regnum hominum* by way of contrast: in Matthew, to the *regnum caelorum*, where the notions of great and small will be turned upside down (*Super Mt.* [*rep.* Petri de Andria], c. 5, v. 19) and, in Hebrews, where the "kingdom of men" comes to an end "with the present life," while the Church that is "His kingdom," having endured all the way to the end of the world, is handed

instructive.[21] In addition to the kingdom of God and the kingdoms (multiple) of this world, there is a kingdom *of* the world, ruled by Satan, to whom the kingdoms (multiple) have been given,[22] and Job fears "especially Satan will try to lead him into pride, ut sic transferretur in regnum ipsius," so that Job will be handed over to his governance.

Let us turn, then, from *regnum* to *regimen*. Aquinas uses the term *regimen divinum* 35 times, including the Job passage, while *regimen humanum* occurs only 12 times, again including the Job passage. These occurrences reveal the argumentative uses of the analogy between divine and human governance as well as its moral and imaginative power. All of these dimensions, nevertheless, ultimately depend on a grasp of the *dis*analogy as well.

First, the analogy to human governance is used to provide *a fortiori* arguments to establish the characteristics of divine rule. In the first chapter of the *Summa contra Gentiles* III, the perfection, mode, and necessity of divine government are unfolded through the words of "the Psalmist." God is the "great king over all the gods, because, even if there were many kings, all of them would be subject to his rule."[23] He, like the best in all types of governance, "oversees the things governed according to their proper mode,

over by Christ to the Father to be consummated and perfected (*Super Heb.* [*rep.* vulgata], c. 1, l. 4. 3) This leaves one instance of the term *regnum hominum* in Aquinas's own voice, where the reigns of "such men" as David and Solomon are said to prefigure the "reign of Christ," where the things said of them will actually come to fruition and completion (*Super Psalmos*, pr.). We can conclude, therefore, that *regnum hominum* is a term of limit and contrast, suggesting that the "mustard seed" can tell us more about the *regnum Christi* or the *regnum caelorum* than the deeds of David or Solomon.

21. *Super Iob*, c. 41, 442–57: "Et quia haec videntur ad superbiam pertinere, ostendit consequenter quod Diabolus non solum in se superbus est sed omnes in superbia excedit et est aliis superbiendi initium, unde *subdit ipse est rex super universos filios superbiae*, idest super eos qui superbiae subiciuntur, qui omnes sequuntur eius ducatum. Ubi considerandum est quod dominus operationem suam quam exercet in malos circa superbos manifestare incepit et in superbis narrationem terminat, ut ostendat hoc praecipue Iob fuisse timendum ne Diabolus, qui eum expetierat ad tentandum, praecipue eum ad superbiam inducere conaretur ut sic transferretur in regnum ipsius, et ideo cavere debebat affectum et verba quae superbiam saperent."

22. Ibid., c. 40, 312–24: "Descripta igitur convenientia Vehemot cum homine, describit proprietates ipsius, et ut hoc primo ad figuram referamus, tria videtur circa Vehemot describere: primo quidem cibum ipsius cum dicit *Fenum quasi bos comedet*: ad litteram enim non est animal comedens carnes sed herbas et alia huiusmodi ad modum bovis. Et quia herbae nascuntur in terra, per hoc figuratur quod Satan pascitur, idest delectatur, in terrenorum dominio, unde et iactanter de se dicit Luc. IV, 6 'Mihi tradita sunt, scilicet regna orbis terrae,' et cui voluero do illa."

23. *SCG* III, c. 1, n. 6: "Hoc igitur, divino repletus spiritu, Psalmista considerans, ut nobis divinum regimen demonstraret, primo describit nobis primi regentis perfectionem: . . . auctoritatis, in hoc quod dicit rex magnus super omnes deos, quia, etsi sint multi regentes, omnes tamen eius regimini subduntur. . . ."

for in this consists the justice of the regime." Subsidiarity, therefore, is present in the divine rule as well: allowing effects to occur per the nature of the agents, even though this is the route through which "corruption and evil" enter into the scheme of things.[24] Some creatures are merely "directed," others "direct themselves through their proper actions to a fitting end," who, if they submit themselves to divine rule, will be admitted to that end.[25] Again, on the analogy with human governance, the dignity of God would seem to require that he have many ministers and diverse executors of his providential rule,[26] and that its perfection entails "that through those which participate more fully in the divine goodness the execution of divine rule should be fulfilled."[27]

The pattern of demonstrating the perfection and mode of divine governance by comparison with human rulers is found in the commentary on the *De causis*, as well. "Any ruler of a multitude attempts to lead the many he rules to unity; and this is found fully in divine rule, which is one in itself and is not diversified in its effects except through the diversity of his subjects, a kind of diversity of fitness."[28] This diversity supports not only the analogy with human rulers but with angelic ones as well,[29] a rule of sec-

24. Ibid., c. 71, n. 4: "Optimum in gubernatione qualibet est ut rebus gubernatis secundum modum suum provideatur: in hoc enim regiminis iustitia consistit.... Ex hoc autem quod creaturae sic agunt, sequitur corruptio et malum in rebus: cum, propter contrarietatem et repugnantiam quae est in rebus, una res sit alterius corruptiva."

25. Ibid., c. 1, n. 5: "Quaedam namque sic a Deo producta sunt ut, intellectum habentia, eius similitudinem gerant et imaginem repraesentent: unde et ipsa non solum sunt directa, sed et seipsa dirigentia secundum proprias actiones in debitum finem. Quae si in sua directione divino subdantur regimini, ad ultimum finem consequendum ex divino regimine admittuntur: repelluntur autem si secus in sua directione processerint."

26. Ibid., c. 77, n. 4: "Ad dignitatem regentis pertinet ut habeat multos ministros, et diversos sui regiminis executores: quia tanto altius et maius ostendetur suum dominium, quanto plures in diversis gradibus ei subduntur. Nulla autem dignitas alicuius regentis est comparabilis dignitati divini regiminis. Conveniens igitur est quod per diversos gradus agentium fiat divinae providentiae executio."

27. Ibid., c.77, n. 5: "Cum igitur perfectio universi requirat quod quaedam aliis abundantius divinam bonitatem participent, ut supra ostensum est, exigit divinae providentiae perfectio ut per ea quae plenius divinam bonitatem participant, executio divini regiminis compleatur."

28. *Super De causis*, l. 2: "Ad hoc enim tendit quilibet rector multitudinis quod reducat multos quos regit in unum; et hoc maxime invenitur in divino regimine, quod est unum secundum se et non diversificatur in effectibus nisi secundum diversitatem, quasi secundum diversa merita, subditorum."

29. *Super De causis*, l. 24: "Postquam ostendit modum divini regiminis et sufficientiam ipsius ad regendum, hic incipit ostendere quomodo divinum regimen diversimode participatur a diversis. Et primo manifestat hoc in generali, secundo prosequitur in speciali de diversitate rerum quae subsunt divino regimini, 25 propositione, ibi: substantiae unitae etc."

ond causes or intelligences, following upon "the power of the first cause."[30]

In the *De malo*, by contrast, we hear of the deviants from "the order of divine rule," including its very executors, which is possible because "it is not necessary that the angel by knowing its essence, understands the whole order of the divine rule."[31] Therefore, while, as an intellectual being, it cannot think the true to be false, "nothing impedes its intellect from having failed in sufficiently apprehending the divine rule, and in this way sin followed in its will,"[32] because "its will was not measured by the measure of the divine rule."[33] Any "defect," "deviation" or "inordinance," whether of the celestial bodies—which are subject to the measurement of the divine rule "not as if moving themselves, but as moved by another"—or of intellectual or rational beings, who are subject "as directing themselves according to the divine measure," implies no defect in the indefectible ruler.[34] In sum, the diversity of divine rule, while crucial to its justice, appears to threaten its order and unity: angelic intelligences, although "not utilizing phantasms or discursive reasoning"[35] do not understand *in toto* the providential order, and so can fail to will it, and, thus, demonic rule is introduced into the cosmos. Human intelligence, as originating in phantasms and proceeding discursively,

30. Ibid, l. 23: "Postquam tradidit modum divini regiminis et ostendit sufficientiam Dei ad regendum, hic agit de regimine secundae causae, scilicet intelligentiae, quod quidem regimen fit ex virtute causae primae."

31. Thomas Aquinas, *Quaestiones Disputatae, Opera Omnia,* V. 23, ed. Leon., 1982 (hereafter cited as *De malo*), q. 16, a. 2 ad 10, 452–56: "Causa autem prima excedit modum substantiae, angeli vel demonis, unde non oportet quod angelus cognoscendo essentiam suam apprehenderit totum ordinem diuini regiminis."

32. Ibid., a. 2 ad 5, 375–84: "Ad quintum dicendum, quod ex hoc quod demon non utitur fantasia nec discursu rationis et per alia huiusmodi potest haberi quod in his que ad naturalem cognitionem pertinent non errat ut estimet aliquid falsum esse verum. Quia cum Deum propter eius infinitatem comprehendere non potest, nihil prohibet quod intellectus eius defecerit in apprehendendo sufficienter ordinem divini regiminis: et ex hoc consequtum est peccatum in eius voluntate."

33. Ibid., a. 2 ad 7, 424–32: "Ad septimum dicendum, quod peccatum demonis non prouenit ex defectu rationis qui haberet rationem contrarietatis—non enim approbauit malum pro bono nec verum pro falso—set solum ex defectu habente rationem negationis, in quantum scilicet uoluntas eius non fuit regulata regula diuini regiminis; ui quidem defectus potest habere locum in natura intellectuali contrarietate carente."

34. Ibid., a. 2 ad 8, 433–42: "Ad octavum dicendum, quod corpora caelestia subduntur regule diuini regiminis, non quasi se agentia, set quasi ab alio acta uel mota; et si in motibus eorum esset aliquis defectus uel deuiatio ab ordine diuinae regule, non hoc redundaret in defectum Dei ordinantis, qui non potest deficere. Set intellectuales et rationales nature subduntur diuino regimini, quasi se dirigentes secundum regulam diuinam; unde potest inordinatio in eis accidere ex eorum defectu absque defectu regentis."

35. V. supra, n. 32.

will *a fortiori* fall still further short of grasping divine order and so introduce tyranny into human affairs. Even the celestial bodies, ruled but not ruling, can be imagined, in comparison with their divine ruler, to exhibit some "defect or deviation in their motions."[36]

In the *De regno,* the analogy between divine and human rule is used to set a standard and measure for human governance. We find here the analogy between the *regimen universale* by which God governs the world and the form of *regimen particulare*

> which is found in the human, who, on account of this, is called a 'microcosm,' because in him is found the form of universal rule. For just as all corporeal creatures and all spiritual powers are contained under the divine rule, so also the parts of the body and the other powers of the soul are ruled by reason, and thus in this way reason is in the human being as God is in the world.[37]

But this is not the only way in which "the likeness of divine rule" is found in human beings; it is so "not only because each one is ruled by reason, but insofar as through the reason of one person the multitude is ruled," because, like bees, we are social. And so, the one who undertakes the office of king should understand that he is to the kingdom what reason is to the body and God is to the world.[38]

This analogy points to "three orders" in which reason must rule and to which the human will must submit: to the ordering of its own reason, to exterior governance whether spiritual or temporal, and finally to the "universal order of divine rule"; a perversion of any of these orders is an act against all of them.[39]

36. V. supra, n. 34.

37. *De regno,* Bk. 2, c. 1, 464, 11–19: "particulare autem regimen, maxime quidem diuino regimini simile, invenitur in homine, qui ob hoc minor mundus appellatur, quia in eo inuenitur forma universalis regiminis. Nam sicut universa creatura corporea et omnes spirituales uirtutes sub divino regimine continentur, sic et corporis membra et cetere vires anime a ratione reguntur, et sic quodammodo se habet ratio in homine sicut Deus in mundo."

38. Ibid., 20–35: "Sed quia, sicut supra ostendimus, homo est animal naturaliter sociale in multitudine uiuens, similitudo divini regiminis invenitur in homine non solum quantum ad hoc quod ratio regit ceteras hominis partes, sed ulterius quantum ad hoc quod per rationem unius hominis regitur multitudo; quod maxime pertinet ad officium regis, dum et in quibusdam animalibus, que socialiter uiuunt, quedam similitudo inuenitur huius regiminis, sicut in apibus, in quibus et reges esse dicuntur, non quod in eis per rationem sit regimen, sed per instinctum naturae inditum a summo regente, qui est auctor naturae. Hoc igitur officium rex suscepisse cognoscat, ut sit in regno sicut in corpore anima et sicut Deus in mundo."

39. *ST* I-II, q. 87, a. 1: "Unde secundum tres ordines quibus subditur humana voluntas, triplici poena potest homo puniri. Primo quidem enim subditur humana natura ordini propriae

With the office of king also comes the *triplex cura,* analogous to the cares of God. First, the king must insure the succession of persons in civil offices, the way that God has provided for the succession in corruptible things through generation, so that he may secure the common good as God secures the "integrity of the universe." Second, the king must constrain the people from iniquity and lead them to virtue, following the example of God, who gave the law and rewards and punishes in accordance with it. Third, the king must keep the people safe from their enemies.[40] The only *dis*analogy we find here is the limit of human virtue: "to lead [human beings] to eternal life is not the end of human, but of divine rule."[41]

Nevertheless, in the Mirror of Princes that Aquinas gives us in the *De regno,* divine exemplar and human copy shows its cracks and splinters when viewed in the light of salvation history. In the 3rd Book of his *Commentary on the Sentences,* he recounts how the *regimen humanum,* which is based on a natural law, became so weakened and obscured by sin, that the *lex vetus* is given to support it. Soon, however, love grows cold, *refrigescente caritate,* and the *remedium* of the incarnation becomes necessary, and, mercifully, before we totally freeze up, will come the glory.[42] Lack of order in

rationis; secundo, ordini exterioris hominis gubernantis vel spiritualiter vel temporaliter, politice seu oeconomice; tertio, subditur universali ordini divini regiminis. Quilibet autem horum ordinum per peccatum pervertitur, dum ille qui peccat, agit et contra rationem, et contra legem humanam, et contra legem divinam."

40. *De regno,* Bk. 2, c. 4, 467, ll. 89–468, l. 116: "Igitur contra tria praedicta triplex cura imminet regi. Primo quidem de successione hominum et substitutione illorum qui diuersis officiis praesunt, ut sicut per diuinum regimen in rebus corruptibilibus, quia semper eadem durare non possunt, prouisum est ut per generationem alia in locum aliorum succedant, ut uel sic conseruetur integritas uniuersi, ita per regis studium conseruetur subiecte multitudinis bonum, dum sollicite curat qualiter alii in deficientium locum succedant. Secundo autem ut suis legibus et praeceptis, poenis et praemiis homines sibi subiectos ab iniquitate coherceat et ad opera uirtuosa inducat, exemplum a Deo accipiens qui hominibus legem dedit, obseruantibus quidem mercedem, transgredientibus poenas retribuens. Tertio imminet regi cura ut multitudo sibi subiecta contra hostes tuta reddatur."

41. Ibid., c. 3, 466, ll. 94–98: "Sed quia finem fruitionis divine non consequitur homo per uirtutem humanam, sed uirtute diuina, iuxta illud apostolic "Gratia Dei, uita aeterna", perducere ad illum ultimum finem non est humani regiminis, sed divini."

42. *Super Sent.,* Bk. 3, d. 1, q. 1, a. 4: "... a principio generis humani indita est mentibus hominum lex naturalis, per quam homines Deo subjecti essent: postmodum vero invalescente consuetudine peccatorum, lex naturalis adeo tenebrata est in pluribus, ut jam non videretur ad regimen humani generis sufficere; et ideo tunc additum est aliud remedium, scilicet vetus lex, et ea quae ad ipsam pertinent: qua etiam processu temporis in hominum cordibus debilitata, oportuit aliud perfectius remedium per incarnationem apponi usque ad tempus illud, cum multorum caritas refrigescet, et tunc succedet per secundum adventum visio fidei, et status gloriae statui praesentis Ecclesiae."

the individual occurs when reason follows the "sensual powers." Likewise, "in human government lack of order arises from the coming to power of someone not because of intellectual preeminence, but either when someone seizes it in virtue of his bodily strength or when someone is put in power because of sensual feeling."[43] Even the wise ruler lacks the wisdom by which God rules the world, "because it exceeds the reasoning of human government," as in Job 12, 24: "He takes understanding from the leaders of the land, till they grope in the darkness without light; he makes them stagger like drunken men."[44] Nevertheless, "human government is derived from divine government and ought to imitate it, e.g., by allowing "some evil," lest greater goods be lost or greater evils ensue.[45]

Among human governments, there is a *dis*analogy between the rule of tyrants and divine rule, since the *regimen tyrannicum* is "the worst," the "most unjust," sustained only by fear, and, because it seeks the private good of the ruler rather than the common good, inordinate to the point of being "most seditious."[46] In sum, for Aquinas, while there is government by tyrants, there is no *tyrannicum regnum*; the term "regnum" is reserved for that rule by *one* which resembles the kingship of God.[47]

43. *SCG* III, c. 81, n. 6: "... ita et in regimine humano inordinatio provenit ex eo quod non propter intellectus praeminentiam aliquis praeest, sed vel robore corporali dominium sibi usurpat, vel propter sensualem affectionem aliquis ad regendum praeficitur."

44. Thomas Aquinas, *Super I Epistolam B. Pauli ad Corinthios lectura* (http://www.corpusthomisticum.org), c. 2, l. 2: "Saeculares enim principes hanc sapientiam non cognoverunt, quia excedit rationem humani regiminis. Iob XII, 24: qui immutat cor principum populi terrae, et decipit eos, ut frustra incedant per invium."

45. *ST* II-II, q. 10, a. 11: "Respondeo dicendum quod humanum regimen derivatur a divino regimine, et ipsum debet imitari. Deus autem, quamvis sit omnipotens et summe bonus, permittit tamen aliqua mala fieri in universo, quae prohibere posset, ne, eis sublatis, maiora bona tollerentur, vel etiam peiora mala sequerentur. Sic igitur et in regimine humano illi qui praesunt recte aliqua mala tolerant, ne aliqua bona impediantur, vel etiam ne aliqua mala peiora incurrantur."

46. Ibid., q. 42, a. 2 ad 3: "Ad tertium dicendum quod regimen tyrannicum non est iustum, quia non ordinatur ad bonum commune, sed ad bonum privatum regentis, ut patet per philosophum, in III Polit. et in VIII Ethic. Et ideo perturbatio huius regiminis non habet rationem seditionis, nisi forte quando sic inordinate perturbatur tyranni regimen quod multitudo subiecta maius detrimentum patitur ex perturbatione consequenti quam ex *tyranni* regimine. Magis autem tyrannus seditiosus est, qui in populo sibi subiecto discordias et seditiones nutrit, ut tutius dominari possit." *De regno*, lib. 1, c. 3, 452, 1–2: "Sicut autem regimen regis est optimum, ita regimen tyranni est pessimum." Ibid., 41: "regimen igitur tyranni est iniustissimum." Ibid., c. 10, 462, 106–11: "Fortassis autem nec fidelitati contrarium reputabitur secundum opinionem multorum, si tyrannice nequitia qualitercumque obuietur. Restat ergo ut solo timore tyranni regimen sustentetur, unde et timeri se a subditis tota intentione procurant. Timor autem est debile firmamentum."

47. Aquinas defines the tyrannical regime as the *corruptio regni* in *Sententia Libri Ethicorum,*

However, in the first redactions of *Summa Contra Gentiles* III, Aquinas proposes another *dis*analogy: namely, "in what ways the divine rule differs from tyrannical rule *and* from the rule of kings." The tyrant takes as his end his own utility, for which his subjects are the means; the king, by contrast, takes the utility of his subjects as the end, so that "they may be well-ordered each to the other." But divine rule over human beings is more than this, for it is like paternal rule:

For the father also has the care of the child, not only with respect to those things through which he or she is ordered to others, but also with respect to those things pertaining to him or her *secundum se*, as has also been shown concerning God above. And this [likeness] is rational, because just like God, the natural father gives the human child his natural beginning. Wherefore divine and paternal rule is extended to some person not only because he or she is political, but insofar as he subsists in his nature. Nevertheless, the two [forms of] rule differ, because paternal rule is only able to encompass those things which appear in this child on the outside, while divine rule also encompasses interior things. The care or responsibility of the father cannot reach to those things which are hidden from him, for the secrets of the heart are concealed from human beings which are shown to God.... For God demands an accounting from the human person not only concerning what he may perform exteriorly, but also for how he is interiorly disposed, both what he wishes to do and what he intends through what he does.[48]

Opera Omnia, V. 47, pt. 2, ed. Leon., 1969, Bk. 8, l. 10, 51–52: "Et dicit quod transgressio sive corruptio regni vocatur tyrannus. *Super I Epistolam B. Pauli ad Timotheum lectura* (http://www.corpusthomisticum.org), c. 2, l. 3. "Eccle. XXV, 30: mulier si primatum habeat, contraria est viro suo. Et philosophus dicit, quod dominium mulierum est corruptio familiae, sicut tyranni in regno. Et sic prohibet duo contra duo, quae competunt eis, sed primum repetit, scilicet sed esse in silentio."

48. Thomas Aquinas, *Primae redactiones Summae contra Gentiles*, Bk. 3: "Quod lege Dei non requiritur ab homine solum ut sit bene ordinatus ad alios, sicut legibus regum iustorum. Non solum autem divinum regimen tyrannorum regimini dissimile est, qui propriam utilitatem a subditis expetunt, sed etiam multum differt a regimine regum qui subditorum utilitatem intendunt. Reges enim ad socialem vitam inter homines conservandam constituuntur: unde publicae personae dicuntur, quasi publicum bonum procurantes." Primae redactiones *Summae contra Gentiles*, Bk. 3: "Quod divinum regimen/ ad homines/ est sicut regimen paternum. Videtur autem paternum regimen aliquam similitudinem habere cum divino regimine, nam etiam pater curam habet de filio non solum quantum ad ea in quibus ordinatur ad alios, sicut rex, sed etiam quantum ad ea quae pertinent ad ipsum secundum se, quod/ etiam/ de Deo etiam supra ostensum est. Et hoc rationabiliter accidit, nam sicut Deus ita et pater naturalem originem homini praestat. Unde divinum regimen et paternum ad aliquem hominem extenditur non solum secundum quod politicus est, sed etiam secundum quod in sua natura subsistit./ in/ hoc tamen/ inter/ utrumque regimen differt quod paternum regimen ad illa tantum se extendere potest quae in/ hoc/ homine apparent exterius, divinum autem regimen etiam ad ea quae interius sunt: cura enim alicuius non potest esse de his quae ipsum latent, homines autem occulta cordium latent,

These restrictions remind us of those things that human law and human rulers cannot do and, therefore, should not attempt, as Aquinas outlines them in *ST* I-II 91, 4: it cannot direct citizens to their final end, because this end is not proportioned to reason, and so human law must defer to divine law in this area; it is restricted by the "uncertainty of human judgment, especially on contingent and particular matters"; it is "not competent to judge of interior movements, that are hidden, but only of exterior acts which appear," and therefore it cannot successfully encourage or repress them; finally, and on account of the first three, it cannot forbid all evil nor enjoin all good.[49]

When, therefore, Aquinas differentiates divine rule or providence from human rule in the *Expositio* on Job, calling providence "secret" and "manifold," he is not talking about characteristics that human rule may seek to imitate. Human rulers do not fail at ruling only by defecting from the divine order, like some angelic rulers. The king seeks the common good, in imitation of God, and the tyrant perverts this, seeking his own, private good. However, the king should not seek to rule the interior movements of the soul or seek control over details he cannot hope to understand, let alone direct. The manifest inadequacies of our language should modify human ambition in this direction. We speak of "the invisible things of God," His secrets, yet God is really completely transparent; it is we who see through

---

quae Deo sunt manifesta, ut ex/ dictis patet/ superioribus patet. Requirit igitur Deus ab homine non solum quid exterius agat, sed etiam qualiter interius afficiatur, et quid facere velit, et quid ex his quae facit intendat."

49. *ST* I-II, 91, 4: "Sed quia homo ordinatur ad finem beatitudinis aeternae, quae excedit proportionem naturalis facultatis humanae, ut supra habitum est; ideo necessarium fuit ut supra legem naturalem et humanam, dirigeretur etiam ad suum finem lege divinitus data. Secundo, quia propter incertitudinem humani iudicii, praecipue de rebus contingentibus et particularibus, contingit de actibus humanis diversorum esse diversa iudicia, ex quibus etiam diversae et contrariae leges procedunt. Ut ergo homo absque omni dubitatione scire possit quid ei sit agendum et quid vitandum, necessarium fuit ut in actibus propriis dirigeretur per legem divinitus datam, de qua constat quod non potest errare. Tertio, quia de his potest homo legem ferre, de quibus potest iudicare. Iudicium autem hominis esse non potest de interioribus motibus, qui latent, sed solum de exterioribus actibus, qui apparent. Et tamen ad perfectionem virtutis requiritur quod in utrisque actibus homo rectus existat. Et ideo lex humana non potuit cohibere et ordinare sufficienter interiores actus, sed necessarium fuit quod ad hoc superveniret lex divina. Quarto quia, sicut Augustinus dicit, in I de Lib. Arb., lex humana non potest omnia quae male fiunt, punire vel prohibere, quia dum auferre vellet omnia mala, sequeretur quod etiam multa bona tollerentur, et impediretur utilitas boni communis, quod est necessarium ad conversationem humanam. Ut ergo nullum malum improhibitum et impunitum remaneat, necessarium fuit supervenire legem divinam, per quam omnia peccata prohibentur."

a glass darkly. The oft-repeated claim that God permits small evils so that greater goods are not lost or greater evils do not occur is an admission that the multiplicity of events and their meaning is impossible for us to read: "the height of the ruler exceeding the entire proportion of the creature."

This phrase, *excedens proportionem*, which occurs only ten times in Aquinas's writings, has a very precise frame of reference: the relation between God, as the final end of human life, and natural human capacities. The "felicity of which the philosophers speak" is proportioned to human nature and "obtainable through their natural powers." But "there is another good of man, exceeding the proportion or capacity of human nature."[50] And "nature is not capable of an act exceeding the proportion of its own power," so that, while human beings can love God above all things, they cannot "produce meritorious acts proportionate to eternal life," because it is "an end exceeding the capacity or proportion of human nature . . . ;"[51] thus, while being an end to which they are "divinely ordained," human beings require the gift of grace and "virtues above natural inclination" in order that it does not exceed their grasp.[52] Indeed, even with the attainment

50. *De veritate* V. 22, II, fasc. 2, 441, q. 14, a. 2, 147–61: "Est autem duplex hominis bonum ultimum quod primo voluntatem movet quasi ultimus finis, quorum unum est proportionatum naturae humanae, quia ad ipsum obtinendum vires naturales sufficient, et hoc est felicitas de qua philosophi locuti sunt, vel contemplativa, quae consistit in actu sapientiae, vel activa, quae consistit primo in actu prudentiae, et consequenter in actibus aliarum virtutum moralium. Aliud est bonum hominis naturae humanae *proportionem excedens* quia ad ipsum obtinendum vires naturales non sufficiunt, nec etiam ad cognoscendum vel desiderandum; sed ex sola divina liberalitate homini repromittitur . . ."

51. *ST* I-II, q. 109, a. 3 ad 2: "Sed intelligendum est quod natura non potest in actum vitae aeternae, sed ad hoc exigitur altior virtus, quae est virtus gratiae *excedentem proportionem* suae virtutis. Talis autem actus non est diligere Deum super omnia, hoc enim est naturale cuilibet naturae creatae, ut dictum est. *ST* I-II, q. 109, a. 5: Vita autem aeterna est finis excedens proportionem naturae humanae, ut ex supradictis patet. Et ideo homo per sua naturalia non potest producere opera meritoria proportionate."

52. Ibid., q. 114, a. 2: "Actus autem cuiuscumque rei non ordinatur divinitus ad aliquid *excedens proportionem* virtutis quae est principium actus, hoc enim est ex institutione divinae providentiae, ut nihil agat ultra suam virtutem. Vita autem aeterna est quoddam bonum excedens proportionem naturae creatae, quia etiam excedit cognitionem et desiderium eius, secundum illud I ad Cor. II, nec oculus vidit, nec auris audivit, nec in cor hominis ascendit. Et inde est quod nulla natura creata est sufficiens principium actus meritorii vitae aeternae, nisi superaddatur aliquod supernaturale donum, quod gratia dicitur." *De virtutibus*, q. 1, a. 12 ad 6. "Ad sextum dicendum, quod respectu finis qui est naturae humanae proportionatus, sufficit homini ad bene se habendum naturalis inclinatio; et ideo philosophi posuerunt aliquas virtutes, quarum obiectum esset felicitas, de qua ipsi tractabant. Sed finis in quo beatitudinem speramus, Deus, est naturae nostrae *excedens proportionem*; et ideo supra naturalem inclinationem necessariae sunt nobis virtutes, quibus in finem ultimum elevemur."

of eternal life, "the divine essence is a form that exceeds the proportion of any creature whatsoever."[53] God, in sum, "is the exemplar exceeding all proportion or capacity of the creature."[54] One God, therefore, can rule the world, but not one prince. Aquinas indeed implies, in his commentary on the Apostles' Creed, that the limitations of the analogy between divine and human kingship contribute to the failure to understand that there is but one God.[55]

IV. History and Providence

The historian Henri Marrou has said that arriving at the complete truth of history, the what-it-is-that-has-happened, requires rendering the singular transparent, which is only possible for God.[56] On Marrou's understanding, for the same reason that He is the exemplar ruler, God would be the perfect historian. Is the study of history, then, a remedy for the opacity of the singular heart and the singular act, which baffles both individual prudence and human governance? Let me move from Marrou to Maritain's *On the Philosophy of History,* for the outline, at least, of an answer.

Here Maritain interprets Aquinas's statement in *De veritate* that "the judgment of the intellect ... is dependent on [the senses] as on a final terminus with reference to which the resolution of the judgment takes place"[57]

53. *ST* III, q. 9, a. 3 ad 3: "Ad tertium dicendum quod cognitio beata non fit per speciem quae sit similitudo divinae essentiae, vel eorum quae in divina essentia cognoscuntur, ut patet ex his quae in prima parte dicta sunt, sed talis cognitio est ipsius divinae essentiae immediate, per hoc quod ipsa essentia divina unitur menti beatae sicut intelligibile intelligenti. Quae quidem essentia divina est forma *excedens proportionem* cuiuslibet creaturae. Unde nihil prohibet quin, cum hac forma superexcedente, simul insint rationali menti species intelligibiles proportionatae suae naturae."

54. Thomas Aquinas, *Quaestiones disputatae de potentia* (http://www.corpusthomisticum.org), q. 7, a. 4 ad 5 (hereafter cited as *De potentia*): "Ad quintum dicendum quod exemplata non semper repraesentant perfecte exemplar; unde quandoque quod est in exemplari deficienter et imperfecte invenitur in exemplato; et praecipue in his quae exemplantur a Deo, qui est exemplar omnem creaturae *proportionem excedens.*"

55. Thomas Aquinas, *Expositio in Symbolum Apostolorum* (http://www.corpusthomisticum.org), a. 1: "Cuius ratio est, quia illa dispositio rerum humanarum est bene disposita, in qua multitudo invenitur disponi et gubernari per unum. Nam multitudo praesidentium inducit saepe dissensionem in subditis: unde cum divinum regimen praeeminet regimini humano, manifestum est quod regnum mundi non est per multos deos, sed per unum tantum. Sunt autem quatuor, ex quibus homines inducti sunt ad ponendum plures deos."

56. Henri Marrou, *Time and Timeliness* (New York: Sheed and Ward, 1969), 18.

57. *De veritate* V. 22, II, fasc. 1, 378, q. 12, a. 3 ad 3, 395–99: "Ad tertium dicendum quod iudici-

to require a necessary return to the senses at each degree of knowledge, and similarly "with respect to philosophical knowledge as a whole." He explains the going forth and return of all knowledge to the singular perceived through sense using one of his famous diagrams: "starting from experience, i.e., the level of the singular" the human mind arises first to the sciences, then to natural philosophy, and "at the supreme level of natural wisdom," metaphysics. But, he says, "the curve is not finished—after ascending it descends, it has to come down" first to moral philosophy, then "in brackets we have history facing the sciences. And finally, I propose, we have the philosophy of history as the final application of philosophical knowledge to the development of human events."[58]

Maritain invites the philosopher to consider history, to look at the "entire movement of humanity,"[59] "the very succession of time.... the singularity of the entire course of events,"[60] what Pieper describes as "that happening which takes place through time upon active and passive humanity and through its agency."[61] In sum, he asks the philosopher not only to think *about* God's providence, at the height of the philosophical curve, but to think *providentially* as that curve bends back down to the mystery of human existence. Thomas Aquinas appears to follow a parallel process, when, as lector at Orvieto (1261–65), he writes about providence simultaneously in the *Summa Contra Gentiles* III and the *Expositio super Job*.

The historian's perspective on the singular event is itself singular. He, *qua* singular, attempts to explain the singular, as Maritain notes, through "singular circumstances, motivations or events."[62] The formal object of the historian "is not scientific—it is not universal, not necessary, not raised to the level of abstract intelligibility."[63] If any philosophy of history is possible, it must, to avoid distortion, take "an indirect intellectual approach ... to the singular ... not in its singularity ... but as a meeting point of general typical aspects, which are to be found in a given individual and which may help us to understand" it.[64] It cannot be a milking of "essences" from the sin-

um intellectus non dependet a sensu hoc modo quod actus iste intellectus per organum sensibile exerceatur; indigent autem sicut extremo et ultimo ad quod resolutio fiat."

58. Jacques Maritain, *On the Philosophy of History* (New York: Charles Scribners and Sons, 1957), 13.

59. Ibid, 17.

60. Ibid., 35.

61. Josef Pieper, *The End of Time* (London: Faber & Faber, 1954), 13.

62. Maritain, *On the Philosophy of History*, 3.

63. Ibid., 5.

64. Ibid., 15.

gular event,[65] which produces not a philosophy, but a "Gnosticism of history" à la Hegel and Comte.[66] Maritain sees it as subalternated to political philosophy as it studies human groups, and to ethics, insofar as it studies decisions and activities of individuals as well. This relation to moral philosophy, however, comes with a familiar Maritainian twist: because of its practical object, moral philosophy must take into account the human existential condition, including that evidence only available from revelation, e.g., creation, original sin, grace, and the prophecy of the end. This is still philosophy, not theology, in Maritain's *didascalicon*, because it will take the point of view of the world or the City of Man, humble as that may be.[67]

Aquinas would have approved Maritian's "turn" to history; indeed, he makes it himself in the *Expositio.* In addition to his concern to establish that Job was an historical person, he approves the methods of history in testing hypotheses concerning divine providence. Baldath, who begins by proposing that those who have been punished for sin will return to prosperity if they have a conversion of heart, wants to confirm this through experience. St. Thomas considers this approach very appropriate: "For experience is the most efficacious kind of proof in the case of particular things, and the more so the longer it has been observed and found without error. But those things which take time are best double-checked through the recollections of the ancients."[68] To lengthen and strengthen our experience, we must turn to the memories of the living (patres) and, beyond them, to the interrogation of the dead (*pristini* or *antiqui*), reading "accounts of ancient deeds and learning what concerning past peoples has been transmitted by report." Further, because "much is written and told in the mode of fables about ancient deeds," the avoidance of error requires that one have recourse to "the elders who are able to speak of what they saw."[69]

65. Ibid., 14–16.

66. Ibid., 31.

67. Ibid., 39, 133–36.

68. *Super Iob* c. 8, 127–43: "Experimentum enim in rebus particularibus maxime efficax est ad probandum, et tanto magis quanto diuturnius est observatum et infallibile inventum. Ea autem quae diuturnitatem temporis requirunt per antiquorum memorias maxime comprobantur, et ideo ad propositi probationem recurrit ad antiquorum memorias, et quantum ad antiquos cum dicit *interroga enim generationem pristinam,* et quantum ad immediate praecedentes cum dicit *et diligenter investiga patrum memoriam,* idest ea quae patres tui in memoria habent. Interrogatio autem generationis pristinae est considerando antiquorum gestorum scripta et ea quae de antiquis per famam feruntur; et quia de rebus antiquis multa fabulose et scribuntur et narrantur, ne ex hoc aliquis se falli reputaret, remittit ad patres qui narrare possunt ea quae viderunt."

69. Ibid. See Sommers, "*Manifestation:* The Historical Presencing of Being in Aquinas' *Exposition Super Job,*" *Proceedings of the American Catholic Philosophical Association* 62 (1988): 147–56.

Upon Aquinas's interpretation, the theories of divine governance put forward by Job and his friends are defended by appeals to observation and experience. Eliphaz understands himself "to have proved through experience" that "adversity does not touch the innocent and the upright."[70] In discussing the prosperity of wicked men, Sophar considers it to be *certissimum et experimentum probatum* that their rejoicing is short-lived,[71] while Job argues that some of the wicked really prosper while others really suffer *quod experimentum apparet.*[72] Indeed, Job, according to Aquinas, describes the method by which "the surpassing greatness of God" comes to be known by humanity "through the experience of divine power and wisdom in human affairs."[73]

Whence he shows first in what way human beings come to the knowledge of things through experience, saying "does not the ear distinguish among words? Do not the jaws of the one eating discern flavor?" Because experience is from sense, the power of experience is appropriately revealed through the judgment of the senses, and especially through hearing and taste, because hearing, among the senses, is the most productive of knowledge, whence it has great value for the contemplative sciences. Taste, on the other hand, is discerning of the foods which are necessary to human life, whence, through the judgment of taste, experience signifies that which is had for the things of the active life. Whence through the judgment of these two senses is shown the power of experience, both in speculation and action.[74]

70. Ibid., c. 4, 131–37: "Posito ergo quod innocentibus et rectis adversitas non contingat, consequenter adiungit quibus adversitas contingat dicens *Quin potius vidi eos qui operantur iniquitatem et seminant dolores et metunt eos, flante Deo perisse et spiritu irae eius esse consumptos.* In hoc autem quod dicit vidi dat intelligere se ista per experimentum probasse."

71. Ibid., c. 20, 32–36: "Hoc autem videbatur ei certissimum et experimento probatum quod mali etsi aliqua prosperitate gaudeant, tamen illa sit brevis et cito in hac vita etiam finiatur vel per festinam mortem vel per aliquam subsequentem adversitatem. . . ."

72. Ibid., c. 21, 270–72: "Erat autem opinio amicorum Iob quod ratio praedictae diversitatis esset ex diversitate meritorum, quod est contra id quod experimento apparet de hoc quod impiorum quidam prosperantur, quidam adversa patiuntur."

73. Ibid., c. 12, 163–68: "*Nonne auris verba diiudicat* etc. Quia superius posuerat Iob ea quae Sophar de excellentia divinae magnitudinis dixerat esse omnibus manifesta, intendit hic ostendere quod hoc ad notitiam hominum pervenire potest per experimentum divinae potentiae et sapientiae in rebus humanis."

74. Ibid., 168–82: "Unde primo manifestat quomodo homines per experimentum in rerum cognitionem deveniant, dicens nonne auris verba diiudicat, scilicet dum ea audit? Et fauces comedentis saporem nonne diiudicant? Quia experimentum a sensu est, convenienter per iudicium sensuum virtutem experimenti manifestat, et praecipue per auditum et gustum, quia auditus inter omnes sensus est disciplinabilior, unde plurimum ad scientias contemplativas valet; gustus autem est perceptivus ciborum qui homini sunt necessarii ad vitam, unde per iudicium gustus experimentum significat quod de rebus activae vitae habetur. Et propter hoc ex iudicio duorum sensuum ostendit virtutem experimenti tam in speculativis quam in operativis."

What is it that through experience, given "much time," we can discover about God? There are four things: his understanding, i.e., that he knows the hidden things; his counsel for the finding of appropriate means; his wisdom, which is shown in right judgment; and his fortitude, which is the powerful execution of those things that he judges ought to be done.[75] Aquinas next delineates specific experiences, both in human affairs and in nature, which illuminate each of these divine characteristics. One example, of the "divine strength," will suffice:

> For we see that some men are completely destroyed, either through death with respect to their natural being or through complete degradation in their civil being, even though they have many protectors; whence since they are not able to be aided such that they avoid destruction, it is clear that this occurs from some hidden and divine cause, excelling human power, since no human power is able to resist it.[76]

Thus, acting as historians, confronted by a puzzle, a *collation* of human affairs, we may catch a glimpse of God governing. While it may be in accordance with the divine dispensation "that this sheep is killed by this wolf," this does not occur "because of some merit or lack thereof of either this wolf or this sheep, but because of the good of the species, since it is divinely ordained that each species should have its proper food."[77]

However, since each human being is divinely governed *for his own sake*, Job cannot be a generic victim of predators, natural or otherwise. Human tragedy, as opposed to ovine, must be personalized. His friends interpret his vicissitudes according to a simple rule, "their straightforward moral cal-

75. Ibid., 188–203: "Sic igitur manifestata experimenti virtute, subiungit quid homines de Deo experiri possunt cum dicit A*pud ipsum est sapientia et fortitudo*, ipse habet consilium et intelligentiam. Ubi quatuor Deo attribuit quae se per ordinem habent: nam primum quidem est occulta cognoscere, quod ad intelligentiam pertinet; secundum autem est, ex his quae homo intelligit, invenire in activis quidem vias accommodas ad aliquem finem, quod ad consilium pertinet, sicut et in speculativis, per ea quae homo intelligit, rationes deducit ad aliquas conclusiones cognoscendas; tertium autem est ut de his quae homo adinvenit rectum iudicium habeat, quod ad sapientiam pertinet; quartum autem est ut ea quae aliquis iudicat esse facienda potenter exequatur, et ad hoc pertinet fortitudo."

76. Ibid., 209–17: "Videmus enim quod aliqui homines totaliter destruuntur, vel per mortem quantum ad esse naturae vel per omnimodam abiectionem quantum ad esse civile cum tamen habeant multos manutentores; unde cum adiuvari per homines non possunt ne ad destructionem perveniant, manifestum est quod ab aliqua occulta causa et divina et excellente humanam virtutem hoc contingit, cum ei virtus humana resistere non possit."

77. Ibid., c. 7, 385–90: "... quod haec ovis occiditur ab hoc lupo vel aliquid aliud huiusmodi, non dispensatur a Deo propter aliquod meritum vel demeritum huius lupi vel huius ovis, sed propter bonum specierum, quia divinitus unicuique speciei ordinatus est proprius cibus."

culus,"[78] whereby sin, public or hidden, is their necessary cause. Job, nevertheless, understands his own history as an argument against this rule: that he is not being punished for his sins is clear "from the rectitude of his life." While it is desirable for the judgments of human rulers and their ensuing rewards and punishments to be public and comprehensible, Job maintains that "no certain and demonstrative proof can be produced concerning divine judgments, since the divine will is incomprehensible."[79] Therefore, the justice of divine governance, which extends to the whole, yet still perfectly measures the smallest motions of the human will with respect to its end, eludes those who, like Job's friends, do not see the limits of its analogy to human governance.

V. Conclusion

However important what we have learned from being attentive to the evidence of Job's life, it is, on balance, very little. While constructing a narrative that makes sense for him out of cattle raids conducted by Sabeans and Chaldeans and the collapse of a house on Job's children, we have to let slip through our fingers their significance for the lives of his wife, the dead children, not to mention those of his friends, Eliphaz, Baldath, and Sophar. And, if we struggle with these interlocking narratives, perhaps some clue to what the savagery of the Sabeans and the Chaldeans could possibly mean will come to light. One narrative leads inexorably to another and defeat stares us in the face; or, alternatively, the specter of heresy like Brother Juniper in Thornton Wilder's *The Bridge of San Luis Rey*. The devout Franciscan friar, who thought "that it was high time for theology to take its place among the exact sciences,"[80] saw the collapse of the bridge, this "sheer Act of God" as "a perfect laboratory," where "one could surprise His intentions in a pure state."[81] The resemblance of this "experimental method" to Satan's proposal to strip Job of his family, wealth, and bodily well-being in order

78. John Yocum, "Aquinas' Literal exposition on Job" in *Aquinas On Scripture: An Introduction To His Biblical Commentaries*, edited by Thomas G. Weinandy, OFM Cap., John P. Yocum, Daniel A. Keating (London and New York: T. & T. Clark, 2005), 35.

79. *Super Iob*, c. 23, 207–12: "Et ne aliquis diceret hanc probationem quam induxit ex rectitudine suae vitae non esse convenientem, ostendit consequenter quod de divinis iudiciis certissima et demonstrative probation induci non potest propeter incomprehensibilitatem divinae voluntatis. . . ."

80. Thornton Wilder, *The Bridge of San Luis Rey* (New York: Albert & Charles Boni, 1927), 19.

81. Ibid., 20.

to test God's assessment of Job's God-fearing character, is unmistakable, if imperfect. Brother Juniper did not doubt divine providence, "[h]e merely wanted to prove it, historically, mathematically, to his converts ... so slow to believe that their pains were inserted into their lives for their own good."[82] He is confident in the power of science to reveal "the hidden and multiple governance of God." In the wake of a plague, "he secretly drew up a diagram of the characteristics of fifteen victims and fifteen survivors, the statistics of their value *sub specie aeternitatis*. Each soul was rated upon a basis of ten as regards its goodness, its diligence in religious observance, and its importance to the family group."[83]

The collapse of the Bridge "prompted him to busy himself for six years, knocking at all the doors in Lima, asking thousands of questions, filling scores of notebooks, in his effort to establish that each of the lives lost was a perfect whole."[84] The resulting book "deals with one after another of the victims, cataloguing thousands of little facts and anecdotes and testimonies, and concluding with a dignified passage describing why God had settled upon that person and upon that day for his demonstration of wisdom."[85] Wilder uses the subsequent burning of the book and its Rationalist author to affirm the gap between human science and divine wisdom, which the great and perilous suspension bridge seems to symbolize. Neither statistics nor history is adequate to capture the full meaning of the divine governance that brings just five persons together in death.

God, nevertheless, intends that history disclose something of the providential narrative. Aquinas is clear about this. When Job concludes that he is being tried as "gold through fire," Aquinas comments that gold does not become true gold by being subjected to the fire, but is tested so "that its truth may be manifested to men."[86] Job's reversal of fortune does not make him virtuous; it does not establish him as virtuous in the judgment of God, who already knows what Job is. Its cause, its whole purpose, is that the virtue of Job "become manifest to everybody": to his friends, who construe adversity as "evidence" of vice, and to Satan, the technician of his misfortune.[87]

82. Ibid., 20–21.

83. Ibid., 213.

84. Ibid., 22.

85. Ibid., 23.

86. *Super Job*, c. 23, 166–70: "Et sicut aurum non fit verum aurum ex igne sed eius veritas hominibus manifestatur, its Iob per adversitatem probates est non ut eius virtus appareret coram Deo, sed ut hominbus manifestaretur...."

87. Ibid., c. 1, 575–77: "Patet igitur ex praedictis hanc fuisse causam adversitatis beati Io but eius virtus omnibus fieret manifesta...."

God, to rule the world, has to be everywhere at once, or better, *with* everyone at once, like the figure of the Fool from the Tarot pack in Charles Williams' novel *The Greater Trumps*.[88] As in many Williams' novels, a Platonic form breaks through the wall of the physical universe to transform or destroy. At the end, the eidetic tarot cards are at last glimpsed in motion: not as the fortune-teller's static map, but as a dance choreographed by the Christ/Fool, who comes to any one point on the floor "from all sides at once, but is only One." This is, perhaps, as close as we can get to the "feathery delicacy" of providence,[89] a governance both universal and multiple, usually hidden, but revealed sometimes in the midst of great tragedies and greater joys.

88. Charles Williams, *The Greater Trumps* (http://gutenberg.net.au/ebooks06/0608881.txt), c. 10:"She knew where the golden light came from among the images; it came from the figure of the Fool who moved so much the most swiftly, who seemed to be everywhere at once, whose irradiation shone therefore so universally upward that it maintained the circle of gold high over all, under which the many other rays of colour mingled and were dominated now by one, now by another.... the vivid figure of the Fool."

89. Gerard Manley, Hopkins, SJ, "The Wreck of the Deutschland, stanza 31, ll. 246: "Well, she has thee for the pain, for the/Patience; but pity of the rest of them!/Heart, do and bleed at a bitterer vein for the/Comfortless unconfessed of them—/No not uncomforted: lovely-felicitous Providence/Finger of a tender of; O of a feathery delicacy, the breast of the/Maiden could obey so, be a bell to, ring of it, and/Startle the poor sheep back! is the shipwreck then a harvest, does tempest carry the grain for thee?"

JAMES V. SCHALL, SJ

How Evil Is Evil? How Good Is Good?*

All the love cast for centuries on the roads of time—is it possible that it is forever lost? To exist would be worse than absurd if there were not eternal life.

—Jacques Maritain[1]

The devil has the widest perspectives for God, and that is why he keeps so far away from him—the devil being the oldest friend of knowledge.

—Nietzsche[2]

Morality demands that before evil is done by a man we should do everything to prevent it; and afterwards everything to undo it without inducing a greater evil; but if that is impossible, it demands that we recognize that which is: the existence of the evil that this man has committed, and which is there, which has been committed, which has taken its place in the course of the events of this world, together with the good on which it preys.

—Jacques Maritain[3]

I

Nietzsche remarks, recalling Genesis, that the devil is the "oldest friend" of "knowledge." The tree in the Garden was named the "Tree of

*This essay originally appeared online in the ISI Web Journal, *First Principles* (December 8, 2009).

1. Jacques Maritain, *Notebooks* (Albany: Magi Books, [1965] 1984), 153.

2. Friedrich Nietzsche, *Beyond Good and Evil* (Harmondsworth: Penguin, [1886] 1976), #129, 81.

3. Jacques Maritain, *Integral Humanism* (Notre Dame: University of Notre Dame Press, [1934] 1973), 221.

Knowledge of Good and Evil." The devil tempted Adam and Eve to partake of its fruit, contrary to the prohibition of God, the only one given to them. Had they not eaten of the tree, they would not, presumably, have had this kind of knowledge that comes to us when we actually do something evil, a concrete, not abstract, knowledge. The command was for their good. It gave them responsibility over their own fate, without which they would not have been free. We presume also that this famous aphorism of Nietzsche does not, in principle, suggest that the primary meaning or cause of evil is knowledge itself, but what we do with it. They understood what the prohibition required of them.

We likewise hesitate to identify the devil with knowledge and God with something else that is not knowledge. *Deus Logos Est.* The knowledge that an angel can have and God's own knowledge are not in principle in opposition to each other. How could they be? The "truth" in the being of an angel is ultimately located in the creative knowledge of the Godhead about what is not God Himself, or better about what is known in Himself that can be imitated and chosen to exist outside of Him. The angel does not cause himself either to exist or to exist as an angel. The angel knows his relative rank in being.

Maritain, early in *An Introduction to Philosophy,* writes of the Zoroastrian or Manichean notions of evil. It is located in a separate god of evil. In the light of Nietzsche's remark about the "oldest friend of knowledge," Maritain's comments are worth noting:

> By his failure to perceive that God is the sole supreme principle and the source of everything which exists, so far as it partakes of being, and that evil is mere privation of being without positive existence, and therefore that no creature is evil by nature, Zoroaster ended in *dualism* and taught the existence of two principles uncreated and eternal, the principle of Good (*Ormuzd*) and the principle of Evil (*Ahriman*), who share the dominion over the universe and whose unrelenting struggle constitutes its history. So far as Ahriman is to be identified with the rebel angel of primitive tradition, Zoroastrianism tended to make the devil a god striving against God.[4]

Often we picture the devil as wanting to replace God, to himself become the one God.

Strictly speaking, the devil cannot think this way. He knows clearer

4. Jacques Maritain, *An Introduction to Philosophy,* trans. by E. I. Watkin (London: Sheed & Ward, [1930] 1946), 20.

than any other creature that he is not God. But he can, as Maritain put it, "strive against God." His fallenness does not reduce him to nothing. His being remains what it is. This striving, to the extent that it succeeds, is his evil. He uses his being to corrupt other free beings. He seeks to interfere with God's good and plan as it exists in creation and in creation's purpose as it passes through the descendants of Adam and Eve. And the striving against God is not possible without the use of what is good. Good and evil are not two gods. The drama takes place within the souls of finite human beings in their own personhood among beings who are good. Evil remains primarily a lack of what is good as caused by a free being.

These views of knowledge and the devil's friendliness to it are close to the Socratic affirmation that evil is really but ignorance. All we have to do to rid ourselves of evil is to know the truth. If we know it, we will do it. Learning itself ironically can thus become a kind of god, a cure of evil in the world. This approach is certainly tempting and often tried. It is "intellectual" without being "moral." It bypasses personal responsibility. If we could locate evil in lack of knowledge alone, we could solve the human problem by progress in knowledge and the sciences, by simply building more schools and hiring more tenured faculty. This solution indeed is what Strauss called "the modern project," the effort to solve all human problems by rearrangements of differing bodies of knowledge that would find the golden key to perfection.

This non-moral solution has zealously been advocated since the modern era began. No indication exists, however, that evil has declined in the light of increasing knowledge. We would, in this view, need no "repentance," self-discipline, or grace before evil. We only need accurate knowledge. Knowledge alone would cure evil's consequences. Instead of saying "I'm sorry for what I did," we would say "I know now what I did." Morality would become similar to correcting an error in a mathematics examination. It would only involve a correct understanding of the formulae, not our acknowledgement of our own contribution to what went wrong.

The stating of such propositions about evil is enough to give us pause. The history of politics shows that those who do the worst of evils are not the dumb, greedy, and stupid. The evils due to simple ignorance or dullardness are nowhere near as damaging as those stemming from what I call the philosophical politicians of this world. The Lenin's, Mao's, and Hitler's were not ignorant men who happened to acquire power. They were invariably men with a vision of how to make the world better and what prevented their cause to triumph. This ameliorative or visionary purpose is why they took the trouble of acquiring power in the first place. Their most terrible crimes had a rationale about them, a logic, a knowledge component. Their immediate followers were enthusiastic and excited to participate in world transforming forces, as they thought. Followers were not innocent of the same temptation of leaders. When their theories resulted in violations of human dignity or the Commandments, they preferred their theories.

We do know, however, that a basic knowledge component is found within anything evil, which is never just a "thing" but the lack of what should be there. Evil, though itself a lack, a nothing, must exist in a something which is good. Nietzsche's devil is not such a bad character with whom to begin the questions of "How evil is evil?" "How good is good?" The devil makes it clear that the worst evil did not have its origin solely in the conflict of spirit and body as it uniquely exists in human beings. This diversity of parts does cause us problems if we do not relate the parts of our being properly to our end. But really great evils, as Aristotle had already intimated, are found in philosophic minds. The bringing together, or the failure to do so, of knowledge and good in freedom is the essence of the human drama.

But the remarkable thing about evil is not that it only occurs with the great tyrants and sinners. We are sobered by the Christian instinct that evil is present and possible wherever there are men and women, either to chose or to reject it in whatever situation of life they find themselves. Dostoyevsky, in *Crime and Punishment,* asked whether it was all right with impunity to eliminate an evil old lady who had no redeeming characteristics. He did not think so. Huck Finn is always wrestling with his conscience over what is right and wrong. Hannah Arendt caused something of a scandal in her treatment of the Nazi prison commander who was banal, who was just following orders but who caused enormous evils. She was following a thesis of Augustine. She called it "the banality of evil." She meant that evil was found everywhere, not just in the great and powerful, where we can see it more easily.

All of our literature depicts something of the extent and nature of evil, not just of evil alone but of the responses to it. The drama is no less poignant and burdensome among the ordinary people and among the poor than it is among the great and powerful. The reason for this is that all are called to salvation on the basis of their lives, no matter in what sort of polity or economy they live. If there is anything that is strange about evil, it is the response to it. The whole dramatic interest of Christianity itself is the life of Christ. He came into the world, it is said, not to abolish evil directly, but to enable us to have our sins forgiven, almost as to say that by removing evil as such, something greater would also be removed, namely our freedom. The removal of evil could not be a one-way operation on the part of the Godhead.

This very fact suggests, at first sight, that sins are more important than suffering. Adam and Eve did not suffer in the Garden. It also suggests the Socratic principle that it is "better to suffer evil than to do it." At this point, Christ and Socrates are in full agreement. Both Socrates and Christ suffered evil unjustly imposed on them. They endured suffering when they had to rather than do something that seemed easy and simple, but wrong. They did not seek some "higher good" by doing evil to attain the good.

Something very democratic hovers about evil. It neglects no actual life. Each person decides in his thoughts and deeds where he stands before it. We see its consequences, if we will, in most divorces, however high-minded they are pictured to be. We see it in the effects on children, on the spouses. We see it in the tremendous extent of the illegal drug business with its profits and ruined lives, the murders it takes to get contraband into various countries. We see it in the enormous cost to society when individuals refuse to reject what they usually understand perfectly clearly to be bad for everyone. We see that modern medicine and politics conceive themselves as agents to remove "suffering" as the sole human problem. They are not, however, agents to forgive the sins that cause the suffering.

II

In his *Gulag Archipelago,* Solzhenitsyn tells of a Soviet official by the name of Yagoda. It seems that near the bathhouse on his estate, he used to set up Icons stolen from Russian Churches as objects of target practice with his pistols. Solzhenitsyn wonders if this shooting is an act of an "evildoer?" How are we to understand it? He wonders whether such people, evildoers, really exist.

> We would prefer to say that such people cannot exist, that there aren't any. It is permissible to portray evildoers in a story for children, so as to keep their picture simple. But when the great world literature of the past—Shakespeare, Schiller,

Dickens—inflates and inflates images of evildoers of the blackest shades, it seems somewhat farcical and clumsy to our contemporary perception. The trouble lies in the way these classic evildoers are pictured. They recognize themselves as evildoers, and they know their souls are black. And they reason: "I cannot live unless I do evil. So I'll set my father against my brother! I'll drink the victim's sufferings until I'm drunk with them!" Iago very precisely identifies his purposes and his motives as being black and born of hate.[5]

We moderns think that such evildoings are really exaggerations. The great writers stretch the point. We read about them. At bottom, however, they talk of something we know in our own souls but we do not want to admit it. The evildoing does not exist outside of us.

Our "contemporary perceptions" will not see the truth in classic writers' descriptions of evil. Partly, they want to prevent us from vividly seeing the evils that we ourselves have put into the world, especially those against life and love, the kind that most often, we think, lets us do what we want. This reason is, I suspect, why abortion, say, is never seen in its reality on television. In a world where everything is open, it is hidden. Classic evildoers, however, know and admit that they do evil. They hate. They choose to do their deeds. It becomes their life. Such life is "born of hate." "Hatred of whom?" we wonder. Themselves? Every sin is also an offense against God. This is the root of this hatred, as it is the root of the redemption.

The only thing to hate would seem to be something that is the opposite of their own hatred, something that everyone calls good but they call evil. Further, we cannot just hate an abstraction. Hatred must be personal. God is normally "hated" under the rubric of being the cause of the evil we call good. The essential point of the account of the Fall of Man in Genesis, in fact, was nothing less than man wanting the divine power of being himself the one who defines what is good and what is evil. The point was that this desire already implicitly was a turning away from the good that was prepared for him had he obeyed and understood that good, though from another, was for him. Like the fallen angel who knows he is not God, man, at least in his own acts, can put into existence acts that are evil, that is, that lack the good that should be in them. Once these acts are chosen and put into existence, they remain in existence in their effect. They may or may not eventually be repented, but they remain, as "lacks," among the ongoing

5. Alekesandr Solzhenitsyn, *The Gulag Archipelago* Part I, C. 4, in *The Solzhenitsyn Reader*, edited by E. Erickson and D. Mahoney (Wilmington: ISI Books, 2006), 233.

complexities of actual existence. Human society is a web of actions interrelated as good and evil.

The strangest thing about actual human nature is that its own good was intended to be something more than its own natural good. As Aquinas said, *"Homo non naturale sed supernaturale est."* This is an existential statement. It is not a denial that man is man. It is a denial that he is only what man would be were he not caught up, from his beginning, both as a species and as an individual within that species, in something greater than he can imagine. "Nothing is more human than for man to desire naturally things impossible to his nature," Maritain wrote in his *Approaches to God.*

> It is, indeed, the property of a nature which is not closed up in matter like the nature of physical things, but which is intellectual or infinitized by the spirit. It is the property of a *metaphysical* nature. Such desires reach for the infinite, because the intellect thirsts for being and being is infinite. They are natural, but one may also call them trans-natural. It is thus that we desire to see God; it is thus that we desire to be free without being able to sin; it is thus that we desire beatitude.[6]

What is Maritain saying here? It is "more human" to desire things "naturally beyond" our nature? Is this desire not the very *hubris,* the pride for which we took pains to blame the devil, that "friend of knowledge?"

Maritain's happy phrase "infinitized by the spirit" means both that man's finite nature is called to be more than nature assigns to it, noble as that is. His being "infinitized" is not of his own doing. It is the doing of what is not himself, by the Spirit; but it is not contrary to his given nature. The very nature of his intellect and love leaves him open to something higher. So, though he is that, man is more than the "microcosmos" to which status the Greeks assigned him. He is literally invited, in his very first creation, to participate in the inner life of the Godhead, something that is not natural to him. Yet it is something his nature can be called to by God, but only on condition of its being freely accepted. We are, as Maritain put it, "natural," but also "trans-natural." "Intellect thirsts for being and being is infinite." But the being we encounter, finite being, is not itself "infinite" except in logic. In being it is only infinite if that is its source.

The questions I am asking are "How good is good?" "How evil is evil?" These are not static questions. Being is not just another thing. As Solz-

6. Jacques Maritain, *Approaches to* God, translated by Peter O'Reilly (New York: Collier, [1954] 1962), 98.

henitsyn put it, the classic evildoer says "I cannot live unless I do evil." "So I'll set my father against my brother. I'll drink the victim's sufferings until I'm drunk with them!" (*The Brothers Karamazov*) Notice that the evildoer, the devil, cannot "drink" the victim's sins. But he can enjoy the victim's "sufferings." Sufferings are the consequences—what becomes visible because of the lack that is in the action that contains the evil. "How good is good?" What is striking about Christ is His relation, in this matter, to the Socratic principle that "It is better to suffer evil than to do it." We, including Christ, would just as soon not have to suffer anything, no doubt. Since we do suffer, the question becomes how do we suffer?

The point is that the goodness of the good is shown both by the enjoyment and delight of the good that we know and also by the suffering of evil rather than the doing of it. "Greater love than this no man hath than he who lays down his life for his friend." Thus, not only does good present us with our own suffering in its name, but it leads us to friendship. This relationship can ask of us suffering for another. In the case of Christ, the friendship with God is something whose possibility Aristotle worried about. Christ laid down His life as our friends, as He told us. He laid it down to redeem our sins. His suffering was a result which He accepted.

III

"How good is good?" In the *Gospel according to Peanuts*, a Schulz strip is reproduced that begins with Lucy and Charlie at the Stonewall. Both look straight ahead, but Charlie has his head on his elbow and hand. He says to Lucy: "All it would take to make me happy is to have someone say he likes me...." As they walk away, Lucy asks him, "Are you sure?" Charlie stops and tells her, "Of course I'm sure." She replies, "You mean you'd be happy if someone merely said he or she likes you?"

In the next scene, Charlie is at the water fountain in the park. Lucy, looking on, continues, "Do you mean to tell me that someone has it within his or her power to make you happy merely by doing such a simple thing?" They walk on in the park, both with eyes straight ahead. "Yes! That's exactly what I mean," Charlie affirms.

Obviously thinking of herself, Lucy admits, "Well, I don't think that's asking too much.... I really don't." Lucy then looks directly at Charlie. "But you're sure now? All you want is to have someone say, 'I like you Charlie

Brown. . . '. And then you'll be happy?" Charlie, echoing her words, throws up his arms in elation, "And then I'll be happy!" In the final scene, to a totally deflated Charlie Brown, Lucy walking away says firmly, "I can't do it!"[7]

This amusing scene contains a good bit of philosophy when sorted out. In a sense, it presupposes the whole content of Christian revelation also. No doubt, there is something pleasantly naïve about Charlie and preternaturally hardheaded about Lucy, who is often said to represent the Protestant notion of the Fall and salvation by faith alone. Happiness, of course, is the result of receiving that good for which we are created. Charlie is always a bit forlorn, looking for someone, anyone to love him. The very idea that he is loveable gives Lucy much pause. Every football season he puts his trust in her, and every season she betrays his confidence by removing the ball just before he kicks it off.

Lucy for her part, while credulous of Charlie's innocence about just one friend, is forced to admit that if this is what he wants, it is just a little thing. What can harm anything if she tells him she wants to be his friend? This whole conversation presupposes the "We are to love one another as I have loved you" of Scripture. It also portends the judgment scenes of Matthew where we do not do such a simple thing as give a glass of water to a little one. Lucy is quite sure Charlie is a little one. Lucy is the woman of the world. She cannot stand naïveté. Charlie is just babbling pious phrases. "Are you sure all you want is for someone to say 'I like you Charlie Brown?'" He is sure, but she just cannot do it. Lucy herself, of course, finds herself in the same situation when Beethoven, the pianist of whom she is most fond, won't give her the time of day.

Ralph McInerny has written of the mind of the modern philosophic atheist who wants easily to write off these questions of good and evil by a simple syllogism. It goes: "Evil exists. It can only exist if God permits it, because he is omnipotent. But if he is omnipotent and permits evil he cannot be good. The suggestion is that, if two of the divine attributes, omnipotence and goodness, cannot coexist, God as believers think of Him is impossible" (*Catholic Thing*, June 16, 2009). But these tired old arguments serve to deflect attention from our input into the evil of the world. They also miss the fact that good things are given to us as well as the sufferings

7. Robert Short, *The Gospel according to Peanuts* (Louisville, Kentucky: Westminster/John Knox Press, 1965), 36.

that we experience. Our understanding of good and evil "would make utterly no sense if earthly life were all we could expect."

A correspondent by the name of "Willie" wrote to McInerny that both moral and physical disasters have to be reconciled with God's love. We are to pray to be "delivered from evil." Why? I guess the bottom line of our question is "Why do we die?" We are told we are here only temporarily. I ask, 'What did man do to deserve this?'" It is this question that Benedict XVI deals with in *Spe Salvi*. We did not do anything to deserve our existence. Death is both a punishment and a blessing. It prevents us from living the endless this-worldly life that modern science and ideology proposes to us as an alternative to what God has promised us. "Even the goods we work for rely on their achievement on unexpected twists and turns. If we in a whimper recognize the role of God in our lives when things go wrong, the psalmist is there to tell us that all of the works of the Lord bless the Lord. Creation is a chorus of gratitude and praise that drowns out complaints" (*Spe Salvi*, 10).

IV

How good is good? How evil is evil? "What *formally constitutes* His (God's) Nature, so far as we can conceive it, is the act of intellection," Maritain wrote in *A Preface to Metaphysics*,

> But the privilege of God which most astounds our reason, His *Glory*, is the fact that in Him the ultimate and principal overflow—that of whose very nature it is to be an overflow—namely His Love, is identical with His essence and His existence. For God's fundamental love is itself His elicit love and His *esse*. Therefore, from this point of view, when we regard God in the aspect of His glory, subsistent *Love* is his true and most secret Name, as subsistent *intellect* is His true Name when He is regarded in his aspect of His essence taken as such. *Ergo, sum qui sum—Deus caritas est.*[8]

The "glory" of God astounds our reason. His love is identified with His essence and existence. It constitutes an "overflow," as Maritain put it. The very superabundance of God is already present in His being. *Deus est. Deus Logos est. Deus caritas est.* What did we do to deserve our temporariness? Why do we die? Is that the worst evil? It is if Christ did not die and did not die for our sins. How good is good? It is good enough to restore what is lost

8. Jacques Maritain, *A Preface to Metaphysics* (New York: Mentor, 1962), 75.

by those who listen to "the greatest friend of knowledge." But it is not great enough to make a free being not to be a free being. Nor would we want it to be. It is great enough to redeem a free being who commits evil. It is not great enough to save him if he chooses not to be saved, for that would mean that he would cease to be what he is.

How good is good? It is good enough to create and invite other free creatures to live within its own inner life. How evil is evil? It is evil enough to reject this invitation. In the overflowing abundance of God's inner love, His only choice was to create a world in which He would give being and respond to the free responses of the free beings He created. Outside these parameters, there could be no love or no overflow of His glory, because His being cannot contradict itself or the beings that are rooted in his knowledge that results in *what is*. And so we return to our prologue.

"It demands that we recognize that which *is*: the existence of the evil that this man has committed, and which is there, which has been committed, which has taken its place in the course of the events of this world, together with the good on which it preys."

> "The devil is the oldest friend of knowledge."
> "To exist would be worse than absurd if there were no eternal life."

SIOBHAN NASH-MARSHALL

Evil, Pain, and the Problem of Properties

One of the curious "properties" of the contemporary Anglo-American discussion of the problem of evil—where by the "problem of evil" I mean the claim that there is something contradictory about the co-existence of God and evil[1]—is its approach to evil itself. Evil, in this discussion, seems to be the only constant in what is otherwise a jungle of variable terms. Thus, while those who participate in this discussion admit that the term "God is [and can be] used with a variety of different meanings,"[2] and that such other terms as "omnipotence"[3] and "moral goodness,"[4] both of which also play significant roles in that problem, can be defined in a variety of dif-

1. Michael Tooley, "The Argument from Evil," *Philosophical Perspectives*, Vol. 5: *Philosophy of Religion* (1991), 90: "Any version of the argument from evil claims that there is some fact concerning evil in the world such that the existence of God—understood as an omnipotent, omniscient, and morally perfect person—is either logically precluded, or rendered unlikely, by that fact."

2. Michael Tooley, "Problem of Evil," *The Stanford Encyclopedia of Philosophy* (Winter 2009 Edition), edited by Edward N. Zalta.

3. For a discussion of this point see, for instance, Alvin C. Plantinga, *God, Freedom, and Evil* (Grand Rapids: Wm. B. Eerdmans Publishing Co., 1974), 17: "What does it mean to say that a being is omnipotent? That he is *all-powerful,* or *almighty,* presumably. But are there no limits *at all* to the power of such a being? Could he create square circles, for example, or married bachelors.... Theologians and philosophers may hold that there are no *nonlogical* limits to what an omnipotent being can do ... some theists, on the other hand—Martin Luther and Descartes, perhaps—have apparently thought that God's power is unlimited even by the laws of logic."

4. For a discussion of this point see, for instance, Nelson Pike, "Hume on Evil," *The Philosophical Review*, 72.2 (April, 1963): 180–97. Pike's discussion is historically helpful on this point. He illustrates how the contemporary Anglo-American problem of evil stems from nineteenth century utilitarian definitions of morality.

ferent ways, no one—or at least hardly anyone[5]—questions the meaning of the term "evil."[6]

An excellent illustration of this point is Marilyn Adams's definition of the Gordian knots of the problem of evil.[7] These, she claims, are eight "polarities" or what I might more readily call *aporiae,* since she describes them in much the same way as Aristotle does his *aporiae* in *Metaphysics* B.[8] These polarities concern such things as:

1. the "foci for God's attention: (P3)[9] that of the world as a whole, versus (P4) the context of an individual created person's life;"

and

2. the role of "(P5) Divine versus (P6) created agency in creating and resolving the problem of evil."

They do *not* include mention of the polarities inherent in evil, such as might be:

1. the "foci" of human acts: (AP11),[10] all of which aim for the good versus (AP12) the destructiveness of some human acts;

5. There are some attempts in recent literature to understand evil. See, for instance, John Kekes, "Understanding Evil," *American Philosophical Quarterly,* Vol. 25, No. 1 (January 1988), 13–24. Only very rarely do these attempts enter into discussions of the problem of evil. See, on this point, H. J. McCloskey, "The Problem of Evil," in *Journal of Bible and Religion,* XXX (1962), 188–90. See also G. Stanley Kane, "Evil and Privation," *International Journal for Philosophy of Religion,* Vol. 11, No. 1 (1980), 43–58.

6. A most interesting example of this phenomenon is J. L. Mackie. In "Evil and Omnipotence," *Mind* 64 (1955): 200–12, Mackie admits that there are different views of the nature of evil. "Some," he claims, "have said that what we call evil is merely the privation of good, that evil in a positive sense, evil that is really opposed to good, does not exist" (201). He also admits that the challenging view would make for an "adequate solution to the problem of evil" (202). But then he simply dismisses the claim that evil is a privation, asserting that those who adopt it might not do so completely, or indeed that they might reify privations—think that "privation of good is *an* evil."

7. Marilyn Adams, "God and Evil: Polarities of a Problem," *Philosophical Studies: An International Journal for Philosophy in the Analytic Tradition,* Vol. 69, No. 2/3, Papers Presented at the American Philosophical Association Pacific Division Meeting 1992 (March 1993): 167–86.

8. Ibid., "eight pairs of polar theoretical considerations merit the same sort of dialectical attention. My hunch is, in each case, that one should not eliminate either pole without immersing oneself in it and mining it for all it's worth; indeed, that repeated oscillation between the poles may be the best way to assess their complementarity as well as to measure their opposition."

9. P is Adams's abbreviation for polarity. Thus, P3 stands for polarity 3, P4 stands for polarity 4, and so forth.

10. Following Adams's cue, AP is an abbreviation for Added Polarity. These polarities are ones that I am adding to the picture.

or again:

3. the "foci" of the subsistence of the universe: (AP13) that must contain an inherent order in order to be able to continue to exist, versus (AP14) it contains the disorder of evil.

Adams mentions no such polarities in the case of evil. Thus, although she acknowledges that there are aspects of the problem of evil that are *aporetic,* Adams does not seem to believe that any of these aspects concerns evil itself. In her view, evil is not, to use Scheeben's term, a mystery.[11]

This silence on matters concerning the nature of evil is not altogether surprising. Evil, on the view of those who participate in discussions of the problem of evil, seems so self-evidently to be necessarily existent and to have a specific nature and cause that thinkers do not on the whole consider it necessary to define evil, to delineate reasons why a given act, event, or thing is evil, or even to tackle the reasons why evil exists.

Quentin Smith's "An Atheological Argument from Evil Natural Laws" beautifully illustrates each of these points. The article's prologue begins with a description of what Smith takes any sane person immediately to recognize and to acknowledge is obviously evil:

> Not long ago I was sleeping in a cabin in the woods and was awoken in the middle of the night by the sounds of a struggle between two animals. Cries of terror and extreme agony rent the night, intermingled with the sounds of jaws snapping bones and flesh being torn from limbs. One animal was being savagely attacked, killed and then devoured by another. A clearer case of a horrible event in nature, a natural evil, has never been presented to me.[12]

Since he believes the event that he witnessed to be a "clear case of evil," Smith does not explain what he takes to be the evil that is present—or, to put the point in his own language, what evil is exemplified or instantiated—in the event that he describes. Nor does he explain why we should consider that something evil in the event to be evil. Rather, immediately after having described his "clearly evil event," he claims that it seems "self-evident" that this "evil" is an instance of an evil that exists necessarily: an "evil natural law." This apparently "self-evident" "evil natural law," he then argues, is "sufficient evi-

11. Mattias Joseph Scheeben, *Die Mysterien des Christentums* (Freiburg im Breisgau: Herder & Co Verlagsbuchhandlung, 1911), 206–61.

12. Quentin Smith, "An Atheological Argument from Evil Natural Laws," *International Journal for the Philosophy of Religion,* 29 (1991), 159.

dence" for the claim that God does not exist: "It seemed to me self-evident that the natural law that *animals must savagely kill and devour each other in order to survive* was an evil natural law and that the obtaining of this law was sufficient evidence that God did not exist."[13]

Smith does not explain why he believes that the "clear evil" that he has witnessed exists necessarily—why it is an instance of a "natural law"—any more than he explains what the evil that he witnessed is, or why that evil is an evil. He simply assumes both that it is necessary for this evil to exist and that his readers will readily realize that this is so. Thus, after he has strung together his "self-evident" and "clear" examples and deductions in his prologue, he simply turns to validly, and with sophistication, formulate his atheological argument. The bulk of his article focuses on the logical niceties of this argument.

What Smith and Adams demonstrate with respect to evil can be banally expressed in the claim that the primary disputants in the contemporary debates on the problem of evil take evil to be a "primitive," something in itself that does not need explaining.

This latter is a claim that I have often heard—and observed—in past years.[14] It is also a claim that I have had trouble with for some time,[15] and for a number of different reasons. Here are some of the reasons. I am listing them in no particular order.

1. I am not really sure what a primitive is, nor have I discovered an adequate discussion or definition of "primitive." Contemporary thinkers seem to take the word and notion "primitive" to itself be a primitive.[16]

13. Ibid., 159.

14. Those who use the term "primitive" in order to describe something which they take to be self-evident apparently do so because they are inspired by Roderick Chisholm.

15. See my "Is Evil an Ontological Primitive?" in *Social Justice: Its Theory and Practice. Proceedings of the ACPA*, 79 (2006): 157–71.

16. Apparently, the notion of a primitive is similar to the notion of Cartesian *clear and distinct* ideas: it is a self-evident idea (or reality) that is apparently noetically–or at least not rationally–grasped. The mathematical notion of a prime number seems to me to be the paradigm for the notion of the philosophical "primitive." A number is prime, mathematicians tell us, when it cannot be defined in terms of anything other than itself. That is, a prime number is one that cannot be "decomposed," as Borevich and Shafarevich's definition would claim, into factors other than itself. Thus, the number 13 is prime because it cannot mathematically be "decomposed" into different factors x and y, where both x and y are whole numbers. In the absence of such "decompositionability," the number 13 cannot be defined in terms of anything other than itself. It is simply defined as the product of itself. 13 is 13*1. 13 is, mathematically speaking, a "primitive." In philosophy, I take it, a "primitive" is likewise an epistemic or metaphysical reality that cannot be decomposed into

2. Whatever evil is, or is not, it is highly suspect to close the door on discussions of its nature, or lack thereof, cause, or lack thereof, by claiming, rather than demonstrating, that it is a primitive, or by treating it as a primitive without showing why it is.

3. If a primitive is, as the name would indicate, a necessary aspect/attribute/characteristic of reality, then the claim that evil is a primitive would entail that evil is a necessary aspect/attribute/characteristic of reality—this is deeply troubling.[17]

4. If Thomas Nagel can dismiss theism by claiming that although he can neither disprove the claim that God exists, nor positively demonstrate that He does not exist, he nonetheless feels justified in claiming that God does not exist because he does not like a universe in which God does exist,[18] I can dismiss the claim that evil is a primitive because I do not like a universe in which it is.

I do not want directly to address here any of the above points, although all of them should be discussed. The first two points are both related and urgent. Contemporary philosophy increasingly includes claims that certain facts and events need not be explained but are just to be accepted.[19] This

factors other than itself, where the factors are existing things. This reading of the notion of "primitive," and its application to evil, is, I think, confirmed by Rosamund Kent Sprague's definition of evil. She defines ontological evil as "an ever present feature of reality" (564) whose "essential characteristic is "badness" (562). See Rosamund Kent Sprague, "Negation and Evil," *Philosophy and Phenomenological Research* 11 (1951): 561–67.

17. Thinkers like Alvin Plantinga seem to have no trouble accepting this point. See, for instance, his notion of *transworld depravity*—i.e., the claim that it is possible for a person necessarily to be evil, in *God, Freedom, and Evil*, 48: "What is important about the idea of transworld depravity is that if a person suffers from it, then it wasn't within God's power to actualize any world in which that person is significantly free but does no wrong—that is, a world in which he produces moral good but no moral evil."

18. Thomas Nagel, *The Last Word* (Oxford/New York: Oxford University Press, 1997), 130: "In speaking of the fear of religion, I don't mean to refer to the entirely reasonable hostility toward certain established religions and religious institutions, in virtue of their objectionable moral doctrines, social policies, and political influence.... I am talking about something much deeper—namely the fear of religion itself. I speak from experience, being strongly subject to this fear myself: I want atheism to be true and am made uneasy by the fact that some of the most intelligent and well-informed people I know are religious believers. It isn't just that I don't believe in God and, naturally, hope that I'm right in my belief. It's that I hope there is no God! I don't want there to be a God; I don't want the universe to be like that."

19. The most spectacular formulation I know of the sort of contemporary reasoning that grounds the claims in points (1) and (2) is John Searle's in *Minds, Brains and Science* (Cambridge Massachusetts: Harvard University Press, 1984), 23: "The best way to show how something is possible is to show how it actually exists." I am not quite sure what that phrase means, but Searle

tendency must be addressed. It involves just the sort of flight from reason that one can see in Nagel's dismissing the existence of God because he does not *like* it (see the fourth point above).

In this paper, I want to concentrate on the belief that evil so evidently has a determinate and recognizable nature that it is not necessary to delineate the reasons why a given event, act or thing is evil. I want, in other words, to concentrate on the modern and contemporary belief that it is *self-evident* what evil is.

In the context of the problem of evil—the attempt to analyze the logical compatibility of the terms "God" and "evil"—this belief has wreaked havoc. Not only has it made the problem of evil *per se* insoluble, it has contributed to the strange state of affairs in which scholars believe that everything involved in the co-presence of evil and God can be questioned except evil itself. Or to state the point more simply, this view of evil has led to the belief that the problem of evil is really the problem of God.[20] George Chryssides actually states this point explicitly at the outset of his rendition of the problem of evil:

> What I shall contend is that it is the traditional concept of God which generates this area of philosophical and theological perplexity, not the nature and function of evil. In particular, I shall attempt to show that the problem admits of a much more acceptable solution if the Christian believer abandons the notion of God as "a person" or a disembodied agent, and conceives of God in a less overtly "personalistic" manner.[21]

This strange state of affairs must be addressed. I would like to begin to do so in this paper by raising and briefly attending to three basic questions:

a. What do contemporary thinkers believe the self-evident nature of evil to be?

b. Why do contemporary thinkers believe that nature to be evil?

c. Why are contemporary thinkers wrong on this point?

---

seems to think that it grounds his claims that consciousness and life need no explanation. "Once we understand how the features that are characteristic of living beings have a biological explanation [viz. description], it no longer seems mysterious to us that matter should be alive."

20. See, on this point, Mary Midgely, *Wickedness* (London/Boston/Melbourne and Henley: Routledge & Kegan Paul, 1984), 1: "This book is about the problem of evil ... often treated as the problem of why God allows evil. The enquiry then takes the form of a law-court, in which Man, appearing both as judge and accuser, arraigns God and convicts him of mismanaging his responsibilities."

21. George D. Chryssides, "Evil and the Problem of God," *Religious Studies*, Vol. 23, No. 4 (December, 1987): 467–75.

I. What Do Contemporary Thinkers Believe the Self-Evident Nature of Evil to Be?

To clarify my first question, let me return to Quentin Smith, his cottage, his nocturnal adventure, and his case of self-evident evil.

> Not long ago I was sleeping in a cabin in the woods and was awoken in the middle of the night by the sounds of a struggle between two animals. Cries of terror and extreme agony rent the night, intermingled with the sounds of jaws snapping bones and flesh being torn from limbs. One animal was being savagely attacked, killed and then devoured by another. A clearer case of a horrible event in nature, a natural evil, has never been presented to me.[22]

I am not a great fan of nocturnal beastly sounds or aggression, whether they come from mosquitoes or larger non-rational—or even rational—animals. Nor do I particularly like killing, although I confess that I do not at all mind it when it comes to mosquitoes. Apparently, however, I am missing some sort of intellectual dimension in my apprehension of beastly sounds, aggression, and killing. As gruesome as the event that Smith describes is, it is not immediately evident to me at least what he takes the evil exemplified in that event to be, or why he considers that evil to be evil. To make the reasons for my confusion clearer, let me contrast Smith's nocturnal adventure with one of my own.

The summer before last I was dining in a villa on an island and heard the gruesome sounds of a catfight. It was not pleasant. When the sounds began, I and everyone else at the table looked at each other. We quickly put down our forks and napkins and rushed to check what the sounds were. Cat screams can sound ominously similar to the cries of an infant. Before we understood what we were hearing, we were very agitated. My stomach was doing flips. Visions of infants being tortured were dancing in my head. When we got to the scene and discovered that the source of the gruesome sounds was a pair of cats, one of which was biting, clawing, and scratching the other, I—and everyone else—heaved a sigh of relief. We shooed away the attacker, returned to the dinner table, and thought no more of it. The food and company were excellent.

22. Quentin Smith, "An Atheological Argument from Evil Natural Laws," 159–74.

What were we collectively missing? What was the "clear case of a horrible event in nature" exemplified in our adventure? What was the clear "natural evil" that we all—the company included four professors, three of whom were professors of philosophy—failed to notice on that balmy August night? One would be tempted to claim that we missed what was not there: death. Or perhaps, again, that what we failed to be struck by was the destructiveness, the rapaciousness, inherent in the catfight, that destructiveness that we have come to take for granted in nature. Yet again, our habits might have made us dull to the disorder that beastly fights clearly demonstrate. Surely, the fact that they did so was wrong, as was our obvious indifference to destructiveness and rapaciousness. Death, destructiveness, and disorder can all be identified with evil. Death—which was present in Smith's experience and absent in mine—is a terrible natural evil.[23] So too are destructiveness, rapaciousness, and disorder. Tidal waves, rats, the ebola virus, and children scratching and biting each other all make me mentally scream, "this should not be." So perhaps Quentin Smith was alerting me—and all those like me who heave sighs of relief when they realize that those sounds that rent the night only belonged to fighting cats—that we have become immune to the evil in nature: death, destruction, rapaciousness, and disorder.

This was not his intent. None of the characteristics that I listed as identifiable with evil is the one that Quentin Smith would claim that we failed to grasp on the way back to the dinner table that August night. What Quentin Smith thought was the clear natural evil exhibited in his nocturnal adventure was the *suffering* of the attacked animal. He makes this clear in the page following his prologue, in which he discusses the case of a zebra being "savagely attacked, wounded and killed" by a tiger:

> This event, considered by itself, is evil. When I say "considered by itself," I mean this strictly, so that the statement "the zebra's being savagely killed is good since the zebra was suffering severe agony from a broken leg and it is good that the zebra be put out of its misery" counts as considering the event *the zebra's being savagely*

23. This claim too has been questioned. Smith questions it. See the passage quoted in the lines following this footnote. Smith is by no means the only person to do so. See also John Martin Fisher, editor, *The Metaphysics of Death* (Stanford: Stanford University Press, 1993), 193. The volume contains a series of articles, some of which question the very claim that death is an evil. See also Thomas Nagel, *Mortal Questions* (Cambridge/London/New York/New Rochelle/Sydney/Melbourne: Cambridge University Press, 1979).

killed at t in relation to another event that has negative value, namely, *the zebra's suffering agony from a broken leg at t.*[24]

Indeed, such is Smith's conviction that the suffering of the zebra is the evil instantiated in his example—the "suffering severe agony from a broken leg"—that he is willing to claim that death is a good thing: "the zebra's being savagely killed is good since the zebra was suffering severe agony from a broken leg and it is good that the zebra be put out of its misery."

II. Why Do Contemporary Thinkers Believe that Nature to Be Evil?

Smith does not give his readers a reason why he believes that suffering—"suffering severe agony from a broken leg"—is itself evil, so great an evil, in fact, that it makes death good. He assumes both that it is, and that his readers will readily accept that it is. The latter of these assumptions is completely justified. Smith is by no means the only modern and contemporary thinker to claim that suffering is necessarily evil. Hume,[25] Mill,[26] Conway,[27]

24. Smith, "An atheological argument,"161.

25. Cf. e.g., David Hume, *Dialogues Concerning Natural Religion*, ed. Richard H. Popkin (Indianapolis: Hackett Publishing Company, 1980), 65: "If pain is less frequent than pleasure, it is infinitely more violent and durable. One hour of it is often able to outweigh a day, a week, a month of our common insipid enjoyments; and how many days, weeks, and months are passed by several acute torments?… pain often, good God, how often! rises to torture and agony; and the longer it continues, it becomes still more genuine agony and torture. Patience is exhausted, courage languishes, melancholy seizes us, and nothing terminates our misery but the removal of its cause or another event which is the sole cure of all evil, but which, from our natural folly, we regard with still greater consternation." See also on this point, Nelson Pike, "Hume on Evil," *The Philosophical Review*, 72.2 (April 1963): 180–97.

26. See Mill's complaint against God in "Theism," in *Three Essays On Religion* (London: Longmans, Green, Reader, and Dyer, 1874), 181: "We may ask why the human race should have been so constituted as to grovel in wretchedness and degradation for countless ages before a small portion of it was enabled to lift itself into the very imperfect state of intelligence, goodness and happiness which we enjoy." This complaint conforms to Mill's definition of evil in *Utilitarianism*, edited by George Sher (Indianapolis: Hackett Publishing Company, 2001), 7: "by unhappiness [is intended] pain and the privation of pleasure."

27. David A. Conway, "The Philosophical Problem of Evil," *International Journal for Philosophy of Religion*, 24, (1988): 35: "A child suffers agonies as a malignancy inexorably spreads; an elderly person freezes to death, sick, hungry, and alone, in an unheated city apartment; yet again, one person tortures, rapes, and murders another. Since even a human who could prevent these evils but willfully does not do so would be subject to the most severe moral condemnation, such occurrences certainly appear to be at odds with the theistic belief that a wholly good, all-knowing, and all-powerful 'father' is watching over us."

Tooley,[28] McCloskey, Rowe,[29] Draper,[30] and legions of others all clearly claim (or endorse) the same belief. Some of these thinkers equate suffering and evil. Mill seems to, and so does Hume. A good case can be made that Tooley does, and Draper too. Some of these thinkers are, like Smith, willing to think of death as a good thing because it relieves suffering.[31] Nor are those who embrace the Anglo-American analytic *weltanschauung* the only ones to do so. Daryl Koehn, who most certainly is not an analytic philosopher, begins her *The Nature of Evil* with the claim that "evil is suffering."[32]

I would like to know why they do so. Why do so many thinkers believe that it is self-evident that suffering is necessarily evil? Why do so many thinkers simply assume that one can and should equate suffering and evil and sally forth and fill our minds and libraries with arguments that claim that God cannot exist because people and animals suffer?

I believe that Mary T. Clark answered this question in the best and most succinct possible way. Over dinner one night, I asked her why she believed that so many contemporary thinkers equate evil and suffering. She looked at me and, without blinking, fired back, "because it makes them *feel* bad." There is something deep about this claim.

Consider H. J. McCloskey's definition of evil in his article "The Problem of Evil":

28. See Michael Tooley, "The Argument from Evil," *Philosophical Perspectives*, Vol. 5: *Philosophy of Religion* (1991): 90. Tooley's case is interesting. Against Swinburne, he claims that evil cannot be objectively defined—"moral judgments have no truth values"—(99), but nevertheless is willing to claim that "that suffering which is endured by sentient beings that are morally innocent is always intrinsically evil" (106). This position with respect to evil leads Tooley to claim that the best atheological arguments "appeal to more detailed facts concerning the evil that is present in the world—such as the fact that innocent children suffer agonizing deaths, or that animals suffer, or that animals did so before there were any persons to observe their suffering, or that the suffering that people undergo apparently bears no relation to the moral quality of their lives, or that it bears a rather clear relation to the wealth and medical knowledge of the societies in which they live" (91).

29. See, e.g., William L. Rowe, "Ruminations about Evil," *Philosophical Perspectives*, Vol. 5: *Philosophy of Religion* (1991): 69–88. Rowe does not even make the explicit claim that suffering is evil. He simply assumes it.

30. Paul Draper, "Probabilistic Arguments from Evil," *Religious Studies*, Vol. 28, No. 3 (September 1992): 303: "any of the following or countless other statements reporting the existence of evils of certain kinds or in certain amounts or distributed in a certain way might be thought to be better suited for the job: E2. The world contains instances of suffering and immorality. E3. The world contains instances of suffering that do not result from human immorality. E4. Many animals suffer intensely for prolonged periods of time. E5. Human suffering is not distributed according to merit."

31. See n. 22 above.

32. Daryl Koehn, *The Nature of Evil* (New York: Palgrave McMillan, 2005), 5.

It [evil] is essentially something unpleasing, shocking, disgusting, and vile. Consider such physical evils as the diseases of cancer, tuberculosis, hydrocephalus, or meningitis. They are not challenges to those who helplessly endure the sufferings they cause. Similarly, there is nothing trivial or challenging about the excruciating pain of the slowly dying child whose body has been bruised and broken by a landslide. Again, insanity in most of its forms is a distressing, shocking, and unpleasing spectacle for the observer and anything but a challenge for the victim and his relatives. The same is true of moral evil. Gross moral evils disgust, revolt, and distress the observer, and simply make the morally evil man worse. There is nothing trivial or challenging in a particularly cruel, brutal murder. The spectacle of cowardice and panic in another arouses in us at best, pity; at worst, contempt and disgust. And the knowledge that there are men in our community who choose to exist by exploiting the weak, the uninformed, and the helpless—for example by swindling old women of their savings, or by enticing or coercing young girls into prostitution—is a challenge, not to the victims nor to the observer, but only to the police. The contemplation of such moral evils is the contemplation of something vile, which the world would be better without.[33]

The number of times McCloskey refers to feeling in this definition is shocking. The definition begins with three emotional responses to evil: "unpleasing, shocking, disgusting." It continues with a reference to "excruciating pain" and three more emotional responses to evil: "distressing, shocking, and unpleasing." Nor does the definition use emotional states merely to define physical evils. The first thing McCloskey claims about moral evils is that they "disgust, revolt, and distress." He continues his description of moral evils by claiming that they are not just trivial or challenging because they arouse "pity at best; at worst, contempt and disgust." Pity, contempt, and disgust are all responses that minimally require emotions.

McCloskey's treatment of evil throughout his article makes continuous reference to emotions. He rejects the claims that evil is an illusion and that evil is a privation simply for emotional reasons: evil causes pain. And while we may well accept that evil is not an illusion because it has real effects, the same thing cannot be said for privations. Holes in the ground cause effects, as every New Yorker who has twisted an ankle on one of the sidewalks knows. Nonetheless, McCloskey insists that pain demonstrates that evil is not a privation:

Pain is not an illusion, nor is it simply the absence of a good, e.g., pleasure. Pain is positive. It has a real nature, and its evilness flows from that nature, not from its

33. H. J. McCloskey "The Problem of Evil," *Journal of Bible and Religion*, 30.3 (1962): 187.

being the absence of something else. It is pointless to tell the child whose body is bruised and broken by the landslide, and who is wracked by pain, that he is experiencing simply a privation of the proper good of the body. His suffering may be associated with a privation of the proper good of the body, but it is much more and other than this. And its existence needs to be justified.[34]

One hardly knows how to respond to this argument. How does the claim that it is pointless to tell "a child who is wracked by pain" that "he is experiencing a privation of the proper good of the body" demonstrate that his suffering "is much more and other than this?" How does it demonstrate that pain "has a real nature, and its evilness flows from that nature, not from its being the absence of something else?" One is tempted to respond to McCloskey's argument by claiming that my intellectual "displeasure," "shock," and "distress" at his argument demonstrate that his point is not false simply because it exhibits a marked absence of truth. My intellectual "displeasure," "shock," and distress" demonstrate that his argument's falseness is *much more and other than this*! After all, intellectual shock *has a real nature, and its falseness flows from that nature,* whatever this may mean!

The key word in Mary T. Clark's description of the reason for the identification of suffering and pain with evil is, I believe, "feel." As odd as it may seem, given the training of those people who make this identification, what is driving the identification itself is emotion. Emotions are surely the foundation of both Hume's belief that evil is suffering and his transmission of that belief. Hume's, Mill's, Rowe's, Smith's accounts of evil are gruesome. They make you *feel* bad. Note McCloskey's arguments for establishing that evil is something positive. It is a shameless guilt trip. It boils down to the claims that evil must be a positive thing because the child feels pain, and that we should feel bad for the child. Feeling bad is, after all, a bad thing. It is, on both Hume's and Mill's account, an *immoral thing.* It is precisely for this reason that Draper claims that "pain and pleasure ... have intrinsic moral value. Pain is intrinsically bad, and pleasure is intrinsically good."[35]

There is more. It is precisely because the foundation of the modern and contemporary identification of suffering and pain with evil is human emotions that so many modern and contemporary thinkers believe that evil is a primitive notion. No emotion has rationally distinguishable components.

34. Ibid., 189.

35. Paul Draper, "Pain and Pleasure: An Evidential Problem for Theists," *Noûs,* 23. 3 (1989): 336.

III. Why Are Contemporary Thinkers Wrong on this Point?

If Sr. Clark—and I—are right, and the foundations of the contemporary identification of evil with suffering are indeed emotions, then those of us who have become increasingly irritated by emotional manipulation have a difficult task in combating that identification. Emotions are tricky foundations for intellectual claims for at least three reasons.

1. they cannot be directly intellectually questioned qua emotions—no one can tell a person who is feeling some emotion—rage, let us say—that he is not feeling that emotion—rage;[36]

2. they feel right—they feel unquestionable;

3. they lead to outrageous claims that make those of us who suspect them even more emotionally involved; they infuriate us.

All of these points are demonstrated by our apparent inability to respond to the contemporary "problem of evil" in a convincing way. We respond to this problem intellectually. This means that we often do not see the contemporary problem of evil. And since this is so, our responses to that problem often miss the mark.

So what are we to do? How are we to respond to those thinkers who shamelessly argue that God does not exist because there are people who suffer, and animals too, and want us to become so drunk with emotions that we might even consider God unjust?

One is tempted in these cases to fight fire with fire: to counter the identification of suffering and evil with what is still the emotional trump card in ethical matters: Hitler. As Hannah Arendt points out in her *Eichmann in*

36. Clearly I am presupposing that the emotions in question are strong emotions: pain, rage, fear, joy, ecstasy, and so forth. Strong emotions are immediately clear to the person who is feeling those emotions and cannot consequently be questioned either by the person who is feeling the emotions, or by others, insofar as they are emotions. A person who is feeling rage cannot question whether or not he is feeling rage. He is engulfed by it. Likewise, saints who are overwhelmed by ecstasy cannot question whether or not they are feeling ecstasy, they are enraptured by the sight of God. To claim that we cannot directly question emotions is to claim that we cannot question whether or not we are feeling that given emotion at the moment in which we are feeling that emotion. To be sure, emotions can (and should) be indirectly intellectually questioned. We should ask ourselves if we should be feeling the specific thing that we do when we do. Emotions are not necessarily properly ordered. As any student of Aristotle knows, the life of the *phronimos* requires a great deal of emotional training.

Jerusalem, Hitler and his death squads used the very argument that Smith used in the zebra case above in order to justify Auschwitz, Chelmno, and Treblinka:

> Eichmann, asked by the police examiner if the directive to avoid "unnecessary hardships" [for those transported to the extermination camps] was not a bit ironic, in view of the fact that the destination of these people was certain death anyhow, did not even understand the question, so firmly was it still anchored in his mind that the unforgivable sin was not to kill people but to cause unnecessary pain. During the trial, he showed unmistakable signs of sincere outrage when witnesses told of cruelties and atrocities committed by S.S. men ... and it was not the accusation of having sent millions of people to their death that ever caused him real agitation but only the accusation ... of one witness that he had once beaten a Jewish boy to death.[37]

One is tempted to point out that if one continues emotionally to define evil, Auschwitz will return. One is tempted to point out that we are already well on the way to getting there precisely because our society emotionally defines evil.

Emotional trump cards, however, actually do not solve the problem. They keep alive the very foundation that is feeding the modern identification of suffering and evil. If that foundation is nurtured, breaking that identification is difficult indeed.

What we must do is what Aristotle did in the *Nicomachean Ethics* when he argued that pleasure and pain cannot, Eudoxus to the contrary, be good and evil respectively. We must minimally show that pain/suffering and evil are not co-extensive. We can begin that difficult task by showing how certain evils do not involve suffering, and certain forms of suffering cannot be evil. There has never been a more crucial time for this task. Euthanasia is spreading. Abortion is rampant, and confessionals are empty. Remorse and repentance are painful, after all, so they must be evil!

37. Hannah Arendt, *Eichmann in Jerusalem. A Report of the Banality of Evil* (London: Penguin Books, 2006), 107–08.

JONATHAN J. SANFORD

On Vice and Free Choice

Significant work on the nature and role of the virtues has gained traction over the last fifty years, and Christian philosophers have been some of the major contributors to these efforts. Elizabeth Anscombe, Peter Geach, Alasdair MacIntyre, and Stanley Hauerwas, amongst others, have done much to recover the resources of the Christian tradition's reflections on virtue and bring them to bear on debates both within the academy and beyond it. More still needs to be done, not just in clarifying the nature, role, and purpose of the virtues, but in bringing greater clarity to that murkier and too often underexplored dimension of virtue theory, that of vice.[1]

There are no doubt good reasons for this tendency toward the oversight of vice, such as the fact that clarifying what we are to aspire to seems more pressing, and what we are to avoid would seem to follow with ease once that is done. There is also the unfortunate and common impression that there is simply not much to investigate about vice: one simply takes one's virtue theory, reverses it, and *voilà*, what one wants to know about vice is ready at hand. But the matter, surely, is not nearly so simple; and one reason for its complexity has to do with difficulties concerning the role of free choice in vicious actions. It is just this that I investigate here, asking: to what extent are vicious actions freely chosen actions?

It seems that we are far readier to acknowledge the role of free choice in

1. This is not to suggest that important work on the vices has not been done recently. Recent and significant scholarship on the subject includes Rebecca Konyndyk DeYoung's *Glittering Vices: A New Look at the Seven Deadly Sins and Their Remedies* (Grand Rapids, Michigan: Brazos Press, 2009), Gabrielle Taylor's *Deadly Vices* (Oxford: Oxford University Press, 2006), and Christine McKinnon's *Character, Virtue Theories, and the Vices* (Peterborough, Canada: Broadview Press, 1999).

those acts that proceed from virtues than in those acts that proceed from vice. Just think of how "vice" is used in common English: bad dogs are vicious, but bad people make mistakes. We have relegated vice to what the *Oxford English Dictionary* defines as "an automatic reaction to a specific situation, acquired by learning or repetition."[2] The operative word in this definition is "automatic," and that which is automatic would seem to be at odds with that which is freely chosen. Of course, much of the reason for this usage has to do with 19th and 20th century psychological theories, where the stress has been on unconscious and stimulus-response acquired motives for acting. Such theories fit all too well our tendency toward self-deception, whereby we are far quicker to commend our good actions than we are to condemn our evil ones. However, there are difficulties with the role of freedom in vicious actions even from the position of action theories that are more robust in their acknowledgment of the role of a free will in constituting the grounds for human agency, such as in Aristotelian and Thomistic theories.

There seem to be two related problems at work that make even this group of thinkers skittish about acknowledging the full freedom of vicious actions: such actions run contrary to our natural inclinations, and they would seem to make our object of choice to be a non-being, an action *insofar as* it is evil. But Aristotle and especially Aquinas do indeed have much to offer by way of explanation for how we knowingly and with malice aforethought do wrong, despite our natural orientation towards goods and despite the fact that we cannot but choose something under the auspices of its goodness. It is my contention that we stand to learn much from both of them, but especially Aquinas, about the nature of vice and the role of the will in performing actions that proceed from those habits that are properly designated as vicious.

There are three key distinctions that are central to Aquinas's solution to the difficulties about freely chosen evil acts: (1) that between metaphysical as opposed to moral accounts of evil, where the privation theory remains metaphysically relevant even in those actions that are defined properly as evil;[3] (2) that between the will causing actions directly (*per se*) as opposed to indirectly (*per accidens*), whereby the will can directly intend some ac-

2. *Oxford English Dictionary*, 5th Edition (Oxford: Oxford University Press, 2002).

3. Thomas Aquinas, *De malo*, q. 1, a. 1 ad. 4; *Summa Theologiae* [hereafter cited as *ST*] I-II, q. 18, aa. 2 and 5.

tion that is good in some way but nevertheless specifically (by definition) evil;[4] and (3) that between two moments in the will's movement toward evil-doing whereby the first, prior to choice, ignores the rule that ought to guide it and so introduces defect into the will, and the second in which the will proceeds to choose some mixed good without bringing to bear on that choice its proper rule and so completes an evil deed.[5] By these distinctions, Aquinas is able to produce his sophisticated treatment of evil-doing in a manner that both respects the metaphysics of the privation theory of evil and recognizes the reality of evil in sinning.[6] My task is not to analyze these distinctions in detail, but rather to rely on them in order to pursue our main prey, which is understanding what vice is, and in understanding what vice is, understanding as well why acting through vice is necessarily acting with that nefarious species of free choice that is designated as acting from malice.[7]

I. Acting from Incontinence Is Not Acting Maliciously

There is a widespread misperception that can be noticed amongst those who give some, but not enough, thought to Aristotle and Aquinas's moral theories, the effect of which misperception is the judgment that neither of these thinkers can explain how we knowingly do wrong. The source for this mistaken claim seems to be the way recent and much older commentators alike have regarded Aristotelian and Thomistic strategies for explaining incontinent actions. Considerable attention in the recent literature has indeed been given to Aristotle and Aquinas's treatments of incontinent actions, ac-

4. Ibid., q. 1, a. 3; q. 2, a. 1; *ST* I-II, q. 8, a. 1.

5. Ibid.

6. Ibid., q. 2, a. 11 ad. 13. On this point, and others relevant to a consideration of malice, see Gregory M. Reichberg's "Beyond Privation: Moral Evil in Aquinas's *De Malo*," *Review of Metaphysics* 55 (2002): 751–84.

7. One need not act through a vice, even with regard to evil actions that are done and that one's vice makes perversely lovable, both because a bad habit does not altogether corrupt reason, and it could be the vicious man's passion that directs him towards a certain evil act, rather than his vice. (See *ST* I-II, q. 78, a. 2.) This is connected to the distinction Aquinas makes in *De malo* q. 3, a. 12 ad 12, between sinning from choice (*peccare ex electione*) and sinning while choosing (*peccare eligens*). The distinction is given more explanation in *ST* I-II, q. 78, a. 4 ad. 3. Bonnie Kent reflects on this distinction in "Transitory Vice: Thomas Aquinas on Incontinence," *Journal of the History of Philosophy* 27 (1989): 199–223.

tions in which passion militates against our freedom of choice and our full knowledge of the actions we undertake. The impression given in much of this literature, however, is that Aristotle and Aquinas's treatments of incontinence are tantamount to their general treatments of wrong-doing, and this, as Gavin Colvert has argued, seems to be whence the misinterpretation derives.[8]

This judgment about the scope of the explanation for incontinent actions is both unfortunate and mistaken.[9] To begin with Aristotle: his discussion of *akrasia* is by no means intended to cover every sort of evil-doing.[10] Aristotle repeatedly asserts in his *Nicomachean Ethics* that virtue and vice are contraries, and so, just as moral virtue always implies choice, so too does vice: "That vice [κακία] then is not incontinence, is evident (but perhaps in some way it is): on the one hand the former is according to choice whereas the latter is contrary to choice;"[11] and:

> For virtue on the one hand preserves the principle whereas vice [μοχθηρία] destroys it, and in actions that for the sake of which is the principle, just as in mathematics are the hypotheses; neither there nor in the other case is reason teaching the principles, but virtue, whether natural or habitual, generates right opinions about the principle.[12]

8. This misinterpretation of Aquinas when he deals with the problem of incontinence in *ST* I-II, q. 77, a. 2 is one that Gavin T. Colvert has sought to put aright in "Aquinas on Raising Cain," *Proceedings of the American Catholic Philosophical Association* 71 (1997): 203–20, especially 212–15.

9. Colvert notes that this controversy goes back to the very first encounters with Aquinas's action theory. He also observes that two of the notorious 219 Parisian condemnations (numbers 129 and 130) deal directly with this misinterpretation of Aquinas, and he explains how Henry of Ghent and John Duns Scotus both sought a more voluntaristic account of the will to correct this perceived error. Much more recently, Donald Davidson promotes this false interpretation in "How is Weakness of the Will Possible," in *Essays on Actions and Events* (Oxford: Clarendon Press, 1990).

10. Nevertheless, some interpreters have claimed that since *akrasia* always involves some degree of ignorance, either about general principles or about particulars, Aristotle has no way to treat wrongdoing in a manner that overcomes the Socratic identification of all wrongdoing with ignorance.

11. Aristotle, *Nicomachean Ethics* (hereafter cited as *NE*), VII 8, 1151a5–7: "ὅτι μὲν οὖν κακία ἡ ἀκρασία οὐκ ἔστι, φαωερόν (ἀλλὰ πῇ ἴσως). τὸ μὲν γὰρ παρὰ προαίρεσιν τὸ δὲ κατὰ τὴν προαίπεσίν ἐστιν." The Greek text is Bywater's, Oxford Classical Texts, 1954 [1894]. Translations of this, and all Greek and Latin texts to follow, are my own.

12. *NE* VII 8, 1151a15–19: "ἡ γὰρ ἀρετὴ καὶ μοχθηρία τὴν ἀρχὴν ἣ μὲν φθείρει ἣ δὲ σῴζει, ἐν δὲ ταῖς πράξεσι τὸ οὗ ἕνεκα ἀρχή, ὥσπερ ἐν τοῖς μαθηματικοῖς αἱ ὑποθέσεις. οὔτε δὴ ἐκεῖ ὁ λόγος διδασκαλικὸς τῶν ἀρχῶν οὔτε ἐνταῦθα, ἀλλ' ἀρετὴ ἢ φυσικὴ ἢ ἐθιστὴ τοῦ ὀρθοδοξεῖν περὶ τὴν ἀρχήν." See also, *NE* III 12, 1119a20–34; IV 5, 1113b15–22; VII 6, 1150a1–8; 7, 1150a16–23.

The incontinent person, just as the continent, preserves his knowledge of the first principle of action, that principle that correctly directs us to those goods constitutive of our proper end. His is not a mistake on the level of basic principle, but rather on that of its application, a mitigated ignorance achieved by the persuasive promptings of a disordered passion. Not so is this for the vicious man; for the vicious man has managed to destroy the very principle that ought to guide him, taking now some disordered good, some evil, as though it were his genuine good.

Aquinas's aim, as well, is more limited than a general account of wrongdoing in his treatment of incontinence, for his goal there is to show how passion and ignorance can both be causes of sin. But, even in the case of passion or ignorance as causes of sin, the principal subject of sin is the will: "Since moreover it is proper to moral acts that they are voluntary … it follows that the will, which is the principle of voluntary acts, whether of good ones or of evil ones, which are sins, is the principle of sins."[13] The will is the principal subject of sin, but of course not the only power of the person involved in sins:

> Whence not only is the will able to be the subject of a sin, but also all those powers which are able to be moved towards their acts, or from them restrained, through the will; and these same powers also are the subjects of moral habits, whether good or evil, because it is the same for act and habit.[14]

So, evil acts must necessarily proceed principally from the will, but they can certainly involve any number of other powers movable by the will. Moreover, the same analysis of the will as subject, which extends through the will's agency into the other powers, applies not just to good and bad *acts* of the will, but also to good and bad *habits*.

The will is not only the principal *subject* of sin; it is also the principal *cause* of sin. Aquinas makes a significant distinction between internal and external causes to underline this point:

13. *ST* I-II, q. 74, a. 1: "Cum autem proprium sit actuum moralium quod sint voluntarii, …; sequitur quod voluntas, quae est principium actuum voluntariorum, sive bonorum sive malorum, quae sunt peccata, sit principium peccatorum." The Latin text is the Leonine (Rome: 1895), edited by Roberto Busa, SJ: *Sancti Thomas opera omnia,* 7 vols. (Stuttgart: Frommann-Holzboog, 1979), on-line at http://www.corpusthomisticum.org/iupetera.html.

14. *ST* I-II, q. 74, a. 2: "Unde non sola voluntas potest esse subiectum peccati, sed omnes illae potentiae quae possunt moveri ad suos actus, vel ab eis reprimi, per voluntatem. Et eaedem etiam potentiae sunt subiecta habituum moralium bonorum vel malorum, quia eiusdem est actus et habitus."

> [T]he internal cause of sin is both the will, since it accomplishes the act of the sin, and reason, as to not making use of the due rule; and the sensitive appetite inclining. So therefore something extrinsic is able to be a cause of sin in three ways, either because it moves immediately the will itself; or because it moves reason; or because it moves sensitive appetite.[15]

Aquinas argues that God is the only external cause who *could* move our wills immediately, but that it is impossible for God to so move our wills to sin, for doing so would be contrary to his nature, and so therefore there is in fact no external cause of sin that moves the will directly. Nevertheless, reason could be enticed to sin, either by another man or a devil, and of course any number of sensible objects could move our appetites. None of these external movers, however, can so move the reason or sensitive appetite in such manner as to vitiate the will's role as the principal cause of sin, and so Aquinas concludes, "Whence something exterior is able to be some cause moving to sin, not however sufficiently inducing to sin, but the sufficient completive cause of sin is the will alone."[16]

The important difference between incontinence and vice might be thought, however, not to overcome the suspicion that the vicious man is nevertheless acting in ignorance. It is Aristotle who seems to suggest this possibility with his claim that the vicious man's vice is, so to speak, like a disease—he gives the examples of dropsy and consumption—where the disease itself is hidden from the sufferer of it, remarking, "for on the one hand vice is unknown [to the vicious], whereas incontinence is not unknown [to the incontinent]."[17] In Aquinas's commentary on the *Nicomachean Ethics*, it becomes emphatically clear that this is a fully culpable, and indeed, chosen, ignorance. That is to say, it is a species of self unawareness that the vicious self is entirely responsible for. The vicious man's subsequent evil choices are grounded on an earlier choice, that of supplanting the good he naturally knows for a false good of his own making. As Aquinas remarks in his commentary, "the intemperate man is not penitent, be-

15. *ST* I-II, q. 75, a. 3: "... causa interior peccati est et voluntas, ut perficiens actum peccati; et ratio, quantum ad carentiam debitae regulae; et appetitus sensitivus inclinans. Sic ergo aliquid extrinsecum tripliciter posset esse causa peccati, vel quia moveret immediate ipsam voluntatem; vel quia moveret rationem; vel quia moveret appetitum sensitivum."

16. *ST* I-II, q. 75, a. 3: "Unde aliquid exterius potest esse aliqua causa movens ad peccandum, non tamen sufficienter ad peccatum inducens, sed causa sufficienter complens peccatum est sola voluntas."

17. *NE* VII 8, 1150b36: "ἡ μὲν γὰρ κακία λανθάνει, ἡ δ' ἀκρασία οὐ λανθάνει."

cause he sins from a choice in which he remains by which he chose bodily pleasures as if an end."[18] In insisting on this, Aquinas is careful to ensure that we do not lose sight of the persistent choice arrived at by deliberation on the part of the vicious man, and seems at the same time subtly to correct what he sees as a possible miscue in Aristotle's reflections on vice, continuing to use intemperance as the example thereof:

> And this argument was induced above about incontinence and intemperance. The same argument was used before in the case of the incontinent and the intemperate man, as if the incontinent man deliberated beforehand, but not however the intemperate. And this is false, for because the intemperate man also deliberates beforehand, he indeed sins from choice.[19]

It is no accident, and no matter of simple ignorance, that has led to the vicious man's self-deception with respect to his diseased state. He has already subverted the right rule with regard to true goods, and done so on multiple occasions so that such subversion has become a persistent state. The ignorance that results is then in the class of feigned ignorance, an achievement that eases the conscience and forestalls regret. The vicious man's actions are, then, framed by choice on both sides, for, "He has indeed a permanent habit through which he chooses evils,"[20] the establishment of which habit was forged in the nefarious fires of repeated abnegation of the right rule of his actions. It is in *De malo* that Aquinas gives his most thorough treatment of how this right rule comes to be subverted.

Though less developed than Aquinas's position, Aristotle does explore vice as a sort of wrongdoing that does not involve the same sort of clash of passions against reason as we find in the case of incontinence. Aquinas's clarification of Aristotle's position does nothing more than to display the consistency of Aristotle's own treatment, a position he had elucidated already in the third book of the *Nicomachean Ethics* when claiming that the vicious man is responsible for being in the state he is in.[21] Moreover, Aristotle remarks that a bad man, a vicious man, is in a far worse moral position

18. Aquinas, *Sententia libri Ethicorum* (Leonine, 1969), Bk. 7, l. 8, n. 2: "... intemperatus non est poenitivus, quia peccat ex electione in qua permanet eo quod eligit delectationes corporales tamquam finem."

19. Ibid, n. 5: "Et haec ratio supra inducebatur de incontinente et intemperato, quasi incontinens esset praeconsiliatus, non autem intemperatus. Et hoc est falsum, quia etiam intemperatus praeconsiliatus est, peccat enim ex electione, ..."

20. Ibid, n. 3: "Habet enim habitum permanentem per quem eligit mala."

21. *NE* III 5, 1113b14–24; 1114a3–21.

than a brute because his vice magnifies rather than weakens his ability to do evil.[22] It is true enough in one sense that a brutal man is more depraved than both an incontinent and a vicious man, insofar as the brutal man's reason is corrupted, but the vicious man is worse precisely because he still has use of his reason and yet this reason is unhinged from those principles that ought to guide its moral deliberations. Such a man will set himself towards his bad designs with great urgency and efficacy. Indeed, a vicious man is marked by his ability to make choices for what is in fact evil, and Aristotle rightly assesses the extent of the damage he wreaks by exercising his human powers in these activities.[23] There is the same note struck between Aristotle and Aquinas in arguing that the truly evil act is a willful act, not merely one that is due to a more or less correct reason being overcome by passion, but by a reason and will so corrupted as to reject the right rule of reason.

II. Acting from Vice is Acting Maliciously

Despite their similarities, Aquinas's treatment of vice has more depth to it than does Aristotle's, and this has much to do with the benefit Aquinas receives from having Augustine's accounts of the will and evil at his disposal. This depth is manifest in a consideration of the distinctions Aquinas makes between three different, so to speak, moral moments: sin, malice, and vice. To understand better the distinctions among these three, we should bear in mind that for Aquinas, "a habit imports a disposition which is in relation to the nature of a thing, and to its operation or end, following which something is placed well or badly towards this disposition."[24] Moral habits, including those properly called virtues and vices (as opposed to such non-moral habits as health or beauty),[25] are distinguished from each other with respect to their suitableness, or lack thereof, to human nature:

And in this way good and bad habits are distinguished by species, for a good habit is said to be one which disposes to an act fitting to the nature of the agent; a bad

22. *NE* VII 6, 1150a7–8.

23. *NE* VII 7, 1150a16–1150b6.

24. *ST* I-II, q. 49, a.4.: "... habitus importat dispositionem quandam in ordine ad naturam rei, et ad operationem vel finem eius, secundum quam bene vel male aliquid ad hoc disponitur."

25. Aquinas follows Aristotle in calling continence and incontinence habits (see his commentary, 1434, and *Nicomachean Ethics* VII 8, 1151a27–28).

habit however is said to be one which disposes to an act unfitting to nature. Just as virtuous acts are fitting to human nature, so far as they are according to reason, acts truly of vice, since they are contrary to reason, are in discord with human nature.[26]

In thinking, then, about what is opposed to virtue, Aquinas notices that it is not enough to point only to vice—though as a habit it is indeed vice that is opposed to virtue *as such*—since one also has to consider the acts to which virtue orders us, as well as that from which the notion of moral goodness is derived, which is the employment of reason in thinking about what is suitable to our nature. Sin and malice, then, are the terms used to refer to these other two moral categories. Sin, writes Aquinas, "is that which is opposed to virtue itself from that part to which virtue is ordained, for sin properly named is an inordinate act, just as an act of virtue is an ordered and owed act;"[27] whereas, "With respect however to that which is consequent to the account rendered for virtue, which is a sort of goodness, it is malice that is opposed to virtue."[28] The relation between habit and act, in this case between vice and sin, should already be sufficiently clear. Permit me, however, to note a few things about the relationship between vice and malice, for it is this relationship that points most directly to the premeditated and persistent choice that lies behind every vice and upon which subsequent malicious choices are made.

When one sins through malice, the defect is not through the intellect, as when we sin through ignorance, nor is the defect through the sensitive appetite, as when we sin through passion, but rather through a defect in the will itself. In acting with malice, a man chooses evil knowingly. But what is the knowledge in question here? It is the knowledge that he has departed from that very rule to which the will ought to bind itself, which is the order of reason:

And through this manner, at any time some inordinate will loves some temporal good more, for example wealth or pleasure, than the order of reason or the divine

26. *ST* I-II, q. 54, a. 3:"Et hoc modo distinguuntur specie habitus bonus et malus, nam habitus bonus dicitur qui disponit ad actum convenientem naturae agentis; habitus autem malus dicitur qui disponit ad actum non convenientem naturae. Sicut actus virtutum naturae humanae conveniunt, eo quod sunt secundum rationem, actus vero vitiorum, cum sint contra rationem, a natura humana discordant."

27. *ST* I-II, q. 71, a. 1: "... quod opponitur sibi ex parte eius ad quod virtus ordinatur, nam peccatum proprie nominat actum inordinatum, sicut actus virtutis est actus ordinatus et debitus."

28. Ibid.: "Secundum autem quod ad rationem virtutis consequitur quod sit bonitas quaedam, opponitur virtuti malitia."

law, or the charity of God, or something of such a kind; it follows that it is willing to suffer the loss in some spiritual goods, so that it may obtain some temporal good.[29]

The spiritual goods whose loss are willingly suffered are precisely those that follow from being bound to the order of reason, which binding is the very source—because itself derived from Eternal Reason[30]—of goodness in human action. The malicious man sins in acting in a way that has departed from that good suitable to his human nature, and does so knowingly.

It is on understanding the freedom of this act, that it is indeed an act of the created freedom of a dependent being negating its uncreated source of freedom, that Maritain's reflections in *St. Thomas and the Problem of Evil* are so instructive. Maritain writes:

Evil lies in acting without reference to the rule; and in this concrete whole, acting without consideration of the rule, there are two moments to be distinguished, not with regard to time but according to ontological order: *first moment, not considering the rule,* which is a negation, an absence, the lack of a good which is not yet due; and *second moment, acting with that negation,* which, from the sole fact that one acts with it, becomes a privation, an absence of a due good in the action.[31]

The first moment of the malicious will, as Aquinas and Maritain both argue, is not yet sin, for no action has yet been done. It is, simply, the ignoring of the rule to which the will ought to be bound, an absence, when the will "does nothingness," as Maritain paradoxically remarks.[32] But, in the second moment, where we have the beginning of the evil act, the sin itself, there we find the privation of the due good. Malice is to be found in the will that knowingly has departed from its right rule *and* prefers to elevate lesser goods above those superior ones. It is, in short, the subversion of our natural *telos*.

Malice is also, and unfortunately, common. For, it is precisely such malice aforethought that Aquinas argues is at work whenever one acts viciously. It is not always the case that a vicious man sins precisely *out of* or *from*

29. *ST* I-II, q. 78, a. 1: "Et per hunc modum, quando aliqua inordinata voluntas aliquod bonum temporale plus amat, puta divitias vel voluptatem, quam ordinem rationis vel legis divinae, vel caritatem Dei, vel aliquid huiusmodi; sequitur quod velit dispendium pati in aliquo spiritualium bonorum, ut potiatur aliquo temporali bono."

30. *ST* I-II, q. 19, a. 4.

31. Maritain, *St. Thomas and the Problem of Evil* (Milwaukee, Wisconsin: Marquette University Press, 1942), 31.

32. Ibid., 34.

the vice, for he might commit a sin that a vicious man would do through ignorance or passion. However, whenever a vicious man does act through or because of his vice, it is necessarily the case, Aquinas argues, that he sins *ex certa malitia*, out of certain malice. Aquinas reasons as follows:

> Because to whomsoever has a habit, that which is through itself lovable is fitting to him according to that particular habit, because it becomes for him, in a sort of way, connatural, according to which custom and habit are changed into nature. That however which is fitting to someone according to his vicious habit, is that which excludes a spiritual good. From which it follows that a man chooses a spiritual evil, so that he might obtain a good which is fitting to him according to his habit. And this is to sin out of certain malice. Whence it is manifest that whosoever sins from habit, sins out of certain malice.[33]

It is vice that makes the evil thing seem lovable, channeling, so to speak, the vicious man's powers towards goods unsuitable to his nature. Sin arises when that disposition is acted upon; and it is the bad will, the will that has knowingly departed from the right rule, in other words the malicious will, that executes the sin.

Though every action done through vice is done with malice, necessarily, it is not the case that every malicious action is done through habit. Aquinas gives as examples of preconditions for malice other than vice certain sickly conditions of the body and a moment of despair. One does not need, then, a habit of sinning to sin with malice. But, certainly malice is most common in those who have acquired such habits, and their malicious actions are given fuel by the sorts of complements to habit one would expect, that is, doing them with pleasure and without regret.[34] The distorted goods that have become lovable to the malicious man and have achieved, as Aquinas notes, a sort of connaturality with him, become the very sources of the pleasures he takes through his malicious choices. He no longer regrets his evil actions, and this is the sign of the sort of self-deception to which the vicious are prone, that of not being conscious of their corrupted state. But

33. *ST* I-II, q. 78, a. 2: "Quia unicuique habenti habitum, est per se diligibile id quod est ei conveniens secundum proprium habitum, quia fit ei quodammodo connaturale, secundum quod consuetudo et habitus vertitur in naturam. Hoc autem quod est alicui conveniens secundum habitum vitiosum, est id quod excludit bonum spirituale. Ex quo sequitur quod homo eligat malum spirituale, ut adipiscatur bonum quod est ei secundum habitum conveniens. Et hoc est ex certa malitia peccare. Unde manifestum est quod quicumque peccat ex habitu, peccet ex certa malitia."

34. *ST* I-II, q. 78, a.3.

we see now why Aquinas insists that this self-deception is not a matter of ignorance, nor acting through ignorance, but rather a special sort of negligence: the vicious man's principle, his rule, has become corrupted, and he becomes hell bent, and gleefully so, on pursuing those goods that only worsen his state. But make no mistake, Aquinas reminds us, this is done knowingly, with malice aforethought.

III. The Counterfeit Success of Vicious Actions

Does Aquinas's account go far enough to explain what can be thought of as the creative energy of vice? Looking at two recent and public examples of this phenomenon can help answer this question by putting Aquinas's account to the test. Take first the case of Bernard Madoff, the former financier and current convicted felon. By all accounts, he was a charismatic figure who lived comfortably among the power brokers in New York and Washington, D.C. I do not suppose that one can think of his career-long efforts at bilking money from friends and associates as the chronic actions of an incontinent man. He was, rather, committed to the principle of making vast amounts of money, at least of making that money for himself, at nearly any cost. He knew it was wrong to lie and steal, but these moral absolutes were put aside in favor of his relatively long-term strategy of taking things that did not belong to him while giving the appearance that he was a fair dealer.

Consider second the case of Arnand Jon Alexander, the former fashion designer recently convicted of multiple acts of rape. Well respected in his field, it has apparently come as a shock to those who knew him that Alexander was a rapist. Like Madoff, one cannot reasonably argue that Alexander's is the case of a man occasionally overcome by his sexual passion. He knew it was wrong to force himself on women, but nevertheless used his position of power in the world of fashion (of which, for the record, I know nothing) to lure different women on various occasions to his apartment with false promises. He was committed to the principle of having sex with whomever he wished, whenever he wished, and took what he considered the necessary steps to protect himself from their charges, largely relying upon his status as cover, and his ability to prevent these women from advancement in their chosen field.

These examples are not those of the pathetic individuals we normally call to mind when thinking of the incontinent, those who cannot help themselves to avoid the things they know they should avoid. The alcoholic, the shopaholic, the teenager addicted to pornography are all enslaved despite their better intentions. The two cases I described are rather each of men who were extremely successful in their fields, who were generally well liked, and who were exceptionally effective in their nefarious undertakings. This success was in no small measure due to their lack of regret and self-recrimination. They did not spend time wishing they could overcome their miserable attachments the way the incontinent do. They were fully committed to their evil ends, the goals of money, sex, fame, and power. Their natures, in other words, were marked by vice, and their actions were the products of a malicious will.

Aristotle calls vicious characters incurable precisely because there is no gap to be found between their disordered passions and their disordered reason. They lack, amongst many other things, the virtue of integrity that enables them to be the same person in whatever situation they find themselves. In order to keep up their evil activities, they need to hide behind different masks in different situations. Madoff has to pretend to be a friend to those who have entrusted him with their money. He is whatever he needs to be to secure his position of influence, a chameleon-like shade flitting from one venue to the next. The same thing must be true of Alexander, sycophant to the more powerful, false friend to those women of whom he took advantage. Nevertheless, each of these characters has something that looks like the virtue of integrity, for one can tie together the disparate pieces of their lives by seeing those lives as focused on some false good that has become lovable to them, even connatural to them, through the perverse second nature they have acquired.

Another virtue clearly lacking in their lives is a virtue that MacIntyre, reflecting on Jane Austen, has given pride of place to, constancy.[35] To be constant is to pursue in a whole-hearted manner the same goods in whatever circumstances one finds oneself. Here, however, in a more forceful way than with the false integrity, we seem to find something rather like constancy in our two vicious characters: they are wholeheartedly committed to domination, whether in finance, sexual relations, or any other number of

35. Alasdair MacIntyre, *After Virtue*, 3rd Edition (Notre Dame, Indiana: University of Notre Dame Press, 2007), 183. Both integrity and constancy make regular appearances in MacIntyre's reflections on the virtues in his post-*After Virtue* works.

areas of their lives. There is, however, this crucial difference: the good pursued so single-mindedly by the vicious man is merely an apparent, and so no real, good. They possess, then, not genuine constancy, but its mockery.

We are struck, all the same, by the success achieved by means of these mimicries of integrity and constancy at work in these vicious men. There is something, moreover, that we can recognize as creatively genius in their ability to do what's wrong while appearing to be always in the right. They are like Glaucon's depiction of the unjust man with the greatest reputation for justice in Book II of the *Republic*: they get what they want, which is always to outdo others, while everyone sings their praises (at least until they are caught). Plato has Socrates make the case that a vicious man is unhappy even though he gets exactly what he wants, and the reason he is ultimately unhappy has nothing to do with him getting his legal comeuppance for his unjust actions. Aquinas, should he have had the chance to read *The Republic*, would I think approve of this approach: remove the consequences for viciousness and one still can see that vice is its own punishment. But why is that so?

Vice, as we have seen, is a moral habit, and as such entails a certain development of a person that is action motivating. It is then a settled disposition to act, and so a coordination of a person's passions, reason, and will towards that which is opposed to the actual good of a person. Nevertheless, the collection of such vices constitutes the character of the vicious man, which is his second nature, and so those very evils that are contrary to the vicious character's true good appear connatural to him. It is for this reason, the reason of a subverted principle, that the vicious man schemes, connives, and does so with a cleverness that rivals the rightly ordered cleverness of the prudent man.

IV. The Chains of Vice

Vice, then, presents itself as a settled disposition of a person, and it seems to take on a creative force that directs a man's actions wrongly. However, the dispositional status of vice is only able to present itself as virtue's opposite because it is not in every way virtue's opposite. That is to say, vice lacks in itself the natural and teleological underlayment one finds in the virtues. Rather, it draws upon virtue's underlayment—the natural powers of the person—to mimic the positive and creative aspects we find in their true form in the lives of the virtuous. To say this is to remind ourselves that habits are not the same things as powers. A vicious habit is the corruption of a power; yet that corruption is not itself an additional something deposited upon some combination of human powers, but rather the very disordering of those powers to evils. But those evils, in turn, are not, so to speak, pure evils. Rather they are lesser goods that have become preferred *at the expense* of higher. It is only the virtues, then, that are constitutive of our happiness. We cannot say the same thing about vice and remain the happy eudaimonists we ought to be. That is to say, although it is true that we are not by nature virtuous or vicious, it *is* in accord with our nature that we develop the virtues; whereas it is contrary to our nature that we develop vices.

This is why the vicious man is rightly observed to be at war with himself. Aristotle argues that vicious men hate themselves, and that:

> Factious is the soul of those ones, and on the one hand according to its wickedness it grieves when desisting from some things, on the other hand it takes pleasure; and on the one hand it drags hither and on the other hand thither as though pulling it apart.... It certainly does not seem that the bad man [ὁ φαῦλος] is disposed lovingly towards even himself on account of his having nothing that ought to be loved.[36]

There is nothing left to love in the second nature forged by the vicious man's repeated choices. He is at war with himself, and, perhaps most sadly of all, this is a war that he can no longer really know himself to be party to. He has lost, by his own repeated acts of malice, the principle that should guide his nature to its proper fulfillment, or that at least in the case of the incontinent man informs him that he is engaged in actions that will bring him to ruin. He is absolutely miserable, unable to know himself, unable to love himself, and unable to discern why he is so unlovable.[37]

36. *NE* IX 4, 1166b19–22, 25–26: "Στασιάζει γὰρ αὐτῶν ἡ ψυχή, καὶ τὸ μὲν διὰ μοχθηρίαν ἀλγεῖ ἀπεχόμενόν τινων, τό δ' ἥδεται, καὶ τὸ μὲν δεῦρο τὸ δ' ἐκεῖσε ἕλκει ὥσπερ διασπῶντα.... οὐ δὴ φαίνεται ὁ φαῦλος οὐδὲ πρὸς ἑαυτὸν φιλικῶς διακεῖσθαι διὰ τὸ μηδὲν ἔχειν φιλητόν."

37. Sarah Broadie, in *Ethics with Aristotle* (New York: Oxford University Press, 1994), rightly points out that the vicious hate themselves (see *NE,* IX 4, 1166b 7–29). She also contrasts the vicious with the incontinent. The incontinent has practical alternatives, whereas the vicious does not: "Now if the vicious person comes to hate himself and his modes of practical acceptance, it does not follow that he knows in a practical way *how else to be* or even how to begin to change. At the moments of choice and action he has no other moves to make, and other ways of seeing and classifying this particular circumstances, than those which express his detested character.... The incontinent's alternative to incontinent behaviour is to do *what* he knows he should; the vicious person hates what he is, but knows no practical alternative" (161).

Finally, we find an extremely significant difference between Aristotle and Aquinas with respect to the deplorably self-hating state of the vicious man. Aristotle thinks the vicious man unsalvageable precisely because of his destruction of the principle or rule by means of which, in measuring his actions aright, he might become aware of his own evil-doing. Aquinas, however, in insisting on the role of the will's negation of the true rule that ought to lie behind every action, sees even in the vicious person the seeds of the perfectible traits of a rational nature whose rule can be restored, although it is a restoration that can only be accomplished through the ministrations of salvific grace. This means that Aquinas sees a way out of the prison of vice, whereas Aristotle does not. Aristotle is correct to see no natural salvation in store for the vicious, but wrong about there being no help whatsoever for such as them. Aquinas does not need to reject the Aristotelian analysis of vice to disagree with Aristotle's judgment that there is no saving the vicious. Aquinas has met the vicious man's liberator, and finds hope precisely where Aristotle despairs. Nevertheless, a reflection on the relationship between free choice and vice, even within the hope-filled context of Aquinas's Christian Aristotelianism, is not without its edge of sadness; for we humans love what we make, even when we hate it, and few choose to leave the vicious prison of their own construction.

≈II≈

JACQUES MARITAIN ON MORAL EVIL: SOME DISPUTED QUESTIONS

JOHN F. X. KNASAS

Maritain and the Cry of Rachel

Reiterating the thought of Georges Sorel, Jacques Maritain remarked: "If philosophers lived up to their calling in the new age into which we have entered, the crucial work for them would be to renew the theory of evil, that is to say, by examining it more profoundly."[1] It is safe to say that the philosophers Maritain especially had in mind were Thomists. And, with many thinkers exploiting evil as the Achilles heel of classical theism, is the urgency of Maritain's remark any less today?[2] Maritain addressed the problem of evil with a singular relentlessness.[3] His first formal treatment of the issue was his Marquette Aquinas Lecture of 1942. Twenty years later, in his *God and the Permission of Evil,* he was still arguing the point. Maritain's treatment won him high praise.[4] Certainly anyone who read Maritain observed the honesty

1. Jacques Maritain, *God and the Permission of Evil,* translated by Joseph W. Evans (Milwaukee: Bruce Publishing Co., 1966), 4.

2. See David R. Griffin, *God, Power, and Evil: A Process Theodicy* (Westminster: John Knox Press, 2004). For a popular presentation of the process perspective, see Harold S. Kushner, *Why Do Bad Things Happen to Good People?* (New York: Avon Books, 1981). In passing, a distinction ought to be made in the "problem of evil." First is the issue of *whether* there can be both evil and an all-good, powerful, knowing God, and second is the issue of *how* this can be so. Aquinas solves the first quite easily. At *Summa Contra Gentiles* III, 71, Aquinas even asserts that evil proves the existence of God; since evil is a privation in a being and God is the first cause of beings, then, if evil exists, God exists. Logically speaking, the second *how* issue can remain problematic without need to go back on the resolution to the first. For these two senses of the problem, see my "Aquinas and Finite Gods," *Proceedings of the American Catholic Philosophical Association,* 53 (1979): 93–94. In his *Why Does Evil Exist?* (Hicksville, New York: Exposition Press, Inc., 1974), 67, Cohn Connellan acknowledges the same "whether" versus "how" distinction in the evil problem.

3. For an indexing of Maritain's treatments of evil, see Charles Journet, *The Meaning of Evil,* translated by Michael Barry (New York: P. J. Kenedy, 1963), 295–96.

4. Speaking of his extensive use of Maritain, Journet remarks, "An apology must be made for

and sincerity with which he faced the issue. Maritain realized that the stakes were high and expended himself to clarify the matter.

I. Maritain's 1942 Marquette Aquinas Lecture

I wish to begin with Maritain's critique of a Thomistic text on physical evil. As I will note, the critique's use of Rachel wailing for her lost children is, in the minds of other contemporary discussants, an archetypal form of the evil problem. Also, Maritain's critique illustrates a crucial ambiguity whose clarification is valuable for discerning a truer resolution of the evil problem.

The Thomistic text upon which Maritain focuses is *Summa Theologiae* I, q. 48, a. 2: "Whether evil is found in things." For Maritain, the text is a failure philosophically. For its argument to follow, the text must be taken up into a larger theological context. The body of the text goes as follows:

> ... the perfection of the universe requires that there should be inequality in things, so that every grade of goodness may be realized. Now, one grade of goodness is that of the good which cannot fail. Another grade of goodness is that of the good which can fail in goodness. These grades of goodness are to be found in being itself (*in ipso esse*); for there are some things which cannot lose their being (*suum esse*), as incorruptible things, while there are some which can lose it, as corruptible things. As, therefore, the perfection of the universe requires that there should be not only incorruptible beings, so the perfection of the universe requires that there should be some which can fail in goodness and which sometimes (*interdum*) do fail. Now it is in this that evil consists, in the fact that a thing fails in goodness. Hence it is clear that evil is to be found in things in the way that corruption also is found; for corruption itself is an evil.[5]

In sum, God permits evils for the perfection of the universe. Evils are a concomitant of corruptible things. And corruptible things belong to the perfection of the created order. Now, according to Maritain, this text poses a danger to Thomistic commentary. The danger is that the text will be regarded "... in a merely philosophical sense, and as a satisfactory answer given by the philosopher."[6]

---

the constant quotations from his works—but we consider these to be rich and coherent, traditional yet full of innovation, and containing the most penetrating teaching on evil written in our own times from the Christian viewpoint" (Ibid., 14).

5. Thomas Aquinas, *Summa Theologiae* I, q. 48, a. 2; edited by Anton Pegis, *The Basic Writings of St. Thomas* Aquinas (New York: Random House, 1945), I, 467.

6. Jacques Maritain, *St. Thomas and the Problem of Evil* (Milwaukee: Marquette University Press, 1942), 8.

But Maritain finds the philosophical explanation unsatisfactory. Maritain confronts the perfection-of-the-universe solution with the Biblical personage of Rachel. The full text that Maritain has in mind is from Matthew 2, 16:

> Then Herod, seeing that he had been tricked by the Magi, was exceedingly angry; and he sent and slew all the boys in Bethlehem and its entire neighborhood who were two years old or under, according to the time that he had carefully ascertained by the Magi. Then was fulfilled what was spoken through Jeremias the prophet, "A voice was heard in Rama, weeping and loud lamentation; Rachel weeping for her children, and she would not be comforted, because they were no more."

Though human agency is responsible for the death of these innocent children, Maritain intends Rachel to be any mother who suffers the loss of a child from any source, human or natural. What consolation can the philosopher give this parent? Little or none. Maritain poignantly writes,

> ... tell her this thing was necessary in order that every degree of being should be filled, and she will answer that she cares not one whit for the machine of the world,—let them give her back her child! And she will be absolutely right; for such questions are not resolved by the machine of the world ...[7]

Appealing to a mother's intuition, Maritain effectively embarrasses any "perfection of the universe" reply to this tragedy. What can be the value of the perfection of the universe in comparison to the existence of this young and innocent human being? There is nothing more precious. Is there not? Does God not see and understand this? If God does, why does God permit such gross transgressions in his created universe? To speak of the perfection of the universe as somehow excusing God only entails that God is value blind or insensitive to the value even a created intelligence can acknowledge.

Maritain also provides Rachel's reply a Thomistic elaboration. What is wrong with the above reply to Rachel is that the human being is considered a mere part of the whole universe and hence expendable for the universe's perfections. But human beings are *persons* and

> ... in that light not parts but real *wholes*; for the person signifies in itself, wholeness. Neither man nor even the angels are persons in the perfect and absolute state, but they are in a real sense persons,—however wretchedly that condition of person is realized in man.
>
> And from this point of view the existence of evil in things injects into being

7. Ibid., 9.

an incongruity from which nothing can console us. *Et noluit consolari.* (And she refused to be consoled.) ... The suffering of a man is the suffering of a person, of a whole. Here he is considered no longer as part of the universe, but insofar as he is a person he is considered as a whole, a universe to himself; to suffer that pain as part of the universe in the perspective of nature or of the world taken as God's work of art, does not do away with the fact that as far as the person is concerned it is an utter anomaly.[8]

Maritain's thinking is this. Like the universe, the human person is a whole, so for itself. The person's extinction, then, is in principle unredeemable, inconsolable. Justifying a person's destruction by good brought about elsewhere just misses the point, for the justification treats a whole as merely a part of a larger scheme.

But in virtue of what is the person such a whole, a universe unto itself? The self-sufficiency and autonomy of the person is rooted in its freedom. Maritain speaks of "... the moral and spiritual relations of created persons to one another and with God, which relates to the universe of *freedom* and presupposes the world of nature, but is quite distinct from it."[9] In *The Person and the Common Good* Maritain provides some Thomistic texts for the above.[10] They are both from the *Summa Contra Gentiles* and concern God's governance of the rational creature for itself and not for anything else. In this respect, the rational creature is like a whole. Because of its self-determination, this special providence is appropriate to the rational creature.

From such thoughts, Maritain criticizes the traditional explanation of evil. That explanation is insensitive to the "utter anomaly" of the person suffering and dying. With a sense of the person's dignity, a reader cannot help but to experience the explanation as "insufficient," "enigmatic," "hanging in the air," and "discordant."[11]

After critiquing the traditional explanation, Maritain begins the positive work of filling its lacunae. Maritain first argues for the human's creation in the state of grace.

We see there the most profound reason of suitability for the elevation of the intelligent creature to the supernatural order; I say reason based on fitness! Not on

8. Ibid., 11–12.

9. Ibid., 10.

10. Jacques Maritain, *The Person and the Common Good,* translated by John J. Fitzgerald (Notre Dame: University of Notre Dame Press, 1966), 19, n. 8.

11. For these characterizations of Aquinas's explanation, see Journet, *The Meaning of Evil,* 54, 239–40. In *God and the Permission of Evil,* 1–2, Maritain mentions his approval of Journet's book.

> necessity, nor on justice. God could, without the least injustice, have created man in a state of pure nature, man would have been defrauded of nothing which his nature as such demands; but in actual fact God has created man in a state of grace; let us say that in actual fact he would not have created nature if He had not destined it for grace,—and this word carries us very far. Very far from Leibniz.[12]

Later, Maritain repeats, "... God, in actual fact, would not have made nature if He had not destined it to grace."[13] How, then, does Maritain answer Rachel's cry? Maritain asserts that sorrow and suffering are the retinue of the intellectual creature's free refusal of supernatural beatitude. Maritain writes:

> Without fallible freedom there can be no created freedom; without created freedom there can be no love in mutual friendship between God and creature; without love in mutual friendship between God and creature, there can be no supernatural transformation of the creature into God, no entering of the creature into the joy of his Lord. Sin,—evil,—is the price of glory.[14]

In other words, "sin ... [is] not permitted for the greater perfection of the machine of the world, but for the consummation of a work of love which transcends the whole order of the world."[15] So, to Rachel Maritain's reply is as follows. Sorrow, suffering, and death are the results of man's refusal of God's love. God has willed to love us; in fact God created humans, i.e., Adam and Eve, in what theologians call the supernatural "state of innocence." But man refused God's love. The consolation is that God still loves us and will bring us to himself.

As gripping as Maritain's critique of 48, 2 is, analysis of his position reveals some inconsistencies that invite deeper reflection. For Maritain, 48, 2 fails as a piece of philosophy. Its reasoning comes to wreck on the understanding of the human as a person. In the perspective of that understanding, Maritain's complaint is uncompromising—the death of a human as a person is an "utter anomaly." Since 48, 2 is a philosophical argument, Maritain's complaint should also be philosophical. And it seems to be. For the dignity of the person Maritain appeals to human freedom. Human freedom is a thesis of Maritain's Thomism. Also, even though Rachel is a biblical

12. Maritain, *St. Thomas and the Problem of Evil*, 13. Maritain's problem with Leibniz is that Leibniz makes all evils suffered by free agents "simply instrumental in regard to the universal order." For Maritain's texts, see Journet, *The Meaning of Evil*, 52.

13. Ibid., 17–18.

14. Ibid., 19.

15. Ibid., 18.

personage, Maritain makes it clear that he intends Rachel to stand for all mothers, not simply for mothers who believe in biblical revelation. Hence, in the apparently philosophical perspective of the human as person, 48, 2 treats the human inappropriately. As a person, the human is a whole; but 48, 2 considers the human as a part. Sticking to the human as a person, one cannot explain evil by viewing the human as a part of a larger whole. Rather, one must realize that humankind somehow has only itself to blame for the evils that it suffers. This thought creates the opening for the introduction of Original Sin and the person's spurning of the creator's love.

Yet Maritain's position includes some back peddling that can only confuse the reader as to his actual position. As "utterly anomalous" as death is for the human person, Maritain insists that the human's desires not to die and not to suffer are "conditional and inefficacious." Still within the perspective of the human as person, not within the perspective of Original Sin, Maritain described the desires as only a profound "reason of suitability" and of "fitness" for the elevation of the intelligent creature to the supernatural order. As Maritain was quoted above, these desires create no reason for supernatural elevation based upon "necessity" nor upon "justice." Hence, the reader would pose the following questions. First, if in the philosophical perspective of the person, human death is an utter anomaly, why is the desire not to die and not to suffer conditional and inefficacious? Should not the desires be the opposite? In other words, why does not the human as person provide a reason for supernatural elevation that is based upon necessity and justice? Does not "anomalous" mean inconsistent, contradictory, and improper? Do not those meanings of "anomalous" imply that a refusal of supernatural elevation is inconsistent, contradictory, and improper?

Second, granting Maritain's avowal that the human as person provides only a fitting reason for supernatural elevation, how can Maritain claim to know that God would not have created nature if God had not destined it for grace? A philosopher can reason only on the basis of the natures known by natural reason. If the nature of the human as person provides only a reason of fittingness, then all the philosopher can claim is that perhaps creation includes the offer of supernatural elevation.[16]

16. "If [God] wills to make a man, He must give him an intellect. But if there is anything which is not necessary for that which God wills, then that thing comes from God, not as something due, but simply as a result of His generosity. Now, the perfections of grace and glory are

Third, if the concept of the human as person does not eliminate the possibility of a state of pure nature, since (as Maritain says) supernatural elevation is only fitting and not necessary, then what is fundamentally wrong with the reasoning of 48, 2? Rather, 48, 2 would be explaining evil from this possibility that Maritain grants. Also, does not the same possibility undercut his use of Rachel? Given that the state of pure nature would have "defrauded" the human of nothing, is not Rachel overreacting?

In sum, if Maritain's remarks about inefficaciousness and conditionalness of human desire and about the possibility of pure nature are to be taken seriously, then Maritain should remove his mention of Rachel and erase his remark of "utter anomaly." But Maritain does neither. Hence, this reader is confused. Which of the above textual sets express Maritain's position? If the philosopher grasps the human as person, then the gratuity of the supernatural is removed. If the theologian grasps the human as person, then surprisingly Maritain is not giving a philosophical critique of 48, 2.

II. Maritain's *The Person and the Common Good*

Yet not long after, in *The Person and the Common Good* (1946), Maritain revisited the understanding of the human as person. Maritain's treatment is noteworthy for a number of reasons. First, it provides Thomistic texts. The texts derive from the *Summa Contra Gentiles* III, 111 and 112, in which Aquinas argues that in God's providence rational creatures are governed for their own sake. Second, the remarks about the person only cement in the reader's mind the above questions.

On the one hand, in a lengthy note 7, Maritain in part says:

> Using a distinction established further on, we may say that as individual or part, the intellectual substance is first willed and loved for the order of the universe and the perfection of the created whole; as person, it is first willed and loved for itself. Yet, like every creature, it differs from God, or Personality in pure act, more than it resembles Him. Hence, absolutely speaking, it is part or "individual" more than "person" and before it is a "person." (It is this that Kant failed to see.) It follows there from that, absolutely speaking, the intellectual substance is loved and willed for the order of the universe of creation before being loved and willed for itself.

goods of this kind, because nature can exist without them inasmuch as they surpass the limits of natural powers" (Aquinas, *De Veritate,* q. 6, a. 2; translated by Robert W. Mulligan [Chicago: Gateway Edition, 1961], 116).

This in no wise hinders it, in contrast to irrational beings, from being really for itself and referred directly to God.

Let us add that if we pass to the supernatural order, the order of formal participation in the deity, this priority of the universe of created nature over the person is reversed. Each person is here willed and loved for its own sake, that is, to find bliss in God (He truly died for each of them), before being willed and loved for the order and perfection of *this* world or of the universe of nature and creation.[17]

Here, it seems clear that the philosopher does not consider the human as a person, hence as a whole. First, Maritain mentions the mistake of Kant. In his *Groundwork for the Metaphysics of Morals*, Kant delineated a view of the human in which it was always wrong to treat the human as a means to an end.[18] For Maritain, Kant's view fails to realize that every creature differs from God more than it resembles God. In light of this difference, the human is more part than whole and so is loved and willed for the order of the universe. Second, at the start of the second paragraph, Maritain says that by passing to the "supernatural order," we reverse the priority of nature over the person. Now, the person is willed and loved for its own sake. As the term "supernatural" indicates, this pivot to the human as person is a theological consideration. If the notion of person is theological, then Maritain's Marquette Aquinas lecture critique of 48, 2, was not philosophical but theological. But is that fair? Should not the critique of a philosophical position be philosophical also?

But an answer to that question does not seem to matter. Unfortunately, when Maritain goes on in Chapter Three to describe expressly the consideration of human as individual, or part, and as person, or whole, he produces further confusion for the reader. Maritain presents the distinction between individual and person as "belonging to the intellectual heritage of mankind"[19] and speaks of the "philosophical discovery of personality"[20] to which the most apposite approach is through the self-donation that char-

17. Maritain, *The Person and the Common Good*, 17–18.

18. "For, to say that in the use of means to any end I am to limit my maxim to the condition of its universal validity as a law for every subject is tantamount to saying that the subject of ends, that is, the rational being itself, must be made the basis of all maxims of actions, never merely as a means but as the supreme limiting condition in the use of all means, that is, always at the same time as an end" (Immanuel Kant, *Groundwork of the Metaphysics of Morals* II [German Academy edition, vol. 4, 440]; translated by Mary Gregor [Cambridge: Cambridge University Press, 1998], 45).

19. Maritain, *Person and the Common Good*, 34.

20. Ibid., 38.

acterizes love. It is noteworthy that within this philosophical context Maritain claims that "the person is directly related to the absolute."[21] Finally, to cement the impression that the Chapter Three discussion of person is philosophical, Maritain follows the above with the remark: "Finally, we turn to religious thought for the last word and find that the deepest layer of the human person's dignity consists in its property of resembling God—not in a general way after the manner of all creatures, but in a proper way." He goes on to speak of the effects of grace. My point is that only now, in Chapter Three, does the discussion of the human as person become theological. Previously, the discussion should have been philosophical.

So, is the notion of the human as a person, as a whole, philosophically attainable? Note seven of Chapter Two appears to say no; Chapter Three appears to say yes. This oscillation repeats the wobbling noted in the Marquette lecture. In the lecture, the claims of personality are presented as known to all mothers. Also, to develop the understanding of the human as person, Maritain uses the philosophical theme of human freedom. Nevertheless, in the end, our philosophical consideration of the human seems to sink to the level of the individual, to use language from *The Person and the Common Good*. Maritain conceded that the consideration uncovers only reasons of fittingness for supernatural elevation.

III. The Great and the Small and the Play of Being

Maritain's inability to make up his mind about the philosophical or theological character of the human as person when he critiques 48, 2 is not a reason to dismiss him, but a reason to think profoundly. As I will note, some excuse for the wobbling is found in Aquinas's texts cited by Maritain, though Aquinas will be much clearer. At *Summa Theologiae* I, 29, 3, Aquinas does describe the person as the most perfect, but Aquinas adds "in all of nature." As far as I know, Aquinas, unlike Maritain, never ascribes to humans the exalted sense of person used by Maritain. Rather, at *Summa Contra Gentiles* III, 112, Aquinas says that, as an intellector of being, the rational creature "comes closer to a whole" (*maiorem affinitatem ad totum*). Other descriptions in the same chapter include: the rational creature is "a principle part" (*partes principales*) and is "closest to existing always" (*maxime*

21. Ibid., 42.

accedunt ad hoc quod sint semper). Moreover, I do not find Aquinas making Maritain's argument that as free the person is a universe unto himself. For Aquinas, freedom is not autonomous but is related to the intellection of being. Up and against being, things appear as goods, not the good. Hence, we can will things, but we do not have to. But, as just noted, the intellection of being brings the rational creature only closer to being a whole.

In my opinion, the true source of Maritain's wobbling goes deeper. The notion of being, the *ratio entis*, can become associated with things in a way that invests the things with the implications of being itself. One of these implications is being as the good. Since, unlike a univocal intelligible object, being does not abstract from the differences of its instances, the mind apprehends being as an intelligible concrescence of perfection. As such, being is the desirable *par excellence* and so is denominated the good. So, for example, the contemplation of the gargantuan can unwittingly enlist the aid of being, up and against which the gargantuan can be profiled and so objectified. Hence, the gargantuan can take on all the preciousness of being itself. That is why, to an American Indian on the western plains, the mountain is something mystical. The Indian unknowingly mixes the experience of the mountain with his intellection of being. The scientist's insistence that the mountain is just a basalt dome is so focused on the minute that the association of the mountain with being is lost. Yet, if the scientist is not careful, being can break though in the scientist's consideration of minutiae. For to contemplate the small everything else must be gotten rid of. The result is that the small stands alone with being. Because of that cognitive association, the small can become invested with the preciousness of being itself. Hence, one finds the reverential and awe-filled remark of that popularizer of current science, Carl Sagan, that we are all "star stuff."

Not only spatial minutiae but temporal minutiae can suffer the same association with being. Consider the experience of viewing old photographs. Even if the subjects bear no relation to the viewer and even if the subjects are ordinary, at certain moments the pictures can take on poignancy. Out of all possible moments we, the viewers, are at that moment. Just as the contemplation of physical minutiae enlists the aid of being, so too does the contemplation of temporal minutiae. Moreover, because we know that we are looking at a moment in the past, the poignancy includes a note of sadness. Why? By its association with what is past, being is experienced as suffering an eclipse.

This psychology of an association with the *abstractum* of being, in my opinion, is the explanation of an experience related to me by a graduate school friend. The friend would contemplate himself standing at the opposite side of the school yard and then enjoy making it real by walking to that side. What was the fun in this apparently trite exercise? I think that the exercise drew its joy from the fact that out of all possibilities, my friend was picking out that one. In his mind, the picking out left the possibility alone with being and so allowed it to draw some of the preciousness of being. Making the possibility actual was then appreciated as making something very precious actual, hence his joy.

Yet, in these cases, it must be insisted, the relation to being is not quite accurate. Certain features of the data inappropriately aggrandize the relation of the data to being. If one does not realize what is going on, then the data can take on all the value of being itself. Again, consider the spontaneous reaction of adults to a young child or baby. Both the child and the baby are "so precious." Just as the consideration of minutiae entails a vacating from consciousness of everything else so that the minutiae stand alone with being, so too does the fragility and helplessness of the child and baby. Their perceived vulnerability is a reaction to their isolation. Unlike an adult, they have not yet effected relations that establish them in existence. But even though as yet they are isolated from everything else, they are not in our awareness isolated from being. In fact, the association with being is intensified the greater the dissociation from other things. Here, the experience of the children as precious has everything to do with their association with being.

The above analysis illustrates that some of the most striking perceptions of human dignity do not always derive from the correct source. The unwitting psychic association of the child or infant up and against being seems sufficient to generate in everyday experience a modicum of respect for these small humans. In fact, it is a more persistent and pervasive source of human dignity than Kantian reflections on the autonomy of the will, Aquinas's understanding of the person as an intellector of being, and even Christian revelation on the direct relation of the person to God. This psychology may also be intermittently operative in Maritain's mind, so that the vacillation in his philosophical estimate of the human as whole and as part is traced to its true source. Nevertheless, the "wildness" of this psychology, i.e., its applicability to any thing, belies it as truly locating the basis of human dignity. That true philosophical source of dignity for all humans, Thomistically speaking, is the intimate relation of the rational soul to the *ratio entis*. But that source establishes the person to be not a whole but, to use Aquinas's designation, "a principle part."

The point that I wish to make is that knowing the correct relation of being to a thing is crucial for understanding the reactions of our will and ultimately for understanding Aquinas's thoughts on evil. Is the thing a true epiphany of being as is the human intellector, the creator, spousal union, and society (and still distinctions are necessary here)? Or is the thing merely a *faux* epiphany of being? In other words, with an epiphany of being, the nature of the thing involves being. There is an intrinsic intensity of the *ratio entis*. On the other hand, the thing's relation to being can be more superficial. Certain accidents like physical or temporal size can prompt a use of being in our awareness of the thing. I have argued that knowing when the latter is taking place is crucial for understanding many of Aquinas's remarks on why evil exists. For the merely associative play of being always leads to an inaccurate estimate of things. It always invests things with a worth out of all proportion to the truth. A thing's preciousness can become so exaggerated that nothing will console us at its loss. Hence, Aquinas will argue that happiness is not to be found in the motions of the will. Joy and delight are not to be trusted. Aquinas explains,

> Now, in their relation to the will act, true happiness does not differ from false happiness. In fact, the will, when it desires, loves or enjoys, is related in just the same way to its object, whatever it may be that is presented to it as a highest good, whether truly or falsely. Of course, whether the object so presented is truly the highest good, or is false, this distinction is made on the part of the intellect.[22]

The intellect's discerning work consists in differentiating an epiphany of being from a mere, albeit intense, association with being. This effect is what Aquinas's explanations of evil achieve. We are not left prey to our psychology. Yet such are, I believe, the quandaries of sorrow, joy, and anger suffered by Rachel.

22. *Summa Contra Gentiles* III, 26, as translated by Vernon J. Bourke, *Summa Contra Gentiles*, III–I (Notre Dame: University of Notre Dame Press, 1975), 195.

LAURA L. GARCIA

Does Maritain Solve the Problem of Evil?

Forty-seven years ago Jacques Maritain delivered three lectures to a group of Dominican-trained Brothers in Toulouse, France; these lectures evolved into a book with the title *God and the Permission of Evil*.[1] While their training in Thomism was doubtless demanding and thorough, one wonders what the Little Brothers of Jesus made of these intricately-argued lectures. For contemporary readers, false hopes may be raised by the author's foreword, where he assures us that he has "kept the tone of simplicity and freedom" characteristic of the original talks.[2] If this is Maritain's simple style, one trembles to imagine the complex!

While I find Maritain's theory of the cause of evil appealing in many respects, my tentative assessment is that the account he proposes does not succeed in avoiding the difficulties afflicting competing explanations of evil. One of Maritain's vivid metaphors accuses his opponents of "running smack into insurmountable difficulties" on which one is bound to "break one's teeth."[3] I will argue that the same could be said of virtually every assault on this subject by philosophers and theologians who wish to preserve the axioms that I believe Maritain and most defenders of Western theism would adhere to. I make this argument with fear and trembling, especially given John Cahalan's enthusiastic endorsement in the collection of essays edited by John Knasas: "Jacques Maritain solved the problem of predesti-

1. Jacques Maritain, *God and the Permission of Evil,* translated by Joseph W. Evans (Milwaukee: Bruce, 1966), hereafter cited as *Evil.*

2. Ibid., vii.

3. Ibid., 25.

nation.... We should consider it one of the great intellectual achievements of all time."[4] So I am aware that I may be missing something.

The dearth of persuasive resolutions to the problem of evil is, I believe, largely due to the problem to which Maritain brings our attention in his introductory remarks. There is at least an apparent tension, he explains, between two axioms that must be endorsed by all who accept the traditional (or orthodox) concept of God. He relies for both of these axioms on St. Thomas's *Summa Theologica,* and he phrases them as follows:

1. God is absolutely not the cause of moral evil, directly or indirectly.
2. The creature has the first initiative of moral evil.[5]

Maritain argues that many Catholic philosophers and theologians go astray by compromising one or the other of these axioms when attempting to explain the origin of sin or moral evil; and he further believes that such compromises arise from a failure to appreciate what he calls the "*dissymmetry, the fundamental, irreducible dissymmetry, between the line of good and the line of evil.*"[6] This dissymmetry is described by St. Thomas in *De Malo,* q. 3, a. 2: "If those with free choice be properly disposed and rightly ordered to receive movement by God, good acts will result, and we completely trace these acts to him as their cause. But if those with free choice should defect from the requisite order, disordered acts that are acts of sin result .... [O]nly free choice, not God, causes what regards the deordination or deformity [of these acts]."[7]

Maritain's goal, then, is to explicate the difference between the causal histories of morally good and morally evil actions and to argue that the two major competing explanations of moral evil go astray in one of two ways: either they focus on the genesis of good actions and attempt to explain evil actions from that same perspective, or they focus on the genesis of evil actions and attempt to explain good actions from *that* perspective. Since "the good is being, and plenitude or completion of being" and "evil ... is ab-

4. John C. Cahalan, "Making Something out of Nihilation," in *Jacques Maritain: The Man and his Metaphysics,* edited by John F. X. Knasas (Mishawaka, Indiana: American Maritain Association, 1988), 191.

5. *Evil,* 6. Axiom (1) is from St. Thomas Aquinas, *ST* I-II q. 79, a. 1; (2) is drawn from *ST* I-II q. 79, a. 3 ad. 2. For an elaboration of axiom (1), and thus its tension with axiom (2), see n. 10 and following.

6. Ibid., 9.

7. *On Evil,* translated by Richard Regan and edited by Brian Davies (New York: Oxford, 2003), hereafter cited as *De Malo.*

sence of being, privation of being,"[8] Maritain finds it virtually self-evident that the causal history of good (which is the same as the causal history of being) must lead back to God, while the causal history of evil (or non-being) must lead back to man. While every action is good *qua* action, since it inhabits the realm of being, evil acts incorporate the privation of a good that is fitting or proper to them. Such a lack or privation of being in the act must be traced not to the will of God, but to the human will. The erring human being is the first cause, not of evil acts in their totality, but of "the evil itself which vitiates these acts."[9]

Maritain's description of the first axiom adds to it the positive claim that "God is the first … cause of our liberty and of free decisions, so that the free act is wholly from God as the first cause and wholly from us as second cause."[10] Maritain accepts this claim but disagrees with many traditional Thomists about what follows from it. Suppose we restate axiom (1) to include the positive thesis:

> 1. God is the cause of everything outside himself down to the last detail, yet he is not the cause of moral evil directly or indirectly.

Maritain reasons that since God knows himself perfectly, he knows everything of which he is the cause. However, given that evil is in no way caused by God, he does not know evil by knowing himself as the creator and cause of all things.

Instead, Maritain proposes to reconcile the total causality of God *vis-à-vis* creatures with the presence of moral evil by claiming that free creatures themselves are the *first cause* of evil. This is not to say that creatures can cause something independently of God, since evil has the ontological status of a lack or privation of being. While speaking about evil may tempt us into thinking of it as a thing, the truth is that evil is ontologically parasitic on the good and can only be described in relation to a good. As a lack of something due, it is simply an absence or a failing-to-be of some good.

I. Lopsided Thomism

Maritain begins his critique of the inadequate views with what he calls the "traditional" school, that is, disciples of St. Thomas. Broadly speaking,

8. *Evil*, 9.
9. Ibid., 10.
10. Ibid.

this group includes Maritain himself, although he finds the views of some of his fellow traditionalists odious in the extreme. Focusing on axiom (1) regarding divine causality, as just elaborated, the traditional school derives from it two important theorems that Maritain also endorses:

3. God is the primary cause of every human act in its totality.
4. God knows every creaturely action by knowing himself as its cause.

Principle (3) captures the familiar Augustinian and Thomistic claim that God's knowledge is the cause of everything that is and is in no way dependent upon creatures. Unfortunately, Maritain tells us, the traditional school sometimes fails to bear in mind the equally important implications of axiom (2) regarding the source of the evil of sinful acts. Two such implications are:

5. The free creature, not God, is the first cause of evil.
6. God knows evil without causing it, directly or indirectly.

Maritain's complaint against some traditional Thomists, particularly Dominic Bañez and company, is that they focus so narrowly on propositions (3) and (4) that they lose sight of (5) and (6). Thus, many erstwhile followers of St. Thomas (the excessively "rigid") conclude that God is "the initiator of the evil which he punishe[s] as well as of the good which he reward[s]."[11] A lopsided emphasis on God's role in causing free actions, combined with the doctrine that God knows such actions because he causes them, has led these thinkers to the scandalous conclusion that God must be the cause of everything that occurs, and so of evil actions as well as good. Such a theory of evil actions steers disturbingly close to the views of John Calvin, whose emphasis on the sovereignty of God sometimes inclined him toward holding that no causality whatever, including that exercised by the human will, could do anything contrary to the express intentions of God. Indeed, some of Calvin's disciples dispense with secondary causes altogether on the grounds that attributing separate powers to creatures detracts from the sovereign power of God.[12]

Maritain offers several objections to the logically valid but morally

11. Ibid., 14.

12. On this point, I once heard a chapel speaker at Westmont College tell about a plane crash that claimed the lives of a missionary couple who were his dear friends. As we pondered this tragedy, the speaker went on to insist that, given the sovereignty of God, we had to accept the conclusion that it was God who crashed their plane into the side of the mountain.

repugnant view he has just described. At its most dismal, this account of moral evil depicts God as punishing some of his free creatures for sins they cannot avoid committing and, presumably, rewarding others for virtuous deeds they cannot avoid performing. While the injustice here is apparent with respect to any morally significant act, Maritain focuses on those acts that are fraught with eternal consequences. He accuses lopsided Thomists of making God the cause of sin, not directly by inclining an agent's will toward sin, but indirectly by withholding from that agent the grace necessary to produce salvific acts of faith, hope, and love.

Given this pseudo-Thomistic theory, God knows who will be saved and who will be lost by knowing, "prior" to his creative act, which creatures will receive his supernatural grace and which will not.[13] Withholding such grace from some persons guarantees that they will not be able to perform the supernatural acts necessary to obtain salvation. Further, at least after the Fall, their sinful natures guarantee that they will commit sins of their own so as to merit eternal damnation. Hence, the fate of the damned is not *directly* intended by God, but occurs as a foreseen and inevitable effect of his failing to give them the same graces he gives to others. To add insult to injury, the Bañezian school denies that this separation of the sheep from the goats has anything to do with facts about the creatures themselves; it is wholly independent of their foreseen merits or demerits, and even of their foreseen cooperation with grace or resistance to it.

While Maritain's scorn for this version of Thomism is evident, his sword falls more gently on some of its more recent defenders, including Father Reginald Garrigou-Lagrange and Maritain's good friend and frequent interlocutor Father Jean-Hervé Nicolas. Father Nicolas attempts to preserve both God's innocence and his infallible knowledge of every action by drawing on St. Thomas's distinction between an agent's failure to pay attention to a moral rule and, on account of this inattention, his making a sinful choice.[14] While Thomas holds that inattention to the moral rule is not in itself sinful, it is an absence that causally suffices to render the subsequent act of choice a sinful one.[15] Here, Maritain draws on an analogy St. Thomas

13. Since God is timeless, the priority here should not be understood as a temporal one. It is rather a priority of causal dependence, sometimes referred to as a relationship to God among "instants of nature" or "moments of reason." Maritain makes this point in *Evil*, 25, n. 14.

14. In *ST* I-II, q. 75, a. 2 ad. 3, St. Thomas declares that "the will in failing to apply the rule of reason or of the Divine law is the cause of sin."

15. See *De Malo*, q. 1, a. 3: "Not actually attending to such a [moral] rule is itself neither

uses in *De Malo,* comparing inattention to the moral rule as a cause of acting sinfully to a carpenter's neglect of his ruler as a cause of sawing crookedly. Leaving the ruler in the toolbox is not in itself a woodworking sin, but sawing without it yields defective results. Similarly, inattention to a moral norm is not sinful in itself, but acting without considering that norm results in an evil act (one that deviates from the true good of the agent).

A major advantage of Thomas's and Maritain's theory is its ability to trace the evil in free actions back to a cause that is in itself morally neutral. This means that God can have infallible knowledge of Jones's evil acts by knowing that at a given moment (call it *t1*) Jones is paying no attention to a relevant moral rule *R* and that, at a subsequent moment (*t2*), Jones makes a moral choice while continuing to ignore *R*. Hence, Jones's action at *t2* deviates from the moral good in a way that is culpable, even though his inattention to rule *R* at *t1* is not a moral fault. What is a *simple absence* at *t1* only becomes sinful at *t2*, where the absence becomes a *lack of something due*. For our purposes, it makes no difference whether *t1* and *t2* are distinct temporal moments, as long as one retains the causal dependence of the sin on the ignoring of the moral rule.

On all of these points, Maritain and his friend Nicolas appear to agree, but appearances turn out to be deceptive. It seems that Nicolas treats the initial inattention to the moral norm at *t1* as itself morally blameworthy. For Nicolas, the failure to consider the relevant moral rule is not merely a negation or absence (where these terms have no moral valence); it is a *privation,* a lack of something due, which is by definition an evil.[16] But Maritain criticizes Nicolas's account (which he calls neo-Bañezianism) for failing to explain the cause of evil. If inattention to the moral rule is already an evil, a culpable act of omission, we still have no explanation of what causes *that* evil. Perhaps inattention to the relevant moral rule is due to a culpable failure to consider a higher-order moral rule, for example, a rule enjoining constant and diligent attention to all moral rules. But then failing to attend to this higher-level norm is also culpable, and we will be caught in an infinite regress, never reaching a cause of evil that is in itself good or at least morally neutral. In any case, St. Thomas wisely insists that there is no duty

moral wrong nor punishment.... But not attending to the rule first takes on the aspect of evil because the soul proceeds to make a moral choice without considering the rule."

16. *Evil,* 21–22.

to hold the moral law constantly in view, "since the soul is not held, nor is it able, always actually to attend to such a rule."[17]

Maritain considers the following possible response from Nicolas: at *t2*, the moment of sin, inattention to *R* and the sinful choice form one ontological whole. The two are separable only conceptually, or by "a distinction of reason."[18] Hence, inattention to *R* is a constitutive part of an act that is sinful, making it sinful as well. To this suggestion, Maritain replies that, if failure to attend to *R* is supposed to be the cause of the sinful choice, it must be ontologically distinct from that choice, since a cause cannot be identical with its effect. So, even if inattention to *R* and the sinful decision exist simultaneously at *t2*, there must at least be a relationship of dependence between them such that inattention is the cause of the sin and not vice versa. Conflating these two merely reproduces the original puzzle, leaving an evil act that has no explanation from the side of being. The upshot is that Nicolas's theory fails to provide a convincing account of axiom (2); it does not succeed in explaining how free creatures can be the first cause of moral evil.

But there is more—Nicolas's theory also fails to preserve axiom (1), the unassailable innocence of God. Nicolas and company contend that sinful inattention to the moral rule at *t2* is a result, not of a direct divine intention, but of a *pre-ordained permissive decree* whereby God allows Jones's failure to consider a moral rule at *t1* and so his falling into sin at *t2*. God is not the *cause* of sin, on this view; but he includes sinful acts, as it were, in his plan or intention in creating the universe. Maritain finds this account repugnant, complaining that, on this neo-Bañezian view, the non-consideration of the rule occurs because "the creature has been left to its fallible liberty.... God has not given it at that moment the motion or activation under which, and under which alone, its fallible liberty would not have failed. He has of his own initiative decided not to do that without which evil will infallibly occur. God has *withdrawn his hand*."[19]

It might seem that Maritain is overreacting here; does not God have to withdraw his hand in some sense in order to allow his creatures to choose freely? Of course; but the choices paramount in Maritain's mind here are those determining a creature's eternal destiny. Choices leading to salvation

17. *De Malo*, q. 1, a. 3.

18. *Evil*, 24, n. 12.

19. Ibid., 28–29.

can only be made with the assistance of God's supernatural grace, so to withhold such grace from a person is to ensure that he or she will miss out on eternal bliss. In fact, that person will spend eternity in hell experiencing the just punishment for his or her sins. It is also true, of course, that without God's supernatural grace human beings cannot help but fall into sin at some point. So some sinners will be left in their sins, having no chance at salvation, while some will be given supernatural graces enabling them to enter into eternal life. Since the decision about which creatures wind up in each camp is made prior to creation, it seems to contradict the insistence of Scripture that God wills all men to be saved.

If Maritain's description of Nicolas's theory is accurate, that view does seem to compromise divine justice. The decision to give grace to some and not to others can only appear as arbitrary, showing insufficient concern for the damned and punishing creatures for sinful acts that were unavoidable for them. If Nicolas attributes God's punishment of the wicked to his foreknowledge of their sins, Maritain responds that the sins themselves occur only because God has previously decided to withhold the grace necessary to prevent them. Furthermore, in creating free creatures and withdrawing his hand of grace from them, God in effect ensures that those creatures will fail, making him at least indirectly the cause of evil. Hence, Nicolas's theory runs afoul of axiom (1).

Finally, Maritain argues that even if God's antecedent permissive decree is *not* an indirect cause of sin, God's decision to create a world that not only permits some creatures to fail but effectively guarantees that they will is itself unjust. Nicolas responds that God's withholding grace from the lost is a due punishment for their sins. But this results in the following absurdity: God withholds his saving grace from some creatures and so *brings it about* (indirectly) that they fall into sin, yet God withholds his grace from these creatures *because* they fall into sin. While many Calvinists seem to be able to live with this view on the grounds that God's ways are not our ways, Maritain insists that it is an unacceptable attack on divine justice.

II. Lopsided Anti-Thomism vs. Genuine Thomism

Maritain's discussion of the non-Thomistic theory of action proposed by Luis de Molina is intertwined with his defense of his own view, which he of course insists is the true Thomistic view. In this section, then, we will consider an alternative approach to God and the permission of evil that Maritain finds even more distasteful than the first. Along the way, I believe a clear picture of Maritain's own view will emerge as well. What all the failed theories have in common, according to Maritain, is their neglect of the inherent dissymmetry between good and evil actions. The rigid Thomistic school, as we have seen, while tracing good actions back to God as their complete primary cause, twists itself into knots trying to avoid tracing evil actions back to the same cause.

In the major alternative view, that of Luis de Molina and friends, Maritain finds the opposite error; while it succeeds in tracing morally evil actions to free creatures alone, it then offers the same account of morally good actions and so ends up surrendering the positive claim in axiom (1), that God is the cause of everything outside himself down to the last detail. Molina claims that some aspect of free human actions, the good and the evil alike, is due to the human agent alone.

Maritain is willing to countenance the claim that some aspect of evil actions is due to the human agent alone, since his own account of evil includes some kind of interference from the side of the creature. But he insists that such interference must not be construed as bringing something about, as that would make the human agent a secondary cause of the existence of the evil act, which means God is the primary cause of an evil act; he causes evil indirectly, which violates axiom (1). Further, if God is not the cause of every aspect of human actions in their totality (at least as primary cause), theorems (3) and (4) are also nullified.[20]

One might wonder why (3) is so important for Maritain, and indeed for traditional theists generally. Many reasons might be offered here, but the one most salient for our purposes is that (3) is logically entailed by (4). If God does not know free actions in their every detail by knowing himself as their cause, then "prior" to God's act of creation he does not know everything that the created order will include. As one of the earliest defenders of (3), St. Augustine unequivocally denies that God's knowledge

20. Ibid., 16: "The human causality *adds itself* to the divine causality. It is the human will which gives a final determination, in one direction or the other, a last finishing touch to an indeterminate divine motion." I believe Molina would have accepted this characterization of his view, though he may have wanted to clarify the meaning of "indeterminate." The divine motion may be indeterminate in permitting some specifying causality to the human will, or it may be indeterminate by removing all divine influences from the will, leaving it completely unguided. Molina would accept the former, but not the latter, kind of indeterminacy.

of creatures depends in any way on the objects of his knowledge. God does not know creatures because they are, he writes in *De Trinitate* (XV.13.22); rather, they are because God knows them. God learns nothing about creatures from the creatures themselves. Notice also that if God were to learn something new about creatures following his act of creation, this would constitute a change in God and so would compromise divine immutability. Further, failing to know exactly how things will turn out means that God, prior to creating, is not omniscient and cannot guarantee the details of his providential plan for the world. So the importance of (3) for traditional theism cannot be overestimated.

However, principle (3) introduces a conundrum of its own. Since free creatures are unable to surprise God with any of their free choices, and God's perfect and immutable knowledge does not *reflect* such choices but causally *produces* them, what metaphysical room is left for the human will? Pondering such questions might lead one, along with Molina, to try to find a way of preserving God's comprehensive knowledge of the created order without compromising creaturely freedom. The Molinist understanding of human freedom is a libertarian one, holding that a person is free with respect to an action only if that action is not a causally necessary outcome of prior events. That is, Molinists accept:

7. An agent is free with respect to an action only if that action is neither a chance event nor causally necessitated by prior events, whether internal or external to the agent.

The libertarian position obviously entails that every free action is in some dimension or other caused by the agent alone, and this will apply to good and evil actions alike. So, if God's knowledge of a morally good action causes it to be the very action that it is in all of its specificity, it is hard to see how that action is genuinely voluntary or within the power of the created agent. It would seem to be God's causal input and not that of the created agent that specifies what the action will be.

On the other hand, Molina clearly sympathizes with Maritain's view that God is not the cause of free *evil* actions. In other words, he wishes to preserve axiom (1) as well as axiom (2). Molina also endorses, along with Maritain, the following claim:

8. God's eternal punishment of some creatures is based upon his foreknowledge of their voluntary and unrepentant resistance to grace.

Proposition (8) recommends itself as a necessary consequence of God's perfect justice. As Maritain points out, "[God] wills that all be saved *if only* they do not refuse, for all this is an affair of love, and love necessarily implies liberty and free gift."[21]

Where Molina parts ways with Maritain, and *a fortiori* with St. Thomas, is over the free agent's role in morally *good* actions. As we have seen, Maritain subscribes to a principle that he takes to be a logical implication of (3):

9. Free agents make no specifying causal contribution to morally good acts.

In one of his diagrams, Maritain depicts the causal influence of God on the agent's will as a straight line with an arrow at the right-hand side to illustrate the claim that both the natural tendencies instilled in the agent and additional graces provided by God move the agent's will in the direction of the good (i.e., toward the agent's true good). However, this motion toward the good can be resisted by the agent when he or she prefers an inferior, merely apparent, good to the genuine good. Maritain calls this act of resistance a "shattering" of the motion that was pointing the agent in a positive direction.

The reason God is not the cause of the will's resistance to grace (or to nature, as the case may be) is that the shattering is not strictly speaking a complete act. In fact, it results (causally) from an absence in the agent (a non-consideration of the relevant moral rule) that becomes, at the time of the action, a lack of something due. The result is an act that is caused by God in all of its ontological reality but is vitiated by a failure in the agent, for which the agent alone is responsible. When the will shatters a motion toward the good, Maritain holds, that motion ceases to exist and is replaced by God's general concurrence with the operation of secondary causes.[22]

What is it about this picture, then, that Molinists reject? Primarily, I believe, it is the account of God's causality vis-à-vis human actions of every sort, whether these are good, evil, or morally neutral. In the case of evil actions, as we have seen, Molinists accept axiom (2), the claim that human agents are the sole cause of the evil in such actions, and this by turning away from their genuine good. The deficiency in such actions, therefore, does reside in the human will rather than in the divine will. But since there

21. Ibid., 104.
22. Ibid., 57.

is more than one way of sinning, it would seem that the will is also free in choosing among merely apparent goods. Where Maritain speaks of an evil act as shattering a motion toward the good, Molinists picture such an act as more of a swerving from the good toward some lesser good. Of course, one can swerve in many different directions. If you're planning a robbery, you still have to decide which bank to target.

The swerve metaphor coincides with St. Augustine's account of the pear tree caper in the *Confessions*. The idea is that the will turns away from the good in choosing an improper good—in Augustine's case, the good of human respect: "*Who can understand sins?* .... Someone cries, 'Come on, let's do it'—and we would be ashamed to be ashamed!"[23] This turning of the will is not an Epicurean swerve, since it has as its object a good of some kind and hence at least a partial explanation. The swerve metaphor has certain advantages over Maritain's image of shattering: it includes an explanation of why the will deviates from natural and supernatural predispositions toward the good, and it allows for the possibility that an agent might in fact consider the relevant moral principle and act against it anyway. As Aristotle points out, right reason does not always lead to right action.[24]

Maritain might respond that the swerve theory has problems of its own in that it credits the human will with producing an act (and hence some being) independently of God's causality, thus violating principle (3). That is, while shattering results in an evil act that is vitiated by a mere absence (non-consideration of a rule), swerving involves adding a direction or final determination to the act—and determining the ultimate term of an act is a positive causal contribution to it, not merely an absence or a lack of something due. Hence, while Molina's insistence on libertarian freedom in principle (7) may save axiom (2) and its corollaries of (5) and (6), it runs afoul of axiom (1) and its corollaries of (3) and (4). In fact, I believe that Molina simply rejects principle (9), although his own account of God's pre-creation knowledge of free actions is (so far) unexplained. Without such an account, Molina may also lose principle (8), since that principle draws on God's pre-creation knowledge to explain divine predestination.

23. Augustine, *Confessions*, 2.9, translated by F. J. Sheed (Indianapolis: Hackett, 1993).

24. This also seems to coincide with St. Thomas' claim in *De Malo* q. 6, a.1: "[The denial that human acts are voluntary] is also to be counted among the oddest philosophical opinions, since it is not only contrary to faith but also subverts all the principles of moral philosophy.... For if nothing is within our power ... deliberation, exhortation, precept, punishment and praise and blame ... are destroyed."

There are at least two possible Molinist replies to Maritain's accusations. First, Molinists could argue that swerving is no more a positive action than is shattering; both involve a resistance to nature or grace, and both include a diversion toward a good that is inappropriate in the circumstances. Maritain traces this resistance back to a lack of due consideration, though Molina believes that such a lack of consideration does not fully explain the resulting evil act. An action always aims at an object, so an evil act is partly a shattering and partly a seeking. Further, the seeking, however misguided, would seem to be the cause of the shattering rather than the other way around. Hence, Molinists might argue that Maritain's own theory must include a swerving as well as a shattering, giving it no advantage over Molinism as regards the agent's causal contribution to evil.

Second, Molinists could claim that swerving is not an action outside the divine causality. After all, the power to act voluntarily and the exercise of that power depend on God's sustaining causality at every moment. To swerve is to exercise this power against the divine motions toward the good implanted in one's nature or bestowed by supernatural grace. Presumably, then, the human will is still the first cause either of resisting such motions or of cooperating with them, but this involves at most some *partial aiming* of the will's powers rather than an addition of ontological heft. Unless the human will is able to contribute at least this much to an action, Molina believes, it will be impossible to save axiom (7) with its insistence on libertarian freedom. Lest one think that the stakes are minor here, Molinists argue that (7) is logically entailed by (8), and to surrender (8) would compromise divine justice.

Now let us consider Molina's own analysis of morally good actions. As Maritain rightly notes, Molina's account of good acts is virtually the same as his account of evil acts. In good moral actions, Molina claims, the will freely chooses in keeping with the agent's genuine good and so in cooperation with the forces moving it in that direction. However, just as evil actions involve choosing among a variety of *unsuitable* goods, so good actions involve choosing among a variety of *suitable* goods. For instance, even if an agent considers and obeys the moral rule that giving testimony in a court of law requires telling the truth, there are many ways of fulfilling this obligation, since the witness decides which facts are relevant, which words to use in describing them, and whether or not to assume a British accent in hopes of impressing the jury. Here too, then, the agent aims the will in a particular direction, exercising the power of voluntary action bestowed on free agents by God in giving them a rational nature.[25]

Hence, while Maritain accuses Molina of flouting principle (3), Molina would accuse Maritain of flouting principles (7) and thus (8). If one accepts Maritain's account of good actions, Molina might ask, how have those who have not shattered motions toward the good (in salvation-significant situations) contributed personally in any way to their salvation? And if one accepts Maritain's account of evil actions as a free agent's decision to shatter a motion toward the good, it follows that the agent is also free to *refrain* from shattering such motions. In short, the agent is free to *cooperate* with grace (or nature) as well as to *resist* it, which seems to imply that there is *something* the human will "adds" to divine causality even in a person's good actions. Beyond this, unless good actions are *wholly necessitated* by divine causality, the human will may still decide among equally acceptable ways of realizing the good.[26]

On this last point, Maritain admits in an "Additional Note to the Third French Addition" of *God and the Permission of Evil* that there is more than one way of opting for the good, that is, of not shattering a divine motion. To take an example from the Gospels, Jesus praises the widow who places two mites into the temple treasury as having done more than all the others, since they gave out of their abundance while she gave out of her need. Presumably all parties were doing something good by making a contribution, but the widow acted out of heroic generosity and total trust in God. In order to accommodate such cases, Maritain proposes that perhaps even good actions may fall short of the end intended by God, not by shattering a motion toward the good but by defecting in some way from a motion toward the best or most perfect action in the circumstances. Given the total perfection of God, it may be that divine motions always aim at the most perfect act possible, even one that is morally heroic.[27]

This proposal, however, is both puzzling and problematic. Given Maritain's earlier analysis, why not say that God is the cause of every good act in its entirety, even when it is not a *perfectly* good act? After all, the language

25. *De Malo,* q. 6, a. 1: "Regarding the performance of the act, the will moves its very self."

26. *De Malo,* q. 6 ad 1: "A cause indeed effects this change [from potential choice to actual choice] as the will moves itself to act and also as an eternal cause, namely, God moves the will. And yet the will is not moved necessarily, as I have said [in the answer and reply to objection 15]."

27. *Evil,* 115.

of "best action" fits better with utilitarian moral theories than with the virtue ethics espoused by St. Thomas and Maritain. But, since Maritain rejects the claim that creatures causally contribute to the specification of good actions, his theory as it stands entails that God is the complete and total cause of ungenerous almsgiving and good acts that are performed merely out of a sense of duty. Therefore, if Maritain is to preserve the claim that the human will is the first cause of an action's deficiencies, his only option is to treat morally good but deficient actions as incorporating some kind of negation or nihilation. Hence Maritain conjectures that all divine motions aim at the highest or most perfect act, allowing him to ascribe any imperfections to the human will's "remissive nihilation" of the divine impetus. As he explains, "[The imperfect morally good act] could have in an altogether other sense a first initiative of nothingness ... by reason of which it would render *less high and less perfect* (although still good) the object to which the (not-shattered) shatterable motion inclined it. In other words, the shatterable motion would be also a lowerable or diminishable motion."[28]

But difficulties arise for Maritain's revised view as well. While I am not convinced that there *is* a best action a finite agent could choose at a particular moment, let us grant this assumption for the sake of the argument. Then, on Maritain's view, whenever the agent departs in the slightest degree from this best action, he or she fails to cooperate fully with God's will. Even though Maritain hastens to add that failures of this kind do not constitute sins, even venial sins, they still involve acting contrary to the will of God, which seems like a relatively serious matter. Perhaps God does not really expect creatures to carry out his will perfectly, but it is a little discouraging to find out that one is failing to realize God's will in virtually every decision one makes. On such a view, it is as though God creates finite agents with an inherent fallibility that ensures that the vast majority of their actions will fail to fulfill his antecedent will.

Before leaving Maritain's theory of action, it might be instructive to give some brief consideration to morally neutral actions. St. Thomas insists that there are some kinds of actions for which no moral rule is applicable; they are neither required nor forbidden.[29] Examples of such choices are de-

28. Ibid., 116.

29. *De Malo*, q. 2, a. 5: "Some acts considered in their species are morally indifferent." St. Thomas does go on to say that particular acts are never morally indifferent, since "the act is or is not the way it ought to be." On the other hand, it seems there may be more than one option in a given situ-

ciding which shoe to put on first, which gallon of milk to put in one's cart, and whether to paint the living room puce or mauve. Since all such actions partake of being, it would seem that, on Maritain's view, God must be the sole specifying cause of them with the creature contributing nothing of its own.

But this implies that God chooses mauve for the living room. Perhaps a finite agent can "shatter" this divine preference for mauve, but why accept the claim that God moves the agent toward a specific color in the first place? Further, any shattering of a divine motion toward either a perfectly good action or a morally neutral action is likely to be done out of ignorance. While we may fairly assume that the natural law is knowable by all, the natural law does not require that one choose the most perfect action possible, nor (as far as I know) does it have anything to say about interior decoration.

III. Middle Knowledge

We turn now to spell out Molina's theory, thereby taking what Maritain describes as "a plunge into the absurd."[30] As we have seen, Molina places a very high premium on principle (7), the claim that humans possess libertarian freedom, since he believes (7) is entailed by (8). Molina thus accepts that there is something that human agents contribute on their own initiative to genuinely free actions, perhaps in specifying which means to use in pursuing a good. Maritain worries that this view leads to Pelagianism, but I believe Molina is innocent of this charge. Pelagius held that the human will by its own natural powers could perform deeds worthy of salvation. But Molina would reject that claim, holding rather that God's causal concurrence is necessary both to the will's existence and to its exercise, and that only supernatural grace makes possible saving acts of faith, hope, and love. To allow the human will some causal initiative with respect to free actions does not exclude the presence of other causal factors, as long as these additional factors do not necessitate the resulting actions.

Molina's primary aim, I submit, is not to preserve axioms (1) and (2) but to reconcile principles (7) and (8), divine foreknowledge and human

ation that is the way it ought to be, i.e., that is not morally objectionable by being done in the wrong way, at the wrong time, with the wrong motives, and the like.

30. *Evil*, 15.

freedom. Still, it is important to recognize the close connection between these two goals. If (7) turns out to be incompatible with (8), it follows (in Molina's opinion) that (1) and (2) are also incompatible. His argument is this: Maritain's model declares that God knows morally good and neutral actions in their every detail by knowing his own will, while he knows evil and deficient actions by discerning an interruption in the direction he gives to the will. Molina argues that neither good nor evil actions are adequately explained in this model. As regards sinful choices, Molina deems inattention to a moral rule as neither necessary nor sufficient to explain such actions, since a person may act against a recommendation of reason (the moral rule) whether or not he keeps it in view, and shattering a divine causal predisposition toward the good does not explain why the evil action aims at *x* rather than *y* (where *x* and *y* are two different unsuitable goods). Molina may certainly be mistaken in his opinions, of course; but given these beliefs, he can see no way of reconciling (1) and (2) without first reconciling (7) and (8).

Turning now to Molina's own solution to this dilemma, we find that the pivotal element is his introduction of so-called "middle knowledge." This concept is no doubt familiar to most philosophers today, either from acquaintance with Molina's work or with that of contemporary Molinists like Alvin Plantinga, who employs middle knowledge as part of his free will defense against the logical problem of evil.[31] First, we should note that all parties to the present discussion agree that God's knowledge "prior" to creation includes perfect knowledge of his own essence, and hence a perfect knowledge of (a) all necessary truths and (b) all contingent possibilities. But Molinists add to these two categories of divine knowledge a third set of propositions (c), which Molina calls "*futurabilia*" and contemporary Molinists call "counterfactuals of freedom" or "counterfactual conditionals."[32]

Futurabilia take the form: "In *C*, *S* would choose *A*," where *S* is a free creature, *C* is the set of circumstances in which *S* acts (including the fact that *S* has libertarian freedom with respect to *A*) and *A* is what *S* would freely choose if God were to create *S* and bring it about (directly or indirectly) that *S* encounters situation *C*. Propositions asserting what a creature would freely do in various possible situations thus fall between God's

31. Alvin Plantinga, *Warranted Christian Belief* (New York: Oxford, 2000), 460–62.

32. For a comprehensive treatment of this view, see Thomas Flint, *Divine Providence: The Molinist Account* (Ithaca, New York: Cornell University Press, 1998).

knowledge of necessary truths and his knowledge of other contingent truths (which depend on knowing his own creative causality). Molina calls God's apprehension of such counterfactuals "middle knowledge," since it falls between categories (a) and (b) above.

Critics have raised numerous objections to Molina's theory, and Maritain pities St. Francis de Sales for having been tempted into it. Here we consider two of the strongest objections to the middle knowledge proposal. The first of these finds middle knowledge incompatible with (4), the claim that God's knowledge is in no way dependent on creatures. Principle (4) seems to entail that the truth-value of every contingent proposition is decided by divine creative causality. This principle thus rules out the possibility of middle knowledge, since *futurabilia* are contingent propositions having truth-values that depend on creatures. Indeed, as Plantinga points out, Molinism entails that there are some contingent states of affairs that God is unable to bring about. In the above example, for instance, if *S* would choose *A* in *C*, God cannot bring it about that *S* would freely *refrain* from *A* in *C*. Of course, God decides whether to create *S* and whether to permit *S* to encounter *C*, but the truth or falsehood of the relevant counterfactual is up to *S* rather than to God.

It would seem, then, that God's middle knowledge depends on possible finite beings and their choices, a result that flies in the face of (4). However, I believe Molina would reject that conclusion. He holds that God's knowledge of every free action that occurs in the created world, in every one of its details, is due to his knowledge of his own causality, informed in part by middle knowledge. In creating, God decides which creatures will exist and in which circumstances they will find themselves, so it is his own causality that determines every feature of the created order, even though there are some contingent scenarios that he *cannot create*. Thus, the truth of a contingent counterfactual proposition, combined with God's causal contribution (creating *S* and allowing *S* to encounter circumstances *C*) entails that *S* chooses *A* in *C* (in the existing world). But just as the counterfactual proposition is contingent, so is the corresponding factual proposition.

It is hard to imagine that critics like Maritain would be satisfied with this response to the first objection. Even though God's creative act is informed by his knowledge of the truth-value of every possible contingent proposition, his knowledge of *futurabilia* remains dependent on (hypothetical) creatures and their decisions rather than on divine causality alone, and this is (I assume) unacceptable to Maritain. But perhaps Molina can find a way of saving theorem (4) without abandoning middle knowledge. Perhaps God's knowledge of counterfactuals of freedom is grounded in his knowledge of himself and of all the ways his being can be shared in by creatures, including rational creatures who possess libertarian freedom and exercise it one way in *C1* and another way in *C2*.

That suggestion, however, leads us to the second major objection to middle knowledge, namely, the claim that infallible knowledge of *futurabilia* is logically impossible. Sometimes this criticism takes a weaker form, arguing that defenders of middle knowledge have the burden of proof in showing that infallible middle knowledge *is possible*. We may take the weaker form of the objection as asking for a description of the method or mechanism by which God knows counterfactuals of freedom. To this request, notorious Molinist Alvin Plantinga replies that even if there is no ready explanation of God's knowledge of *futurabilia*, the same could be said for God's knowledge generally speaking. Still, if counterfactuals of freedom *have* truth-values, it is crucial to divine omniscience that God knows those truth-values, whether or not we can explain how he knows them.

Plantinga's position assumes that counterfactuals of freedom are either true or false. It is possible to reject this assumption, of course, but here the burden of proof seems to fall on the critic. Generally speaking, the only propositions without truth-values are those that make no meaningful assertions, such as the line in Lewis Carroll's poem *Jabberwocky*: "All mimsy were the borogoves/ And the mome raths outgrabe." An unperceptive reader might wonder whether or not the borogoves were indeed mimsy, but there is no truth of the matter in this case. *Futurabilia,* on the other hand, seem meaningful enough, and it also seems that there *is* some choice a given free agent would make in a particular situation, even though that agent could have made a different choice in the same situation.

For believers, the stakes are even higher, since Scripture seems to imply that God has middle knowledge. In I Samuel 23: 10–13, we read:

> David then said: 'O Lord God of Israel, your servant has heard a report that Saul plans to come to Keilah, to destroy the city on my account. Will they hand me over? And now: will Saul come down as your servant has heard: O Lord God of Israel, tell your servant.' The Lord answered, 'He will come down.' David then asked, 'Will the citizens of Keilah deliver me and my men into the grasp of Saul?' And the Lord answered, 'Yes.' So David and his men left Keilah and wandered from place

to place. When Saul was informed that David had escaped from Keilah, he abandoned the expedition.[33]

In this passage, it seems that God knows at least two counterfactuals of freedom, namely that, had David remained in Keilah, Saul would have come there in search of him, and that, if Saul had come, the citizens of Keilah would have handed David over to Saul. Since these actions of Saul and the Keilahites would be evil ones, we assume that they would be free actions. But since the circumstance of David's remaining in Keilah was not realized, neither Saul nor the men of Keilah performed those evils. Thus, since God knows the truth-values of at least two counterfactuals of freedom, perhaps Molinists can be permitted to slide over the fact that they do not understand the mechanism by which God could know such propositions with certainty.

There are some Scripture passages that suggest that God changed his mind, which seems to entail that some counterfactual proposition, perhaps *If the citizens of Ninevah behave odiously, God will destroy their city*, is true at one time and false at another. This contradicts the logical principle that every proposition has a (determinate) truth-value. (It also compromises claims about God's immutability, but that is not our focus here.) While this is a conditional rather than a counterfactual proposition, it presents similar problems. Is there a specific action God will perform when faced with the grievous behavior of the Ninevites?

Traditionally, theologians have solved this dilemma by interpolating further conditions into the antecedent. For example, perhaps the relevant proposition is: *If the citizens of Ninevah behave odiously and fail to repent, God will destroy their city*. This conditional can be true while the following is false: *If the citizens of Ninevah behave odiously but repent, God will destroy their city*. The goal is to avoid making a proposition both true and false (which is logically impossible), or neither true nor false until God either does or does not destroy Ninevah. As noted above, the latter approach contradicts the axiom that every proposition has (at all times) a determinate truth value.

We now turn to the stronger objection to middle knowledge, the claim that such knowledge is logically impossible. Maritain offers a version of this objection in his criticism of the Molinist position, stating that, on Molina's

33. This citation is taken from *The New American Bible: The New Catholic Translation* (Camden, New Jersey: Thomas Nelson, 1971).

view, "God knows the free act by . . . the *super-comprehension of causes* which is the privilege of his intelligence. As if the impossibility of being foreseen with absolute certitude was not a property of the free act as such, whatever comprehension or super-comprehension of causes one may have."[34] Perhaps Molina would have been better off to adopt Plantinga's strategy of pleading inculpable ignorance instead of proposing a mechanism, super-comprehension, which has nothing going for it but the name. Be that as it may, Maritain's remarks suggest a claim something like the following:

i. Knowing that p implies that p is true, one believes p, and one is justified in believing p.[35]

In order to understand the second premise of Maritain's argument, we must distinguish between stronger and weaker forms of justification. Let us stipulate that one can be weakly justified in believing a proposition even if that proposition turns out to be false, but one can be strongly justified in believing a proposition only if one's grounds for that belief render the truth of the proposition absolutely certain. Thus, strong justification requires infallible knowledge. Given this distinction, the next premise will be true by definition:

ii. If a person is strongly justified in believing a counterfactual of freedom, his belief is infallible.

But, as Maritain points out, prior infallible knowledge of genuinely free actions seems impossible. One way to capture that intuition is the following:

iii. Strong justification of a counterfactual of freedom is possible only if God's actions, or some properties or features of the subject or of his circumstances causally necessitate the truth of that counterfactual.

However, since counterfactuals of freedom as understood by Molina incorporate libertarian freedom, it is true by definition that:

iv. Every counterfactual of freedom is such that no act of God and no properties or features of the subject or of his circumstances causally necessitate the truth of that counterfactual.

34. *Evil*, 16.

35. While these three conditions may not be sufficient as a complete definition of human knowledge, most philosophers would agree that they are at least necessary conditions of human knowledge.

v. Therefore, strong justification (infallible knowledge) of counterfactuals of freedom is impossible (from iii and iv).[36]

This argument is open to challenge, of course, especially regarding the first premise. Defining knowledge as justified true belief may not be applicable to divine knowledge (nor am I suggesting that Maritain himself thought it to be applicable). Premise (iii) might also raise questions, since perhaps there are means of acquiring infallible knowledge of counterfactuals of freedom that are not included in (iii). "Super-comprehension" is not particularly illuminating here, but it does point to the truth that God's ways of knowing infinitely exceed our own.

IV. Conclusions

Where does this discussion of God and the permission of evil leave us? In my (quite fallible) opinion, we are left with the same puzzles with which we began. This is not because of any intellectual deficiencies in Maritain's theory. In fact, his careful analysis of good and evil actions and his depiction of evil acts as "shattering divine motions" and "introducing fissures of being" lend significant clarity and theoretical substance to the Augustinian insight that evil is a privation of being rather than a part of being. On the other hand, it is possible that Maritain's enthusiasm for treating evil actions as nihilations and shatterings makes it difficult for him to present a fully persuasive account of the voluntary nature of good and morally neutral actions.

Just as Molina's punt to super-comprehension does not solve the problem of middle knowledge, so Maritain's claim that human actions are both

36. Alfred J. Freddoso discusses two other versions of this objection, one mounted by Reginald Garrigou-Lagrange in *God: His Existence and Nature* (St. Louis: Herder, 1936), 465, and a more technical version advanced by Robert Adams in "Middle Knowledge and the Problem of Evil," *American Philosophical Quarterly* 14 (1977): 109–17. See Alfred J. Freddoso, "On Divine Middle Knowledge" in *Philosophy of Religion: A Reader and Guide,* edited by William Lane Craig (New Brunswick, New Jersey: Rutgers, 2002), 257–64. That essay is reprinted from the introduction to Luis Molina, *On Divine Foreknowledge,* translated by Alfred J. Freddoso (Ithaca, New York: Cornell, 1988), 47, 68–75. Freddoso claims that there are adequate metaphysical grounds for the truth of future contingents, but these obtain only at the time when the circumstances described in the antecedent are fulfilled. Along similar lines, *futurabilia* have adequate metaphysical grounding if they would have such grounding if the antecedent were to become actual. This is an interesting strategy, but it provides no explanation of how God could have infallible knowledge, prior to creating, of either of these kinds of propositions.

"contingent and free"[37] is not enough to save libertarian freedom. Indeed, the above argument against middle knowledge would serve equally well as an argument against infallible foreknowledge of future contingent propositions. Simply replace "counterfactual of freedom" with "future contingent proposition" in that argument. Most theists, including Maritain, believe that God knows prior to creating that, at a particular moment in this world's history, King Henry VIII freely orders Thomas More's execution. But an argument exactly analogous to the one above will conclude that prior (atemporally) to creating, it was impossible for God to know what Henry VIII would freely choose at that moment. Of course, Maritain could always borrow Molina's strategy here and insist that there is some way God knows infallibly what his free creatures will do with their freedom, even if we cannot understand how such knowledge is possible.

Unsurprisingly, Maritain rejects the "mystery" solution to God's infallible knowledge of future contingent propositions. Rather, he proposes that God knows which sinful acts his creatures will perform because all of these are present to him. Though events in the created world occur successively, since God is outside of time, he is able to grasp each of these events by his "science of vision." Maritain explains, "[God] is capable in his eternal instant of shaping, forming, and ordaining everything in a single glance by taking account of all that which happens at each moment of time in created wills."[38]

Unfortunately, this explanation of God's knowledge of evil acts in all their specificity fails to resolve the tension between God's knowledge and free sinful actions. The reason is that God's science of vision does not precede[39] his creative act; rather it is his knowledge of what he has already (as it were) caused to exist. Further, God's science of vision cannot be grounded on what free creatures actually choose, since such knowledge would be received passively and would constitute a change in God, from what he knows before to what he knows after creating. "Vision" is thus a misleading

37. *Evil*, 73.

38. Ibid., 113.

39. Since divine immutability entails that the various aspects of God's creative act occur "simultaneously," the priority mentioned here is one of logical dependence. Unless God's knowledge of a given world informs his act of creating, his knowledge of what occurs in the world will partially depend on what happens in it. He will not know "ahead of time," as it were, every event the world will contain. This scenario also seems to introduce a change in God, since the knowledge he has of the created order would be more extensive after he creates than it was before.

metaphor in this context, and it leads Maritain to offer a proposal that is inconsistent with his deeper convictions.

In the interest of full disclosure, I should say that I agree with Maritain that Bañezian theories are morally repugnant. This is largely because I accept principle (8) while it seems that Bañez is forced to reject it. To be fair, however, Bañez can cite some parts of the *Summa Contra Gentiles* that seem to promote a view very close to his own. St. Thomas's discussion of predestination in Question 161 of Book III, for example, is titled "That God Frees Some Men from Sin and Leaves Others in Sin." Here Thomas explains that God gives his grace to some sinners "so that they may be turned away from evil and toward the good." But since all human beings are sinners (with two notable exceptions), why does God not give this same grace to everyone? Thomas answers only that "this depends on his will alone." Distressingly, he even cites the same Scripture passage that John Calvin cites in support of his (Calvin's) doctrine of double predestination, Romans 9:21: "Or hath not the potter power over the clay, of the same lump to make one vessel unto honor and another unto dishonor?"

Thomas's main point here, I believe, is to deny that the elect are chosen because of their foreseen merits. However, that denial, we may hope, is compatible with his earlier claim (in chapter 159) that "those alone are deprived of grace who offer an obstacle within themselves to grace." We may also, it seems, conclude that those who resist grace do so freely, rather than because they were previously chosen to be deprived of a motion of grace that was given to others.

Setting aside rigid Thomism, then, we are left with Thomism *á la* Maritain or with some version of Molinism. I find myself wandering nomadically between these views, unable to pitch my tent permanently in either camp. From our discussion, it would seem that Molina's view risks surrendering principles (1), (3), (4), and certainly (9); but he would say that this is in the interest of saving the remaining principles. Similarly, Maritain's view risks running afoul of (2), (5), (6), and probably (7); but again he would claim that this is in the interest of saving the remaining principles. Clearly, neither thinker is willing to compromise (8), a shared commitment that inspires both Maritain's crusade against rigid Thomism and Molina's spirited campaign for libertarian freedom.

It seems, then, that one will lean to one side or the other of this dispute depending on which principles one takes to be non-negotiable. But I am convinced that somewhere in the vicinity of these two proposals lies a solution to the mystery of God's permission of evil. My indecision results from a persisting dissatisfaction with both of these theories in their worthy attempts to preserve robust accounts of both divine omniscience and human freedom. And, like them, I would rather be impaled on the horns of this dilemma (metaphorically speaking, of course) than save my philosophical hide by letting go of either one.

My ultimate conclusion, then, is that philosophical attempts fully to resolve the tension between divine omniscience and human freedom are bound to fail. While that skeptical conclusion is sure to disappoint, there is a silver lining in it (or at least a pewter lining). Recall that Maritain began his discussion by insisting on two axioms that are essential to the correct conception of God, and all who accept those claims as axiomatic will find many theories about God's permission of evil wholly unacceptable.

Consider (in brief) four such theories. Peter Geach's insistence that even God cannot have infallible knowledge of future contingents compromises divine providence, omniscience, immutability, and simplicity.[40] Eleonore Stump and Norman Kretzmann's appeal to God's timeless instantaneous vision of the entire history of creation does nothing to explain how such knowledge could (atemporally) *precede* God's act of creating, nor does it preserve God's immutability and pure actuality.[41] Hugh McCann's suggestion that God moves the human will "from the inside" only shifts the locus of God's causality and fails to retain libertarian freedom.[42] Finally, Peter van Inwagen's proposal that the universe is open to randomness so that many free actions are neither foreknown nor redeemable by God, vitiates divine goodness as well as God's providence, omniscience, immutability, and simplicity.[43] Exposing the flaws in theories like these is a worthy, if humble, philosophical task, and on this mind-bending problem, it may be the only task philosophers can profitably pursue.

It is just possible that God's innocence in permitting moral evils is an

40. See Peter Geach, *Providence and Evil* (London: Cambridge, 1977).

41. See Eleonore Stump and Norman Kretzmann, "Eternity," *Journal of Philosophy* 78 (1981): 429–58.

42. See Hugh McCann, "Divine Providence" in *Stanford Encyclopedia of Philosophy* (Spring 2009 edition), edited by Edward N. Zalta, http://plato.stanford.edu/archives/spr2009/entries/providence/divine/. Accessed on September 22, 2009.

43. See Peter van Inwagen, "The Argument from Evil" in *Christian Faith and the Problem of Evil*, edited by Peter van Inwagen (Grand Rapids: Eerdmans, 2004), 55–73.

article of faith that belongs to the mysteries rather than to the preambles of faith. In his illuminating encyclical letter *On the Relationship between Faith and Reason,* John Paul II commends the attitude expressed by St. Anselm in the *Monologion,* where that champion of divine perfection asks, "'If prior thought has concluded rationally that one cannot comprehend how supernal wisdom knows its own accomplishments … who then will explain how this same wisdom, of which the human being can know nothing, or next to nothing, is to be known and expressed?'"[44] The Holy Father adds: "Faith asks that its object be understood with the help of reason, and at the summit of its searching, reason acknowledges that it cannot do without what faith presents."

V. Appendix: Theses Relevant to God's Permission of Moral Evil

Maritain's Thomistic Axioms

1. God is the cause of everything outside himself down to the last detail, yet he is not the cause of moral evil directly or indirectly.
2. The creature has the first initiative of moral evil.

Theorems derived from axiom (1)

3. God is the primary cause of every human act in its totality.
4. God knows every creaturely action by knowing himself as its cause.

Theorems derived from axiom (2)

5. The free creature, not God, is the first cause of evil.
6. God knows evil without causing it, directly or indirectly.

Thesis regarding libertarian freedom

7. An agent is free with respect to an action only if that action is neither a chance event nor causally necessitated by prior events, whether internal or external to the agent.

44. Anselm, *Monologion* (64: PL 158, 210), cited in John Paul II, *Fides et Ratio,* 42. The encyclical was promulgated on September 14, 1998.

Thesis regarding divine justice

8. God's eternal punishment of some creatures is based upon his foreknowledge of their voluntary and unrepentant resistance to grace.

Maritain's theorem derived from (3)

9. Free agents make no specifying causal contribution to morally good acts.

Argument for the Impossibility of Middle Knowledge

Logical form of a counterfactual of freedom: *In C, S would do A.*
Logical form of a contingent proposition: *At t, S does A.*

i. Knowing that p implies that p is true, one believes p, and one is justified in believing p.

ii. If a person is strongly justified in believing a counterfactual of freedom, his belief is infallible. (One is strongly justified in believing a proposition only if one's grounds for belief render the truth of that proposition absolutely certain.)

iii. Strong justification of a counterfactual of freedom is possible only if some properties or features of the subject or his circumstances causally necessitate the truth of that counterfactual.

iv. Every counterfactual of freedom is such that no properties or features of the subject or his circumstances causally necessitate its truth.

v. Therefore, strong justification (infallible knowledge) of counterfactuals of freedom is impossible (from iii and iv).

STEVEN A. LONG

God, Freedom, and the Permission of Evil

The following remarks, concerning the teaching of St. Thomas Aquinas regarding God, freedom, and the permission of evil, derive from a plenary lecture given to the Maritain Association in 2009. I had initially thought to offer preambular remarks about the convertibility of being and good; the nature of evil as a deprivation of good owed to the subject; and also regarding Thomas's teaching, taken up by Maritain, on the role of a pure negation, a pure "non-consideration" of the rule of reason, in the genesis of moral evil. St. Thomas's analysis, and Maritain's rendering, of this last point are of great intelligible value. However, the constraints of the lecture format led me to presuppose these analyses for the sake of addressing a question that I believe to be extremely important. On reflection, this same limitation necessarily conditions the following essay. The problem that these remarks address is not an introductory sort but one that pertains to Thomas's doctrinal synthesis, and so certain judgments bearing upon this problem must be presupposed: the whole itinerary of metaphysical study cannot be reproduced in capsule prior to each application.

In the following considerations I will, first, address St. Thomas's teaching regarding divine simplicity, a teaching whose implications regarding human freedom are indispensable if we are to understand what St. Thomas teaches about the divine permission of evil. His understanding of divine simplicity forms his principal reason for not reposing his analysis upon a purely libertarian view of freedom such as is widely held by many today. Second, I will further explore Thomas's substantive account of the nature of human freedom and of the nature of the divine permission of evil. Third, I will identify a general modern objection to St. Thomas's teaching, and subsequently consider and respond to two strategic Thomistic adaptations or revisions of his teaching aimed at redressing this difficulty. These revisions are widely and well received, and their authors undertake to develop them along Thomistic lines. Nonetheless, I shall argue that these creative gambits fall short of the excellence of Thomas's teaching both exegetically and doctrinally.

The authors of the revisions whom I have in mind are important Thomistic figures—Jacques Maritain and Bernard Lonergan. Before proceeding further, I would like to observe that they are perhaps the last major theological and philosophical figures solidly to engage with the antecedent Thomistic tradition on the points in question. Their teachings often are thought to be tantamount to the pure doctrine of St. Thomas Aquinas, and to provide the most propitious responses to criticisms of his teaching. For this reason, their attempted development of St. Thomas's teaching offers a favorable place to observe what I take to be a common departure from certain difficult but significant insights achieved by Thomas Aquinas.

I. The Divine Simplicity

The first point concerning the divine simplicity bears implications that are crucial for understanding Thomas's treatment of freedom and of the divine permission of evil. This is a teaching that has suffered criticism both from the quarters of process theology and personalism. As Thomas articulates the matter in *ST* I, q. 28, a. 2 ad 1:

> ... nothing that exists in God can have any relation to that wherein it exists or of whom it is spoken, except the relation of identity; and this by reason of God's supreme simplicity.

God is Pure Act, and His perfection is elevated infinitely beyond the perfection of any real or possible finite being or beings, infinitely transcending the perfection of the entire universe. This is one reason why no perfection designates God save as *incomprehending God* and as *exceeded by Him*, as Thomas argues in *ST* I, q. 13, a. 5. For our knowledge of perfections always grasps them as distinct from other perfections, whereas God possesses in one infinite and simple Act all transcendental and pure perfections whatsoever. Likewise is this the foundation of the truths that St. Thomas argues in *De Veritate* q. 23, a. 7 ad. 9, where he writes that there is and can be no proper *proportion* between God and creature. Rather, creature and God have a "proportion" only in the improper and general sense in which any one thing can be said to have a proportion according as it is related to another. But, since God is not *really related* to the creature, but only the creature *really related* to God, there can be neither any proper proportion between God and creature nor any determined relation of God to the creature.[1]

God is infinitely simple and has no determined real relation to the creature; for God does not create out of necessity, and creation is not something real in God. In other words, it does not essentially belong to God to be "Cause of Steve." Indeed, being "cause of Steve" does not even rise to the dignity of an *accident* in God, Who is subject to no further enhancement and articulation through accident. Had God never created, His perfect repose in infinite good would in no way have been limited or deprived. After creation, there are more *beings*; but there is not *more perfection of being*, because the supereminent and infinite perfection of being is wholly actual in God.

From all of this follows a formal and crucial implication regarding creation as such—*including the created actuality of free acts*—namely, *that the only difference between God causing X, and God not causing X, is the being of X*. There is no change whatsoever in God whether I do or do not exist. Likewise, with respect to the reality of our free acts of will, the only difference between God willing our free act and God not willing our free act is the *reality* of the free act itself. The doctrine of divine simplicity makes impossible any account of human freedom as a liberty of indifference with respect to divine causality; it makes impossible any definition of human freedom that requires free acts to stand outside the providential causality of God. For either God simply wills a free act, or God does not; and if God simply wills the free act, the free act is, and if He does not, the free act is not. Any other account must posit a real relation of God to the creature,

1. Accordingly, while one may in an improper and general sense speak of an analogy of proportion between creature and God, as Thomas puts it in that same article, this is only an analogy of *transferred proportion*. And analogy of transferred proportion always translates backwards—or so Thomas tells us in *De Veritate*—into analogy of proper proportionality. For God is *incomprehended by* the perfections we affirm of Him, and *exceeds them* not merely by any *fixed ratio* of act, but rather *infinitely*.

such that the divine causality does not extend to the totality of being and is, like the causality of a creature, *limited*.

This is of course crucial for understanding freedom. The only free acts that exist are those that are eternally ordained by God. Created human freedom is an *effect* of divine causality and *cannot exist* outside of the divine causality. Further, every free act in all its concreteness is an *effect* not merely of human causality but first—and as a condition of it being an effect of human causality—*of divine causality*.[2] As St. Thomas puts it in *Summa Contra Gentiles III*, Chapter 67: "In everything that operates, God is the cause of its operating" ("*Quod Deus est causa operandi omnibus operantibus*"). The view that God proposes and man disposes—that the will has a liberty of indifference to divine causality—is not consistent with the divine simplicity. Whereas one can imagine a finite cause *beginning* to effect something but *failing* to achieve it owing to an impediment—like a strong man struggling to move a wagon that he cannot move—God either does, or does not, bring about an effect. To repeat: the *only* difference between God causing X and God not causing X is the reality of X. The creation in all its concreteness and variety, including in all the concreteness and variety of its free acts, is the *effect* of God's efficacious providential causality.

This leads us to a fuller consideration of Thomas's understanding, first, of the nature of freedom and, second, of the nature of the divine permission of evil.

II. A Fuller Consideration of Thomas

A. The Nature of Freedom

St. Thomas teaches that free acts only occur *within* the providential causality of God and that whatever God wills is realized precisely according

2. It is quite clear that, for Thomas, the causality of the first agent extends to universal being, to anything that exists in whatsoever manner. One notes Thomas's words in *ST* I, q. 22, a. 2: "Unde necesse est omnia quae habent quocumque modo esse, ordinata esse a Deo in finem." Further, it is without doubt of God's *agent causality*—of God as First Efficient Cause—that St. Thomas is speaking when he says, in the same place: "Cum enim omne agens agat propter finem, tantum se extendit ordinatio effectuum in finem, quantum se extendit causalitas primi agentis."—"For because every agent acts toward an end, the ordering of effects toward that end extends as far as the causality of the first agent." And: "Causalitas autem Dei, qui est primum agens, se extendit usque ad omnia entia"—"But the causality of God, who is the first agent, extends to all being".... Insofar as our free acts are actual or in any way exhibit perfection, that actuality and perfection are caused first by God, and only secondly by man.

to the *mode* in which He wills it—God wills that necessary things happen necessarily, that contingent things happen contingently. Thomas's frequently reiterated position is that necessity and contingency are modes of universal being and that as God is the cause of universal being, God is the cause both of the necessary and of the contingent.

Because God is the ultimate cause of everything, if we denominated contingency and necessity by that fact, *everything would be contingent*—because dependent on God—*and also necessary*—because infallibly brought forth by God. Hence the distinction between natural necessity and contingency is a function *not* of the relation to God as ultimate cause but rather a function of the *nature of the proximate cause*. As Thomas puts it in *ST*, q. 25, a. 3 ad. 4: "For it is according to the condition of the proximate cause that the effect has contingency or necessity." This is, of course, also his express teaching in *De Malo* q. 16, a. 7 ad. 15, wherein he expressly denies that necessity and contingency are discriminated *in relation to God;* for as the first, final, and exemplary cause of all that is, God transcends this distinction. Necessity and contingency are wholly a function of the proximate cause. Hence the contingency of the free act of the will is not negated by the fact that its prime cause is God.

The freedom of rational volition as a contingent cause is not specified in relation to God—Who is alike the cause both of the necessary and the contingent—but rather *in relation to the nature of the rational will* which, as ordered to the universal good, cannot be compelled by any finite good. Whether the will is free or not is not a function of whether it can exist and operate outside of, or in resistance to, divine causality: because nothing can exist and operate outside of or in resistance to divine causality *as such*. Man can resist any finite good as an object—and this includes *grace,* taken as an object of choice that can be fended away[3]—but this is not the same thing as being able to resist the divine causality absolutely. It makes no more sense to say that man can resist the divine causality, as such, than to say that grace can resist the divine causality. Man, his operations, and grace are all in differing ways *created divine effects*. This is why St. Thomas says in *ST* q. 22, a. 2 ad. 1 that no effect can occur outside the range of God's universal causality. The being, the true, and the good of every act is caused first by God and only secondarily by creatures.

3. E.g., one may speak of grace as an object, as in "it would be a grace to go to Mass" where "going to Mass" is the object of a choice which hence as a finite good *cannot compel the will.*

St. Thomas teaches that the human will is subject to divine motion not only with respect to the divine gift of the natural motion of the will toward the good in general, but also with respect to the *application* of the will in choice, which requires that the will be moved from potency to act with respect to its own self-determination in freedom. His use of the term "motion" is illustrative of this point.[4] The application of the act/potency distinction to the will by Thomas is manifest in his own words, although some of the most direct of these I will withhold until the moment arises to dispel the contrary view. For now, however, a few texts should suffice. Thomas notes in *ST* I, q. 83, a. 1 ad. 3, that:

> Free-will is the cause of its own movement, because by his free-will man moves himself to act. But it does not of necessity belong to liberty that what is free should be the first cause of itself, as neither for one thing to be cause of another need it be the first cause. God, therefore, is the first cause, Who moves causes both natural and voluntary. And just as by moving natural causes He does not prevent their acts being natural, so by moving voluntary causes He does not deprive their actions of being voluntary: but rather is He the cause of this very thing in them; for He operates in each thing according to its own nature.[5]

Likewise, Thomas arrestingly teaches in *De Malo*, q. 3, a. 2 ad. 4 that "When anything moves itself, this does not exclude its being moved by another, from which it has even this that it moves itself. Thus it is not repugnant to liberty that God is the cause of the free act of the will."[6] In *ST* I-II,

4. But Thomas insists upon it with a metaphysical rigor that is frequently missed by readers who approach his work without the requisite awareness of the centrality of his teaching that being is divided by act and potency. The centrality of this axiom is manifest in that in *De ente et essentia* it implicitly provides the key premise for Thomas's argument that were a being to exist in which existence and essence were one, there could be only one such being; and this because *ex hypothesi* such a being would be Pure Act and so lack all potency, whereas all the ways in which plurification accrue to being require potency. Without the prior understanding of being as divided by act and potency, this central premise in the universalization of the real distinction of essence and existence to all of finite being—including even the angels—would not occur.

5. *ST* I, q. 83, a. 1 ad. 3: "Dicendum quod liberum arbitrium est causa sui motus; quia homo per liberum arbitrium seipsum movet ad agendum. Non tamen hoc est de necessitate libertatis, quod sit prima causa sui id quod liberum est; sicut nec ad hoc quod aliquid sit causa alterius, requiritur quod sit prima causa eius. Deus igitur est prima causa movens et naturales causas et voluntarias. Et sicut naturalibus causis, movendo eas, non aufert quin actus earum sint naturales; ita movendo causas voluntarias, non aufert quin actiones earum sint voluntariae, sed potius hoc in eis facit; operatur enim in unoquoque secundum eius proprietatem."

6. "Similiter cum aliquid mouet se ipsum, non excluditur quin ab alio moueatur a quo habet hoc ipsum quo se ipsum mouet. Et sic non repugnat libertati quod Deus est causa actus liberi arbitrii."

q. 109, a. 1, he writes of the divine application of the natural motion of the will in choice:

But it is clear that, just as all corporeal movements are reduced to the motion of the body of the heavens as to the first corporeal mover, so all movements, both corporeal and spiritual, are reduced to the absolutely First Mover, Who is God. *And hence no matter how perfect a corporeal or spiritual nature is supposed to be, it cannot proceed to its act unless it be moved by God.* Now this motion is according to the plan of His providence, and not by a necessity of nature, as the motion of the body of the heavens. *But not only is every motion from God as from the First Mover, but all formal perfection is from Him as from the First Act. Hence the action of the intellect, or of any created being whatsoever, depends upon God in two ways: first, inasmuch as it is from Him that it has the form whereby it acts; secondly, inasmuch as it is moved by Him to act* [emphasis added].

One notes the language: both the will that does not proceed to act and the will that does proceed to act enjoy the natural motion of the will; but the will that proceeds to act *cannot do so* unless it is further moved by God. This makes clear that it is not merely the natural motion of the will, but the *application* of this natural motion in choice, that Thomas holds to require prior divine motion. This is compatible with his well-known teaching (found, for example, in *SCG* III, q. 67), that "every application of power to action is chiefly and primarily from God" ("*Sed omnis applicatio virtutis ad operationem est principaliter et primo a Deo*"). Thomas's example is that of a cook applying fire in heating: "For the artisan applying the power of a natural thing to some action is said to be the cause of that action, as the cook is of the cooking that is done by fire."[7] Clearly it is about God's direct *efficient causality* that Thomas is speaking: as the cook is the efficient cause of cooking by applying the power of fire to act—he ignites and applies the flame for the sake of cooking—so God is the primary efficient cause of the application of *every* natural power to action (inclusive, one notes, of the power of free choice). The *application* of the natural motion of the will in our self-motion in choice derives first and primarily from the efficient causality of God (for we must be moved from potency to act with respect to moving/determining ourselves freely, as the earlier quoted *De Malo* q. 3,

7. Here is the passage including the earlier cited line: "Quicquid applicat virtutem activam ad agendum, dicitur esse causa illius actionis: artifex enim applicans virtutem rei naturalis ad aliquam actionem, dicitur esse causa illius actionis, sicut coquus decoctionis, quae est per ignem. Sed omnis applicatio virtutis ad operationem est principaliter et primo a Deo."

a. 2 ad. 4 makes clear: "When anything moves itself, this does not exclude its being moved by another, from which it has even this that it moves itself"). One notes also in *ST* I-II, q. 109, a. 1 Thomas's use of *motio* referring to the will. There is precisely no suggestion that this is not a real motion, a point to which I will return.

The will must be moved from potency to act for willing to occur, and this is not contrary to human freedom, first, because no finite object can fully actuate the whole potency of the will so as to command the will, whose object is the universal good in general—this is the teaching of St. Thomas in *ST* I-II, q. 10, a. 2 ad. 1. Thus, even when the will is moved by God, it retains a *power* susceptible of diverse actuation. *Objectively*, at the level of all the terrestrial objects of the will, no finite good can compel the will. Nonetheless, for the will to move in the least requires that God move the will—not merely in authoring our natural motion toward the good in general, but in actualizing our potential to apply this natural motion in any given intention or choice. The effect of the will is *willing*, but the will must first be moved from potency to act with respect to its own willing in order to will, because nothing moves from potency to act save by virtue of that which is in act. Hence "no matter how perfect a corporeal or spiritual nature is supposed to be, it cannot proceed to its act unless it be moved by God."

Insofar as God moves the will, then, the will is moved, but the will is said to be a contingent cause, or to be free, because as the proximate cause *of its own willing* it is not merely ordained to one effect or one narrow range of effects, and because no finite or terrestial object can compel it. It is expressly not denominated as free owing to its relation to God, for in relation to God, all creatures and created operations, whether contingent or necessary, are effects of the First Cause.

The will can do otherwise than God wills, in the sense that even when it is divinely moved freely to will something, it nonetheless retains at that very instant *the power* to do otherwise. But *power* is not *act*, and the will *does not wish* to do otherwise insofar as it is freely moved by God. Just as no being can exist outside the divine causality, and as every perfection of being is an effect of God, so the will's own motion whereby it determines itself to act is received from God.

On St. Thomas's account,[8] in the *composite sense*—the sense in which

8. For the distinction of the composite and divided sense, see *Summa Contra Gentiles,* I, c. 67.

one might ask whether one can do two things at the very same instant—one can no more not freely will when God is moving one freely to will, than one can sit and stand at the same instant. But in the *divided sense*—the sense in which *even while sitting* one retains in the present a power to stand—the will retains the power to act differently. The will is not exempt from providential causality; but it is free in the sense that no finite object can compel it, and because it does not have merely a prefixed operative power determined to one effect (as Thomas notes in *ST* I, q. 22 ad. 4) but rather is open to universal good as such. As Thomas puts it in *ST* I, q. 105, a. 4 ad. 3:

> If the will were so moved by another as in no way to be moved from within itself, the act of the will would not be imputed for reward or blame. But since its being moved by another does not prevent its being moved from within itself, as we have stated, it does not thereby forfeit the motive for merit or demerit.

In *ST* I–II, q. 9, a. 4 ad. 2, Thomas similarly writes that:

> For an act to be violent it is not enough that its principle be extrinsic, but we must add "without the concurrence of him that suffers violence." This does not happen when the will is moved by an exterior principle: *for it is the will that wills, though moved by another* [emphasis added]. But this movement would be violent, if it were counter to the movement of the will: which in the present case is impossible; since then the will would will and not will the same thing.

This last line is only to say: insofar as the will is freely moved to will something, it is not *not*-moved to will it. Freedom is not a violation of the principle of non-contradiction. The object of the will being the good in general—universal good—it follows that no finite good is able fully to actuate the will and so to command the will (cf. *ST* I-II, q. 10, a. 2 ad. 1). But nothing that moves from potency to act can do so save by virtue of something that is in act: God must move the will from potency to act with respect to its moving itself.

B. The Divine Permission of Evil

Given these insights, the picture of evil, and particularly of moral evil, becomes clearer. Every being, truth, and good derives from God as its First, Final, and Exemplary Source. Thus, as Thomas argues throughout his career—as, for example, in *ST* I, q. 49, a. 3 ad 5—*there is* no *per se* cause of evil, nothing that *by its very essence* is ordained to evil. Although in a weaker sense we do speak of acts with certain deprivations as *per se* ordered to evil—for example, when we say that an act is evil *ex obiecto*—we mean by this only that *per se mala* acts are so deprived as necessarily to fall short, rather than that some agent is from creation possessed of an essentially damnific nature.

Thus, evil as a deprivation of that which is due or necessary for the perfection of a being must be permitted by God if it is to occur. Further, as for God to cause X signifies nothing in God, but only *the being of X;* for God to "permit" evil is necessarily for Him *not to ordain the contrary perfection.* As we shall see, this is precisely the heart of Thomas's doctrine of reprobation. Granted that there is no *per se* cause of evil, still God must permit evil for it to occur. Simply put, God is omnipotent; and did He simply and efficaciously ordain the contrary, the contrary would freely occur. To deny this is formally to derogate the divine omnipotence on behalf of a liberty of indifference to divine causality that does not exist.

Thomas argues in *ST* I-II, q. 109, a. 2 ad. 2 that:

> To sin is nothing else than to fall from the good which belongs to any being according to its nature. Now as every created thing has no being unless from another, and considered in itself is nothing, so does it need to be conserved by another in the good which pertains to its nature. For it can of itself fall from good, just as of itself it can fall into nonbeing, unless it is conserved by God.[9]

Nota bene—the real capacity to fall is *pari passu,* keeps equal pace with, *non-conservation by God.* In this passage, Thomas argues that the creature *of itself* is operationally deficient as its operative power is proportioned to its ontological finitude. A free, rational creature that, *as* created, *of itself does not exist*—and which hence *is not its own law or rule of operation*—is likewise *of itself defectible in act* unless upheld in act by an extrinsic power, namely by God. It is of itself ontologically deficient in operation, and hence apart from divine aid of itself falls away from the good. This is not sinfulness or moral evil *per se,* but rather *ontological deficiency.* Yet, metaphysically viewed, this is what makes the creature susceptible to evil. No creature is Pure Act, and so every creature must be sustained in the good

9. *ST* I-II, q. 109, a. 2 ad. 2: "Dicendum quod peccare nihil aliud est quam deficere a bono quod convenit alicui secundum suam naturam. Unaquaeque autem res creata, sicut esse non habet nisi ab alio, et in se considerata nihil est, ita indiget conservari in bono suae naturae convenienti ab alio. Potest enim per seipsam deficere a bono, sicut et per seipsam potest deficere in non esse, nisi divinitus conservaretur."

proper to it by God if it is to achieve its good. As St. Thomas puts it elsewhere, in the *Summa Contra Gentiles* III, q. 155, "everything that is changeable of itself needs the aid of an immovable mover in order to stand fast to one thing" (from the chapter titled "*Quod homo indiget auxilio gratiae ad perseverandum in bono*": "*Omne enim quod de se est variabile, ad hoc quod figatur in uno, indiget auxilio alicuius moventis immobilis*"). Or, as Thomas alike puts it, in *ST* q. 20, a. 3, "For since God's love is the cause of goodness in things, as has been said (2), no one thing would be better than another, if God did not will greater good for one than for another." Speaking of the very special good of predestination, Aquinas makes quite clear that he is speaking of the "simple will" of God (*ST* I, q. 23, a. 3 ad. 3).

But why then does God not efficaciously sustain all rational creatures in the good? Thomas's classical answer is given in the *Summa Theologiae*. First, God does not owe defectible creatures that they be preserved from all defect. For if He did owe the creature that it be preserved from all defect, then to permit the creature to suffer defect would be unjust.[10] But God does not owe the creature a guaranteed achievement of the optimal accomplishment possible to its nature: this is his point in *ST* I-II, q. 79, a. 1, where, speaking of imputing sins to God he writes: "For it happens that God does not give some the assistance, whereby they may avoid sin, which assistance

10. *ST* I-II, q. 79, a. 1: "Deus autem non potest esse directe causa peccati vel sui vel alterius. Quia omne peccatum est per recessum ab ordine qui est in Deum sicut in finem. Deus autem omnia inclinat et convertit in seipsum sicut in ultimum finem, sicut Dionysius dicit, I cap. *De Div. Nom.* Unde impossible est quod sit sibi vel aliis causa siscedendi ab ordine qui est in ipsum. Unde non potest directe esse causa peccati.—Similiter etiam neque indirecte. Contingit enim quod Deus aliquibus non praebet auxilium ad evitandum peccata, quod si praeberet, non peccarent. Sed hoc totum facit secundum ordinem suae sapientiae et iustitiae, cum ipse sit sapientia et iustitia. Unde non imputatur ei quod alius peccet, sicut causae peccati; sicut gubernator non dicitur causa submersionis navis ex hoc quod non gubernat navem, nisi quando subtrahit gubernationem potens et debens gubernare. Et sic patet quod Deus nullo modo est causa peccati."—"Now God cannot be directly the cause of sin, either in Himself or in another, since every sin is a departure from the order which is to God as the end: whereas God inclines and turns all things to Himself as to their last end, as Dionysius states (*Div. Nom.* i): so that it is impossible that He should be either to Himself or to another the cause of departing from the order which is to Himself. Therefore He cannot be directly the cause of sin. In like manner neither can He cause sin indirectly. For it happens that God does not give some the assistance, whereby they may avoid sin, which assistance were He to give, they would not sin. But He does all this according to the order of His wisdom and justice, since He Himself is Wisdom and Justice: so that if someone sin it is not imputable to Him as though He were the cause of that sin; even as a pilot is not said to cause the wrecking of the ship, through not steering the ship, unless he cease to steer while able and bound to steer. It is therefore evident that God is nowise a cause of sin."

were He to give, they would not sin. But He does all this according to the order of His wisdom and justice, since He Himself is Wisdom and Justice: so that if someone sin it is not imputable to Him as though He were the cause of that sin; even as a pilot is not said to cause the wrecking of the ship, through not steering the ship, unless he cease to steer while able and bound to steer. It is therefore evident that God is nowise a cause of sin." God is able to uphold the creature in good, but He is not bound in justice to prevent a defectible agent from ever defecting—and the defectibility of the created agent is ontological before and as a condition of it ever becoming moral. Only if God were bound in justice always to preserve the defectible creature from defect would it be the case that by not always and invariably doing so God could rightly be impugned. Second, evil is permitted both for the sake of the common good of the universe, and for the sake of other noble goods, especially for the good of the elect; and God is infinitely powerful, so that just as He can bring forth something from nothing, so it belongs to Him to bring forth good from evil. Thus, Thomas argues in *ST* q. 22, a. 2 ad. 2 that the permission of evil is by divine omnipotence ordered to the production of good, quoting Augustine: "Thus Augustine says (*Enchiridion* 2): 'Almighty God would in no wise permit evil to exist in His works, unless He were so almighty and so good as to produce good even from evil.'"[11] Thirdly, as St. Thomas puts it in Chapter 142 of the *Compendium Theologiae,* "good is rendered more praiseworthy when compared with particular evils, just as in relation to the darkness of black the radiant brilliance of white is more pronouncedly manifest. And so through this—that evil is permitted to be in the world—the divine goodness is more clearly shown forth in the good, just as divine wisdom is more patently manifested in ordering evil to serve good."[12]

Likewise, St. Thomas expressly teaches that election and reprobation

11. Thomas also argues in *ST* I, q. 22, a. 2 ad. 2 that: "Since God, then, provides universally for all being, it belongs to His providence to permit certain defects in particular effects, that the perfect good of the universe may not be hindered, for if all evil were prevented, much good would be absent from the universe. A lion would cease to live, if there were no slaying of animals; and there would be no patience of martyrs if there were no tyrannical persecution. Thus Augustine says (*Enchiridion* 2): 'Almighty God would in no wise permit evil to exist in His works, unless He were so almighty and so good as to produce good even from evil.'"

12. *Compendium Theologiae, Capitulum CXLII:* "Tertio, quia ex ipsis malis particularibus commendabiliora redduntur bona dum eis comparantur, sicut ex obscuritate nigri magis declaratur claritas albi. Et sic per hoc quod mala permittuntur esse in mundo, diuina bonitas magis declaratur in bonis, et sapientia in ordinatione malorum ad bona."

are *prior to prevision of merit,* and that *predestination is gratuitous and so God is free to grant it to whomever He will.* These express teachings—regarding the permission of evil for the sake of the common good of the universe; for the sake of the good of the elect; and for the greater manifestation of the conquest of evil by good—together with the teaching that predestination and reprobation are prior to prevision of merit, are incontrovertibly in St. Thomas's texts, especially in his middle and later work. But should these be considered at full length now, the scope of the consideration might deflect sufficient focus upon the revisions of Maritain and Lonergan, the Thomistic authors whose revisions of Thomas's teachings on this subject I wish to identify and submit to criticism. Suffice it to say that one can find these teachings of St. Thomas in *Summa Theologiae* I, q. 23, a. 5 ad. 3, on predestination,[13] peppered throughout Thomas's *Commentary on the Gospel of John,*

13. "The reason for the predestination of some, and reprobation of others, must be sought for in the goodness of God. Thus He is said to have made all things through His goodness, so that the divine goodness might be represented in things. Now it is necessary that God's goodness, which in itself is one and undivided, should be manifested in many ways in His creation; because creatures in themselves cannot attain to the simplicity of God. Thus it is that for the completion of the universe there are required different grades of being; some of which hold a high and some a low place in the universe. That this multiformity of grades may be preserved in things, God allows some evils, lest many good things should never happen, as was said above (Question 22, Article 2). Let us then consider the whole of the human race, as we consider the whole universe. God wills to manifest His goodness in men; in respect to those whom He predestines, by means of His mercy, as sparing them; and in respect of others, whom he reprobates, by means of His justice, in punishing them. This is the reason why God elects some and rejects others. To this the Apostle refers, saying (Rom. 9:22–23): 'What if God, willing to show His wrath [that is, the vengeance of His justice] and to make His power known, endured [that is, permitted] with much patience vessels of wrath, fitted for destruction; that He might show the riches of His glory on the vessels of mercy, which He hath prepared unto glory' and (2 Tim. 2:20): 'But in a great house there are not only vessels of gold and silver; but also of wood and of earth; and some, indeed, unto honor, but some unto dishonor.' *Yet why He chooses some for glory, and reprobates others, has no reason, except the divine will* [emphasis added]. Whence Augustine says (Tract. xxvi. in Joan.): 'Why He draws one, and another He draws not, seek not to judge, if thou dost not wish to err.' Thus too, in the things of nature, a reason can be assigned, since primary matter is altogether uniform, why one part of it was fashioned by God from the beginning under the form of fire, another under the form of earth, that there might be a diversity of species in things of nature. Yet why this particular part of matter is under this particular form, and that under another, depends upon the simple will of God; as from the simple will of the artificer it depends that this stone is in one part of the wall, and that in another; although the plan requires that some stones should be in this place, and some in that place. Neither on this account can there be said to be injustice in God, if He prepares unequal lots for not unequal things. This would be altogether contrary to the notion of justice, *if the effect of predestination were granted as a debt, and not gratuitously. In things which are given gratuitously, a person can give more or less, just as he pleases (provided he deprives nobody of his due), without any infringement of justice* [emphasis

and generally throughout his middle and later works, the *Scriptum on the Sentences* alone providing a distinct but also a clearly abandoned teaching. Further, in q. 23, a. 5 ad. 3, as well as in the *Commentary on the Gospel of John* (Lectio III, Jn 15 [14–17]), Thomas compares the ordering of predestination and reprobation to the assignation of form upon prime matter for the sake of the "splendor of order in things" (from *Commentary on the Gospel of John*) and flowing from the "simple will of God" (from *ST* I, q. 23, a. 5 ad. 3) saying, in his *Commentary on the Gospel of John*, that:

> The reason why God confers more good on one than on another is so that there might be a splendor of order in things. This is clear in material things where prime matter of itself is uniformly disposed to all forms. Also, before things themselves exist, they are not disposed to this or that existence; rather, they receive different forms and existences from God so that an order can be established among them. *It is like this among rational creatures where some are chosen for glory and some are rejected for punishment* [emphasis added]: "The Lord knows who are his ... In a great house there are not only vessels of gold and silver but also of wood and earthenware, and some for noble use, some for ignoble" (2 Tim. 2:19). And so we see a diversified order: the mercy of God shines forth in those whom, without any previous merits, he prepares for grace; in others we see the justice of God when, because of their own guilt, he allots them punishment, yet less than is deserved. So, I have chosen you by predestining you from all eternity, and by calling you to the faith during your lifetime.[14]

The comparison of the potency of our wills for good with prime matter is not accidental: because it is God Who gives all good gifts, including volitional ones. There is not a word in all of this of a liberty of indifference to divine causality, but rather solely of the ordering wisdom and goodness of the divine plan. One also cannot avoid noting the almost eerie fashion in which St. Thomas foresees, and rejects, the notion that will later be articulated in terms of *scientia media* by Molina:

> Others say that it is true that our actually existing merits are not the cause of our predestination, but those merits preexisting in the foreknowledge of God are. Thus they say that because God knew that certain persons would be good and make good use of grace, he decided to give them grace. But if this were so, it would follow that the reason he chose us was because he foreknew we would choose him.

added]. This is what the master of the house said: 'Take what is thine, and go thy way. Is it not lawful for me to do what I will?' (Mt 20:14–15)."

14. *Super Evangelium S. Joannis,* Lectio III, John 15 (14–17), lect. 3, n. 2024.

And so our choice would be prior to the divine choice; which is contrary to our Lord's statement.[15]

Thus, Thomas's answer to the question as to why God permits evil is as follows: namely, that evil is permitted by God for the sake of the common good of the universe, for the sake of the higher good of the elect (as all things work to the good for those who love God, e.g., as from persecution God brings forth the patience and holiness of the martyrs), and for the sake of magnifying the good by causing even evil to serve it. Just as God brings something out of nothing, so it belongs to Him to bring good from evil. We may add that insofar as the good brought forth is finally the rational creature's vision of God—an infinitely disproportionate good that we cannot *in via* fully fathom—the ground for the permission of evil cannot now and for us be resolved clearly into vision. But in the beatific vision the magnification of the triumph of goodness achieved through God permitting evil while always both further ordering evil to good, and bringing forth higher good from evil—just as He brings forth something from nothing—will be clearly seen.

III. The Problem, and Two Proposed Revisions

This leads us to the modern problem with Thomas's teaching. In essence, one might say that the problem with Thomas's account of the permission of evil is that on this account God is not a Kantian: the singular private good of the creature is not the *ratio* for the creation. Not even the omnipotent God can make it to be the case that the *ratio* for the whole of creation is the private good of any particular creature, precisely because the private good is ordered to the common good.

Yet, to suggest that God loves some more than others, and that this love is the *cause* of the excellence of some as opposed to others—especially in a context wherein some lack of excellence is *damnific*—is a thought that strikes moderns as *fatalistic, incompatible with freedom,* and *contrary to the belief that God loves, and wills the salvation of, all.* In fact, one hears such terms as "morally repugnant" and "rigid" used of this teaching.[16] Feeling acutely the modern repugnance to this teaching, both Maritain and Loner-

15. Ibid., n. 2021.

16. The present author has heard such characterizations of this doctrine, and worse, at several conferences of theologians and philosophers.

gan offer revisions of St. Thomas's account. Here, I will simply identify one proposition essential to the argument of each that in my view falls short both of Thomas's text and of speculative defensibility.

A. The Case of Maritain

Maritain argues that, although God can infrustrably move the will, this is exceptional, and that God normally moves the will first by way of a "breakable" or "fracturable" motion. *If* the creature does not negate or nihilate this motion—does not "break" it—then God normally will perfect it by bestowing an infrustrable motion. But whether the creature does or does not "nihilate" or negate the motion is entirely at the initiative of the creature. Referring to this, Maritain considers the case "... when the creature does not produce nothingness under grace" and then he writes parenthetically: "(this is no merit in its part, for not to take the initiative of nothingness is not to do something, it is only not to move under divine action)."[17] Maritain writes further of not nihilating or negating the divine motion of the will in relation to the rule of reason:

> It is proper to remark here that if 'not to nihilate' and 'to consider the rule' come practically to the same thing, nevertheless there is, formally, a clear distinction between the two, and the first formality is the condition of the second.[18]

The idea is simple: God causes everything positive, but the creature has initiative in nihilation or negation; and God normally bestows graces that can be subject to nihilation or negation. Thus, if and only if the creature does *not* negate the motion bestowed by God, will God ordinarily bestow an infrustrable efficacious motion upon the creature. *And so, whether the creature is lost is a function of the creature's own absolute initiative in evil.* There no longer need be any concern that God must first infallibly permit evil for it to occur.

I think it is undoubtedly true that the creature has the initiative in evil, as only a creature can enact evil. But Maritain forgot something about negation that St. Thomas did not forget in *De Veritate*, III, 28.[19] In that work,

17. Jacques Maritain, *St. Thomas and the Problem of Evil* (Milwaukee: Marquette University Press, 1942), 37.

18. Jacques Maritain, *Existence and the Existent*, translated by Lewis Galantiere and Gerald B. Phelan (New York: Pantheon Books, 1948), 100, n. 10.

19. Leonine *De Veritate*, III, 28: "Quaedam vero opposita sunt quorum alterum tantum est natura quaedam, reliquum vero non est nisi remotio vel negatio ipsius, sicut patet in oppositis

Thomas teaches that where there is a real subject, the negation of a negation is *something positive*, and so it is *not really distinct* from the affirmative to which the original negation is opposed. To put it in St. Thomas's words, "the destruction of non-white is not really different than the coming to be of white." Thomas is saying that when spoken to someone who really exists, the claim that "you do not *not* have a nose" is equivalent to affirming that indeed in reality "*you do have a nose.*" But this is true only because the subject is *real*. If someone says "elephants singing La Traviata do not *not*-fly," this does not mean that there are really existing elephants singing La Traviata and flying, because *there are no really existing elephants singing La Traviata*.

According to Maritain *if* the creature *does not negate, then* God will bestow an infrustrable efficacious motion upon the will. Maritain treats the creature *not negating* as though it were in some way different from the creature being moved by God. But the creature is a *real subject* and so for the creature *not to negate* is for the creature to do something *positive* which is an effect of divine causality. Since everything that is ontologically positive is caused by God, this means that *if the creature does not negate,* this is in reality the same as the creature receiving the gift of divine motion toward the salutary act: *the non-negation of the creature in reality is not different than its being helped by God*. Non-negation is not then, as Maritain thought, somehow "prior" to and the condition of the positive consideration of the rule of reason, but is indeed *identical* with the positive consideration and consideration of the rule. But this brings us back to the original teaching of St. Thomas, according to which God either gives, or God does not give, efficacious aid to the creature: either God gives the efficacious motion toward the salutary act, or He does not. Thus, in this context, it is not as though there is any formal priority to non-negation at all, because non-negation means only *being moved by the divine motion*. The Maritainian adaptation fails by treating the negation of negation in a real subject as though it were

secundum affirmationem et negationem, vel secundum privationem et habitum; et in talibus negatio oppositi quod ponit naturam aliquam, est realis quia est alicuius rei, negatio vero alterius oppositi non est realis, quia non est alicuius rei, est enim negatio negationis; et ideo haec negatio negationis quae est negatio alterius oppositi, nihil differt secundum rem a positione alterius; unde secundum rem idem est generatio albi et corruptio non albi. Sed quia negatio, quamvis non sit res naturae, est tamen res rationis, ideo negatio negationis secundum rationem sive secundum modum intelligendi est aliud a positione affirmationis; et sic corruptio non albi secundum modum intelligendi est aliud quam generatio albi."

something different than the positive gift given by God. While negation of negation is *logically* distinct from real affirmation in a real subject, *it is not really different.* This destroys Maritain's revision, and that of many similar cognate arguments, e.g., Fr. Most, Dom Pontifex, etc.

B. The Case of Lonergan

Like Maritain, Lonergan is in seraphic discourse with the entirety of the Thomistic tradition. It is arresting to see his responses to John of St. Thomas, Bañez, Del Prado, Garrigou-Lagrange, and others. However, in his famed *Grace and Freedom: Operative Grace in the Thought of St. Thomas Aquinas,* he makes several central assertions that I do not believe survive a sufficient encounter with St. Thomas's text. *The most central of these is the arresting claim that, according to St. Thomas Aquinas, the motion in the creature from not acting to acting—and hence derivatively, from not willing to willing—is not a real motion.* This proposition that the motion in the creature from not acting to acting, and hence from *not willing* to *willing,* is *not a real motion,* is arresting. Indeed, the problem about divine causality and freedom would largely vanish if the transition from potentially willing to actually willing were not a real motion requiring a real mover as the condition for our self-motion. As Lonergan puts it in footnote 26 of Chapter Four of his work *Grace and Freedom*: "To later scholastics this seemed impossible a priori: they held that 'Peter not acting' must be really different from 'Peter acting.' They refused to believe that St. Thomas could disagree with them on this; in fact, St. Thomas disagreed."

In the same chapter of that work, Lonergan notes that causing is not something real in the agent causing, but exists rather in the effect, or at most in the relation between or nexus of agent and effect. He responds to the proposition that everything must move from potency to act in order to cause by observing that were this true that then there could be no First Cause.[20] Of course, precisely as stated, *this is true. That is, to causing as such potency is not essential.* Otherwise it would be impossible that God—Who is Pure Act and in Whom there is no potency whatsoever—cause anything at all. Every agency is, as such, *act.* Thus agency, as such, does not make reference to any transition from potency to act, because it is accidental to

20. Cf. Bernard Lonergan, SJ, *Grace and Freedom* (New York: Herder and Herder, 1971), hereafter cited as *Grace,* 65–66.

agency *as such* that it be related to potentiality, which is what the texts from St. Thomas that Lonergan adduces suffice to show.

Yet, although it is accidental to *agency* as such, and to the agent *qua agent,* that it pass from potency to act with respect to acting—because God is the First Cause and there is no potency in Him, and because agency is agency and the definition of agency makes no necessary reference to potency—*nonetheless, it is not accidental to the being that acts* that it is *not Pure Act,* and so likewise *it is not accidental that the finite agent is not identical with its operation, not purely an agent. Consequently,* it is not accidental to the finite agent *as* finite agent that, for *it* to act, it must pass from potency to act. Even angelic knowers require divinely infused species to actuate their knowing. Moreover, the human subject is not always an agent in act—it is not always causing—and in particular, the human agent is not always *choosing*. Granted that there is nothing about *acting as such* that requires potency, a *finite subject that acts is not its agency*; it is really distinct from its agency. *Thus, the finite subject needs to be moved from potency to act in order to attain to the dignity of acting.*

Of course it remains true that to acting or agency *as such* it is accidental that there be transition from potency to act. *Similarly, it is true that to being as such potency is accidental. However, it is not accidental that potency pertains to finite creatures; because the creature, qua creature, is not Uncreated Pure Act.* The point is simple: while agency *qua* agency makes no reference to potency, the created human subject who acts must first acquire *the dignity of being an agent,* which it can only do by passing from potency to act with respect to acting. It is a *tautology* that the agent qua agent is in act, but this does not mean that every agent is pure act and thus in no need of moving from potency to act with respect to its agency.

Thankfully, we have the precise lines of St. Thomas from the *ST* I-II, q. 9, a. 4, pertaining specifically to the need of the will—as in potency to willing at one time and in act with respect to willing, at another—to be *moved* by a *real mover*. These lines pertain chiefly to the need for an initial extrinsic mover—others, as cited above (e.g., *ST* I-II, q. 109, a. 2), pertain to the application of the natural motion to act. But these lines are conspicuous for articulating the requisite principle: that "everything that is at one time an agent actually, and at another time an agent in potentiality, needs to be moved by a mover." It is precisely this principle that also applies to the application of the natural motion of the will in choice. As Thomas puts it:

As far as the will is moved by the object, it is evident that it can be moved by something exterior. But in so far as it is moved in the exercise of its act, we must again hold it to be moved by some exterior principle. *For everything that is at one time an agent actually, and at another time an agent in potentiality, needs to be moved by a mover. Now it is evident that the will begins to will something, whereas previously it did not will it. Therefore it must, of necessity, be moved by something to will it* [emphasis added].

His conclusion is that: "we must, of necessity, suppose that the will advanced to its first movement in virtue of the instigation of some exterior mover, as Aristotle concludes in a chapter of the *Eudemian Ethics* (vii, 14)."

Lonergan makes the further suggestion that "the Aristotelian premotion as understood by St. Thomas affects indifferently the mover or moved, agent or patient".[21] Rather than premotion accounting for the attainment of the dignity of agency, for Lonergan premotion accounts merely for patient or agent being in causal *proximity*. Rather than seeing that the finite agent must be moved from potency to act by God in order to act, Lonergan thinks of agents as just *in act* and of the divine motion as moving creatures in proximity to one another. Lonergan adduces the relation of the sun to an iceberg, arguing that irrespective which moves toward the other, the effect is the same. But the sun is not a subsistent heat, but rather the result of innumerable processes of gaseous explosion, which are motions from potency to act. The fact that acting, as such, makes no reference to *being moved from potency to act* does not mean that the sun is simply in pure act as a heat generator without undergoing any motion from potency to act. It does not mean that causing can occur in finite creatures without them being really moved from potency to act. And such motions require an actual cause.

Lonergan's account fails to acknowledge that what necessitates divine "premotion" is that the finite subject of agency is not always in act and so needs to be moved to act. It is the motion from potency to act with respect to acting that requires premotion, and not merely the providential arrangement whereby things in act are governed so as to be in proximity to others that they thus may affect.

Of course, the emphasis by St. Thomas on the real motion of the creature from potency to act with respect to its own agency also saves theism from the spectre of occasionalism: God causes our motion but *not* in such a

21. *Grace*, 71.

way that we cease to be causes of that motion, because it is our own power to act that is actualized. It is the *will* that *wills;* but as the will is in potency to willing, it must be divinely moved from potency to act in order for willing to occur.[22] Further, the emphasis upon the motion from potency to act

22. Of course, the divine motion is not a *tertium quid,* not a *thing* or *mechanism,* nor a permanent habitude or created form (none of which *could* move the will, since only the divine author of the will can give it either its natural motion or the motion of *applicatio*); rather, this motion is that by virtue of which the agent moves himself, it is the principle of the agent's own transition from potency to act with respect to its self-determination in freedom. It is God Who is the author of the reality of the will—First Cause of *esse,* and for that matter, Exemplar Cause—and who moves the will from potency to act with respect to its own self-motion—God is First Cause of *agere.* If God does not move the creature from potency to act with respect to free self-determination, free self-determination will never occur. It is not as though God required some third reality to cause this motion: God as Pure Act is sufficient to cause this motion in the creature whereby the creature freely determines itself and God causes the perfection of its free act (surely it cannot be said that the will freely determines itself *without moving* from potency to act with respect to determining itself, for the will is not always determining itself). *Pari passu* with God moving the will freely to move itself with respect to a particular act, the will is moved freely to move itself to this particular act. Hence, God and the created rational agent each in different respects is total cause of the free act, God as Universal Cause, and the creature as particular cause. The rational creature is the cause of its own free acts, and it moves itself; but it is not the First Cause of its free acts, nor is it the First Mover. Hence the sage observation of Thomas Osborne that God "predetermines" free acts rather than determining these in the manner of a finite cause (cf. *Nova et Vetera,* English Edition, Vol. 4, No. 3 [2006]: 607–32, "Thomist Premotion and Contemporary Philosophy of Religion"). To quote this author at length (630): "A Thomist should think that compatibilism is at best ambiguous when applied to God and secondary causes. If the relevant concept of necessity is taken from our discussion of the order of secondary causes, then this concept cannot apply to God's premotion. God is the source of contingency and the first mover of contingent events. With respect to free human acts, he both gives the power of free choice and moves the agent to make a decision freely. Thomism is a kind of compatibilism only if by "compatibilism" we mean that free choice is compatibile with predetermination by the first cause. But this kind of compatibilism differs from others in that God causes an event to be either necessary or contingent with respect to their secondary causes. Ultimately, God is the source not only of all his effects, but also of their necessity and contingency.

Indeed, from the Thomist view it is a serious conceptual confusion to assimilate the question of whether human acts are determined to the question of whether God's premotion is compatible with human freedom. An event is contingent with respect to its proximate cause. Disputes over whether events are in themselves necessary or contingent are consequently disputes that are either over that necessity that results from a creature's nature or that necessity that results from an effect's necessarily following upon its proximate cause. If contingency is required for free choice, then human choices cannot be determined by some proximate cause. The question of whether God predetermines is irrelevant to such a dispute. It is not the case that Thomists are libertarians with respect to secondary causes and compatibilists with respect to God's causality, but rather that the terms do not properly apply to God's causality."

I believe that Osborne is correct that critics of premotion preponderantly do not—and, historically, have not—so much as understood the nature of the teaching. God is the first author both of our freedom and of the perfection of our free acts. But the key again is: for Aquinas freedom is not an abyss of libertarian aseity, not a liberty of indifference to divine causality, but a

is necessitated by the absolute centrality of the analogical division of being by potency and act, whose recognition is central to the understanding of the real distinction of essence and existence in finite being.[23] The analogical division of being by act and potency is very close to the first principle of non-contradiction.[24] The widespread loss of metaphysical realism regarding this first principle owing to reductionist logicism in the Anglophone world is one external factor that has contributed to the misconstruction of this vital metaphysical thesis as a mere secondary consideration regarding sensible being, obscuring its importance for crucial metaphysical issues.[25]

---

true function of the very nature of the rational will that no finite good can compel or completely actuate. Freedom of the will is a function of the intellective nature of the will in its modality as a contingent cause.

23. One notes that it is precisely the truth that the plurifiability of being requires *potentia* that enables St. Thomas, in *De ente et essentia,* to conclude that if there were a being in which essence and existence were identical there could be but one, such that, in all but one hypothetical instance (which will shortly be demonstrated as real), essence and existence are really distinct.

24. In brief, it is not a merely conceptual distinction, because wherever a real is distinguished from a non-real, so that one of the poles of the distinction is real, the distinction is real. E.g., even had God never created finite being, it would be true that the nature of God is not a finite nature: the distinction would be a real distinction owing to the real nature of God Himself. Likewise, being is not non-being. Non-being is purely conceptual, but *being* is not. It is this consideration that poses the problem of Parmenidean monism, which is a problem in reconciling the real unity of the first principle—being—with manyness, limit, and change. *That* manyness, limit, and change are real, is obvious to those who trust their senses. Unfortunately, this is where most analytic philosophers terminate their consideration. But the truthfulness of our sensation must be reconciled with the real character of the first principle and with the unity of being that it involves: being is identical with itself and therefore unitary; there is nothing outside of being that can limit it, and therefore it is unlimited; and being is not and cannot be not-being, and so it is changeless. The answer to this problem—not even so much as conceived or conceivable by logicist authors—is developed by Aristotle in the analysis, it is true, of physical beings, but to the point of answering the Parmenidean metaphysical objection. His answer discloses the existence of a principle that is not act, and is not mere negation, but is capacity or potency, which is always founded upon a prior principle of act and is really distinct from it, and according to which manyness, limit, and change accrue to being.

25. Of course, the point here is not that Lonergan was in any sense committed to logicism, but rather that the analytic/Anglophone proclivity thereto is something that easily melds with the Suarezian denial of the real distinction of act and potency, establishing external conditions that make it easier for English speaking Catholic authors to overlook the strategic metaphysical importance of the act/potency distinction, as—on this question—I believe Lonergan did. This is not to imply that there may not be deeper intra-systemic roots to Lonergan's views on this matter. But surely, even if there are, no one could claim that during the preponderance of his intellectual life the act/potency distinction was widely and well understood even within the Catholic intellectual world, much less within secular thought. It would be a parochial error to think of Lonergan as responsible for the loss of understanding of this metaphysical distinction and its central importance. That dubious palm must be ceded to such authors as Suarez, Kant, and Frege, many of whose strategic judgments Lonergan sought to counter.

This has affected even higher level Catholic apologetics, since the apologist often dialectically takes in certain of the limitations of those with whom he is in dialogue.

IV. Conclusion

In conclusion, I would note that many defenders of what I believe Thomas's teaching to be have presented it with a glum visage. Yet the teaching that evil is only permitted for the sake of noble goods—for the common good of the universe, and for the sake of a higher good that finally resolves into the Beatific Vision—and that our salvation lies first in the mercy of God, and only secondarily with our own limited powers—is a profoundly consoling doctrine. Far from being glum or grim, this teaching of St. Thomas articulates the formal motive of hope: the infallible omnipotence of the infinitely good God as opposed to my own defectible and limited powers. It is my conviction that this account of St. Thomas remains superior not only to the Molinist and Congruist alternatives, but also to recent efforts of many of his most learned disciples to improve upon it.

≈III≈

ON JACQUES MARITAIN'S ENDURING CONTRIBUTION

BERNADETTE E. O'CONNOR

Insufficient Ado about the Human Capacity for Nothing, Too Much Ado about the Human Capacity for Being, and Maritain's Dissymmetry Solution

In his 1942 Aquinas Lecture, *St. Thomas and the Problem of Evil*,[1] Jacques Maritain presents the idea of a distinct moment in the concrete whole, which whole consists of acting-without-consideration-of-that-rule-which-ought-to-guide-human-action.[2] This moment is ontologically distinct from the final election in which a person chooses to act without the requisite consideration. With characteristic humility, Maritain considers his rediscovery of this moment—in open view in St. Thomas but to which commentators had adverted superficially, on the level of conclusions rather than of principles—and his application of it to show the innocence of God in the origin of moral evil to be, among all his insights, the one which "perchance" was "some actual contribution to the progress of thought."[3] In this paper, I present Maritain's understanding of this moment and then show

1. Jacques Maritain, *St. Thomas and the Problem of Evil*, translated by Mrs. Gordon Andison (Milwaukee: Marquette University Press, 1942), hereafter cited as *STPE*. While Maritain's title addresses the "problem" of evil, he concedes that evil "in truth is not a problem but a mystery" (Ibid., 14).

2. Jacques Maritain, *God and the Permission of Evil*, translated by Joseph W. Evans (Milwaukee: Bruce Publishing Company, 1966), 36, hereafter cited as *GPE*.

3. In *Jacques Maritain: Correspondence*, vol. 1, 1920–1929, edited by Mgr. Pierre Mamie (Paris: Éditions Universitaires Fribourg and Éditions Saint-Paul, 1996), Maritain, letter no. 93 [to Msg. Charles Journet] (December 26, 1924), 263, as cited by Michael D. Torre in "Francisco Marín-Sola, O.P., and the Origin of Jacques Maritain's Doctrine on God's Permission of Evil," *Nova et Vetera*,

how the dissymmetry this moment implies between the origins of being and good, on the one hand, and of nothing and evil, on the other hand, allows Maritain to navigate between the Scylla of "the embarrassments of the 'Traditional' School'" of Thomism and the Charybdis of what he calls "the absurd ... the system of Molina."[4] In treating Maritain's solution, I refer only to its application in the ontological sphere, that is, as it refers to the ultimate causality of moral evil, and not to its application in the epistemological sphere, that is, to God's knowledge of our evil acts.

Maritain understands St. Thomas's general principle that a certain presupposed defect in the being or the operative powers of an agent, the evil that wounds the *being* of the agent, gives rise to evil of action, the evil that wounds the *operation* or *action* of the agent, to apply not only in nature but also in the origin of moral evil.[5] In the third section of *St. Thomas and the Problem of Evil,* where Maritain traces "the evil of free will" "to its innermost hiding-place," to "the very beginning" from which it is "impossible to go any further back," he considers two ontologically, if not chronologically, distinct moments or in the cause of moral evil.[6] The ontologically prior aspect of the cause of moral evil corresponds to the nothingness that wounds the being itself or the operative powers of the agent; the ontologically posterior aspect corresponds to the privation that afflicts the operation or the action of the wounded agent.

The ontologically prior aspect of the cause of moral evil is a "*voluntary and free* defect." It must be a voluntary defect, for "it is the evil of a free action or a free choice," the ontologically posterior moment, of which it is a cause.[7] And, yes, the word "defect" is used both by Aquinas and by Mar-

English Ed., Vol. 4, No. 1 (2006), 59, and also *GPE*, viii. I note that Michael D. Torre believes that Maritain depended, in what he, Maritain, considers to be an important contribution of his own, upon the work of the Spanish Dominican Francisco Marín-Sola (1873–1932). See Torre's article, loc. cit., 53–94. I note also that John C. Cahalan, in his web-circulated "Reply to Michael's Torre's Comparison of Maritain and Marín-Sola," 2006, especially in Appendix D: "Dissymmetry Between the Lines of Good and Evil," argues forcefully for the originality of Maritain's appropriation of Aquinas and of his use of it to preserve the innocence of God in regard to causality of moral evil.

4. *GPE*, 13 and 15.

5. *STPE*, 20 and 23.

6. Ibid., 20, 35, and 26. It is interesting to note that, in *STPE*, Maritain constantly asserts (26, 29, 31, and 33) that the priority of the first moment is ontological or "of nature" and not chronological or of time. He takes the same position in *Existence and the Existent* (French edition, 1947), translated by Lewis Galantiere and Gerald B. Phelan (Washington Square, New York: Pantheon Books, 1948), 90, hereafter cited as *EE*.

7. Ibid., 23.

itain; I treat, as fully as possible at this stage of my exposition, the issue concerning this usage in a note here and return to the issue later.[8]

This defect of the first ontological moment is "a pure and simple negation," a nothingness or absence, and, following St. Augustine, a "silence" or "darkness."[9] The defect of the first ontological moment is nihilated or non-posited in the active *power* of the rational agent, that is, in the free will, by the will itself. The ontologically posterior moment is the evil of free *action* or *operation*, the evil of choice.

The ontologically prior moment is not itself "*an evil* or a privation."[10] The ontologically prior moment of nihilating, which in turn causes the moral fault, is not an evil or a privation in the sense of the lack of a perfection that ought by nature to be in the will. This means that the ontologically prior moment of nihilating is not an evil or privation afflicting the free will in its *very nature*, that is, as a power of free choice. For, if the will were afflicted with an absence of what belongs to it by right of its very being as will, what would issue from a will so wounded could not be free and voluntary. In this regard, moral evil differs from evil in the world of nature. In nature, "*evil of action* always presupposes another evil—*evil of being*."[11] An example Maritain gives of this principle in nature is that the evil of *action* or

8. There is, of course, a difficulty in describing what is a mere negation, a simple non-being, which is not yet a privation or the absence of a due good, as a "defect." Roy J. Deferrari and M. Inviolata Barry in their *Lexicon of St. Thomas Aquinas* (Washington, D.C.: Catholic University of America Press, 1947), 271, list a narrow sense of "*defectus*" as meaning "*fault, defect, lack*, i.e., *the non-existence of that which should exist*, synonym of *deficientia, infirmitas*, and *privatio*." It is to this narrow meaning that Maritain's friend Jean-Hervé Nicolas, OP, refers when, in criticism of Maritain's use of "*defectus*" or "defect" for the first ontological moment he writes that "the idea of a *defectus*, of a failure which is a mere negation, not the privation of a due good, is therefore entirely inadmissible. It is an idea contrary to Saint Thomas, 'excluded by his whole metaphysics of evil.'" This quotation is Maritain's summary of his friend's criticism from 46 of *GPE*; the last words of the quotation are from Nicolas's article "La Permission du Péché" in *Revue Thomiste*, LX, 2 (Avril-Juin 1960): 204, n. But Deferrari and Barry also list a more general sense of "*defectus*," in which it can mean "absence" and has as a synonym "*negatio*" (op. cit., 271). And it is in this more general sense that St. Thomas, himself, in *De Malo*, 1, 3 ad 13, uses "*defectus*" to identify the mere negation in the first ontological moment: "The defect which is presupposed in the will before sin is neither a fault nor a punishment, but a pure negation" (*St. Thomas Aquinas On Evil*, translated by Jean Oesterle [Notre Dame, Indiana: University of Notre Dame Press, 1995]). The use of "*defectus*" for the simple absence or mere negation of the first ontological moment cannot, therefore, be un-Thomistic, for St. Thomas himself uses it in this way. Why St. Thomas and Maritain think this use is proper will be explained below in the paper.

9. *STPE*, 28.

10. Ibid., 23.

11. Ibid., 21.

operation that is stuttering presupposes evils of *being* that are weaknesses or imperfections in the organs and nerve centers of speech.[12]

Nor can the nihilation of the ontologically prior moment, which is the cause of the evil election in the ontologically posterior moment, be an evil of the will *in its free activity*, that is, a moral fault in itself. To assert that the nihilation is a moral fault would be only to enter into the vicious circularity of asserting that moral fault is the cause of moral fault.[13]

So the nihilating which is the cause of moral evil must be both voluntary and free and a negation. But this nihilating cannot be a privation of the will, neither the privation by which the being of the will, its free nature, would suffer the lack of a perfection it ought to have, nor that privation which is the effect of the negation, the moral evil afflicting a free choice.

This ontologically prior moment, a certain defect or deficiency prior to the act of evil choice, consists in the will's *not* using, *not* referring, *not* attending to reason and divine law, which should be the rule of human actions.[14] The analogy St. Thomas uses for the first ontological moment of non-using or non-attending is a carpenter's non-using or non-attending to the rule or measure that should be used, attended to, in order to cut straight. The carpenter's fault, non-straight cutting, analogous to the privation that is moral evil, consists in cutting without the required reference to the rule or measure.[15] This negating, this *non*-attending, is not evil in the sense of consisting in a fault; for what is absent is not, in itself, a due good. Maritain follows St. Thomas in his *Quaestiones Disputatae de Malo*, 1, 3, in asserting that this non-attending to the rule is not a fault nor a penalty "because the soul is not obliged, nor for that matter is it able, constantly to take the rule into consideration, in act."[16] It is in the second ontological moment that the evil or privation, the absence of the good due, the moral evil, is committed. This consists in the fault of the free will by which, without consideration of the proper rule of its actions, it proceeds to make an act of choice.

Freedom, itself, the will that can act *or not act*, is the cause of this absence, this *non*-attending to reason and divine law in the prior ontological moment. The freedom of the will is "the negative and deficient primary cause" of the non-being, that is, non-attending-to-the-proper-rule-of-human-actions.[17] In

12. Ibid.
13. Ibid., 23–24.
14. Ibid., 25.
15. *De Malo*, 1, 3, and *STPE*, 25.
16. *STPE*, 26.
17. Ibid., 25–26.

Existence and the Existent, Maritain refers to this free non-acting of the will as "not an acting or efficient cause" but rather as a "dis-acting and de-efficient" cause.[18] This not-willing-to-consider the rule is the defect, the simple nothingness, "a mere negation,"[19] in the operative power of the will that causes the moral privation, the evil in the will's free activity. In *God and the Permission of Evil,* Maritain specifies that this mere negation, this simple nothingness is "not, note well, an *act* of non-consideration, but a *non-act* of consideration" and adds that "this non-consideration of the rule is something *real,* since it is the *cause* of sin."[20] And the negation, the non-consideration of the rule, is "the *cause* of the evil of the act of choice only according as the act of choice takes place at an instant when the non-consideration is present."[21]

Maritain emphasizes that, while the non-consideration of the rule arises by "the pure initiative of the created will," there is, in the first ontological moment, as yet no action. The will precisely does *not* act to consider the rule of reason and divine law, and this non-acting is a mere negation, not a privation or the absence of a due good. The lack of consideration of the rule

> is a sort of nothing, it is a mere absence, an *absence of act,* of which created freedom has the initiative: therefore we must join in our minds these two notions, [1] *to have the initiative* [2] not of an act, but *of an absence,* of a negation, of the non-consideration in act of the rule.[22]

Maritain understands the confusions possibly attendant upon our speaking of nothing as if it were something, but he also understands that we can conceive and speak of non-being "only *ad instar entis,* after the fashion of being, and consequently by speaking of it as *some thing.*"[23]

In *St. Thomas and the Problem of Evil,* Maritain makes heroic linguistic efforts to counter our mind's persistent tendency to reify non-being. The will, in the first ontological moment, "has already done nothingness."[24] In this instant, "the will *nihilates,* that is *noughts.*"[25] In this moment, the created will "'does nothingness,' 'makes non-being.'"[26] Or, again: the will "undoes, or non-does, or it noughts."[27] In *Existence and the Existent,* he speaks

18. *EE,* 91.

19. *De Malo,* 1, 3 ad 13, and *STPE,* 29. At this point, Maritain refers to *De Malo* at 1, 3 ad 3, but this is an error of some sort. It is in the reply to the *thirteenth* objection that St. Thomas calls the non-acting of the will a "*mera negatio.*"

20. *GPE,* 35.

21. Ibid.

22. *STPE,* 32.

23. *GPE,* 36; see also *STPE,* 32.

24. *STPE,* 33.

25. Ibid.

26. Ibid., 34.

27. Ibid.

of the absence of consideration as "a 'naught,' a fissure, a lacuna introduced into the warp and woof of being."[28] In *God and the Permission of Evil,* Maritain speaks of "the conceptual equipment that is needed" in order to grasp this mere negation, the initiative of which belongs to our will. Among this equipment, Maritain lists the following concepts that, he says, are to be taken seriously and not "as mere figures of speech": "to nihilate, initiative of nothingness, nihilating or nihilation, fissure of being."[29] Maritain is striving by means of these neologisms to help us understand the mere negation, of which freedom is the deficient cause, and that will cause the evil act of the will to be "bitten by nothingness."[30]

The concept of this negation is present in the texts of St. Thomas, and Maritain believes that it is "one of the most original of his [St. Thomas's] philosophical discoveries."[31] In *God and the Permission of Evil,* Maritain adds that St. Thomas's theory of the non-consideration of the rule is "a metaphysical discovery of first importance, an absolutely fundamental one and one without which no philosophy of evil is possible."[32] But Maritain suggests that the "lofty and magnanimous genius" of St. Thomas does not permit or require him to draw attention to the originality of his discovery and, hence, that "he gives us this treasure only in passing."[33] It is Maritain's full appropriation of the originality of this discovery that will enable him to make his own contribution to the development of thought about the origin and cause of moral evil.

To conclude this study of the mere negation that St. Thomas discovered and Maritain reappropriates, we should consider how the negation, the non-act-of-considering-the-rule-that-should-guide-free-acts, is *both* the prior moment in the concrete whole that is "to act without considering the rule" *and,* with the application of that negation to action, the privation, the lack of a good that becomes due with the acting, and thus the moral evil. Maritain writes:

Within this concrete whole, acting without consideration of the rule, there are two moments to be distinguished ... : *first moment, not considering the rule,* which is ne-

28. *EE,* 91.

29. *GPE,* 11.

30. *STPE,* 22.

31. Ibid., 23. Maritain makes references to three places in St. Thomas's works, in addition to *De Malo,* 1, a. 3, where this non-consideration of the rule is treated: *Summa Contra Gentiles* III, c. 10, [especially (17)]; *ST,* I, q. 49, a. 1 ad 3; and *ST,* I-II, q. 75, a. 1 ad 3.

32. Ibid.

33. Ibid.

gation, an absence, the lack of a good which is not yet due; and *second moment, acting with that negation,* which, from the sole fact that it acts with it, becomes a privation. . . .[34]

Maritain identifies the mere negation of the first moment with the privation of the second moment most explicitly when he writes in *God and the Permission of Evil*: "this *same mera negatio* which is the non-consideration of the rule as cause of the sinful election becomes a *privation,* the absence of a due good, in the sinful election itself."[35] The same non-consideration is, in one ontological moment, a mere negation and, in the other ontological moment, with its application to acting, the privation that is moral evil.

This identification of the mere negation, through its application to action, with the privation or sin allows us to understand the explanation for St. Thomas's and Maritain's use of the term "*defectus*" or "defect" for the *mera negatio* of the first ontological moment. Maritain explains in *God and the Permission of Evil* that the word "defect" attaches itself to the *mera negatio* "from the front," as it were, because it is this very same absence that in the first moment is a mere negation, the absence of a not-due good, and in the second moment is a privation, the absence of a due good.[36] The difference in the two moments is not in the nature of the absence in one moment from the other; the sole difference is that in the second moment the absence is applied to acting.

Maritain continually asserts the ontological priority of the *mera negatio* over the privation that is the evil act itself; because the *mera negatio* is the negative and deficient cause of sin, it precedes, at least in nature, the sin that is its effect.[37] Maritain also discusses the chronological priority of the *mera negatio* over the privation or sin. While he does not declare himself "*ex professo*" on the chronological priority of the *mera negatio,* he finds himself "decidedly" in favor of a chronological as well as of an ontological priority of the non-act-of-considering-the-rule over the sin.[38]

Maritain's appropriation of the Thomistic doctrine of a mere negation as the negative and deficient cause of the privation that is sin enables him to read the scripture passage "without me you can do nothing" (John 15:5) in a new way: without me you *can do* nothingness, you can nihilate, cause—in a negative and deficient way—the negation of the first ontological moment,

34. *STPE,* 31.
35. *GPE,* 47.
36. Ibid.
37. Ibid., 35.
38. Ibid., 51–54.

which itself, applied to action, causes the sin.[39] Maritain sees in the fact that our free will, itself, is the negative and deficient cause of this non-being the starkest and sharpest manifestation of St. Thomas's dictum that "what comes from nothingness tends by its nature toward nothingness."[40] Our created freedom itself comes from nothingness, and because "this nothingness is in the very entrails of the creature ... [the creature] is constantly tending toward that nothingness under the hands of God."[41] In the language of *St. Thomas and the Problem of Evil*: "the creature slinks ...—from the influx of the First Cause,—which influx is loaded with being and goodness."[42] Only in "the universe of freedom ... can the creature do something by itself alone, but that something consists in non-being, and that 'doing' is an absence of action."[43]

With this ability of the creature on its own to "not-do" something and thus to be the first cause of the nothingness that, afflicting acting, becomes sin, Maritain grasps the dissymmetry that exists between the lines of good and evil human acts.[44] And from the first he understands the dissymmetry between good and evil in terms of the dissymmetry between being and non-being. The dissymmetry between the line of good and the line of evil "consists in the fact that whatever concerns the line of good is presented in terms of being, whereas whatever concerns the line of ... *evil as such* is presented in terms of non-being, of nothingness or of nihilation."[45] He elaborates on the metaphysical basis of the dissymmetry between the line of good and the line of evil:

> *Ens et bonum convertuntur*. The good is being, and plenitude or completion of being. When we reason in the line of good, we reason in the line of being, of that which exercises being or bears being to its accomplishment.

39. *STPE*, 35–36 and *GPE*, 33.

40. *De Veritate*, q. 5, a. 2, and *STPE*, 34.

41. Maritain, letter no. 93 [to Msg. Charles Journet] (December 26, 1924, op. cit., 262, as cited in Torre, loc. cit., 58).

42. *STPE*, 34.

43. Ibid., 34–35.

44. It is true, as Torre points out, that Maritain would have read of Marín-Sola's distinction between the lines of good and evil in the article, "El sistema tomista sobre la moción divina," which the Spanish Dominican published in the July-August (32), 1925, edition of *La Ciencia Tomista*, 5–54; Marín-Sola may have, indeed, used the words "dissymmetry between the lines of good and evil." Cahalan contends, op. cit., 32–34, however, that it is Maritain who deepens the appropriation of the dissymmetry that exists between the lines of good and evil by understanding them metaphysically, that is, in relation to being and non-being.

45. *EE*, 89.

> Evil, on the contrary, of itself or insofar as evil, is absence of being or of good. It is a nothingness which corrodes being. When we reason in the line of evil, we reason in the line of non-being, for evil is in nowise being; evil is only a vacuum or a lack of being, a nothingness and a privation.[46]

And Maritain emphasizes the fact that, given the dissymmetry between being-and-good and non-being-and-evil, "we must reason in two different ways according to whether we are considering the line of evil or the line of good."[47] The reasoning Maritain is referring to is the reasoning necessary to address the question of the cause of moral evil. For, in this matter, reasoning is tortured in the traditional Thomist school and has fallen into absurdity in the Molinist school.

Maritain believes that St. Thomas's indication of the mere negation, the non-considering of the rule of reason and God's law, in the first ontological moment, which becomes privation and sin with its application to acting in the second ontological moment, is what allows us to answer the question of the first cause of moral evil. Maritain sets forth what he calls "our two most sacred axioms," concerning the origin of moral evil found in St. Thomas:

> "First axiom: 'God is absolutely not the cause of moral evil, neither directly nor indirectly.'"[48]

> "Second axiom: 'the first cause ... of the absence of grace comes from us.'"[49]

In setting forth these axioms, Maritain emphasizes the import, in the first axiom, of the words "absolutely not" and "neither directly nor indirectly" and, in the second axiom, of the words "the *first* cause." The first axiom means that "every shadow of indirect causality [understood to be exercised by God] must be excluded." The second axiom Maritain understands according to the reasoning appropriate to the line of evil and non-being: "it is in the creature that the first cause of moral evil (first cause in the order of non-being or of nothingness) is to be found."[50] Maritain is certain that "every Catholic whether simple man of faith, philosopher, or theologian, is ready to die for the two axioms."[51] But sometimes learned people, philosophers and especially theologians, "can happen unwittingly to compromise these axioms more or less seriously."[52] Enter from opposite wings the "Cyclopean Thomists" of the traditional school and Molina.

46. *GPE*, 9.
47. *STPE*, 38.
48. *GPE*, 6, citing *ST*, I-II, q. 79, a. 1.
49. Ibid., citing *ST*, I-II, q. 112, a. 3 ad 2.
50. Ibid., 6.
51. Ibid., 7.
52. Ibid.

In order to avoid the errors, on the one hand, of the traditional school, that is, Bañez, John Poinsot, the Carmelites of Salamanca, and, on the other hand, the absurdity of the system of Molina, Maritain asserts two truths that are metaphysical and concern causality in the line of good and causality in the line of evil.

The metaphysical truth in the line of causality *of being and the good* is this: "God is the first and transcendent cause of our liberty and of our free decisions, so that the free act is wholly from God as first cause and wholly from us as second cause."[53] And the metaphysical truth in the line of the causality *of non*-being *and evil* is this: "God is absolutely not the cause of the evil of our free acts; it is ... [the human] who is the *first cause* and who has the *first initiative* of moral evil."[54]

Maritain understands the error of the traditional school as being so singularly fixed on the line of being and the good that it understands, wholly appropriately, that God is the first cause of being and goodness but also, however much it tries to resist it, that God is in some way the first cause of the non-being that is moral evil. The largely traditional school failed to understand fully that the two dissymmetrical lines, being-and-good and non-being-and-evil, must be reasoned about dissymmetrically. It employed "logical artifices"[55] by which, while trying to preserve the innocence of God, he becomes the first cause of moral evil (however much it resists this conclusion).

One such artifice is the theory of God's "antecedent permissive degree." Its purpose was to spare God—who is the first Cause—the guilt of our moral evil. But this theory could not "hide the break in the armor"[56] caused by the traditional school's failure to think deeply enough of moral evil from the perspective of non-being. In trying to shield God from guilt for our evil acts, the traditional Thomists posited "an antecedent permissive degree" that preceded the sin of the creature and "in virtue of which the evil act took place, as did the good free act, at once infallibly and freely."[57] On this view, a creature had the power to do good given by sufficient grace but, in not doing good, found itself deprived of efficacious grace. But what does this mean?

For Maritain, it means that "God has not given the creature the help,

53. Ibid., 10.

54. Ibid., 10.

55. Ibid.

56. Ibid., 15.

57. Ibid., 17.

assistance, support, however one wants to say it, by which He could have moved its will and caused in it the good in question, so that it did not evade His grace."[58] And for Maritain two facts follow on this: first, God must be the indirect *cause* of evil—however much, "thanks to the resources of logic and of skillfully elaborated definitions and distinctions one succeeded in completely eliminating the concept and the word 'cause,' even indirect."[59] The analogy Maritain uses to show how the antecedent permissive decree makes God the indirect cause of evil is that of one's ability to enable a child to write straight and to prevent the child's scribbling by holding the child's hand in one's own. If the person, so able, withdraws the guiding hand and the child therefore scribbles, the child's hand will be the only *direct* cause of the scribbling, but is not the person who withholds the guiding hand the *indirect* cause of the scribbling?[60]

The second fact that follows from the antecedent permissive degree according to which God withholds from the rational creature the help by which that creature's will could be moved to choose the good is that God, Himself, "has first willed, with a will not causative but permissive," that the failure that is moral evil "occur in the world." For the moment of God's permissive decree had, according to the traditional school, "a priority of nature over the failure of the creature."[61]

And, while these facts follow with the necessity of logic from the premise of an antecedent permissive decree, the traditional school at the same time contrives:

> by a system of appropriate distinctions, to have the whole responsibility of these sins and crimes fall on the sinner and to exonerate God, who was not sorry to wash His hands in the basin [the concept of an antecedent permissive decree] which His zealous servants thus presented to Him.[62]

Maritain, however, cannot see in "the antecedent permissive decrees," "taken in themselves," "be they presented by the most saintly of theologians," "anything but an insult to the *absolute innocence of God*."[63]

And Maritain's vehemence in defending God against the unwitting and unwilling imputation, by the traditional school, of guilt for being the indirect cause of moral evil clearly reveals his own sensitivity to the innocence

58. Ibid., 28.
59. Ibid., 29.
60. Ibid.
61. Ibid.
62. Ibid., 18.
63. Ibid., 31.

of God, which sensitivity he so admires in the poet Comte de Lautréamont (Isidore Lucien Ducasse) at the end of his short life.[64]

The traditional school's error was to try to see the non-being that is evil in the manner that one sees and understands the being that is good: God is the first cause of goodness, and so God must be the first, though indirect, cause of evil. And by its rigid adherence only to the perspective of being and good, the traditional school, however it wished to avoid this outcome, seemed to call into question human freedom.

Maritain asserts, however, that "one will break one's teeth" trying to use the line of being and the good to explain evil and nothingness.[65] This error is corrected by a deeper appropriation of the doctrine of St. Thomas, according to which the cause of moral evil is not God, not even indirectly, but the creature's nihilating. In the line of non-being and evil it is, in fact, "the liberty of the creature" that is "the first cause or the inventor of moral evil *in the existential reality* of the world."[66] Without God, the creature *can* and does, in fact, "*do*" nothing and evil. In both the first ontological moment, in the *non*-consideration of the rule, and in the second ontological moment, in acting with that pure negativity and thus sinning, it is not the fallible nature of the creature but rather "an actual failure of the creature," a creature's initiative, that causes non-being and evil. This is the creature's "initiative of non-being, of deficiency in being," what Maritain calls "nihilation."[67] And the negativity, precisely of the first ontological moment, does not even need a cause; for it is a pure negation or absence that arises voluntarily from the will's inaction.[68]

In the line of being and good it is otherwise, dissymmetrical. In the universe of being and good, "the creature has doubtless the initiative of its good act, without which it would not be a free cause; but it is not the *first initiative*. It is God Who has the first initiative of the good act."[69]

If the traditional school erred in viewing evil from the perspective of being and good, Molina erred in the opposite way:

64. Ibid., 5.

65. Ibid., 25.

66. Ibid., 33.

67. Ibid.

68. "Now we are masters in respect of to act and not to act, to will and not to will," *ST*, I-II, q. 6, a. 3. "We apply the word voluntary not only to that which proceeds from the will directly, as from its action; but also to that which proceeds from it indirectly as from its inaction," loc. cit., ad 1, in *Summa Theologica*, translated by Fathers of the English Dominican Province (New York: Benzinger Brothers, Inc., 1947).

69. *STPE*, 37.

Molina, too, disregarded the principle of dissymmetry between the line of good and the line of evil, but on behalf, this time, of the type of explanation appropriate to the case of evil, and in order to put the good act as well as the evil act under the dependence of a first initiative of the creature.[70]

If the traditional school unwittingly and unwillingly undermined the freedom of the human will in making God the indirect cause of evil, Molinism exaggerated the freedom of the human will. Molina wanted to give an explanation of moral evil that would preserve the creature's freedom and responsibility for it. Thus he began from the perspective of non-being and evil. It was proper for Molina to insist on "the role of created liberty in the destiny of the creature."[71] And it was admirable of him to insist that no human is condemned antecedently. But Molina insisted "to excess" "on the role of created liberty." And, in attempting to understand the cause of being and of the good from the perspective of the human cause of non-being and evil, Molina assigned to human beings "in the line of good first initiatives which ... [they] have only in the line of evil."[72]

In Molinism there is an implicit and unintended Pelagianism; the difference between efficacious and sufficient grace depends entirely on the use human freedom makes of them. To leave to human freedom alone the choice to respond to grace is to give human freedom a greater role in salvation than it has. In the system of Molina:

human causality adds itself to the divine causality. It is the human will which gives the final determination, in one direction or the other, a last finishing touch to an indeterminate divine motion. And to this extent, in this same measure, the good free act, the free act of the saints escapes the divine universal causality.[73]

In the Molinistic over-emphasis on the power of human free will, the "admirable" Thomistic theory of the subordination of causes is set aside. In the theory of St. Thomas *concerning the line of being and good*, "the transcendent causality of God ... moves each created agent according to its own mode, and consequently free agents according to their liberty itself."[74] According to this theory, God is the first cause of the good free act "*in its entirety*" and the human free will, "moved or activated by God," is the second cause of the free act "*in its entirety*."[75] For St. Thomas, the divine and human causes

70. *GPE*, 15.
71. Ibid.
72. Ibid.
73. Ibid., 16.
74. Ibid., 15–16.
75. Ibid., 16.

of a good act are "concurrent causalities, each of them causing, for its part, the total effect."[76] But, in Molinism, there is an addition, in the line of being and the good, from the human side to the divine causality.

It is the non-acting to consider the rule, of which the free creature is first and deficient cause, of which St. Thomas speaks—that is, the creature's nihilating the influx of the divine motion, loaded as it is with being and goodness, of which Maritain speaks—that truly preserves human freedom in the line of non-being and of evil and thus obviates the correlatively excessive theory of what human freedom can do of itself in the line of being and good.[77] By carefully distinguishing the order of being and goodness from the order of evil and nothingness, Maritain is able to show how God is the first cause of all being and goodness while absolving God of being even the indirect cause of evil. What God causes, directly or indirectly, is being and goodness. The moral privation—the absence of the due good that results when a human acts in the absence of attention to reason and the divine law—follows not on God's creative activity, but rather on human nihilating activity, the non-adverting to the rule or measure. It is the human who initiates the non-being that becomes moral evil when he or she acts in the absence of attention to the rule or measure. By emphasizing the dissymmetry between the line of being and goodness and that of non-being and evil, Maritain finds a way to avoid both the error of the traditional Thomist school that unwittingly made God the indirect cause of human moral evil and the Molinist error that, while absolving God from causing, even indirectly, human moral evil, tended to see human agency in choosing the good as independent of God's first causality.

The question at issue in what John C. Cahalan calls "400 years of grief and confusion," and that manifested itself in the acrimony of the *De Auxillis* controversy, was, in Cahalan's clear language: "how can the first cause of everything create a secondary cause that can sin?"[78] In answering this question, the traditional school of Thomists, though unwittingly and unwillingly, made God the first, though indirect, cause of moral evil. Molinism, for its part, answered this question by allowing, though unwittingly and unwilling, something to exist, an act of the human will, that escapes dependence upon the Creator's first causality.

76. Ibid.

77. *EE*, 99, n., and *STPE*, 34.

78. Cahalan, op.cit., 21 and 26.

The answer to this question is in the text of St. Thomas and was discovered there and reappropriated by Maritain. The human will, of itself, is free not to act, to not-be a cause of the consideration of the rule in the first ontological moment. And the mere negation resulting from this non-acting is, when applied to acting in the second ontological moment, the privation that is moral evil. God creates our free will in the line of being and good, and that free will can cause or not cause; but we, alone, in the line of non-being and evil, are the deficient cause of the initial non-causing, of the nihilation, that becomes sin in our will's choosing to act with that nihilation.

MICHAEL D. TORRE

The Grace of God and the Sin of Man

The Drama of Man Before God

I. Introducing the Drama

I will attempt to present here Aquinas's account of the "drama" of man before God: an account centered on man as the cause of his own sin. It rightly begins with Genesis. From The Gospel of Mark to John Paul II's "Theology of the Body," Christians have ever affirmed that "in the beginning it was not so:"[1] the horses that came "whinnying ... on to the fields of praise"[2] at their creation were not the four horses of the Apocalypse (Apocalypse 6:1–8); likewise, our first human ancestors who looked out with wonder onto what God had wrought possessed a nature that was "very good" (Genesis 1:31), and not in its present condition: no longer healthy, but sick, weakened in its natural tendencies. We may wonder why this is so, but we do not need God's revealed word to recognize that it is so,[3] and it is a fact moral philosophers of all times and places have ever decried.

1. The words quoted are from Matthew 19:8, but the identical doctrine is given in Mark 10:6, referencing Genesis 1:27. The injunction against divorce is also found in 1 Corinthians (7:11), where the "one flesh" union of Genesis (2:24) is again referenced (in 6:16). For John Paul II's interpretation of these passages in his "Theology of the Body," see *Man and Woman He Created Them: A Theology of the Body*, translated by Michael Waldenstein (Boston: Daughters of St. Paul, 2006).

2. Dylan Thomas, "Fern Hill," in *Collected Poems of Dylan Thomas* (New York: New Directions, 1957), 179: "so it must have been after the birth of the simple light/In the first, spinning place, the spellbound horses walking/warm/out of the whinnying green stable/on to the fields of praise."

3. Aristotle, for example, when he takes man's mean "moral temperature," in *Nicomachean Ethics* (hereafter cited as *NE*) VII, 7, 1150a 10–15, finds that our usual moral state is neither di-

In the beginning, however, we were not as we now are and we could have been other than we now are: it was *really possible, in fact, to avoid the sin* into which we fell.[4] Thomas so firmly holds we could have avoided sin that he devotes seven questions of the *Summa* to what would have been the case had our first parents not fallen.[5] And, just because we could have avoided it, sin is *our* FAULT, *our* doing. As the Gospels universally affirm, sin can only come from within, by giving ourselves to it.[6] Aquinas of course teaches this fundamental truth of Catholic faith; and he thus affirms, "technically" yet profoundly, that we are the *first cause* of our sin, and that it is impossible for God to be either its direct and proper, or even indirect and accidental, cause.[7]

Note well that the "dialogue" or "drama" between God and man in Paradise occurs not because of man's free will *per se*. Thus, after God tells Adam he is *free* to name the animals as he chooses, we do not see God intervening to object, say, to the name of "giraffe" being given to this animal or "baboon" to that other. To specify this or that animal's name freely raises no

---

vine (or perfect) virtue, nor the human (or imperfect) virtue that would permit an occasional un-virtuous act; nor is it even one of moral continence, in which we usually contain our baser urges; rather, it is a state closer to incontinence; it is a state of being "morally soft," in which we are more likely to act immorally when any difficulty presents itself than we are to resist it and rise to the occasion.

4. Thus, Augustine held that Adam possessed an aid *sine qua non*, a grace with which he could in fact have acted well (cf. *De Corruptione et Gratia*); and Chrysostom (in his commentary on Ephesians 1:5) declared at the same time that God's will of good pleasure was for man's salvation and not his judgment: an idea that Damascene famously made his own in the distinction between God's antecedent and consequent will (*The Orthodox Faith* 2, 30). Chrysostom grounds God's salvific will on the passage from Ephesians used later by Western medieval Doctors to ground God's will of good pleasure ("beneplacito"), for he sees God's "antecedent" will as His most *proper* will (and not a metaphorical one or of "sign"). The necessity of such a will is required just by the fact of sin; for sin interrupts and turns us from our *true order*, which *anteceded* it and *directed* us to our true good and salvation. (For Chrysostom's commentary on Ephesians, see the *Nicene and Post-Nicene Fathers*, vol. 13 [New York: Christian Literature, 1889], 52.)

5. See Thomas Aquinas, *Summa Theologiae* (hereafter cited as *ST*) I, 95–101. The English used is that of the English Dominicans found in the Benzinger edition (New York: Benzinger Brothers, Inc., 1947).

6. See Mk. 7:15–23, and Mt. 15:20 and 18–20; see also Lk. 6:45 and 11:39–40, and Jn. 4:23–24.

7. See Thomas Aquinas, 2 *Sentences* (hereafter cited as *SN*) 37, 2, 1: "God can in no way ['nullo modo'] be said to be the author of sin"; *ST* I, 48, 6: "God is the author of the evil of pain but not of the evil of fault"; *De Malo* 3, 1: "It is impossible therefore, that God be the cause of sin"; and *ST* I-II, 79, 1: "God is in no wise ['nullo modo'] the cause of sin." In *ST* I-II 79, 1, Thomas expressly denies that God is sin's indirect cause. The English of the *Sentences* is my own; that of *De Malo* is taken from Jean Oesterle's translation: *St. Thomas Aquinas On Evil* (Notre Dame, Indiana: University of Notre Dame Press, 1995).

issue between God and man. The issue occurs only in relation to the tree of good and evil, and, even more precisely, in relation to the *free choice of evil.* It is only and just the knowledge of *evil* that accounts for the drama: a Biblical "knowing" entwined in the doing, in the choosing of evil, a knowing captured exactly in the words of Darth Vader: "you do not know the power of the dark side."[8] From Genesis on, God presents man with a blessing and a curse and urges him to choose the blessing.[9] The drama between man and God occurs not because man possesses a *free* will, but because he possesses a free and *fallible* will: a will that can freely FAIL to act well, a will free to *turn* to the dark side. Man is the first cause of one thing only: *sin.*

Thomas is certain that God is the first cause of all being, order, and goodness, as should be any theologian who is as much a metaphysician as he is. Yet he also knows that man (and the angel) not only can, but must, be the first cause of the DEFECT of being, order, and goodness that invades God's good world in sin. He signals this point by the use he makes of a famous *dictum* of Dionysius. The latter argued that it belonged to God's providence "not to destroy nature, but to save it," a dictum that becomes a *leifmotif* of Aquinas's entire work. But Dionysius's minor premise was that we are *per se mobile,*[10] and his consequent conclusion was that God saves our nature by leaving it free to move itself in diverse ways. Aquinas does not object to this syllogism and occasionally uses it;[11] but, from the beginning to the end of his work, he usually alters the minor premise to read that man has a nature that can sometimes fail, that "*quandoque deficit et quandoque non,*" or "*possit deficere et non deficere*";[12] and thus that God saves our nature by allowing it to FAIL, or by providing for it so as not to *exclude* from it the *possibility* of *falling* from goodness.[13] Aquinas substitutes "*deficere et non*

8. George Lucas, *Star Wars: The Return of the Jedi,* producers Howard Kazarijian, George Lucas, Robert Watts, Rick McCollum (Lucas Film, 20th Century Fox, 1983); all emphases are mine, here and hereafter.

9. For but one example, see Moses' final discourse in promulgating the Law, in Deuteronomy 28.

10. See Dionysius, *The Divine Names,* chapter 4 and Aquinas's commentary on the same.

11. For one example, see Thomas Aquinas, *Summa Contra Gentiles* (hereafter cited as *SCG*), III, 73.

12. For examples of this use, see 1 *SN,* 39, 2, 2; 1 *SN* 46, 1, 3 and 4; 2 *SN* 33, 1, 2; *De Veritate* 5, 4 ad 4; *SCG,* III, 71; *Commentary on the Divine Names* 4, 33; *Compendium of Theology,* 142; and *ST* I, 48, 2 ad 3; my italics (here and throughout). Long ago, Richard Schenk first called my attention to the way Thomas switches Dionysius's minor premise. See his more recent "Aquinas and Mid-Thirteenth Century Platonisms," *Nova et Vetera* 3 (2005): 307–20, especially 318 ff.

13. This is a rather remarkable conclusion! We are likely to think of God as saving our nature

deficere" for "*per se mobile*" because this situates man *precisely* before God: not as the one who, on his own and as first cause is "*per se* mobile" (for this is impossible); but as the one who, on his own and as first cause, "*deficere*" and "*quandoque deficit*": who can and who sometimes does sin.

The problem this poses for Thomas is how to reconcile the first causality of free creatures in relation to non-being, defect, and sin with the first causality of God in being, order, and goodness *without compromising either truth*. As we shall now see, he does this—good Schoolman that he is—by making full use of a set of philosophical distinctions and concepts.

II. Sin and Its Causes: The Philosophical Analysis

Here, again, the story begins "at the beginning," namely with Socrates' teaching that all of our evil choosing and doing is the result of ignorance. Now, in one sense, this is profoundly true, and it is in fact supported thereafter by Plato, Aristotle,[14] Aquinas, and the entire Dominican tradition.[15] For we can only want something we first apprehend as good, and we can only intend or choose a good that, at that time, we judge is good for us: if we did not judge it preferable when we chose it, then we would not. And thus, if we choose badly, it can only be because we judge something as preferable for us under its given circumstances, when it is not. Thus, every sin supposes an error of judgment: we sin because we are in some sense ignorant.

The above requires further precision; for it is too much a matter of human experience that we "knew better," and that we chose things we knew

---

by *delivering* us from evil, not by allowing us the possibility of falling into it! Thomas's use of Dionysius indicates why God did allow this: because it pertains to His *wise* providence to govern His creatures in accord with their natures, and man (and the angels) are *naturally fallible* in the moral order.

14. Aristotle follows Socrates in holding that we choose what we actually judge to be good (and thus choose badly because we judge falsely); he merely argues we could know something habitually and yet not follow it, because we fail to make use of what we habitually know: "since science or knowledge is of two sorts, one the possession, the other the use of knowledge, the man who has but does *not use* knowledge *is in a sense justly called ignorant*" (*Eudemian Ethics* II, 9, 1225a 10–13). He here acknowledges what might be missed from his treatment in the *NE*—see the classic text quoted in n. 16: Socrates was correct, albeit qualifiedly or with the necessary distinction.

15. Suarez and some other Jesuits depart from this tradition when they hold that one can freely choose otherwise than one's final judgment. (For an analysis of Suarez's position, see Louis Leahy, SJ,'s *Dynamisme Volontaire et Judgement Libre* [Paris: Desclée, 1963], 51–59.)

we should not choose. This might occur because we knew something in a way that was only "skin deep"; but it could occur even though we knew it habitually or more firmly. The *locus classicus* for explaining how we nevertheless reach an erroneous judgment is given by Aristotle's analysis of moral incontinence. He there indicates that we do so because we FAIL TO USE what we habitually know;[16] and, because we fail to do this, we FAIL TO CONSIDER what we knew habitually, before we made our wrong choice.

Aristotle discusses our failure in relation to some bodily passion, or inclination: some desire rooted in our animal nature that distracts us. Yet, whether in the "heat of passion" or not, or whether failing in a small (or venial) way or in a serious (or mortal) way, the *natural structure* of our choosing remains the same. When we deliberate in order to reach a decision, we finally do not pay attention to something that we could have considered and that we should have considered when our final decision was made. Our non-attention or non-consideration occurs in deliberation. From our final judgment, looking back, we can see that we did not consider something we could have and should have in making it.[17] We act, and *then* we realize we *could have* acted differently and that we have erred. As a well-known commercial once graphically put it, "I *could have* had a V-8!" We recognize our error only after we have made the wrong choice.

Aquinas makes Aristotle's entire analysis his own throughout his work.

16. Aristotle, *NE* VII, 7, 1146b 32–35: "We speak of knowing in two ways: we ascribe it both to someone who has it WITHOUT USING it and to someone who is using it. Hence it will matter whether someone has the knowledge that his action is wrong, WITHOUT ATTENDING to his knowledge, or he both has it and attends to it. For this second case seems extraordinary, but wrong action when he does not attend to his knowledge does not seem extraordinary"; my capitalization, here and hereafter. Note that, in his commentary on this passage (section #1338), Aquinas's applies this idea to a "geometer," his favorite example of Aristotle's point: the geometer does NOT USE the rule that should guide his measurement.

17. This is why Thomas uses "praeintelligitur" ("thought of as prior") when speaking of the defect that precedes sin. His point is that, looking *back*, from sin itself, we can recognize its defective cause (and not otherwise). His usual use of this "technical" word concerns the relation between a material disposition and its subsequent effect. Thus, since a substance first exists by its form, this—and whatever accidents are proper to the form—does *not* presuppose matter; whereas corporeity, and any other accident derived from matter, does *presuppose* it (cf. *ST* I, 76, 7 ad 1). Given that the matter exists by the form, it is then presupposed to *its* subsequent effect. Likewise, then, given that the wills acts or chooses, the prior defect in it (its non-use) is presupposed or rightly "thought of as prior" to the defect in sin: its aversion and malice, which it causes. When Thomas uses this word, he understands its reference as *really prior* to its effect, but as only *rendered causative* by virtue of some form or act. See further my *God's Permission of Sin: Negative or Conditioned Decree?* (Fribourg: Academic Press Fribourg, 2009), 355–57.

He only makes one, but one very important, point: *prior* to our making our final decision, our not considering or paying attention to the higher good is not a moral fault.[18] So, technically, it is not a "privation," but a "negation";[19] that is, when we are still deliberating and not paying attention to the good in question that should finally rule our choice, this non-attention does not deprive us of some good. Now, this actually is quite an obvious point. We cannot consider every good simultaneously. The process of deliberation is just that: one in which we move from considering one good to another. Thus, there is nothing wrong, nothing immoral, about considering that a fresh mountain stream will quench our thirst and is good precisely for being able to meet that need. When a hiker is considering this good, he is *not*, at that time, considering another good: he is not then considering the good of health, of not risking a serious illness (since, let us suppose, the mountain streams have been compromised by the presence of giardia). This non-consideration, at the time it occurs, is not immoral: it does not deprive the agent of something that ought to pertain at that time.

That this is quite obviously and evidently the case is clear from this: in any number of situations, we go on precisely to consider the higher good that should govern our choice and we choose rightly. The fact, then, that we are not always considering this good (but considering another, albeit

18. Aquinas, *SCG* III, 10: "we must presuppose a defect in the will before moral evil ('oportet *praeintelligere* DEFECTUM in voluntate *ante* peccatum morale') and "this defect is voluntary; but nevertheless it is *not moral evil* ('Est igitur voluntarius. *Non tamen peccatum morale*')"; *ST* I, 49, 1 ad 3: "this defect, however, is not a fault ('culpa'), but fault follows upon it from the fact that the will acts with this defect"; *ST* I-II, q. 75, a. 1 ad 3: "NOT APPLYING [i.e. NOT-USING] the rule of reason or the Divine Law has not in itself the nature of evil, whether of punishment or of guilt, before it is applied to act"; and *De Malo* 1, 3: "this itself, which is actually to NOT-ATTEND to this rule, considered in itself, is not evil, neither punishment nor guilt, because the soul is not held to be nor can it always be actually attentive to this rule; but the nature of fault *first* arises from the fact that one *proceeds to an election* of this kind without actual consideration." The English translation of the *SCG* used throughout is that of the English Dominican Province: *Summa Contra Gentiles* (London, Burns and Washbourne, 1924).

19. Thomas Aquinas, *De Malo* 1, 3 and ad 13: "negatio sola" and "pura negatio." While Thomas only declares this plainly in late texts, he implies it even in the *Sentences*: "all sin [is said to be] pride, because, of the deficient act [sin], a *preexisting* DEFECT is able to be the beginning ('actus deficientis, inquantum deficiens est, aliquis DEFECTUS *praeexistens* initium esse potest')." Contrary to what some may hold, Aquinas explicitly uses the word "defectus" to refer either to a negation or to a privation, as in 2 *SN* 31, 1, 2: "DEFECTUS enim simplicem negationem alicuis boni importat" (whereas privation adds the fact of a negation existing when due: "non potest dici malum nisi sit DEFECTUS eius bonum quod natum est haberi"); and thus, 2 *SN* 35, 1, 1 ad 1, "nomen 'DEFECTUS' potest sumi *vel* negative *vel* privative." (2 *SN* 31, 1, 2's "preexisting defect" to the act of sin must be a NEGATION, and just because it *precedes* sin.)

in-this-instance-lesser good) is no fault, nor need this non-consideration in fact have *any connection* to a false choice; for we can avert to the higher good when we judge and choose and thus make the right choice. Nor is such a non-consideration an imperfection. On the contrary, the human process of deliberation requires that we weigh various goods and consider them in turn; it is perfectly normal that we do so, and there is nothing imperfect about it. It is only when we *terminate* our process of deliberation in a final judgment that our intellect is deprived of its proper order. Until then, we remained free to consider what we should in making our choice; but it *closes* that process and commits us to a false good, a good we choose to make our own.[20]

This analysis, then, locates the psychological failure at issue: we fail just in *not-considering* something we could have considered. And, precisely because we could have, this intellectual failure is rooted in our *will*, in a failure to *use* our intellect to consider something it could have. Yet these negations, of NON-use and NON-consideration, only become damaging and connected to an immoral choice supposing that we *act* or judge with them.

While this locates the *psychological* failures in moral evil, it quite naturally gives rise to this question: why do we fail to pay attention, when we do? Since we could have considered what we should have when we made our final judgment and choice,[21] why didn't we? True, there was another

20. Francisco Marín-Sola, OP, makes this point succinctly, but profoundly, in the following words: "Natural or necessary agents are already *determined* to one effect, and not another, by their own *specific form*.... Fire ... always tends to the effect of burning, not of cooling. That which is for necessary agents their *specific form* is for intelligent or free beings their *ultimate practical judgment* that terminates "consilium" or deliberation. Once this ultimate practical judgment is made, they are already *specified*, and they only require an executive motion or "quoad exercitium," which, save by a miracle, God always gives, and, except for *special* providence, He always gives in accord with the final judgment" (my translation); see his "Respuesta a algunas objeciones acerca del sistema tomista sobre la moción divina" in *La Ciencia Tomista* (January-February, number 97, 1926), note #1 on 57. Maritain seems to take this point in *God and The Permission of Evil* (Milwaukee: Bruce, 1966), 51–54, thereby revising his earlier position of *Existence and the Existent*: there is no "first instant" of non-consideration (followed by a false decision), but only a "final time" in which the non-consideration occurs. For Thomas, the non-consideration that precedes sin only becomes its defective *cause* when one "proceeds to election" (when one makes one's final, "practico-practical," judgment). There is no moment (or "instant") prior to a false judgment that is its defective cause; such a cause only exists in the *final time* that is *terminated* by a final judgment.

21. Throughout, I present what Thomas explicitly teaches and thus do not discuss the precise relation of final judgment and election; for Thomas himself never engages in such a detailed analysis. For Thomas, these always come together, with the latter supposing the former. Nevertheless, I believe that what Marín-Sola says (in the previous note) is correct: there is a natural

good at hand, which we falsely judge is the right one (in the given example, the pleasure of quenching our thirst from a mountain stream); but we did not need to judge so; we could have averted to the higher good in choosing (in this case, the good of our health). Why, then, do we not? One will look in vain in Aristotle either for this question or his answer to it. Thomas, however, both raises it and offers an answer that is, again, disarmingly simple. He comes to terms with its root cause, an answer grounded in his METAPHYSICS OF FAILURE. In order to appreciate his answer, we need to see how he makes use of the full resources of metaphysical reason in order to come to grips with the causes of sin.[22]

One of the most common causes of defect and death had already been analyzed by Aristotle in his physics: the generation of one substance entails the concomitant corruption of another. The introduction of a new form entails the corruption of a former, a process we commonly observe in living things. A carrot supplies life to a rabbit, but, in doing so, it ceases to be a carrot; life for a whale is death to krill. It is thus that physical evil has an accidental efficient, or active, cause: the activity of the animal deprives a plant or other animal of its own form or life. Evil is "beside the intention" of nature: the animal naturally seeks life, not death; nevertheless, death is entailed. Thomas applies this analysis to sin,[23] and argues that it, too, has an accidental active cause. This is the sinner's *conversion* to a perceived good (which he *chooses*); the corruption or the concomitant *evil* is

---

priority of judgment to election (of the intellectual act supposed by the volitional one), and thus God could (miraculously) choose to prevent one from committing one's will to a false judgment. (For evidence that this is also Thomas's view, see *ST* I-II, 75, 2: "the absence of the *due* rule pertains to the *reason* [judgment], whose nature it is to consider this rule; and the *completeness* of the voluntary act pertains to the *will*, so that the *act* of the *will* [choice], *given* the conditions we have just mentioned [judgment], is already a sin"). The mature Thomas recognizes that God not only permits the *possibility* of a false judgment (and thus also the *possibility* of a false election), but also that He permits a false judgment to "run its course" and does not interfere with it, in which case a sinful election *infallibly* occurs; but both God's permission of this sinful election and the election infallibly entailed *suppose* our own defect that is *naturally prior*.

22. Sin requires some cause, is not cause-less; for sin is a disordered act, one opposed to the sinner's nature, depriving it of its proper order: "for that which naturally is and ought to be in a thing is never lacking except on account of some impeding cause" (*ST* I-II, 75, 1).

23. Thomas Aquinas, *ST* I-II, 72, 1: "Two things occur in the nature of sin, namely the voluntary act and its lack of order, which consists in departing from God's law. Of these two, one is referred essentially to the sinner, who intends such and such an act in such and such a manner; while the other, namely the lack of order in the act, is referred accidentally to the sinner, for 'no one acts intending evil,' as Dionysius declares." Aquinas teaches this throughout his works.

the sinner's *aversion* from the rule that should govern his choice.[24] We never directly intend evil as such. It is only in judging falsely that a lesser good should be chosen, and committing ourselves to it, that we turn from God and His order. This aversion from God gives mortal sin its infinite depth and its malice,[25] for we turn *from* that which is infinitely good and lovable; but we do so indirectly, not directly: aversion is the concomitant *effect* of judging falsely and committing ourselves to the judged good.[26]

Now, as true as this analysis is, and as constant as it is in Thomas's account of sin,[27] it can only be a *partial* explanation, and for two quite obvious reasons. In the first place, as the previous analysis has already indicated, the non-use of the intellect and the non-consideration of the higher good both *precede* the final judgment and choice to which this analysis refers. And, in the second place, were this the *only* cause of sin, then God would be its accidental cause; for God is the first cause of *all* activity, including the activity of free judgment and free choice. But God cannot cause sin. Indeed, the whole point of Aquinas's analysis was to locate a prior DEFECT, not an act, as a cause of sin; for God need not be the cause, even accidentally, of all defect, and this is why He is not the cause of sin. The *aversion* from God (again something NEGATIVE, an ABSENCE of order to God where before there was no absence) itself *derives* from something NEGATIVE: a *failure* to use one's intellect and thus a *failure* to consider what one could. Thomas therefore always teaches—from first to last—that sin also

24. Thomas Aquinas, 2 *SN* 34, 1, 3: "Just as a natural agent, by inducing one form, causes the defect of another form, so also the will, by adhering to something that is not its due end as though it were its final end, is averted form the final end that is due it." For Thomas's fullest discussion of the way the two changes are present concomitantly, see *De Veritate* 28, 1 and 6.

25. Some texts: 2 *SN* 35, 1—"Two things occur in the make-up ('ratio') of sin, that is the act and defect itself, from which the notion of evil comes ('ex quo ratio mali incidit') ... [and] from which it has the essential note ('ratio') of evil, namely the privation of something directing to an end ('privatio dirigentis in finem')"; *De Malo* 3, 1—"sin *consists in the aversion* of the created will from its final end"; *ST* I-II, 84 ad 2—"Sin lacks order insofar as it turns away from ('aversio') God, for *in this respect it is evil*"; and *ST* I-II, 152, 6—"Two things are to be observed in sin, conversion to the mutable good, and this is the material part of sin, and aversion from the immutable good, and *this gives sin its formal aspect* and complement."

26. Thomas Aquinas, 2 *SN* 34, 1, 3: "Just as a natural agent, by inducing one form causes the defect of another form, so also the will, by adhering to something that is not its due end as though it were its final end, is averted from the final end that is due it"; and *ST* I-II, 73, 3 ad 2: "from the fact that man turns unduly ('indebita conversione') to some mutable good, it follows that he turns from ('aversio') the immutable good." Again, this is constant to Aquinas's teaching.

27. For Aquinas's treatments of the accidental cause of evil, see 2 *SN* 34–44; *SCG* III, 1–16; *On the Divine Names*, chapter 4; *De Malo* 1, 3; and *ST* I, 49 and I-II, 75.

possesses a DEFECTIVE cause;[28] and this defective cause is ontologically (and temporally) *prior* to the accidental active cause. This is the non-use and non-consideration in deliberation that are not privations, but negations: the ABSENCE of act *in* sin, or the aversion from God that deprives the sinner of his proper order, is *caused* by a NON-ACT that *precedes* it and is not yet sin. The reason why God is not the cause of sin *as sin*, even though He is the cause of the created activity in sin,[29] lies in the fact that God only moves us to what we have *negatively disposed ourselves*, by FAILING to do what we could have done: by our previous non-act.[30]

If one asks "what accounts for this non-act in the sinner," one might be *tempted* to locate a possible answer in Aquinas's metaphysics just where it goes beyond Aristotle's. For Christians—as Jews and Muslims—are "radical" monotheists who know well that the great "dividing line" in Being does not lie between our corruptible nature and the supposed incorruptible nature of the stars (or any spirits that move them); rather, it lies between all creatures—corruptible and incorruptible—and their Creator. All of them are distinguished from their Creator by the fact that their act of existing (*esse*) is not entailed by what they are or their nature, but derives precisely from, and exists in real relation to, God's free will. Their creation is the gift of God's free will, as is their preservation in being. Non-existence, non-action, and defect might thus be caused not only by the generation of a new form in matter, but also by the *non-preservation* or annihilation of the subject's entire being: both its matter and its form.

Aquinas is perfectly aware of this possibility and analyzes it carefully, even though he denies that God would ever in fact annihilate any crea-

28. That sin has a defective cause, as well as an accidental efficient cause, is a constant to Thomas's teaching, as can be seen by consulting the texts given in the previous note. In the *Sentences*, it is identified as the cause on the part of the (defective) instrument, with the accidental efficient cause being identified as the cause on the part of what is intended: 2 *SN* 34, 1, 3. His most detailed and exacting analysis can be found (not surprisingly) in *De Malo* (1, 3).

29. That God causes the activity in sin is again a constant of Thomas's teaching. All activity, *qua activity*, possesses order and is good. It is good for a free creature to have a will and to exercise the power of choosing that belongs to it, and God causes this good, as all other goods. What God does not cause, in any way, is the NON-USE of that power and the DEFECT in the act (or its MIS-USE) caused by this.

30. Here, as in all cases where God moves sinners according to their condition, He is only moving them in accord with what they themselves have *previously disposed themselves* to receive. This is a constant feature of Thomas's doctrine (although he is usually referring to the defects of original or actual sin). For his most trenchant and detailed discussion of this in relation to sin, see *De Malo* 3, 2.

ture.[31] The effect at issue would be the NEGATION of a creature's being.[32] The kind of causality involved would derive from the cessation of God's activity, a type of *accidental causality,* as Thomas explains: "non-being has no cause *per se,* for nothing is a cause except in so far as it is being.... But *accidentally* God can be the *cause* of things being reduced to nothing, by *withdrawing* His action from them."[33] The scholastic tradition calls this type of causality "removing a preventive."[34] All creatures, who in themselves are nothing—ever having their being (*esse*) only in real relation to God—are prevented from falling into nothingness by God's action preserving them; simply by *removing* that action, they would cease to exist. Aquinas's favorite metaphor is the sun and the light we receive from it: darkness (or the absence of light) is instantly caused by the sun's absence.[35]

Now, one might be tempted to apply this metaphysical analysis to the case before us precisely because it concerns NEGATION, not privation, and we are just trying to come to grips with that negation in the creature's will that precedes sin and is its defective cause. One might thus argue that, just as God does not owe being (*esse*) to any creature and need not preserve it from nothingness, neither need He preserve any free creature from the negations of not-using its intellect or not-considering a higher good. However, it should be clear on reflection that it is absolutely impossible to make this application, for the very simple reason that it would make God the *accidental first cause* of sin's DEFECT. And this is impossible, for God would then be the cause both of sin's activity and defect: in short of sin *as sin*; but this is both heretical and absurd. Nor would it be to the point to say that God owes preservation in the moral order to no creature; neither does He owe them preservation in natural *being,* but He would *still* be the accidental *first cause* of any supposed annihilation.[36] It is thus wrong to apply this

31. For Aquinas's discussions of annihilation, see *De Potentia Dei* 5, and *ST* I, 104.

32. Since it would cease to exist altogether, there would be no *privation* or evil, for the latter always supposes a creature, which is *deprived* of its proper order.

33. Thomas Aquinas, *ST* I, 103, 3 ad 1. See also *ST* I-II, 75, 1.

34. See Thomas O'Brien, *Summa Theologiae,* vol. 14 (New York: McGraw-Hill, 1975), 50, note to *ST* I, 104, 3, and Garrigou-Lagrange, *Trinity and God The Creator* (St. Louis, Herder, 1952), 496.

35. Thomas Aquinas, *ST* I-II, 75, 1. The fact that this metaphor contains an element outdated in modern physics—that light travels instantaneously—hardly undermines the point he is making.

36. Because he took this point, Jean-Hervé Nicolas, OP, retracted his original position, against Maritain, in which he argued that God's permission was a non-preservation in the mor-

metaphysical analysis to the moral negation at hand: it is the *wrong conceptual tool* to understand it.[37]

Thomas does, however, make use of this analysis in relation to sin: for he applies it just to the case of a sinful creature *remaining* in his defective condition. God does *leave* free creatures, for various periods, in the fallen condition brought on by sin. We need only think of the story of the Prodigal Son: his loving father lets him "go his sinful way," until he is ready, feeding amongst the pigs, to return again. Thus, Thomas holds that God permits some to remain in sin, a permission that is a will *not* to alter their defective state: from God *not-acting* to draw them from that state, they *continue* in their darkness.[38] Likewise, he holds that a judge need not pardon a

al good: see his "La volonté salvifique de Dieu contrariée par le péché," *Revue Thomiste* vol. 92 (1992): 177–96, especially at 186.

37. Thomas's text in *ST* I-II 109, 2 ad 2 is sometimes cited as evidence for this application: "as every created being has its being from another, and, considered in itself, is nothing, so does it need to be preserved by another in the good which pertains to its nature. For it can of itself fail in good, even as of itself it can fall into non-existence, unless it is upheld by God." (See "Deux inedits du Père Marie-Michel Labourdette [1908–1990]," *Revue Thomiste,* vol. 100 [2000]: 355–83, at 360, followed by Steven A. Long, "Providence, Liberté et Loi Naturelle," *Revue Thomiste* 102 [2002]: 355–405, later published in its original English as "Providence, Freedom, and Natural Law," in *Nova et Vetera* 4 [2006]. For the reference in the latter, see 563.) Thomas is here replying to the idea that, since man is the first cause of sin, he can also be the first cause of virtue (obj. 2); in denying this, the reply does no more than draw an apt comparison: the will can fall from the moral good on its own, just as it can fall into nothingness on its own, but, just as the latter does not mean it is the first cause of its natural being, neither does the former mean it is the first cause of its virtue. One cannot construct a full-blown theory of God's permission of sin from such a scant warrant. If one wishes to construct such a theory, one must begin with texts that are express and extended treatments of the matter at hand. If one goes to Thomas's most extensive treatment of God's permission (1 *SN* 47, 1, 2), one finds him asserting that "it is possible to do the opposite of what is permitted ('potest fieri *oppositum* eius quod permissum est'), but this is still according to the permission ('*secundum* permissionem'), because permission respects the power of the cause for opposites ('*potentiam* causae *ad utrumque* oppositorum se habentem'); and neither of the opposites is against permission, but both are according to it ('*secundum* eam')." Clearly, this is far from the idea of "moral annihilation" being proposed! Furthermore, and decisively, the way Thomas uses "non-preservation" in relation to sin is in fact perfectly plain from many texts, as for example *De Malo* 3, 1 ad 1: "God delivers some up to a depraved way or inclines their wills to evil *by withdrawing* his support or by *not-preventing evil,* not indeed by his activity or movement. Just so, for example, we should say that a person who were to fail to extend a hand *to someone* FALLING would cause the latter's fall. But it is by his *just* judgment that God does not bestow assistance on some to prevent their fall." God's withdrawal of aid (here and *always* in Thomas) is being seen as a *just punishment* for a *previous* defect.

38. Thomas teaches in many places that God permits us to *continue* in the state of sin (which permission *infallibly entails* our continuing in it): see 2 *SN* 36,1, 3 ad 1; *De Malo* 3, 1 ad 1; *ST* I, 22, 2 ad 4; *ST* I-II, 87, 2 and ad 1; and his *Commentary on Romans* 9, 3.

criminal,[39] and a captain need not always steer his ship[40]... any more than he need always preserve its goods, in the example made famous by Aristotle in his *Ethics*.[41] But this is because the ship is already *in extremis*, in a dangerous storm (and a captain might also choose to "abandon ship" in such an event),[42] just as the criminal has already been justly *convicted* of a

39. This is Thomas's classic example from *ST* I, 19, 6 ad 1. Here, and everywhere else in Thomas's entire *corpus*, the *reason* the original or "antecedent" salvific will is not effective (in the reprobate) is due to *sin*, to a person's crime. It is because the original order to salvation has been *impeded* by a creature's FAULT, by *sin* (at least original sin), that a final end is not attained. God's will of this end is a *conditioned* one; for, while God created angels and men *for* their salvation (which is why He creates them in grace or at the least moves them towards that state by the inspiration of the Holy Spirit), nevertheless He only wants them to attain that end *if* they are willing to co-operate with His (conditioned) intention (and movement). God respects the free (and FALLIBLE) will of His creatures. They are free NOT to co-operate with His will and movement. If they freely choose their own order and refuse to co-operate with His invitation (offered many times to men), He may be willing to accept this refusal.

40. In *ST* I-II, 79, 1, Thomas says that God "*does not give some the assistance* whereby they may avoid sin.... But He does all this according to the order of His wisdom and justice ... so that, if someone sin, it is not imputable to Him as though He were the cause of that sin; *even as a pilot is not said to cause the wreck of the ship through not steering the ship* unless he cease to steer while able and bound to steer." Someone might think that Thomas here asserts that God leaves an *innocent* person without means to avoid sin, from whence he infallibly sins. This is *patently* false, and for two reasons. First, a pilot or a captain *is* bound not to abandon his ship when there is no storm or extreme circumstance, and he would be negligent were he to do so. Second, Thomas plainly explains his meaning in the same question, ad 1: "He is said to deliver then up in so far as he does not *hinder them from following* a reprobate sense [that they *already* possess], even as we are said to expose a person to danger if we do not protect him." The one who exposes another to danger and does not protect him is just that captain who exposes the ship to danger by not steering it. But the *reason* he does not do so is that the ship is *already in extremis*, just as the *reason* God gives some up to a reprobate sense is that they are *already following it*, and God does not prevent them. Thomas's meaning is evident in all his texts. (For more on this, see *God's Permission*, 409–15.)

41. Aristotle, *NE* 1110a 10. Thomas's use of a captain not steering is just a variant on Aristotle's captain not protecting the ship's goods. The captain does not protect the ship's goods because to do so would go against the good of the ship and its passengers, just as God does not protect the reprobate because to do so would go against "His glory and the good of the universe" (as the commentators commonly say).

42. Note that the captain intends to get his goods to port and to steer his ship, even though this is conditioned by a willingness not to do so *if* it should endanger the ship. By virtue of this conditioned will, he takes action to guide the ship to port, and it will reach port *if* no extreme circumstance intervenes. Likewise, God intends that a person be saved, and He takes action to guide him to the safety of His "port," and he will be saved *if* he does not turn from Him. There is nothing imperfect about a conditioned will. Thus, God wills to give glory *if* one perseveres or He wills to give further grace *if* one asks for it; but it is God Himself who fulfills the condition: here and whenever the condition is a *good*. God's will to punish a reprobate *if* he deserves to be or *if* he rejects His grace or *if* he continues to do so is likewise a conditioned one; but *this* condition is not fulfilled by *His* will, but by the DEFECTIVE will of the free *creature*, as *first* cause. The

crime. The *locus classicus* here is the "hardening" of Pharoah's heart: a heart *already* "gone bad."[43] That God wills not to extend His aid for some period pertains to His *use* of sin. It is itself a great mystery, and often hard for us to accept;[44] but this analysis does not fit the case before us: it pertains to a creature *remaining* in sin, and not to its *falling into* sin.

Thomas does, however, have one final tool in his metaphysical arsenal, one that can be used to understand the free creature's non-act or failure to act that precedes sin. For Aristotle famously held that there was also a radical difference between corruptible and incorruptible beings (the stars and their movers); he supposed these were everlasting, whereas it was absolutely impossible for corruptible beings to be so: at some time, they would necessarily cease to be, would corrupt. Aquinas is aware of his argument to this effect (in his work on the heavens) and makes it his own from the beginning to the end of his career; indeed, he even provides his own arguments in its defense, in his very late and great commentary on the *De Caelo*.[45] So much is he convinced of it that he excludes all corruptible beings, including all animals, from the incorruptible final world to come. He also makes it the centerpiece of his famous "3rd Way," insisting in it that what will come to be called "Murphy's Law" is not merely a "rueful joke," but a metaphysical truth: anything that can fail at some time will fail.

If one asks why this is so, or what grounds this truth, the evident reason is the *materiality* of corruptible beings. Because their matter is inclined to other forms, as well as to its present form, this can exist only for a limited time.[46] We see and use this particular truth mainly in relation to living

differing condition does not render the will in the second case somehow imperfect. For further discussion of God's conditioned will, see my *God's Permission*, 451–55.

43. See *ST* I-II, 79, 1 and ad 1; 79, 3 ad 1; and 79, 4; see also Thomas's *Commentary on Romans* 9, 3.

44. God's *silence*—His willingness neither to intervene miraculously to turn hearts around nor to "give us an answer" as to why He permits sin to continue to run its ugly course and cause its often-times horrendous evil—is connected precisely to the *use* God chooses to make of sin and can be the occasion for much soul-searching: from Job to the present. And since all human beings have fallen into sin, and since the way God chooses to use our sin finally remains obscure to us, each of our personal biographies and destinies remains *a strict mystery* (to faith as well as to philosophy).

45. Thomas first quotes the argument from the *De Caelo* as early as 2 *SN* (1, 1, 5 ag 3 and 19, 1, 1, 1 ag 5). For his fullest discussion of its arguments, see his *Commentary on De Caelo* I, 10–12. For a discussion of this commentary, see James Weisheipl, OP, "The Commentary of St. Thomas on the *De Caelo* of Aristotle," *Sapienza* 29 (1974): 11–34, especially at 16.

46. This is just how Thomas himself argues in *De Caelo* I, 29, #284. That matter indeed has this inclination or in-built dynamism towards other forms of life is magnificently illustrated in

forms. Each has its *natural span*: fortunately for us, a mosquito's is less than an elephant's! On the supposition that a corruptible being were to reach its maximum life-span, then it would corrupt *from within*, not being able any longer to sustain its life. Again, we point towards this truth in the distinction we make between a violent and a "natural" death. Of a death due to "old age," we might say that the person "just slipped away" or "died peacefully in her sleep." Some organ or other finally failed: brain, heart, kidney, liver, circulatory system or what have you. Or the body had become *so* weakened that it could no longer fend off some exterior agent. Thus, beings can cease to exist for two very different reasons: *all* can cease because a cause *extrinsic* to their natural substance is removed (as would happen in any annihilation); and *corruptibles* can cease to exist because of a cause *intrinsic* to their natural substance: their matter, which limits their time, their "natural span." The difference between these causes of non-being is precisely the nerve of the difference between the 4th and the 3rd Ways.

Now, it is quite evident that Thomas uses *this* analysis as the proper analogue to moral failure. Sin is not analogous to a creaturely *annihilation*, but to material *corruption*; and the main reason this is so is because the sinner *fails from within*, by an *intrinsic* cause (namely its *fallible will*). The analogy is clearly signaled by the language Thomas uses in his appropriation of Dionysius's *dictum*: a fallible creature "*quandoque deficit*" and "*quandoque non*" or "*possit deficere et non deficere*" just as a corruptible being "*quandoque non est*" and is a "possible" being: one that "*possibilia esse et non esse.*" But, just as the commentators often became confused about the argument of the Third Way—confusing the *physical* contingents with which the Way begins with *metaphysical* contingency proper to all creatures (and thereby confusing the 3rd with the 4th Way)—so they *missed* the physical analogue to moral failure that unlocks the "final piece of the puzzle" we are here dealing with. Those who have studied the history of the controversies that have circled around the matter before us will know that almost all of the ideas I have presented (and will present) as Thomas's own are common to the commentary tradition. But Maritain was right to intuit that it had not sufficiently deepened its meditation on one point: Thomas's METAPHYSICS OF DEFECTIBLE BEING. It missed the point I have just noted.

our present view of our universe's evolution, as it developed from the simplest of elements into its now marvelous complexity.

All analogies have an in-built difference or dis-analogy. The one that exists between *natural* corruption and *free* corruption is this: when a physical thing fails from within, this is because it is no longer able to continue to exist; but when a person fails to use his intellect to consider what he could, it was still *possible in fact* for him to do so.[47] This is just what makes him *responsible* for his failure: that he does not do what he in fact could do. And it is obvious that, even though a defectible will *can* fail, this does not mean that all *will* fail; for both the angels and the saints who hold firm and do not fall from grace *could have* failed, but they did not. Thus, the non-use we are analyzing has *no other reason*, cause, or explanation than the creature's *own free will*. And this is *just what Thomas says*: that we need look no further than the creature's own will to explain what occurs: "of something of this sort, that is the aforementioned NON-USE of the rule, it is not necessary to search for a cause, because the *will itself*, by which one can act or NOT-ACT, *suffices* for this."[48] He says this, and he means it! This is just why the will is the *first* cause of sin: because it fails *on its own*, when it need not. Humble as he ever is, Aquinas suggests that Augustine himself had already indicated as much when he said that the will's defect in sin "ought to be compared to silence, which has no efficient cause:"[49] since it is a simple negation, and not sin itself, we need not look *beyond it* for a cause.[50]

47. Note that this remains true even of the sinner whom God leaves for some period in his fallen state. Even in that state, it is possible for him in fact to avoid any *particular* mortal sin (just as it is possible for one restored to a graced state to avoid any *particular* venial sin). This is sufficient to establish responsibility for the sin in question, even though a person in a state of sin cannot for long in fact avoid *some* mortal sin (and a person in a restored state cannot for long in fact avoid *some* venial sin). It is sufficient for responsibility that the person could in fact avoid the sin he commits.

48. Aquinas, *De Malo* 1, 3. Of all the points Maritain makes in *St. Thomas and the Permission of Evil* (Milwaukee: Marquette University Press, 1942), his calling attention to this text is his most crucial achievement: see especially 25 and 32. Thomas is of course supposing the will can act well because it is *moved* to act well, for the will can act *only as moved*; yet it can also *fail* to attain its end when so moved.

49. Ibid. See Augustine's *The City of God*, Book XII, Chapter VII, in the 4th Loeb volume (London: William Heinemann, 1987), 33: "No one then should look for an efficient cause of an evil will, for the *cause* is not one of efficiency, but DEFICIENCY, even as the evil will itself is not an effect but a defect. For to DEFECT from that which has supreme being to that which has less is to make a start in having an evil will. Further, since the *causes* of such defections are not efficient but DEFICIENT causes, to wish to trace them is as if someone were to set his heart on seeing darkness or hearing silence." Sin's "fount and origin" plainly lies in the *created will* itself: "It is with evil will itself that evil starts in the changeable spirit" (Book XII, Chapter IX, 39). Anyone wishing to see the fundamental identity of doctrine between Aquinas and Augustine on the cause of sin should read with attention this entire book of *The City of God*.

50. In *De Malo*, Aquinas raises the following objection (1, 3, obj. 6): "If, therefore, good is

To the question, then, of "why" the will fails to do what it could do, Thomas's disarmingly simple answer is this: *it just does,* even though it need not have. There is no *reason* beyond the *ostensive*: the *fact* that it did. There is an analogy here to God's own *first* causality in creating. God possesses a motive for His free act—namely to share His goodness, and especially with the free creatures He makes to be His friends forever—but He was free to act or not to act on this motive. That He did so derived from His own free generosity and nothing else. Likewise, the free creature possesses a motive for *his* own free failure—the good before him, unruled by, and not subject to, a higher good—but he is free to act or not to act on this motive.[51] That he does so derives from his *first* defectible causality and nothing else. "Look: he failed!" That is all there is to say about it, all the intelligibility there is in it. Indeed, this failure is as ABSURD as anything can be: for we fail to do what would fulfill us and make us happy. Were it not for the fact that we find ourselves engaging so frequently in such absurd action, we might question whether or not this were even possible! But the sad experience of our own mortal sins shows us that it is.

III. Sin As Impeding The Interior Vocation of the Holy Spirit

One who is not "scholastically inclined" might well be smiling by this point: we have gone through all the analysis of the Academy, all the Schoolman's wisdom, only to arrive at a position he held all along: sin is

---

the cause of evil insofar as it is deficient, it follows that good is the cause of evil insofar as it already possesses some evil in itself; and then the question is given again regarding this evil." Thomas responds as follows: "In voluntary matters, the cause of sin *is* the deficient will; but this defect does not have the nature [ratio] of guilt or punishment insofar as it is conceived as *prior* ("*praeintelligitur* peccato") as was explained. Nor is it therefore necessary to seek any cause of this defect, and therefore one need not procede to infinity." (See *ST* I-II 75, 2 ad 3 for the identical point.) Sin is a defective or inordinate *act* and therefore will always require some *agent* cause, even if accidental (in the case of sin, the sinner's *conversion* to the false good or its *act* of deciding on and choosing the false good). But the DEFECT that precedes this act is not a sin, nor a privation, but a pure negation, and *therefore* does *not* require such a cause. For such a DEFECT, the will itself is the *sufficient*, and *necessary*, explanation: it *can* fail on its own and it in fact *does* fail. Since this is a NON-ACT or an ABSENCE of being, one need not look for any *further* cause of it.

51. As can be seen, Thomas's entire analysis locates the origin of a free but false choice in our freedom of judgment: because we can exercise our intellect to judge a motive as finally good or not, choice of a false good is our fault alone. We are responsible because we are free to judge well or not to judge well.

our fault; we *fall* into sin when we *need not* have, when we really *could* have done otherwise; it is from *our will* and our will *alone*. Yes, Thomas has indeed sought to teach nothing other than what any Christian (or any Jew or Muslim, for that matter) might know in his simple faith! Nevertheless, reason can "bewitch" us, and it is easy to "get it wrong" when thinking about sin. Anyone familiar with the 16th to 17th century Catholic dispute on the aids of grace (which came to a head in the Roman congregations *de auxiliis*) will know how true this is. For both parties to the dispute "got it wrong" and (curiously enough) in somewhat the same way. For both, it is *God*, not man, who *first* assures that sin will be introduced into the world. For Molina, God eternally foresees that man (and the angel) would sin in a certain situation, and *He* chooses to put them in that situation ... just in which sin will *infallibly* occur. For Bañez, *God* eternally chooses *not* to aid man (and the angel), from which failure and sin *infallibly* occurs. No, no no!!! It is not the will of *God* that *first* assures that sin will exist, but that of his fallible *creature*!! Thomas ever holds that God's will is related to sin in two ways: making it *possible*, by not excluding sin from the world (Dionysius); and by *using* the sin of the creature to good effect (Augustine). But *no* relation exists between sin *as sin* and God's *will* (for then it would be its *cause*)![52] All the "horrendous evil"[53] of the world, all the accounts that make Ivan Karamazov "return his ticket,"[54] all the outrage that one such as Elie Wiesel describes so poignantly in *Night*,[55] all these are not *God's* doing, and they are not somehow eternally "set up" by God;[56] they are *our* own horror, what we bring into God's good world, *when we need not have*.

Both false positions are again alike in being at pains to explain that God knows sin eternally in knowing *Himself alone*, His *own* mind and will, and thus not needing to suppose the creature in order to know his sin infallibly. No, no, no!!! This is precisely *not* what Thomas teaches!! There is not one single text in Thomas to support either a supposed *scientia media* or a

52. There *is* a relation between whatever *activity* there is in sin and God: He is its first *cause*. But He only is willing to cause what the free and fallible creature on his own has DEFECTIVELY *disposed* himself towards. He *uses* the creature's defect and failure, just as He uses his sin (original or actual).

53. Marilyn Adams, *Horrendous Evils and the Goodness of God* (Ithaca: Cornell University Press, 1999).

54. Feodor Dostoevsky, *The Brothers Karamazov* (San Francisco: North Point Press, 1990), Book 5, Chapter 4: Rebellion, 236–46, especially at 245.

55. Elie Wiesel, *Night* (New York: Farrar, Strauss and Giroux, 1958; 2006).

56. Maritain rightly rejects such an implied position in his *Permission*, 30.

"negative decree" as the means by which God knows sin; and there is not, because this is not his doctrine. Rather, he teaches from first to last that God *sees* sin *as it deforms* the sinner who is *physically present* to His eternity: a solution already given by Boethius and one that Thomas makes his own from first to last.[57] Indeed, he *explicitly* holds that, were this *not* the case and were free future contingents *not* physically before Him or supposed, then God would *not* know them infallibly![58]

But then, it might be objected, God only knows sin *through* the creature, seeing sin *in* the creature, whose defect and sin must be *supposed*. Exactly! That is *exactly* what Thomas himself affirms *verbatim* when faced with this problem. God knows sin in the creature (not in Himself, or knowing *only* His mind); for that is the only way sin can *exist* (in the creature), and *thus* there is no defect in knowing sin that way, *as it is*.[59] That does not

57. See 1 *SN* 38, 1, 5; *De Veritate* 2, 12 and 13, *SCG* I, 66, *The Compendium of Theology* I, 133, and his last work: his *Reply to the Abbot of Montecassino*, interpreting a passage from Gregory the Great's *Morals on the Book of Job* (Book 16, chapter 10). It was a badge of honor of the first Dominican defenders of Thomas against the "*Corruptorii*" to insist that all creatures are *physically* present to God (in their *existence*), and not merely *objectively* or in God's idea of them: see John Quidort's *Correctorium Corruptorii Circa*, ed. Jean Pierre Müller, OSB (Rome: Herder, 1941), a. 3, 26; see further, Julius Groblicki's *De Scientia Dei Futurorum Contingentium Secundum S. Thomam Eiusque Primos Sequaces* (Krakow: University of Krakow Press, 1938); and, for the commentary tradition in general, see Joseph de Finance, SJ, "La prèsence des choses à l'éternité d'après les scholastiques," *Archives de Philosophie* 19 (1956): 25–62. Thomas expressly holds this (cf. *ST* I, 14, 13): "all things that are in time are present to God from eternity, not only because He has the types of things present within Him, as some say, but because His glance is carried from eternity over all things as they are in *their presentiality*." Cajetan was the first Dominican to import into his order's position the Franciscan view that the physical presence of contingents was *not necessary* for God's infallible knowledge of them (a position Bañez would later defend, holding God could know *all* things in His own will, absent their physical presence to Him): see Friedrich Stegmüller's account, in his *Francisco de Vitoria y la doctrina de la gracia en la escuela Salamantina* (Barcelona: Balmes, 1934), 18–19.

58. Thomas opts for his position on this question from the *Sentences* on and never varies in it. And, in the *Sentences* (1 *SN* 36, 1, 2) he goes so far as to say this: "And by this, that God knows His essence, He knows these things that are *from* Him, and *through these* He knows their defect. If however, He were to know *only* His essence as such, He *would know no privation or evil*." This is hardly surprising: there is no evil in God to know. In the *Sentences*, he further says this: "that knowledge, by virtue of the reason of certitude, requires certitude in the thing known is *obvious* in relation to *our* knowledge, which is not the *cause* of things, and *the knowledge of God in respect to evil*" (1 *SN* 38, 1, 5), since, (to complete his syllogism), God is *not the cause* of *this* thing (sin) and thus neither of the certitude of its existing.

59. In *ST* I, 14, 10, Thomas presents the following objection: "What is known *through another* and not *through itself* is *imperfectly* known. But evil is not known by God; for the thing known must be *in the knower*. Therefore, if evil is known through another, namely through the good, it would be known by Him imperfectly; which cannot be, for the knowledge of God is not

mean God's mind is thereby "*in*-formed" or changed by what He sees, for the DEFECT of sin is no form; rather, what makes sin to be sin is a DE-formation, an ABSENCE of due form, just as its root cause is a simple NEGATION. Now *all* creatures are NEGATIONS, or LACK being, by comparison to God's plenitude; yet this does not prevent God from knowing them perfectly, because His perfect essence contains *all that there is of being and intelligibility* in the creatures, who participate these in their *lesser* way. God thus knows *sin's* negation just as He knows *all* creatures: in knowing Himself. Nevertheless, for God to *see* sin, the creature must *exist* AS DEFECTIVE to be seen, and it must be present immediately to His eternal mind in order to be seen infallibly. As Maritain rightly underlines, this is the only way sin *can* be known, since there is no divine idea of sin.[60] This does not bespeak any imperfection in God's mind: rather, the imperfection lies in the object to be known.

And yes, this also means that God's eternal will *supposes* His eternal knowledge of our sin, just as His eternally predestining Christ as our Savior *supposes* both the angel's and Adam's sins (in time or aeveternity), for which He is the remedy. Thomas not only teaches this, he teaches it *explicitly*, and at the very *end* of His career, just as he always teaches that any reprobation of a sinner *supposes* the creature's sin. God's will supposes His *own* eternal essence and His *own* vision of the sin that exists.[61] In the case of sin, *none* of this is *caused* by God's will: God's will causes neither His eternal essence nor His eternal mind, *nor* does it cause the creature's defect and sin. True, *that* the creature *exist* supposes God's active and sustaining will; but that it exist AS DEFECTIVE, as sinful, does *not* suppose God's will, but rather the *creature's*, sin's *first* cause. In this case, and *uniquely* in this

imperfect. Therefore God does not know evil things" (obj. 4). Thomas replies to this objection *not* by denying that God knows evil *in another*; on the contrary, he *affirms* this. Rather, he replies by denying that this bespeaks an imperfection in God's knowing: "To know a thing *by something else* only belongs to imperfect knowledge *if* that thing is of itself knowable; but *evil is not of itself knowable*, forasmuch as the very nature of evil means the privation of good; therefore evil can neither be defined nor known *except by good*." He had just explained by *what* good God does know evil: "[evil] is opposed to the *effects* of God, which He knows by His essence; and knowing *them* [that is, the created *effects*], He knows the opposite evils." Manifestly, then, Thomas holds that the *actual, defective,* creature is *supposed as existing* for God to know it perfectly.

60. Maritain notes this in *Permission*, 5 and 67–76: for Thomas on this, see *ST* I, 15, 3 ad 1.

61. For predestination supposing the foreknowledge of sin, see *ST* III, 1, 3 ad 4 and *Quodlibet* 5, 5, 1; for reprobation supposing sin see, *ST* I, 23, 3 ad 2. For more on the issue of God's eternal will supposing the foreknowledge of created defects (and, possibly, effects), see *God's Permission*, 431–37.

case—the case of DE-formation: the evil malice of sin and its DEFECTIVE cause—a created DEFORMITY exists that God does *not* will.[62]

Finally, both positions again "get it wrong" when it comes to explaining the sufficiency and the efficacy of God's grace. For Molina, God's grace is sufficient in itself to effect a good act, but this grace is only rendered effective by the creature's free consent to it; for Bañez, God's grace is infallibly effective, ensuring the creature's free consent to it. Both of these views fall short of Thomas's full teaching; in effect, each catches sight of only one of its sides. Grasping his whole position on this matter not only helps avoid their mistakes and the unnecessary "contention of schools,"[63] but shows us Thomas's own presentation of the drama of man before God.

We have been speaking about the *natural structure* of human action and failure: of our non-action in the process of deliberation that precedes final judgment, of the latter as terminating that process and committing us to the false good to which we convert, choosing it and thereby averting our-

62. Again, anyone who would hold that there is a *possible* world, *including sin*, which God *wills*, would hold a position *expressly rejected* by Thomas: the evil of sin does *not* belong to the perfection of the universe and is *not willed as such* by God (*ST* I, 38, 1 ad 5). What *does* belong to the universe's perfection is that there should be fallible free creatures, *moved* according to their fallible nature, and that God should *turn* their evil will to some good and order. But sin itself is not something that God wills either directly or indirectly, as somehow perfective of His universe. Such an idea can give rise (and with reason!) to Ivan's rebellion. Sometimes, it is suggested that other evils—such as certain kinds of "pointless" animal suffering—*are* willed directly by God and are not part of the above analysis. This is to take too narrow a view of God's universe. The angels participate in its governance, and fallen angels can wound it as much as (indeed, more than) fallen men. (We need only think of the Gadarene pigs for Scriptural warrant of this angelic abuse of the animal world.) If animals suffer and are abused in an "unnatural" way, we may be confident that the sin of free creatures is involved. The natural world and its defects cannot be isolated from their possible relation to the world of freedom and God's governance of it. That *still* does not mean that we understand *why* God chooses to *use* sin the way He does (the Gadarene pigs might be a case in point!); in fact, we often don't understand why: often a cause for anguish.

63. Dom Illytd Trethowan, OSB, rightly says of Maritain's position that it ends the dispute generated by the *Congregatio de auxiliis*: see his review of Maritain's first book on evil, "St. Thomas and the problem of evil," *Dublin Review* 212 (1943): 175–78, at 176. Trethowan indicates that Maritain was not the first to reach this view, for he cites the work of his fellow Benedictine, Dom Mark Pontifex, OSB. (Indeed, the latter had given a remarkably lucid exposition of the doctrines at issue in "Predestination," *Downside Review* 57 [1939]: 63–76.) Trethowan says that Pontifex's treatment is the first presentation of this position "in English." As I have suggested ("Francisco Marin-Sola, O.P. and the Origin of Jacques Maritain's Doctrine on God's Permission of Evil," *Nova et Vetera* 4:1 [2006]: 55–94), the way to it was clearly laid down by Francisco Marín-Sola, OP. Those not convinced by that article may wish to consult my longer work, *God's Permission*. In truth, Marín-Sola has returned Thomists to the teaching of the Common Doctor obscured by earlier disputes and the sad contentions of orders and "schools."

selves from God and His true order. Yet this whole structure is set within an *existential* situation, one that involves more than just our nature, including as it does God's *gracious* invitation to us (and the angels) to participate in His life, which infinitely transcends that of creatures. The blessing and the promise that God sets before His free creatures is not just any moral good, but is the good of acting by virtue of His love and His holy will, of sharing life with Him, of being His friends. And, although man turns away from God, God does not give up on man. He does not prevent that turning just because He will provide its remedy in the Savior He sends to our fallen race. The drama of man before God, as it is experienced by us *existentially* now, comes first in the form of His *call* to us fallen ones to return to Him. The *locus classicus* of this drama lies in the relation between *preparatory grace* and our free will.[64]

It is Aquinas's doctrine, from the beginning to the end of his career, that our being justified by God's grace involves two quite different preparations.[65] One is the *perfect* preparation that accompanies the infusion of sanctifying grace. For, by this grace, we are *trans-formed* from what we were: from ones born into a "dysfunctional family," whose first parents had turned from God, and from ones whose own personal sins crucified the Lord of Glory, to ones who are His friends, and temples of His Holy Spirit. By His grace, God chooses to give us His own Triune life and love and have us begin to live by it now; this requires that our natural life be *in-formed* by a new reality: the life and the love of His Holy Spirit. The *ultimate dispositions* for this new form, ones *accomplished* by its very infusion,[66] are free and personal acts of charity, filial fear, humility, and contrition: the acts involved in turning decisively to God and away from our past sins. If God gives us His gift, then we infallibly receive it,[67] at the moment of our justi-

64. This situation is then extended by analogy (and by the experience of our own restored nature) to the place where the drama began: at the beginning, with Adam and Eve in Paradise (and, if one also is to include the angels, in their own analogous decision to "serve" or "not to serve").

65. See Thomas Aquinas, *ST* I-II, 109, 2.

66. Every ultimate disposition is of the same order (category) and nature as its form. Since sanctifying grace makes us "deiform," and since our participation in God's very own life entirely transcends our nature (as it does the angels'), the ultimate disposition in our soul for this new and life-giving form (a super-natural quality) must be caused by that form itself. Thomas makes this point in his analysis of the light of glory in *De Veritate* 8, 3. This case is analogous and his point applies here as well.

67. In this lies the truth of "compatibilism": freedom is *per se* compatible with an infallible

fication.[68] God's "justifying grace" is thus infallibly efficacious and causes free and personal acts,[69] as the infusion of a form into matter requires that the latter simultaneously and infallibly receive it. Aquinas ever teaches this, from the *Sentences* through the *Summa*.[70]

Yet the final preparation and perfect conversion effected by sanctifying grace is always preceded by another, imperfect, preparation.[71] (The only exception Thomas ever proposes is the *miraculous* conversion of St. Paul.) This preparation temporally *precedes* the infusion of sanctifying grace. Since the latter is the principle of all merit, this preparation is *imperfect* and cannot itself *merit* that infusion or (consequently) our justification. The younger Thomas held, preeminently with Albert, his teacher, and Bonaventure, his friend, that our fallen nature was capable of making *this* prepara-

---

cause. While this is true, God more commonly does not move the human soul and will in an infallible way.

68. Behind Thomas's teaching lies his view of the sacraments. In each, by the power of the Holy Spirit and the promise of Christ, the proper form transforms the matter: the baptismal formula alters the baptismal water to make it apt for the removal of sins; the Eucharistic words of institution *trans-form* the bread and wine into the body and blood of Christ; and the Penitential words of absolution perfect the contrition of the sinner: a contrition itself brought about by the infusion of the Holy Spirit. In each case, God acts and the matter is instantly and infallibly transformed. In the case of penance, as Thomas expressly teaches (*ST* III, 84, 1 ad 2) human acts function as the sacrament's matter: "in the sacrament of Penance ... human actions take the place of matter, and these actions proceed from internal inspiration ... by God working inwardly, while the minister furnishes the complement of the sacrament, when he absolves the penitent."

69. It is surely of these acts, accomplished under the infusion of sanctifying grace, that Thomas is thinking when he teaches, in the famous passage of *ST* I-II, 9, 6 ad 3 that "*sometimes* God moves some specially to the willing of something *determinate,* which is *good,* as in the case of those whom He moves by *grace*." This contrasts with God's *usual* way of moving the will, which is towards the true good, and under which motion man "determines himself by reason to will this or that, which is *true* or *apparent* good." In the latter case, man can consider or not consider well and hence determine himself for the apparent (i.e. false) good, when he sins and turns away from God's motion towards the true (honest) good. In the former case (of the acts of our justification), however, this is *not* possible, because God's motion *infallibly* accomplishes something "determinate," which can only be a true good.

70. Thus *ST* I-II, 112, 2 ad 1: "A certain preparation of man for grace is simultaneous with the infusion of grace; and this operation is meritorious, not indeed of grace, which is already possessed, but of glory, which is not yet possessed."

71. Thus, all sacraments require that their matter be properly prepared to receive the form: true water for baptism, true bread and true wine for the Eucharist; and, in the case of Penance, a heart that has been prepared by an imperfect preparation to receive the new form of sanctifying grace. There is an analogy here to the spiritual life: the "purgative way" (analogous to our imperfect preparation) involves using our faculties, whereas the "unitive way" (analogous to our perfect preparation) increasingly involves being passive (or, rather, "receptive") before God, who transforms our inner life.

tion[72] (God moving us according to our fallen state); by the *Summa Contra Gentiles*, however, he had altered his view and he then held (with Augustine, his greater master) that this preparation is entirely beyond our nature, and doubly so because it is fallen; for this imperfect conversion involves the turning of our will towards God as our potential friend, which is an end above our nature, and this could only be accomplished by an aid that is above our nature.[73] That Thomas altered his view regarding this imperfect preparation was recognized even by his earliest contemporaries and is not controversial. God's aid is given to produce the first personal and free acts that lead us *towards* the charity and the perfect contrition of justification: the initial act of *servile fear* and the acts of a *faith* and a *hope* not yet formed by the perfect love of God.[74]

Now, Thomas not only teaches the need for God to turn us towards Him this way; he even names this aid and uses it *systematically*: it is the vocation and the "*interior instinct*" or "inspiration" of the Holy Spirit, one that *moves* us towards our true good and end. The younger Thomas recognized that God initially prepared some by just such an *interior* vocation, but he allowed God could also do so by some *exterior* means, such as sending a preacher, or even an angel; the mature Thomas demurs: the latter is insufficient, for our *will itself* must be touched and turned, through the Holy Spirit working within.[75] From first to last, however, Thomas not only affirms

72. For imperfect preparation in these men, see the Angelicum thesis of Joseph Nguyen Tri An, OP: *De Praeparatione Ad Gratiam Apud Divum Thomam* (Manila, 1958).

73. He holds the same regarding the angels, teaching that they were turned towards God either by sanctifying grace or at least by this "gracious turning" of their will towards Him: see *ST* I, 62, 2 ad 3. Because our human nature had to have its body and soul integrated in order to turn to God, Thomas thinks Adam and Eve were created in grace (*ST* I, 95, 1). Had they not been, then they, too, would have been at least moved by the preparatory grace Thomas concedes was possible to the angels; for those doctors (such as Bonaventure) who held that Adam was *not* created in grace still thought he could have *prepared* to receive sanctifying grace (since they thought this was true even of fallen nature). However, just as the mature Thomas demurs on this point, and insists that the aid received to prepare initially is above our fallen nature, so he would have insisted the same *would* have held for Adam. For the end towards which Adam and Eve would have been turned transcended their nature (since they were being prepared for sanctifying grace and friendship with God), and this would have required an actual grace.

74. Thomas Aquinas, *ST* I-II, 112, 2 ad 1: "There is another imperfect preparation, which sometimes [indeed, save by miracle!] precedes the gift of sanctifying grace, and yet it is from God's motion. But it does not suffice for merit, since man is not yet justified by [habitual] grace."

75. Starting with the *SCG* (III, 149) and continuously thereafter, Thomas underlines the *initiative* God takes in our conversion. (For other examples, see *Super Secundam Epistolam ad Corinthios Lectura* II, 3 [#68]; *Super Epistolam ad Romanos Lectura* VIII, 6 [#707] and X, 3

this interior movement of the Holy Spirit, but he *also* affirms that *this* motion and preparation (in distinction from the perfect one accomplished by the infusion of sanctifying grace), *does not always attain its term* and that by virtue of the DEFECT of the one called.[76] This vocation and motion *can in fact* be IMPEDED, and sometimes is impeded, by our sin.[77]

Perhaps one might wonder just what type of active, efficient cause can *effect* an act, and yet be *impeded*. This is no mystery to Thomas. For a *sufficient* cause is just that: one possessing the active power to cause a given end, although it can be impeded.[78] This is an integral part of his teaching

[#849]; *Commentary on the Gospel of St. John*, 1, 6 [#154] and 6, 5 [#937]; *Quodlibetum* 1, 4, 2, sed contra; and *ST* I, 62, 2 ad 3, I-II, 109, 6 ad 1, and III, 85, 5.) From then on, he teaches that to declare otherwise is part of the Pelagian controversy. (See *SCG* III, 152 [7] and 157 [6]; *Super Secundam Epistolam ad Corinthios Lectura* III, 1 [# 86]; *Quodlibetum* 1, 4, 2; *ST* I, 23, 5, and II-II, 6, 1.) From then on, he insists that this *turning* of our heart is to an end that *transcends* our fallen capacities and, indeed, our very nature; and thus, from then on, either implicitly or explicitly, he declares that we can be turned to God only by a motion that is *supernatural*, and therefore that is a *grace* in the *proper* sense of that word. (See *Quodlibetum* 1, 4, 2; *ST* I-II, 109, 6; *ST* I-II, 112, 2; and *ST* II-II, 6, 1 ad 3.) And thus, from then on, he reinterprets *facienti quod in se est Deus non denegat gratiam* to mean that God will not refuse the infusion of sanctifying grace to one who does what he can with the aid of God *graciously* moving his heart to do what he can. (See *Super Epistolam ad Romanos Lectura* X, 3 [#849]; *ST* I-II, 109, 6 ad 2; *ST* I-II, 112, 2, and both ad 1 and ad 2; *ST* I-II, 112, 3 and ad 1; and *ST* II-II, 33, 2 ad 1.)

76. In this lies the truth of "libertarianism": while being moved towards an end, the will has the *de facto* capacity to act or not to act to attain it, such that its failure to act (DEFECT or NON-ACT) is its responsibility. This is in fact the more ordinary way God moves us and thus a form of "libertarian" language is the more obvious and easy "fit" with what Christians (and most religious traditions) teach.

77. This point has been controverted, so some texts seem in order. Here is the younger Thomas, in his first great work, the *Sentences*: "Vocation is twofold: an exterior one, as is sometimes accomplished by a preacher, and this is not justification, but disposes to it. Another interior. *And this sometimes does not attain its end on account of a* DEFECT *of the one called*. And this vocation is nothing other than a certain *instinct* or *motion towards the good*, sent by God. And this vocation is not the same as justification, but disposes to it (4 *SN* 17, 1, 1b)." Here is the mature Thomas teaching the same in his *Quodlibet Questions*, 1, 4, 2 ad 2: "God *moves* the human mind to the good, but he is nevertheless able to RESIST this motion; and *thus* it is from God that man prepares himself for grace, but that he LACKS grace does not have a cause from God but from man." His last, great, polemical work—the *Refutation of the Pernicious Teaching Of Those Who Would Deter Men From The Religious Life*—carefully teaches this interior vocation that we can resist, basing his teaching on the authority of Scripture, the Fathers, and philosophy. (See *An Apology For The Religious Orders*, edited with an introduction by John Proctor, O.P. [London: Sands & Co., 1902], Chapter IX, pages 426–30.) See also 4 *SN* 17, 1, 5 ad 2; his *Commentary on 1 Corinthians*, 12:1; his *Commentary on 1 Thessalonians*, 5:2; *ST* I, 63, 6 ad 3; his *Commentary on John*, 6, 4 and 15, 5; and *De Malo* 16, 4.

78. This answers the determinist objection that nothing created occurs without its "determining" cause. While true, this does not mean that, once this cause is posited, its effect must follow; for, even though the cause possesses the sufficient, active, power to obtain its proper effect,

on causes. Some texts seem in order: "It is false to say that, a cause once posited, it is necessary that the effect take place, *even* if the cause is said to be *sufficient* of itself, because it can be *impeded*, just as the combustion of fire is by the throwing on of water."[79] Thomas's point follows ordinary discourse, as can be seen in this application to medicine: "When that which is ordered to an end is *sufficient* to lead to it, then one such thing suffices for the end; thus one remedy, if it is to be *efficacious*, *suffices* sometimes to restore man to health, and then the remedy need not be repeated."[80] A cause is sufficient, then, when it possesses the active power to effect an end. And, even when this cause is *posited* or *applied*, its effect need not occur, because an impediment may intervene. Thomas applies this concept to the very case we are studying. Thus, in replying to the charge that our *will*, once moved by a *sufficient* cause, will certainly attain the *end* towards which it is moved, he says the following: "... even if it be a sufficient cause ... this cause can be IMPEDED so that its effect does not follow.... So, also, therefore, with that cause that makes the will *want* something; it is not necessary that it produce out of necessity, because *the will by itself can place an impediment* either by REMOVING a certain *consideration* which induces it to will or by considering the opposite."[81] Thomas is *consistent* at every point. God moves our will interiorly to prepare remotely for the gift of sanctifying grace; the motion is sufficient to cause the acts towards which it is ordered; yet these acts may not occur, because we impede this motion, as the *first* cause of our defect and sin: by NOT *considering* what we in fact could have considered, by the gracious motion of God, and thus FAILING to do what we could have done.

In short, just as the perfect preparation simultaneous with the gift of justifying grace corresponds exactly to what will come to be called "efficacious grace"—a grace that causes us infallibly to act—so the gracious interior instinct of the Holy Spirit corresponds exactly to what will come to be

it can be impeded. In the case of free will, it is impeded *from within*, by the will itself *not doing* what, being moved, it *could have done*.

79. Thomas Aquinas, *De Malo* 16, 7 ad 14.

80. Thomas Aquinas, *ST* I-II, 101, 3 ad 1 (and see also *ST* I-II, 98, 1). That Thomas is using "sufficient" in its "ordinary" usage (which denotes a *de facto* capacity, rather than a qualified one or in a "divided" sense) is the brunt of M. D. Chenu's study of the term in Thomas: see his "Sufficiens," *Revue des Sciences Philosophiques et Théologiques* 23 (1933): 251–59.

81. Thomas Aquinas, *De Malo* 6 ad 6; see also *ST* I-II, 75, 1 ad 2: "It happens that a thing is the *sufficient* cause of something else and that the effect does not follow of necessity, on account of some supervening *impediment*"; see also *De Malo* 16, 7 ad 14.

called "sufficient grace"—a grace that moves us within to effect preparatory acts, but in a way corresponding to our defectible nature and that can be impeded. In the first instance, we act as free, yet subordinate causes; in the second instance, we do *likewise*—we act as free and subordinate causes, when we act well; but, in the second instance, we may FAIL to do so, and, instead, become the *first* cause of our sin.

Although Thomas does not divide grace between sufficient and efficacious, this division *maps directly* onto his distinction between imperfect and perfect preparation: *the difference is purely verbal.* We should recall that, when Henry of Gorkum first mentioned this division, about 150 years after Thomas's death (and more than 150 years before the *de auxiliis* controversy), he qualifies it as already a common or "customary" distinction.[82] And since it was also the common (if not indeed the *unanimous!*) view of the Thomistic commentators throughout the 250 years after Thomas's death (up through Cajetan's commentary on the *Sentences*) that some particular ends of God's providence *were not infallibly attained,*[83] the *common* Thomist opinion of that time corresponded with what Thomas teaches here: that God provides means to an end, and moves towards an end, in a way that can be *impeded* by our sin. Likewise, it is the *more common* view of Dominican commentators from Nicolaï to the present[84] that Thomas taught an interior

82. Henry of Gorkhum (Gorinchem) was a Thomist who taught at Cologne (+1431); see his *Supplementum Summae S. Thomae,* folio XXIV a, proposition XV. Gerard Schneemann, SJ, seems to have uncovered this text: see his *Controversiae de Divinae Gratiae Liberique Arbitrii Concordia* (Freiburg: Herder, 1881), 103.

83. For a discussion of Thomist commentators' views on providence, see R. Velasco, CMF, "Providencia y Predestinación: Estudio positivo de una cuestión disputada en la Escuela Tomista, *Revista Española de Teologia* 21 (1961): 125–51 and 249–87. That some ends of providence are fallible and not always attained is the doctrine of Annibaldo of Annibaldis (+1272), Pietro of Tarantase—Blessed Innocent the 5th (1225–1276)—Giles of Rome (1246–1313), Hervé Natalis (+1323), John of Naples (+ c. 1336), Gerard of Siena (+1336), Leonard of Pistoia (fl. 1342), Robert Holcot (+1349), John Capreolus (1380–1444), Paolo Soncino (+1494), Juan de Torquemada (1420–1498), and Diego Deza (1433–1523). Indeed, Capreolus consciously used Thomas's earlier and later texts on this issue interchangeably. Velasco defends this decision, noting that Thomas uses an equivalent distinction, regarding the orders of grace and predestination, in his teaching on the "Book of Life" in the *Summa Theologiae.* It is hardly surprising, then, that when Cajetan held Thomas denied his earlier position on this issue, Silvester Mazzolini de Prierio (1456–1523) should have exclaimed: "*mirum est* quod hactenus *nullus* ex discipulis divi Thomae viderit illam contradictionem!" In fact, none of the early concordances that list positions Thomas later abandoned list this as one such. The earlier commentators also give the *reason* for this distinction: the sin caused by free creatures *opposes* the order of providence founded in God's antecedent will, *impeding* the end of their salvation. Ferrariensis (1474–1528) equally objected to Cajetan: see his *In SCG* III, 94 and also 159.

84. For Nicolaï (1594–1673), see M. M. Gorce, OP's entry on him in the *Dictionnnaire de*

motion of the Holy Spirit that *differed* from efficacious grace and that could be *resisted,* and they held this in part because the Jansenist position led the Catholic *Magisterium* to declare so, repeatedly.[85] Contrary to what some may think, then, the idea that there is such a thing as an *actual* and *moving* grace that is sufficient but *impedible*—and that *sometimes is impeded* by our own first causality of sin—is the *most common* Dominican teaching on sufficient grace.

Some may worry that this doctrine ends by making the creature the *first* cause of something good, namely its *not-impeding* the grace which it is given. However well-intentioned, this worry is misplaced, and for two reasons. First, there is only a *conceptual,* but no *real,* difference between *acting with and by* God's grace and "not-impeding" God's grace. The impediment in question is a NEGATION, a not-acting; and there is no real difference between the NEGATION of a NEGATION (thus a "non-impediment") and a positive act, just as there is no real difference between the negation of

---

Théologie Catholique, XIa, 491; see also his "Nicolaï et les jansénistes ou la grâce actuelle suffisante," *Revue Thomiste* 36 (1931): 761–75 and 37 (1932): 452–504. See, further, Sylvio Hermann de Francheschi's "Le Thomisme au secours du jansénisme dans la querelle de la grâce," *Revue Thomiste* 117 (2007): 375–417. He notes that, for Pascal and other Jansenists of Port-Royale, "authentic" Thomism was identified with that of Alvarez and Lemos, whereas Nicolaï and his followers were "new Thomists" and, false, "Molinizing" Thomists (383). Gonet (1616–1681) clearly agrees with Nicolaï's view and he was followed by the Thomists thereafter who opposed Jansenism. (See Gonet's key text in Marín-Sola's "Respuesta a alguna objeciones," 11–14.)

85. It is sometimes insufficiently underlined that the reason later Thomists developed the positions they did (from 1650 on) derived, at least in part, from responding to what the Church condemned in Jansenism. Thus, having earlier condemned, against Jansen (1653), that interior grace is never resisted (*Denzinger* #2002, and likewise #2005), it then went on against Quesnel, in the Bull "Unigenitus" (1713), to condemn the following three propositions: "Gratia Christi est *operatio* manus omnipotentis Dei, *quam nihil impedire potest* aut retardare" (#2410), "*Quando Deus vult* salvare animam, quocumque tempore, quocumque loco, *effectus indubitalis sequitur voluntatem Dei*" (#2412), and "*Quando* Deus *vult* animam salvam facere *et eam tangit interiore gratiae suae manu, nulla voluntas humana ei resistit*" (#2413). It may be said that Clement XII (1730) and Benedict XIV (1748) affirmed that the condemnation of Jansenism was not meant to include any condemnation of "Thomism" (see *Denzinger* #2509 and #2564); but it can be insufficiently noted that the French *Thomists* involved in the Jansenist controversy (Nicolaï, Gonet, Reginald, Bancel, Massoulié) had by then reaffirmed the *Thomistic* teaching that some actual graces were *impedible.* It is not clear, on the face of it, how Bañez's position, and those who try to follow his line of thought, can appropriate the ordinary, but solemn, teaching of the Magisterium in "Unigenitus," nor is theirs "the" Dominican view; on the contrary, theirs is a *minority* view that *interrupts* a position commonly held from 1275–1525 and from 1650 to the present. It could only be identified as "the" Dominican view because of the quarrel of *de auxiliis.* It is high time this equivocation were put to rest.

86. Thomas says the following in *De Veritate* (28, 6): "the negation of an opposite which posits a natural being is real, because it is the negation of a real being; but the negation of the other

darkness and light.[86] Second, the instinct of the Holy Spirit is *moving* the creature to the good act, and it accomplishes this act *under and by that motion* when it acts well, instead of impeding it. Thomas's theory of action is that once a secondary cause is placed *in act*—as the will is when moved by the Holy Spirit—then the good it achieves certainly does come from it, but only by virtue of the action of God, as first cause.[87]

Indeed, the idea of an impedible motion or an impedible cause is neither strange nor puzzling, and we observe these as a common feature of our world. Agents are constantly being impeded from reaching their ends, by other causes that intervene. And, when these do *not* intervene, we do not think the agent acts well because of such a *non*-intervention or *non*-impediment, but rather by its God-given nature and energies. If the lion manages not to impede the gazelle's rush to the safety of the bushes, it reaches safety not because the lion does not impede it, but because of its own forces. The plant does not thrust its stem through the soil and grow be-

opposite is not real, because it is not the negation of any real being. It is the negation of a negation. Consequently, this negation of a negation, which is the negation of the second opposite, in no way differs from the positing of the other ... the negation of the negation is [only] distinct conceptually or in our manner of understanding it [but not really]." Thus, the "destruction of non-white" is the same as the coming to be of white. Or the negation of darkness is the same as the presence of light. Indeed, the light of God's grace and the darkness of the non-act that impedes it is Thomas's favorite simile for this situation. There is no real difference, then, between "not-impeding" God's grace (negating a non-act or our darkness) and acting with and by it (the light). The English of *De Veritate* is that of Robert W. Mulligan, SJ, in *The Disputed Questions on Truth* (Chicago: Regnery, 1952–54).

87. In his *Commentary on Hebrews* (12: 15), Thomas raises the objection that "if [sanctifying] grace is not given from works, but [still] inasmuch as one does not place an obstacle [to actual grace], then [sanctifying] grace will depend on free will and not from the election of God, which is the Pelagian error." The supposition behind this objection is that somehow our "not placing an obstacle" derives from our free will as *first* cause, and not from God. Thomas replies to this difficulty in these words: "this, that one does *not place* an obstacle, *comes from* [actual, preparatory] *grace* itself. And thus if anyone places an obstacle [either original or mortal sin] and nevertheless his heart is moved so *that it is removed* [e.g. the motion effects its end], this is the grace of God through His mercy.... This gift of grace [e.g. God's imperfect preparation], however, is not sanctifying grace" (my translation). Thomas, then, does not deny his own constant teaching and that of all his contemporaries that God freely but infallibly chooses to give sanctifying grace to those who prepare to receive it; nor does he deny that we can place an obstacle to the interior working of the Holy Spirit that is preparing us. What he *does* deny is that our *not* placing an obstacle is somehow *not* the work of that same Holy Spirit. On the contrary, by *moving us and placing us in act* towards the honest (and potentially saving) good, our will possesses all that is needed (in the way of active virtuality) to choose this good, but *according to its fallible nature*, and thus it possesses it in a way that the act of choice *need not follow*, should the will FAIL to act with what it is given. That a motion is sufficient, yet impedible, perfectly captures the two truths that define this matter: God's first causality in being and goodness and the creature's first causality in non-being and sin.

cause there is no rock impeding it from doing so, but by its organic nature. Likewise, if we can see objects, it is not because we have not closed our eyes to the light (since our eyes could be open and we still see nothing, in the darkness of night); rather, we can see because of the sun's light shining.

The latter is indeed Thomas's favorite metaphor for the situation being discussed.[88] Insofar as it pertains to Him (*quantum in se est*), God makes it possible for us to see His truth and act well, just as the sun makes it possible for us to see. If we do not see, it is because we have closed our eyes or shutters to the light;[89] and if we do not do what God is preparing us to do, it is because we fail to act with and by His gracious movement. The simile is in fact a proper analogy. Light and heat exist preeminently and properly in the sun, according to its nature, just as the grace and fire of the Holy Spirit exist preeminently in God, according to His divine nature. The air becomes luminous when it receives the sun's light (and only when receiving it), just as our own soul becomes "lighted up" and shines with the interior instinct of the Holy Spirit (as long as it continues to move it). And light in the air makes it possible for us to see visible objects, just as the grace of the Holy Spirit makes us able to consider properly. But the sun's light can be prevented from lighting, and we will not see, if we close our shutters or eyes. And so, too, we will not act well by God's interior instinct if we impede it and resist it by our NON-ACT: our not using our intellect as we could and our not considering what we could when we need to consider. *God's light does not fail us; we fail it. We* SUBTRACT *ourselves* from God's good order,[90] "DE-ACTIVATING" it:[91] a neologism that Thomas invents to underline our own priority in causing sin.

88. See 1 *SN* 40, 4, 2, and ad 4, and 41, 1, 1 ad 2; his *Reportatio on Matthew*, 13, 1 and on *Second Corinthinans* 3, 3; *SCG* III, 150 (and especially III, 159); his *Commentary on the Divine Names* (4, 19); the *Catena Aurea* on John 1:9; *De Malo* 3, 1 ad 8; his *Commentary on the Liber de Causis* (chapters 23 and 24); *ST* I, 104, 1 and *ST* I-II, 79, 3; and throughout his late, great, *Commentary on John* (1:7, #121; 6:45, #943; 10, lect. 5, #4; and 12:7).

89. The variant of closing shutters to the light can be found both in Hilary, *Tractatis in CXVIII Psalmum* (Migne 9, page 578 C) and Ambrose's commentary on the same psalm, *In Psalmum CXVIII Expositio* (Migne 15, page 1364 D), probably following Hilary. Thomas no doubt gets it from Ambrose. (He quotes Ambrose's commentary on Psalm 118 in 3 *SN* 33, 2, 1, 1 d, obj. 4.)

90. Already in the 2 *SN* 34, 1, 2 Thomas had spoken of sin's cause as "*subtracting*" the will from the influx of divine goodness and causality "("ex ipsa perfectionis SUBTRACTIONE"), just as clouds *impede* the light of the sun ("*impediunt* lumen solis"). He is even more explicit in the *Summa Theologiae*: "voluntary agents have it in their power to *withdraw* themselves ("SUBDUCERE SE") from what is ordained [by God's providence]" (*ST* I, 17, 1) and thus "insofar as they are sinners, they are not, but *fall away* from being ("AB ESSE DEFICIUNT"), and this is not from God" (*ST* I, 20, 2 ad 4).

91. Aquinas, *De Malo* I, 3 ad 8: the defective agent of sin is corruptive by "DEAGENDO, id

There may also be a worry that this doctrine derogates from God's majesty, making not only His grace, but His holy will, subject to being impeded by the creature.[92] For (and it is a point Thomas himself notes) natural impediments derive from the *action* of other natures, *as these are moved by God,* whereas the DEFECT, or impediment, of *sin* derives from *ourselves,* and not God.[93] Again, however well-intentioned, this is a false worry. For it is *by God's very will* and intention that the free creature has the *possibility* of failing, of impeding His motion, and of sinning. God wisely intends (by His *absolute* will) to move it in a fallible way (which is why it is so moved). Second, He also possesses a *conditioned* will of the end towards which He moves the free creature; that is, He wills that the free creature prepare for sanctifying grace, *if* he does not impede or refuse that invitation. Third, God permits *sin* because He wills (absolutely) to *use* any sin for the good of the universe and His own glory, and thus His will is *finally* irresistible. Thus, whether or not a free creature impedes His motion, it acts *within* the possibilities of God's permissive will.[94] That will is not frustrated *in itself*—as Thomas expressly teaches when dealing with this issue[95]—but *in*

est per DEFECTUM *activae virtute*." In the *SCG* (III, 10), he had already said that the defective agent cause of sin DEFLECTS itself from the order of the first cause ("ab ordine primi agentis DEFLECTI").

92. Thus Jean-Hervé Nicolas, OP, in his "La permission du mal," *Revue Thomiste* 60 (1960): 5–37, 185–206, and 509–46: "the concept of a will that one can resist is taken from creatures. Who can deny that this concept implies an imperfection of will? . . . In relation to a definite objective, the possibility of resistance is an imperfection of will as such" (31). On the contrary, this does *not follow* if one *wills* that another have that *possibility of resistance,* as God does will (and as wise parents often will for their children).

93. When Thomas first develops his mature and complete solution to the problem of sin's cause, in the *SCG* III, 10 (a text that should be read line by line and word by word!), he says that, if the matter is "carefully considered" ("diligenter consideretur"), it will turn out that sin's cause is both similar, yet different, from the cause of natural evils. The two cases are alike in both having a defective cause. In the case of natural evils, Thomas usually cites a defective digestive organ causing indigestion or a broken bone causing a limp. But the difference between the two cases he goes on to develop is this: the material defect in the case of natural evils is itself *caused* by some other *agent*; that is, something first broke the leg or injured the digestive organ. Now, God is the cause of all such action and thus can be the *per accidens cause* of *this* privation. But that is exactly *not* what occurs in the case of *moral* evil (for any prior injury done to our faculties would diminish guilt, as in the mad or those overcome by pain); rather, *no* previous action is the cause of the will's defect *prior* to sin: this is *in no way* caused by God.

94. See Thomas's account of God's permissive will in *God's Permission,* 405–28 and 448–60.

95. See Thomas's first treatment of God's permission in 1 *SN* 47, 1, 2. The following text from *De Veritate* 23, 2 should be pondered line by line: "That to which God has *destined* the creature so far as He is concerned is said to be willed by Him in a *primary intention* or antecedent will. But when the creature is held back from this end *because of his own* FAILURE, God nonetheless

the creature: in effect, what a sinner frustrates and impedes most is his *own* good order and consequent happiness. God allows His *creature* to do this, *if it wills*.

IV. The Drama Concluded

And this brings me to my final point, and the full drama of man before God, as Thomas gives this to us. There might be what I will call a "Reformation worry" about the idea of "sufficient" grace, as though this made the creature somehow *self*-sufficient or no longer a sinner, or someone not in need of Christ's saving grace. This would be just the opposite of what Thomas teaches! The *term* of the sufficient grace that initially prepares our soul is the confession of our *insufficiency*. If we act with God's invitation and do not impede it, what we confess is our own indigence, not our sufficiency: we confess our sinfulness (and thus possess *servile fear*); we confess the inadequacy of our own truth (and thus our need to be guided by a divine *faith*); we confess our own inability to make ourselves right (and thus our need to *hope* in the mercy of God, in order to return to His good graces). Even if we prepare with the grace given, we can only be healed by a *further gift*: by the infusion of His Holy Spirit that makes us right again and justified before God. The "dynamic" of sufficient grace and the spiritual life it traces is just to let go of our false self, of our false order, and to open ourselves to the mystery and mercy of God.

Nor need anyone worry that this spiritual trajectory somehow changes when we are restored to His friendship through sanctifying grace. For we then stand, in relation to our *remaining* in God's grace, in just the same po-

---

fulfills in it that amount of goodness which it is capable. This pertains to His *secondary intention* and is called His consequent will. Because, then, God *has made all men for happiness*, He is said to will the salvation of all by His antecedent will. But because some work against their own salvation, and the order of His *wisdom* does not admit of their attaining salvation, in view of their FAILURE, He fulfills in them in another way the demands of His goodness, damning them out of justice. As a result, falling short of the first order of His will, they slip into the second. And, although they do not do God's will, *His will is fulfilled in them*. But the FAILURE constituting sin, by which a person is made deserving of punishment here and now or in the future *is not itself willed by God* with either an antecedent or a consequent will; it is merely permitted by Him. It should *not*, however, be concluded from what has just been said that God's *intention* can be *frustrated*, because from all *eternity* God has foreseen that the one who is not saved would not be saved. Nor did He ordain that particular one for salvation in the order of *predestination*, which is the order of His absolute will. But as far as He was concerned, He gave that creature a nature intended for happiness."

sition as one who awaits it as a first gift. For that we *die* in grace, and thus *finally* find our way to our Father's house, cannot be merited save by our final perseverance; and this can only be *impetrated* of God's mercy: we can only *pray* for this, again as a gift undeserved.[96] The dynamic of one in grace is given by the affirmation of the centurion ever on the lips of one who (in grace!) approaches the Eucharist: "Lord, I am not worthy to enter under your roof, but only say the word and my soul shall be healed" (Mt. 8:8; see also Lk. 7:1–10). This continued indigence, and the continual need of God's mercy of one *restored* to the grace of God, was likewise true of Adam and Eve in Paradise. The drama that those restored play out is the one that was played out long ago (and that was also played out by the angels at their own creation). There is, however, one great difference between Adam's state and our own: *we have seen the human face of God,* and we have known the depths of His mercy. Both Adam and Eve knew (as those restored to the state of grace know) that they could not merit dying in grace, and that they had to rely upon God's mercy. But those restored to grace through Christ, and knowing the depth of His Love, also know that He will bring them to Him—in His own time and according to His own will—if they do not turn from Him. Similarly, those who do not resist the vocation of the Spirit know that God will unfailingly, and by His own will and promise, give them the further gift of sanctifying grace. Thus there is a *depth* to the "certainty" of their hope—just in the grace, mercy, and love of God *made manifest* to them in Christ, and supremely when He opened His arms wide to *all* on the Cross (no matter *how* sinful, *how* desperate, *how* much at their "last gasp," as was the good thief)—that Adam and Eve did *not* possess. And it is just this difference—the greater mercy poured out and shown us fallen ones who so stand in need of it—that lies behind the good news Augustine joyfully trumpeted: the saints, by the grace of *Christ,* now persevere and return to the Father.

This drama of our vocation, as given to us by Thomas, has been increasingly underlined by the tradition of the Church since his day, so that Vatican II declared that *no one* is without this interior aid of the Spirit, operating in many hidden ways, and that *all* of us (indeed, all free creatures)

96. While one may merit a continuance in the state of grace by acting well with graces given, one cannot merit ending or persevering in grace (or, thus, continuing forever in the state of grace); one must always pray for the aid to do this and thus to have a "happy death." Thomas's doctrine here is neither controversial nor controverted: see *ST* I-II, 114, 3, 8, and also 9 and ad 1.

are part of this same drama. The drama is serious and the stakes are high: nothing less than our eternal destiny and the salvation or loss of our soul. As we would expect, the drama is finally a drama of love. When called by the Holy Spirit to a life with God, we are called to live according to a truth and a good that transcend our ken; we are called to "de-center" ourselves, to live for God, for one Unseen, and not for the good we can see: our own nature, our own truth, our own will. As a free and fallible creature, we *do* possess the ability to be as much "like God" as a creature can be; for we can indeed be the *first* cause of our *own* order: by our NOT doing what we could, by our NON-co-operation with the gracious invitation of God, we can introduce our own DEFECTIVE order into the world, and we can *commit* ourselves to that false order. We, as the fallen angels, can choose to commit ourselves to our false self.[97] We can make ourselves as *independent*, and as much "like God," as a creature can be, living as we do by our *own* order (no doubt one of the chief attractions of this choice). But the cost of this false choice is our own happiness, because we thereby freely choose to *subvert* our nature, which was made for friendship with God, and which can only be made happy by being in His presence.

The drama, then, that Aquinas presents for us is just the "ordinary" one preached from many a pulpit: we can close ourselves in on our own defective order, and love that most; or we can open ourselves to the mystery, the mercy, and the love of God, and place that first and before everything else. We can be "like God" and forever miserable; or we can be the servant of God, see Him "face to face," and be forever blessed. Should we in fact reach His blessed kingdom, we do so (whether we realized it and openly confessed it or not) only by the mercy of our Savior and by the vocation and infusion of His Holy Spirit, God's very own Love. This is the good news, and the drama, that "mere Christianity"[98] has ever preached; and this is likewise the doctrine of Thomas.

97. The fallen angel did this, *once and for all*; man does the same through *serial recommitments*. We can choose to harden ourselves to God's call to us, so that it could then seem "cruel," asking us, as it does, to give up our past choices: our own false order, which we increasingly identify as our true self.

98. C.S. Lewis, *Mere Christianity* (New York: Macmillan, 1952). Lewis rightly argued there is a "common core" to this preached drama: all Christians affirm that all those saved are so through the Incarnation of the Eternal Word and Wisdom of God and through His human life, death, and resurrection (as well, of course, as by His sending the Holy Spirit of Love to guide them to Him, and through Him to the Father).

NIKOLAJ ZUNIC

The Measure of Morality

I. Introduction

Morality rests on the fundamental distinction between good and evil. This distinction can be viewed either objectively or subjectively. The objective distinction between good and evil refers to the difference between the positive and the negative aspects in human behavior that has a basis in reality, in the nature of the thing. On this account, good and evil are ontologically or metaphysically distinct, not only logically or conceptually. The subjective distinction, by contrast, is located in a human being's power to discriminate between good and evil in the realm of human acts. Even given an objective distinction between good and evil, for morality to be efficacious and meaningful it is necessary that human beings recognize this distinction and can judge actions correctly in terms of their moral worth. In the absence of any distinction between good and evil, whether objective or subjective, morality would lose its proper identity as a source of value for human life and human actions. In such a context, morality would cease to exist as a rationally coherent notion.

The main argument that I wish to advance is that morality requires a measure that makes the distinction between good and evil possible. The concept of a measure is an interesting one, because it carries within it the connotations I have suggested regarding the subjective and objective distinctions of good and evil. On the one hand, a measure is a criterion or standard or norm according to which human acts are assessed with respect to their moral value. On the other hand, a measure is the judgment or assessment or evaluation that is carried out by the human subject in relation to the established norm; one measures the moral value of human acts in reference to a measure. A measure subsumes both objective and subjective aspects of morality under its guiding force and produces the basic structure of morality.

My paper is divided into two sections. In the first section, I sketch different ways in which the measure of morality has been conceived in Western philosophy. I selectively discuss different moral paradigms that have been used by various thinkers and also attempt to present the strengths and weaknesses of these approaches. Of particular concern in this presentation is the novelty of modernity, in which the very notion of a measure of morality is challenged and even discarded by a certain line of thinkers beginning with Nietzsche and culminating in his postmodern disciples, such as Heidegger and Foucault. The rise of secularism, political liberalism, and scientism have drastically altered our moral landscape, so much so that we are today faced with a pervasive nihilism in the domain of morality, an alarming development in Western and, indeed, human civilization.

The second section of the paper addresses Jacques Maritain's reflections on the essence of evil as the non-consideration of the rule. I connect Maritain's discussion of evil with his well-known doctrine of moral philosophy adequately considered. By doing this, I wish to argue that the true and absolute measure of morality is God, a claim that disputes the prevailing secularism and atheism of our age and that brings into sharp relief the relation between philosophy and theology, the natural and the supernatural domains. As an illustration of this relationship between human ethics and God's lordship over creation, I conclude my remarks by examining Maritain's views on the vocation of the people of Israel and the scourge of anti-Semitism.

II. In Search of a Measure

I would like to begin this reflection on the role of the measure in morality by quoting from the poem "In Lovely Blue" (*"In lieblicher Bläue"*) by the German poet Friedrich Hölderlin.

> But the gods,
> Ever kind in all things,
> Are rich in virtue and joy.
> Which man may imitate.
> May a man look up

From the utter hardship of his life
And say: Let me also be
Like these? Yes. As long as kindness lasts,
Pure, within his heart, he may gladly measure himself
Against the divine. Is God unknown?
Is he manifest as the sky? This I tend
To believe. Such is man's measure.
Well deserving, yet poetically
Man dwells on this earth. But the shadow
Of the starry night is no more pure, if I may say so,
Than man, said to be the image of God.
Is there measure on earth? There is
None.[1]

In these words, Hölderlin expresses his sentiment that the divine is the measure of the human, as has been the case from time immemorial. Throughout human history, the divine has consistently occupied a paradigmatic status in the human world, offering the normative hermeneutical framework for all things human. But in a world in which God is inscrutable and unknown, or when God's existence is questioned and denied, the human being searches for a different measure. To Hölderlin's question whether there is a measure on earth, the only possible answer is "No." Hölderlin believes that in the absence of God, the divine, no viable alternative can be found that could serve as a measure for humanity.

In his book *Is There a Measure on Earth?: Foundations for a Nonmetaphysical Ethics*, the noted German philosopher Werner Marx takes his lead from this question posed by Hölderlin.[2] Marx's chief concern is to attempt to ground ethics on a non-metaphysical basis with the help of the philosophy of Martin Heidegger, who is renowned for his so-called "destruction" or overcoming of traditional metaphysics and his development of a new foundation for being (*Sein*) in the existential analysis of the human being (*Dasein*). Marx agrees that the most important topic in morality is that of the measure, a topic that is more fundamental than the distinction between good and evil; but he disagrees with Hölderlin's assertion that there is no

1. Friedrich Hölderlin, *Hymns and Fragments*, translated by Richard Sieburth (Princeton: Princeton University Press, 1984), 249–51.

2. Werner Marx, *Is There a Measure on Earth?: Foundations for a Nonmetaphysical Ethics*, translated by Thomas J. Nenon and Reginald Lilly (Chicago: The University of Chicago Press, 1987).

measure to be found on earth independent of "heavenly beings."[3] Such an earthly measure would be a purely secular foundation for ethics, one that did not have any ties to a transcendent domain of meaning. What would such an earthly measure look like? This new beginning for ethics would be founded in human subjectivity. For Heidegger, the human being's authentic thinking of the truth of being opens up or clears the vista on to the basic experiences of human life, namely, anxiety and death. By considering the essential structure of human experience, which is universally shared, as the argument goes, a new foundation for morality can be discovered that is independent of metaphysics and theology.

Heidegger was certainly not the first thinker to attempt to ground morality in the human subject. In the fifth century B.C., the Greek Sophist Protagoras famously proclaimed in a fragment from his work *Truth*: "Man is the measure of all things, of the things that are that they are, and the things that are not that they are not."[4] This statement has been taken to represent a radical relativism, both epistemological and moral. Truth, according to Protagoras, is in the eye of the beholder, and different people arrive at different views about reality given their unique perspectives. This is because they perceive reality differently, and these various appearances will be determinative of the truth of reality that each individual affirms for himself. In short, appearance is reality. Regardless of whether one interprets Protagoras as defending a position of relativism or infallibilism, the point that he drives home is that truth is a form of belief and each individual's beliefs constitute the truth for that individual, a position that excludes any absolute and universal truths.

Plato famously attacked this Protagorean doctrine of measure in the *Theaetetus*.[5] In this dialogue, Socrates aims to show that Protagoras's relativism is self-refuting. He does this by arguing that the claim that nobody can be wrong or in error with respect to their beliefs conflicts with the re-

3. Ibid., 1: ". . . I do not believe that the concepts of 'good' and 'evil' are the 'ultimate' determinants of ethics; the ultimate determinant is rather the concept of 'measure.'" The thinking here is that the possibility of distinguishing between good and evil rests upon some criterion or measure without which there would be no distinction. Hence, the concept of the measure is more basic or rudimentary than the concepts of good and evil in the domain of morality.

4. W. K. C. Guthrie, *The Sophists* (Cambridge: Cambridge University Press, 1971), 183. As Guthrie elaborates, Protagoras's word for measure, *metron*, was interpreted by Plato as meaning *kriterion*, standard of judgment.

5. Plato, *Theaetetus*, in *The Collected Dialogues of Plato*, edited by Edith Hamilton and Huntington Cairns (Princeton: Princeton University Press, 1961), 847–919.

ality that people have different and even diametrically opposed beliefs.[6] Not everyone can be right, for such a situation would violate the principle of non-contradiction: belief A cancels out belief not-A and vice versa. If not everyone can be right, then some must be wrong; and the reason why some beliefs are false is that there is objective truth. Put otherwise, without the premise that truth objectively exists, a situation of incoherence and irrationality arises, one in which all opinions are true, even those that contradict each other.

Plato waged an assiduous campaign against the Sophist rejection of the existence of objective truth. The affirmation of truth, encapsulated in the Theory of Forms, is the necessary pre-condition for all rational inquiry, indeed, for the validity of rationality itself.[7] But what is arguably even more important is the Good, which Plato famously placed above the Forms in Book 6 of the *Republic.* As Plato writes on this point: "you are to say that the objects of knowledge not only receive from the presence of the good their being known but their very existence and essence is derived to them from it, though the good itself is not essence but still transcends essence in dignity and surpassing power."[8] The Good is the cause of knowledge and truth and yet transcends this epistemic domain. It is more foundational than truth, because it lies at the heart of truth and gives truth its being. In this sense, we can infer why Plato believed that rationality and morality belong together and mutually reinforce each other. To be rational is to be moral, and contrariwise, morality implies rationality. The doctrine of the *Meno,* that "virtue is knowledge," rings true in this regard. Plato, however, was adamant that we cannot ever fully know what the Good is because of its transcendent nature. Although it lies at the basis of reason, knowledge and morality, it escapes full comprehension. This explains why the Platonic

6. Ibid., 876, 170c-171a: "SOCRATES: In that case, Protagoras, what are we to make of your doctrine? Are we to say that what men think is always true, or that it is sometimes true and sometimes false? From either supposition it results that their thoughts are not always true, but both true and false. For consider, Theodorus. Are you, or is any Protagorean, prepared to maintain that no one regards anyone else as ignorant or as making false judgments? THEODORUS: That is incredible, Socrates. SOCRATES: That, however, is the inevitable consequence of the doctrine which makes man the measure of all things.... Protagoras, for his part, admitting as he does that everybody's opinion is true, must acknowledge the truth of his opponents' belief about his own belief, where they think he is wrong."

7. See Alasdair MacIntyre, *Whose Justice? Which Rationality?* (Notre Dame, Indiana: University of Notre Dame Press, 1988), 69–87.

8. Plato, *Republic*, in *The Collected Dialogues of Plato*, 744, 509b.

dialogues typically end in *aporias*, that is, inconclusive endings. It must be remembered that Socrates does not teach, but merely prods and questions.

The moral realism that Plato advances in opposition to the relativism of the Sophists becomes the template for all philosophies that strive to defend a moral absolutist or objectivist view. Christian philosophers of the Middle Ages no longer saw the ultimate moral reality in terms of an impersonal Good and instead defended the doctrine of the absolute goodness of God, the ground and source of everything Good. The measure of morality for the medieval tradition is the divine essence, which is thoroughly and absolutely good and does not admit of any evil.[9] But thinkers like Aquinas also recognized that there is additionally a natural foundation for morality, something that non-Christians could also grasp. This is the theory of natural law, which maintains that moral truth is determined by the immutable constitution of human nature. The natural law is accessible to human reason, whereas the divine essence is known on the basis of faith. Morality comes to be construed in the High Middle Ages as incorporating both philosophical and theological elements. The highpoint of this development was the ethical system of Thomas Aquinas and his proposal of two kinds of virtue, the cardinal and theological virtues, the former dealing with those virtues that can be acquired through natural talents and the latter emphasizing the role that divine grace has in elevating human excellence to a supernatural level.[10]

Towards the end of the Middle Ages and the beginning of the modern period, new challenges were posed for morality as well as a fundamental questioning of morality's measure. The impressive progress in the natural sciences and the increasing secularization of society produced a context in

9. An excellent treatment of the place of God in human morality can be found in Rémi Brague, *The Law of God: The Philosophical History of an Idea*, translated by Lydia G. Cochrane (Chicago: The University of Chicago Press, 2007).

10. One could argue that the distinctive feature of a theological ethics is precisely the role of divine grace in human morality. Louis Dupré has emphasized the central role that grace has played in the transformations in culture and morality that occasioned the modern Enlightenment. By rejecting divine grace as a necessary ingredient in human ethical conduct, Enlightenment thinkers were able to establish a novel ethical system that anchored moral goodness in human rationality and autonomy, as can be seen in the thought of Immanuel Kant, which eschews any reliance upon heteronomous sources of moral insight. See Dupré's *Passage to Modernity: An Essay in the Hermeneutics of Nature and Culture* (New Haven: Yale University Press, 1993), *The Enlightenment and the Intellectual Foundations of Modern Culture* (New Haven: Yale University Press, 2004), and *Religion and the Rise of Modern Culture* (Notre Dame, Indiana: University of Notre Dame Press, 2008), especially 17–28.

which God was no longer deemed to be the foundation of morality. Furthermore, as political society sought greater freedom and rights, the notion of natural law gradually lost its appeal. Jeremy Bentham, for instance, as a founder of utilitarianism, a thoroughly relativistic moral system,[11] disparaged natural law, calling it a hopelessly unworkable view of morality.[12]

Immanuel Kant, sensitive to the deep changes overtaking Western civilization, sought to rediscover a solid and stable foundation for morality against the seemingly unstoppable withering away of moral absolutes. His solution was to ground morality in human reason. The fact of reason (*das Faktum der Vernunft*), as he boldly puts it in his *Critique of Practical Reason*, is the true basis of morality because reason is able to formulate the essence of moral truth in its binding universality, expressed in a categorical imperative.[13] At the core of this rational foundation of morality lies the doctrine of the moral law. Morality, for Kant, consists in the adoption of maxims that conform to the moral law. Autonomy or self-determining freedom, it

11. The moral relativism of utilitarianism derives from the principle that human acts are judged morally from the point of view of the consequences that they produce. Specific acts are neither good nor bad inherently, but become so in light of the results that ensue. In this way, the same acts can be good in one context, but bad in another context. The morality of human acts, to be clear, must be determined relative to the contexts and consequences of those acts.

12. In an essay originally published as "Anarchical Fallacies," Bentham mocks the notion of natural rights. See Jeremy Bentham, "Nonsense upon Stilts," in *Selected Writings*, edited by Stephen G. Engelmann (New Haven: Yale University Press, 2011), 328: "Natural rights is simple nonsense: natural and imprescriptible rights, rhetorical nonsense, nonsense upon stilts." Bentham believes that theories of natural law, i.e., the Law of Nature, are ultimately reducible to what he terms the principle of sympathy and antipathy. This means that when someone calls a certain human action unnatural or contrary to the natural law he is simply expressing his personal feelings or distaste of the matter, and conversely, if he were to approve of a certain act, this is nothing more than an expression of personal preference. What is lacking in the theory of natural law, according to Bentham, is an external standard by which acts could be objectively judged to be either good or bad. See Jeremy Bentham, *An Introduction to the Principles of Morals and Legislation*, edited by J. H. Burns and H. L. A. Hart (Oxford: Clarendon Press, 1996), 27: "A great multitude of people are continually talking of the Law of Nature; and then they go on giving you their sentiments about what is right and what is wrong; and these sentiments, you are to understand, are so many chapters and sections of the Law of Nature."

13. Immanuel Kant, *Critique of Practical Reason*, translated by Mary Gregor (Cambridge: Cambridge University Press, 1997), 28: "For, pure reason, *practical of itself*, is here immediately lawgiving. The will is thought as independent of empirical conditions and hence, as a pure will, as determined *by the mere form of law*, and this determining ground is regarded as the supreme condition of all maxims.... Consciousness of this fundamental law may be called a fact of reason because one cannot reason it out from antecedent data of reason, for example, from consciousness of freedom (since this is not antecedently given to us) and because it instead forces itself upon us of itself as a synthetic a priori proposition that is not based on any intuition, either pure or empirical, although it would be analytic if the freedom of the will were presupposed...."

must be said, does not create moral truth; human freedom is supposed to obey the moral law that is given in advance of any act that humans may perform. As admirable as Kant's doctrine of the moral law may be, it is mired in immense difficulties. Kant never sufficiently explains what this moral law is and where it comes from. It seems to linger in reason as some feature of human rationality, but it is also something that pervades the whole moral tenor of life as a kind of feeling or sentiment. In the end, Kant's doctrine of the moral law is much too vague to be accepted as an absolute foundation for morality, especially for an audience that has lost confidence in the powers of reason to uncover moral truth.[14]

The demise of the measure in morality reaches an unprecedented level in the philosophy of Friedrich Nietzsche, whose virulent skepticism seeks to undermine the foundation of morality. In his book *On the Genealogy of Morality*, Nietzsche rejects what seemed to be the enduring distinction between good and evil, describing it as a Christian invention, one produced by a slave morality, and aims to supplant it with the master morality's paradigm of strength, power and cruelty, which results in an alternate distinction of good and bad.[15] The naturalism and nihilism of Nietzsche's view of morality are so complete that the final vision he proposes for human life is unspeakably inhumane—chaotic, oppressive, and violent.[16] With the

14. Kant writes in *Critique of Practical Reason* that "[p]ure reason is practical of itself alone and gives (to the human being) a universal law which we call the *moral law*" (29). The suggestion is that reason is not exactly identical with the moral law, but is that which posits the moral law. Kant goes on to explain that the moral law is "laid down as a principle of the deduction of freedom as a causality of pure reason" (42), emphasizing the a priori status of the moral law as something that is not deducible from reason itself. The moral law also inculcates feelings: "Hence we can see a priori that the moral law, as the determining ground of the will, must by thwarting all our inclinations produce a feeling that can be called pain.... Consequently, respect for the moral law is a feeling that is produced by an intellectual ground, and this feeling is the only one that we can cognize completely a priori and the necessity of which we can have insight into" (63–64). Kant summarizes these various points as follows: "Thus the moral law, since it is a formal determining ground of action through practical pure reason and since it is also a material but only objective determining ground of the objects of action under the name of good and evil, is also a subjective determining ground—that is, an incentive—to this action inasmuch as it has influence on the sensibility of the subject and effects a feeling conducive to the influence of the law upon the will" (65).

15. Friedrich Nietzsche, *On the Genealogy of Morality*, translated by Maudemarie Clark and Alan J. Swensen (Indianapolis: Hackett Publishing Company, Inc., 1998).

16. See Friedrich Nietzsche, *The Will to Power*, translated by Walter Kaufmann and R. J. Hollingdale (New York: Vintage Books, 1967), 458–59: "A declaration of war on the masses by *higher men* is needed!... A doctrine is needed powerful enough to work as a breeding agent: strengthening the strong, paralyzing and destructive for the world-weary! The annihilation of

proclamation of the death of God, Nietzsche ushers in a new paradigm for morality that is completely rooted in human subjectivity, or, as Nietzsche expresses it, the will-to-power. In fact, Nietzsche even rejects the notion of morality *per se*. Rationality is debunked as deceptive, tricking humans into making the false distinctions of good and evil. All we are left with in the aftermath of Nietzsche is a profound emptiness, since there are no measures left to offer moral guidance in human morality. Reason and God are discarded in favor of competition, struggle, and war.

Nonetheless, Nietzsche's philosophy is highly instructive. He demonstrates the logical outcome of human beings' rejection of absolute foundations in ethics. Without reason and the immutable divine essence as measures of morality, the human being turns within himself and seeks to ground moral rightness and wrongness in subjective opinion, what *appears* to be right and wrong, rather than what *is* right and wrong. This relativism, however, ineluctably slides into nihilism and the annihilation of morality itself. Morality becomes meaningless in a universe where there are no absolute measures.

We live in a world where the very distinction between good and evil is in question. Not only do many people not recognize any firm and stable foundation for morality, due largely to a pervasive secularism and skepticism as well as to a lack of confidence in the power of reason to discover truth, but they are also unable to discriminate properly between good and evil in human behavior. This relativism produces a fundamental confusion of good and evil, a grave problem highlighted, for instance, in Pope John Paul II's two encyclicals devoted to moral issues, *The Splendor of Truth* (*Veritatis Splendor*) and *The Gospel of Life* (*Evangelium Vitae*).[17] If we are unable to judge correctly between morally good and morally bad acts, we are truly lost at sea. This confusion of good and evil carries enormous consequences. Not only does it interfere with the fulfillment of our nature and the attainment of our ultimate end in life, but it also leads to the immoral

---

the decaying races. Decay of Europe.—The annihilation of slavish evaluations.—Dominion over the earth as a means of producing a higher type.—The annihilation of the tartuffery called 'morality' (Christianity as a hysterical kind of honesty in this: Augustine, Bunyan)."

17. See Pope John Paul II, *The Gospel of Life* (Boston: Pauline Books & Media, 1995), 44: "The moral conscience, both individual and social, is today subjected, also as a result of the penetrating influence of the media, to an *extremely serious and mortal danger*: that of *confusion between good and evil*, precisely in relation to the fundamental right to life.... When conscience, this bright lamp of the soul..., calls "evil good and good evil"..., it is already on the path to the most alarming corruption and the darkest moral blindness."

treatment of human beings, as in the objectification of persons in scientific experiments and the devaluation of life in abortion and euthanasia. Relativism, as I have attempted to show, easily slips into nihilism, the destruction of moral value as such.

III. The Absolute Measure of Morality in Maritain's Thought

Jacques Maritain's most sustained examination of the problem of evil can be found in two of his works: *St. Thomas and the Problem of Evil* and *God and the Permission of Evil.*[18] His guide in these reflections is Thomas Aquinas, who holds that morality is given its measure in the two poles of human reason and divine law. God is the absolute goodness who serves as the criterion of the distinction between good and evil. Evil is produced when the human being acts in contravention of God's goodness. Aquinas describes the cause of evil as the non-consideration of the rule, the rule being reason and divine law. By not considering the rule of natural law and divine goodness, the human being freely ignores the precepts of morality when he acts and in this way causes evil. However, Maritain delves deeper into this non-consideration of the rule, which he analyzes in relation to the concept of human freedom.

Evil is the product of human freedom. It is not necessitated by any series of material causes, nor does it originate with God, who is pure goodness.[19] It is freely executed; there is no coercion or necessitation involved

18. Jacques Maritain, *St. Thomas and the Problem of Evil* (Milwaukee: Marquette University Press, 1942); *God and the Permission of Evil,* translated by Joseph W. Evans (Milwaukee: The Bruce Publishing Company, 1966).

19. See Thomas Aquinas, *Introduction to Saint Thomas Aquinas,* edited by Anton C. Pegis (New York: The Modern Library, 1948), *Summa Theologiae* (hereafter cited as *ST*) I, q. 6, a. 3, 49–50: "... God alone is good essentially. For everything is called good according to its perfection. Now perfection in a thing is threefold: first, according to the constitution of its own being; secondly, in respect of any accidents being added as necessary for its perfect operation; thirdly, perfection consists in the attaining to something else as the end. Thus, for instance, the first perfection of fire consists in its being, which it has through its own substantial form; its secondary perfection consists in heat, lightness and dryness, and the like; its third perfection is to rest in its own place. This triple perfection belongs to no creature by its own essence; it belongs to God only, Whose essence alone is His being, in Whom there are no accidents, since whatever belongs to others accidentally belongs to Him essentially: e.g., to be powerful, wise, and the like, as appears from what is stated above. Furthermore, He is not directed to anything else as to an end, but is Himself the last end of all things. Hence it is manifest that God alone has every kind of perfection by His own essence, and therefore He alone is good essentially."

in the human being's commission of evil. The main philosophical problem dealing with evil, therefore, becomes how human freedom could be led to choose evil rather than good. Why would the human being forsake divine goodness and freely opt to cause evil in his acts? The answer is found in the nature of freedom itself. Maritain explains that human freedom can be defective, and it is this defect of freedom that brings about evil. How should this defect of freedom be understood?

Neo-Platonism was the inspiration behind the doctrine propounded by thinkers such as St. Augustine that evil is a privation or absence of the good. Evil is not a real substance, as is a tree, stone, or animal. Rather, it is the void occasioned in the domain of human agency when the good that is supposed to occur does not. In this sense, evil is always measured against the good and is interpreted as the absence of the good, a good that is supposed to appear but is not realized. Maritain develops this theme in his reflections on evil by examining the nature of human freedom, which is the efficient cause of evil. As Aquinas explains, freedom is nothing other than free choice, the ability to decide between alternatives.[20] As such, free choice belongs to the act of will, the rational appetite of the soul.

Perfect freedom is realized only in unity with truth. The notion that freedom is simply the ability to choose, the implication being that it is an ability to choose *anything*, is alien to Aquinas. Choosing evil, for instance, over the good, is not the perfect realization of freedom but rather its tragic misuse and diminution. By its nature the will, as a rational appetite, is ordained to the good, and for us the highest good is happiness. There is thus a certain necessity involved in human willing. One does not choose one's ultimate end, that is, the highest good; but one can choose the means that one uses to achieve one's happiness. If the human being knew perfectly his or her ultimate good, then one's choices would tend only in one direction—towards the good. Human beings, however, are not naturally capable of knowing the good in itself. From a metaphysical perspective, this condition is due to human nature not being absolutely or perfectly good. Only God, the first cause of being, is perfectly good, indeed, is goodness itself. As creatures, human beings are derivatively good, and this imperfection defines our relation with the good. Put in different terms, since we are only imperfectly good, we do not have a complete and perfect understanding of good.

20. See *ST* I, q. 83, aa. 1–4.

Both Aquinas and Maritain describe this metaphysical imperfection of human nature as a deficiency or defect.[21] Something is lacking in human nature: a proper grasp of the good. Maritain develops this notion of the deficiency of human nature by explaining that human freedom is constituted by two moments or dimensions. The first moment is the original state of the will prior to any decisions or actions being taken. In this original position, the will is not determined by anything, and as such it resides in an unfettered state. It could be said that the will is free in this original state, that is, "free" in the modern sense of non-interference by external influences, free from reason and divine law. The will's detachment from all influences allows it to dwell in a situation that Maritain describes as "nothingness."[22] If the will is isolated from reason, truth, the good, and even God, that is, all that is real, then it is correct to say that the will is in a condition of nothingness. Since the will is an appetite or inclination and is at the basis of all acts, this nothingness is produced by the will as an effect of its appetitive structure.

In this original moment of nothingness, the will chooses neither good nor evil because it is undisturbed by all external influences. In fact, the will cannot choose anything, because all choice requires rational insight, namely, an object conceived by the mind that is desired and thus pursued; and, in the absence of rational understanding, the will is impotent to execute such a decision. In the second moment of human volition, reason enters the scene and exercises a determinative influence on the will. Now the will can be guided by a vision of its object of desire. In this second stage, the will leaves the tranquility of its original position and manifests itself in the world through decision and act. Due to its dyadic structure, human volition is not necessarily ordained towards the good but is open to choose whatever it will. It is precisely due to the existence of this original initiative of absence and nothingness that the will is not necessarily focused on the good, but is able to choose evil as a possible volition. By not being coerced

21. For a more detailed account of Maritain's understanding of evil, see my article "Maritain on Human Fellowship and the Evil of Genocide," *Maritain Studies* 21 (2005), 97–121, at 105–09.

22. Jacques Maritain, *St. Thomas and the Problem of Evil*, 31: "Well then, the first moment, and this is what is so extremely important especially for the problems touching upon the connection between uncreated freedom and created freedom,—the first moment is voluntary, it is free, and it is not yet sin but the root of sin; it is a certain nothingness, the nothingness of the consideration of the rule, it is a certain nothingness introduced by the creature at the start of his action; it is a mere absence, a mere nothingness, but it is the root proper of evil action."

either way, the will, once it appears in the world, can forsake the dictates of rational truth and divine goodness and choose in defiance of these measures of morality.

Reason and divine law are described as the rules of moral human conduct. They lead the will to the proper good. To ignore or reject these rules is to unleash the will into a situation where there is no longer any normative framework for right conduct. Since perfect goodness is nothing other than God himself, to act in the world not being mindful of God is the prime recipe for evil to arise. Evil, in this sense, is defined as the non-consideration of the rule. If one acts through one's choices and decisions and does not consider the rules of proper moral goodness, namely, reason and divine law, then one's actions will veer away from the good and into the domain of evil. What this Thomistic account of human volition and the nature of evil brings out is that human beings are not unconditionally good, a reality that places us in a dependent relation with the good or the source of goodness, this being God, for our actions to be able to achieve goodness. This rational consideration of the good is a requirement for proper moral conduct. Only by being mindful of God's goodness can we execute morally good acts.

In an increasingly secular and pluralistic society, the claim that God serves as the measure of morality can seem hard for many to accept. Such a claim bears the unmistakable marks of theology and religion, which are arenas of life far too sectarian and parochial to gain universal assent as the ground of morality. This reluctance to entertain a divine order within morality may explain why the reality of evil appears so mysterious and inexplicable to a naturalistic or materialistic worldview. Without the presupposition of divine goodness, other hermeneutical paradigms and frameworks are sought to explain evil, such as in the natural and social sciences. Consequently, evil is understood, for example, as a form of social injustice or a mental illness or physical suffering or a disease.[23] Even worse, in the con-

23. For some examples of such various theorizings about the nature and causes of evil, see the following works: Terry D. Cooper, *Dimensions of Evil: Contemporary Perspectives* (Minneapolis: Fortress Press, 2007); Ervin Staub, "The Roots of Evil: Social Conditions, Culture, Personality, and Basic Human Needs," *Personality and Social Psychology Review* 3 (1999), 179–92; James Waller, *Becoming Evil: How Ordinary People Commit Genocide and Mass Killing* (Oxford: Oxford University Press, 2007); John Kekes, *The Roots of Evil* (Ithaca: Cornell University Press, 2005); Nel Noddings, *Women and Evil* (Berkeley: University of California Press, 1989); Kathleen E. Taylor, *Cruelty: Human Evil and the Human Brain* (Oxford: Oxford University Press, 2009); Arthur G. Miller, editor, *The Social Psychology of Good and Evil* (New York: The Guildford Press, 2004); Steven James Bartlett, *The Pathology of Man: A Study of Human Evil* (Springfield, Illinois: Charles C. Thomas, Publisher, Ltd., 2005).

text of moral relativism and the absence of all absolutes, evil becomes an insuperable puzzle. There is no way to differentiate good and evil from the perspective of strict moral relativism. There is no doubt that moral relativism obliterates the notion of morality as such.

In the practical sphere of morality, as opposed to speculative philosophy or metaphysics, moral philosophy necessarily avails itself of theological truths. Maritain emphasizes that theology is not only relevant, but even indispensable, to a proper understanding of human morality. This is because in the domain of morality we are dealing with the complete human being—mind, body and soul—who seeks to attain his ultimate end, which is located in the Supreme Good of God's being. Morality contains both natural and supernatural elements, requiring the cooperation of philosophy and theology. This is Maritain's well-known doctrine of *moral philosophy adequately considered*.[24] Moral philosophy is subalternated to theology; that is, morality can only function properly if it adopts or borrows the principles operative in theology. The final end of human life lies not in this temporal life, but in the life after death, when the human person enjoys forever the vision of the divine essence.

This view of the ultimate foundation of morality as residing in God is also defended by Josef Pieper in his book *The Concept of Sin*. He argues that moral judgments contain absolutes that point to the real and absolute being of God. For example, whenever we condemn an injustice by asserting that such acts violate fundamental moral principles, in this judgment we are appealing to an unconditional ground of justice that can only be God. As Pieper writes:

> Of course, reason can only possess this power to obligate a person if, in the act of knowledge itself, somehow a kind of participation in the divine Logos is taking place and if the interior word-character of things by which we are cognitively oriented to them simultaneously points to the creative aboriginal Word [*Ur-Wort*] of God himself.[25]

For Pieper, it is the nature of moral absolutes, such as the distinction between good and evil, to refer to an absolute ground that is the source of the absolutes themselves.[26] When human intelligence is able to discriminate

24. Jacques Maritain, *An Essay on Christian Philosophy*, translated by Edward H. Flannery (New York: Philosophical Library, 1955), 38–43.

25. Josef Pieper, *The Concept of Sin*, translated by Edward T. Oakes (South Bend, Indiana: St. Augustine's Press, 2001), 46.

26. See Josef Pieper, *The Four Cardinal Virtues* (Notre Dame, Indiana: University of Notre

between good and evil in moral judgment, it partakes in a higher ground of authority in the divine essence. This argument suggests that moral absolutes by their nature invoke or imply God, who is the Ultimate Absolute.[27] Naturally, this standpoint implies that the rejection of God as the measure of morality entails the erosion and disappearance of moral absolutes.

Maritain's conviction that God is the measure of morality is further illustrated with the example of anti-Semitism. Maritain wrote widely about the identity of the Jews and their meaning for humankind, but none of his works is more important than his little-known book *Antisemitism*, published in 1939.[28] Here, Maritain succinctly expounds his view that anti-Semitism is a scourge against humanity itself, that there is something truly anti-human operating at the basis of this form of evil. The key insight Maritain expresses is that at its core anti-Semitism is not a political or ethnic or racial phenomenon, as if the discrimination and violence against the Jews in Europe in the 1930's and beyond could be remedied by changes to the political and legal structures. Rather, underneath the propaganda and violence of anti-Semitism lies a hidden essence, a tacit and virtually undetected meaning of anti-Semitism that is its root cause. The problem of anti-Semitism is precisely that it is motivated by a complete rejection of God in human society.

To understand this thesis more clearly, it is necessary to take into consideration the Jews' self-understanding as a chosen people of God. According to Revelation, as expressed in the Bible and the living traditions of Judaism, the Jews occupy a special place in human history as the people entrusted with the mandate to reveal God's purposes for humankind. God has chosen the Jews to be an instrument of his self-revelation. Being called by God to this task bestows upon the Jewish nation a particular identity, one that is transcendent to this world, but one that is simultaneously in

---

Dame Press, 1966), 9: "Reason 'perfected in the cognition of truth' is therefore the receptivity of the human spirit, to which the revelation of reality, both natural and supernatural reality, has given substance."

27. See John Finnis, *Moral Absolutes: Tradition, Revision, and Truth* (Washington, D.C.: The Catholic University of America Press, 1991), 30: "To affirm that Bentham, Mill, Marx, and, in his different way, Machiavelli were right in their rejection of the moral absolutes, and that the whole People of God was wrong until yesterday in accepting them as truths integral to salvation (ultimate and integral human fulfillment itself), and that the church's magisterium is wrong in proclaiming their truth to this day, is to take a long step toward denying that God has revealed anything to a people, or ever constituted a people of God at all."

28. Jacques Maritain, *Antisemitism* (London: Geoffrey Bles, 1939).

the world. To be a Jew is tantamount to being in a special relationship with God, to being sent by God on a mission to reveal God's personhood to the world. From this perspective, the Jews are a people with a supernatural vocation and a transworldly identity, something that cannot be expunged from their existence and that they live out in a tangible manner by living in the world.[29] They are, in short, God's people.

The hatred that was directed toward the Jews in Europe in the 1930's, largely at the hands of Hitler's Germany, as evidenced, for example, in the Nuremberg Laws of 1935, took on many forms and justifications. The Jews were labeled variously, from greedy entrepreneurs, to lewd and lascivious artists, to manipulative power mongers, and so on. There have been and continue to be many notions invented and promoted about the Jews and the harm that they bring to human society. However, the common thread tying together all these negative attitudes towards the Jews is a crude materialistic worldview. One's identity is reduced to one's bodily or biological existence, a standpoint that spawned the radical racist ideologies of the Third Reich. Since the Jews represented a distinct group of people, their distinctive character was understood along racial lines, in terms of their "blood" and biological ancestry, rather than in terms of their spiritual essence, that is, as a people of God. Maritain is highly critical of this sort of racism. He rejects the notion that human beings can be parceled out into groups based on "race," for there is no such thing as a pure race or a people that has preserved its biological race in its purity, supposing that such a concept is even coherent.[30]

At its core, anti-Semitism is anchored in a materialistic and ultimately atheistic doctrine of life. It rests upon a rejection of a higher order or supernatural domain of meaning in God. But Maritain goes one step further and

29. Ibid., 19–20: "But what, then, is that vocation of Israel which persists in darkness, and of which we were just speaking? First of all, there is its vocation as a witness to the Scriptures. But more, while the Church is assigned the labour of supernatural and supratemporal redemption of the world, Israel, we believe, is assigned, on the plane and within the limits of secular history, a task of *earthly activisation* of the mass of the world. Israel, which is not of the world, is to be found at the very heart of the world's structure, stimulating it, exasperating it, moving it. Like an alien body, like an activating leaven injected into the mass, it gives the world no peace, it bars slumber, it teaches the world to be discontented and restless as long as the world has not God; it stimulates the movement of history."

30. Ibid., 13: "The truth is that the Jews are not a race in the biological sense of the word. We know that in man's present stage of development there is no group of any importance, even that most favoured in this respect, which is pure in race."

describes the heart of anti-Semitism as a form of hubris. The anti-Semite believes that he does not need anything beyond himself to flourish and prosper, that he can achieve his goals in life all on his own. This element of extreme self-reliance is punctuated by Maritain in the following pregnant passage:

> Thus hatred of Jews and hatred of Christians spring from a common source, from the same recalcitrance of the world, which desires to be wounded neither with the wounds of Adam nor with the wounds of the Savior, neither by the goad of Israel for its movement in time, nor by the cross of Jesus for eternal life. We are good enough as we are, says the world, we have no need of grace or transfiguration, we ourselves will accomplish our own happiness in our own nature. This is neither Christian hope in a helping God, nor Jewish hope of a God on earth. It is the hope of animal life and its power, deep and, in a sense, sacred, demonic, when it masters the human being who thinks himself deceived by the emissaries of the absolute.[31]

When the world has become impervious to things divine, when it has lost its sense of transcendence, when it is no longer tied to a supernatural source of meaning, that is when the evil of hatred and violence perpetrated by man against man rears its head. Maritain considers anti-Semitism as symptomatic of the general phenomenon of the enmity and discord that afflicts humankind. Whenever there is division among human beings, instead of fraternal unity, the cause can usually be traced to the disappearance of a mindfulness of God's presence on earth.

The human being is made in the image of God and possesses an immaterial, spiritual essence. When hatred is directed against a human being, it is due to the spiritual center of the person being disregarded in preference for a materialistic ideological standpoint. The purpose of Maritain's treatment of anti-Semitism is to present a specific understanding of evil as a violation of the truth of the human spirit and the rejection of God's primacy in moral matters. The only recourse for overcoming anti-Semitism and thereby of building up a more loving world, where humans live together in harmony, is to change the tenor of the human heart. Only by a transformation of the human spirit will the evil that separates human beings from each other be defeated.

> There remains for all of us, Jews and Christians, to turn toward the invisible powers residing in the heart of man, toward the springs of history which lie within ourselves, in order to purify those springs. If we but realize to what point external

31. Ibid., 20–21.

events and the forms of things depend on the invisible images which our free wills delineate within us, we would have more confidence in spiritual means. At the same time, we would give up fighting hatred with hatred. We would understand what has been so often affirmed by Gandhi, the real power, even over political and social realities, of love and truth.[32]

IV. Conclusion

I have tried to argue two things: first, that morality requires a measure, *a fortiori*, an absolute measure, in order for the distinction between good and evil to be viable, and second, that God must be regarded as the absolute measure of morality. By availing myself of Maritain's doctrine of moral philosophy adequately considered and his reflections on the evil of anti-Semitism and the divine vocation of the Jewish people, I hope to have shed some light on the validity of the claim that God lies at the very heart of the moral life of human beings. To return, then, to our earlier point, if Hölderlin raises the question: "Is there a measure on earth?" we would have to join him in replying: "There is none." A purely naturalistic foundation of morality does not exist; the only final source of moral insight and judgment is God.

32. Ibid., 53–54.

≈ IV ≈

EVIDENCE, PROBABILITY, AND PRUDENCE

ERIC MANCHESTER

Creation and the Probability (But Not Necessity) of Evil

At first glance, Jacques Maritain's contention in *St. Thomas and the Problem of Evil* (6),[1] derived St. Thomas Aquinas's *ST* I, q. 48, a. 2, that the "Perfection of the universe requires ... that there be some beings who can fall from goodness; and if there are beings who can fall from goodness, the result will be that such defection will in fact sometimes occur in those beings" seems clearly false. Certainly, one can conceive of a logically possible world entailing creaturely freedom (a "free world") where evil actions were genuinely possible but never in fact occurred. In fact, some would assert that an omnibenevolent, omnipotent, and omniscient God would choose to create such a world rather than one such as ours, in which evil was presumably foreknown by God.[2] Consequently, the occurrence of evil is often taken as evidence against the existence of God, or at least one who is omnipotent, omniscient, and omnibenevolent.

Despite first appearances, however, Maritain's contention that insofar as moral evil is possible, it will in fact occur, need not be interpreted as denying the *logical* possibility of a free world remaining permanently evil-free.[3]

1. This work was originally published as the 1942 Aquinas Lecture, sponsored by the Aristotelian Society of Marquette University (Milwaukee, Wisconsin: Marquette University Press, 1942). References to this work, as well as to primary sources from St. Thomas, will be cited internally (with the *Summa Theologiae* cited as *ST*). All other citations will be provided as footnotes.

2. Strictly speaking, because God transcends time, His knowledge of our future is for Him simply "knowledge" rather than "foreknowledge." I retain this term, however, as it is commonplace in discussions regarding God's knowledge of what temporal creatures have not yet experienced in time.

3. Natural evils that afflict human beings will not be considered here, although I assume the

Neither Maritain nor St. Thomas claims that moral evil is "logically necessary" or absolutely unavoidable. Instead, Maritain makes the more ambiguous claim that where "it is in the nature of things that evil can happen, this event will actually happen sometimes" (6), further citing St. Thomas's remark that where things "can be lacking in good, [they] consequently sometimes do lack good" (7, from *ST* I, q. 48, a. 2). Simply stating as a matter of fact that something *will* happen is not logically equivalent to saying that it *must* happen, or cannot *not* happen. Rather, it only expresses a confidence, or a *practical* (as opposed to *logical*) certainty that evil will sometimes occur. In later sections, I will show that this practical inevitability can be explained in terms of astronomically high statistical probabilities, to be distinguished from absolute metaphysical necessity. I therefore side with Maritain's reading of St. Thomas against what Maritain describes as the neo-Bañezian position, where God renders it certain that particular individuals will sin by willfully withholding from them the grace needed to abstain from evil.[4]

Section one of this present work develops Maritain's insights to establish that St. Thomas's conception of evil as privation not only indicates that the practical inevitability of evil differs from its being logically necessary, but that the latter suggestion is outright contradictory. Given this, it is actually logically necessary that any free world, including the one that actually exists, could in principle remain permanently devoid of evil. Nevertheless, later sections argue that, while it is logically necessary in principle that any world can remain evil-free, it is exceedingly unlikely that any world actually will remain permanently devoid of evil. This validates Maritain's and St. Thomas's claim that evil will in fact occur, without taking it to be unavoidable in principle.

Next, section two examines Maritain's view that our finite nature entails that we will sometimes fail to consider the proper rule in acting in a way that serves as a precondition for sin, without this failure itself constituting a sin. Here, Maritain distinguishes between an absence that is a "mere" or "pure and simple negation" from one that involves the deprivation of a "due good" (27–29).[5] From here, section three builds on Maritain's work

traditional Christian view that these arise as an effect of original sin, brought about through an initial immoral act.

4. Maritain, *God and the Permission of Evil*, translated by Joseph W. Evans (Milwaukee, Wisconsin: Bruce Publishing Company, 1966), 26; see also 21–25.

5. Maritain refers here to St. Thomas's *Quaestiones Disputatae de Malo* 1,3. See also *God and the Permission of Evil*, 36, 45, and 50.

by revealing how evil is even more likely in worlds containing a greater variety of creatures. Even so, I maintain that God cannot be faulted for creating a world with this increased probability of evil, since (1) this greater variety also constitutes a greater extent of beauty and goodness, (2) God never renders it absolutely impossible for agents to abstain from evil, and (3) there are no actual beings for whom it would have been better if God had created some other world, or no world at all, rather than one in which He foreknew avoidable evil would occur.

Following this, section four uses statistical probability to illustrate why evil is practically inevitable in any world, and even more so in worlds containing greater created variety, while never being absolutely certain. Beyond this, section five concludes by showing that even if it is overwhelmingly likely that an evil-free world would eventually come about where an astronomically high number of possible worlds is considered, this does not mean that God can choose to bring such an evil-free world into existence rather than one foreknown to entail evil. This analysis therefore supports Maritain's assertion that a divine assurance of a free world remaining permanently sinless is just as contradictory as the notion of a squared circle (16). Moreover, it accentuates the error of those who claim that an omnipotent and omnibenevolent God would not create a world He foreknows will entail evil, as this practically amounts to saying that God cannot create *any* free world. Such a position, however, clearly undermines, rather than exemplifies, omnipotence and omnibenevolence. This is especially true insofar as it is necessarily possible for all worlds to avoid evil.

I. Implications of the Privative View of Evil

The conception of evil as the privation of goodness is well known to those familiar with St. Thomas. By definition, a creature's goodness is defined in terms of its performing its proper function, so as to achieve its intended actuality. A good eye, for instance, is one that sees as an eye should, while a blind or damaged eye suffers various "degrees" of natural evil to the extent that vision is impeded (*ST* I, q. 48, a. 3).

In terms of moral evil, this conception of evil entails that a good or virtuous person is one who acts in a way that contributes to the long-term fulfillment of his or her natural capacities, thereby leading to temporal "happiness" (*ST* I-II, q. 5, aa. 3 and 5). Beyond this, of course, there is also the possibility of supernatural eternal beatitude, requiring grace even beyond what is needed to aid us in attaining earthly virtue (e.g. *ST* I–II, q. 3, a. 8 and *Summa Contra Gentiles* III, chps. 50–53 and 59).

Where evil is conceived as a privation, the question of why God allows moral evil really amounts to inquiring as to why God allows creatures to freely act in ways that impede the fulfillment of their nature, thereby undermining happiness. In considering this question, it is important to note that the privative understanding of evil logically precludes the notion that God can create anything in a way that leads to it necessarily acting against its own good. This is true, in that such a scenario would amount to saying that God designed the creature to fail to fulfill its natural design. In this case, however, an agent failing to fulfill its nature would be both fulfilling its design (as it was designed to fail) and failing to fulfill it (as evil implies), which is contradictory.

Maritain of course realizes that, among impersonal creatures lacking free will, the fulfillment of one entity's function necessarily involves accidentally depriving another of its function, much as fire destroys what is flammable (21–22). Even in these cases, however, the privation results from the relationship between creatures, and not from entities being directed toward evil through determinations of their own nature and activities. Beyond this, however, Maritain emphasizes that the case is fundamentally different for personal creatures possessing free will, for whom evil need not occur, whether through intrinsic determinations, or accidentally (22ff).

It should be mentioned here, in line with the above comment regarding neo-Bañezianism, that the claim that it is logically necessary that any free world could remain evil-free precludes conceptions of the Fall which hold that God predestines some to be incapable of avoiding sin. Nevertheless, the view that sin is necessarily avoidable at the creation of the world does not imply sin is necessarily avoidable once original sin enters the world. It could be that evil was genuinely avoidable before sin occurred but becomes unavoidable after that.

On the other hand, the biblical assertion that all have sinned (except the Blessed Mother and perhaps a few others like Elijah and Enoch) need not mean that even now sin *necessarily* happens, but only, as Maritain and St. Thomas contend, that it will in fact occur (i.e., is *practically* certain), while perhaps still being avoidable in principle. Maritain appears to favor this view, given his conviction that God always provides us with the grace "sufficient" to establish an initiative in us toward what is good (37). Still, he emphasizes that this grace-caused initiative can be "broken" (37) or "shattered,"[6] despite being continually offered by God for all, by a "voluntary and free failure" on our part to not consider the proper rule before acting (37). In any case, one should not equate a postlapsarian propensity to sin simply with a statistical probability for sin nascent to creation; surely, the effects of the Fall resound in our being more deeply than what can be measured by mere statistical eventualities.

Admittedly, one might try to avert the conclusion that it is logically contradictory to suggest that a free agent, at least prior to the Fall, will necessarily sin (even if this is practically certain) by distinguishing between a creature's natural end and God's particular design for it. This distinction is problematic, though, in that we come to know the end of a thing, and hence its nature, by examining what it is best designed to do. Hence, the view that something could be "designed" to act in violation of its "nature" simply constitutes another contradiction. Accordingly, one must conclude that any free world God creates is one where it was logically possible for evil to be permanently avoided. The real question, then, is why would God create a world where evil was even possible, especially if He knows evil will in fact occur?

The next section addresses this issue by examining Maritain's explanation for how our finitude makes it possible for us to commit improper actions due to a failure to consider what constitutes a proper action in a particular situation. After this, sections three and four will demonstrate further that, while it is necessarily possible in principle for all free worlds to remain evil-free, statistically speaking it is practically inevitable that evil will occur at some point. In explaining this, it will also be made clear why God cannot simply choose to have created a free world that He foreknows will overcome these odds. This is true even if it is overwhelmingly likely that such a world would eventually occur if one considers a number of worlds great enough to offset the astronomical odds against any particular world remaining evil-free.

II. Maritain's Account of the Possibility for Evil

While it has now been demonstrated that it is necessarily possible for any free world to remain devoid of evil, the question still remains as to

6. Maritain, *God and the Permission of Evil*, 38–39.

what it is about the nature of free creatures that makes it possible for them to act contrary to the fulfillment of their proper end. Maritain answers this question by developing St. Thomas's conviction that evil results from an agent's failing to consider the proper rule for action in a particular situation (24ff).

As he notes along with St. Thomas, this neglect cannot in itself be evil if it is the cause of evil. Simply put, if this neglect itself was necessarily evil, one would need to hold that the cause of evil was itself evil, leading to a vicious circle (24). Because evil is privation, this failure to consider the rule must therefore be regarded as a kind of absence, or negation, which does not yet constitute a privation (27–29). Citing St. Thomas's *de Malo* (24), Maritain explains that this subtle difference between a mere negation and an outright privation relies upon the distinction between the simple failure to do something ("consider the rule") and the failure to provide a specific "due good" to the action or being in question (27–29 and 31). Put differently, one is not expected to be constantly aware of the proper rule for every possible action, as this is obviously impossible given our natural finitude (26–27). To use Maritain's example, following St. Thomas, there is nothing wrong in a person failing to consider the need to use a straightedge for cutting, except in cases where cutting straight is required (25). Evil results, nevertheless, once one goes on to act in a way that is against the proper rule.

Admittedly, Maritain's explanation here requires a bit more elaboration to address possible objections that he does not explicitly consider. For example, one might contend that while one is not constantly obliged to consider every *particular* proper rule for every possible kind of action, there is a *general* rule that should be considered constantly; namely, the general rule that one ought to consider the particular rule for *any* action, in general, that one performs. On this view, one could say that, prior to one's acting, there is a general obligation due any conscious action to consider which rules apply to the particular kind of act in question.

Though one might suspect that this general good due all conscious actions counters Maritain's claim that the simple failure to consider the proper rule does not in itself constitute sin in depriving something of its due good, careful analysis reveals that this elaboration actually reinforces his account. To explain, Maritain's position that the failure to *act* according to the rule *is* evil essentially agrees with the above insight that we have a general obligation to consider which rule properly applies before acting. Nevertheless, it is just as unrealistic to say that one must be *constantly* aware of a general obligation to consider which rule is proper to any given action as it is to say that one must be constantly aware of the particular rule for a particular kind of act. The due good of considering which rule applies only obtains once one has consciously entertained acting a particular way. Indeed, this obligation basically describes the virtue of prudence ("think before you act"). One has not violated this obligation, however, until he or she actually acts improperly.

Once again, it should be emphasized that our inability to be constantly aware of every obligation renders it possible that we may, without fault, pre-reflectively consider improper ways of acting. In the heat of the moment, it may "cross the mind" of an angry baseball player that the ball would be a handy projectile by which he could protest a bad call, in violation of its proper use within the formal rules of the game. No sin is committed, however, until the player throws the ball at the umpire, or at least develops a conscious intention to do so ("Hey ump, I'm going to take this ball and knock your block off!").

III. Creaturely Variety and the Probability of Evil

The previous section explored how our finitude makes it possible for us to fail to consider the proper rule for action without this failure itself being evil. In this section, I expound on this assessment by conveying that this failure follows not only from our own finitude as agents, but also from the finite nature of the created entities we employ in acting. Accordingly, the diversification of creatures that expands the possibility for good also necessarily increases the various way creatures can be used improperly, resulting in evil.

To understand this point, it is helpful to recall St. Thomas's view that the nature of a thing is known in respect to its final cause, or designated purpose. Every kind of created being has a specific nature, and hence end, distinguishing it from other kinds of creatures. From this, it follows that what is a proper use for one kind of thing may not be proper for another. For example, a plant may be useful for treating one kind of illness, but harmful in treating another condition. At the same time, the fact that there are multiple kinds of creatures entails that the sum total of possible proper uses of all creatures considered together exceeds the number of proper uses for any particular creature. This variety, though, makes it possible for someone to consider using a created being in a way that is appropriate for some other kind of creature but not for it. However, one is morally faulted only if he or she proceeds to act improperly.

This necessary relationship between creaturely finitude and the possibility of evil also elucidates Maritain's agreement with St. Thomas that the perfection of a universe that includes free agents entails that such agents may sin. Because beauty presupposes a rational arrangement of diverse elements, an increased diversity within the natural order is necessarily accompanied by both an increased capacity for beauty and, conversely, an increased capacity for misuse and perversion. Maritain makes a similar point when he notes that the extent of possible evil is commensurate with the extent of personal freedom (18–19).

Once one understands that the failure to consider the proper rule in acting follows inevitably from the fact that the sum total of, or proper uses for, all creatures together exceeds the range of proper uses for any particular kind of creature, one can demonstrate why it is overwhelmingly likely, without being necessary, that evil will occur at some point in any free world. At the same time, section one's insight that this privation cannot be absolutely unavoidable proves that God cannot be blamed for evil.

In addition, the fact that evil is necessarily avoidable also indicates that God cannot be faulted for creating a world in which He foreknows evil would occur. In particular, God cannot be faulted for creating a world of great variety whereby the likelihood and frequency of evil is increased, as this variety also provides the possibility of greater blessings. Much is expected to whom much is given. Indeed, if God had not created a world with as much variety as ours, we would not exist at all.

Obviously, it is absurd to say that *we* would be better off if God had created some other world or no world at all, as in this case *we* would never had existed at all. Similarly, if we take divine impassibility and aseity seriously, we cannot say that God would be better off if He had not created a world in which He foreknows evil will occur; God remains perfectly self-fulfilled regardless of what world He does, or does not, create. Moreover, one cannot say that it would have been better for some other logically possible free world foreknown to entail less evil to have been created, as nothing can be "better for" that which does not actually exist!

IV. Statistical Probabilities and the Likelihood of Evil

Now that it is clear how evil in general is necessarily possible, and even more so where creaturely variety is increased, it is time to examine precisely why it is practically certain that evil will occur at some point in any possible free world, even as it remains necessarily avoidable in principle.

While the number of proper and improper uses for particular kinds of creatures is in fact exceedingly high, for the sake of discussion it is easier to consider a case involving a much more comprehensible number of possible uses for a creature. To explain, suppose that for a given object *O*, there are *P* number of proper uses, and *I* number of improper uses. If one likens, with important qualifications, free actions to statistically random events (the justification of this comparison being addressed shortly), the odds that an improper use will occur increase as the number of actions increases. This increase can occur by considering either additional actors or additional acts by a single agent (or both). Consequently, from a purely statistical point of view, no matter how low the odds were that evil would occur in the earliest stages of a world's creation, over enough time and/or enough actors, the odds that an improper use will occur at some point become astronomically high.

For example, suppose objects O and O^2 each have 10 possible uses, with nine of these being proper and one improper for each. Beyond this, imagine that of the nine proper uses for each, eight of these are proper for both objects, with the ninth proper use for each being proper to one object but not the other. For simplicity's sake assume that no other uses are possible, and that each event is independent of the others. In this case, there is a 90% chance in a particular instance that either object will be used properly. However, where two uses are considered (whether for one or both objects), the odds of a proper use resulting (and an improper use being avoided) in both cases decreases to $(9/10)^2$ or 81%, dropping to $(9/10)^3$ or 72.9% for three instances, below 50% in the case of just seven instances, and so on. Over a mere 100 instances, the probability of an improper use being avoided every time drops to approximately .00266%, or just over 2 in 100,000.

Obviously, where many more actors, instances, and/or the number of possible improper uses increases, the odds of evil being perpetually avoided are infinitesimally small. Certainly, in a world as diverse and with as many actors as ours, the odds of the proper rule being followed in every action would for all practical purposes be zero. Similarly, the probability that moral evil will be repeated also increases over a greater number of instances. Even so, the possibility of permanently avoiding evil will never reach absolute zero, as the absolute necessity for evil implies a contradiction.

Some may challenge the legitimacy of comparing a free will decision to a random event. To be sure, such events are not random in the sense that an agent simply finds itself, as if by surprise, acting in a particular way. Rather, in many cases one *chooses* to act in a certain way.[7] From the perspective of observers, however, these choices *can* be compared to random events, with proper qualifications added, to the extent that free acts are not strictly determined, and thus necessarily retain an aspect of unpredictability. This comparison is even more apt in the case of people whose past behavior is unknown to the observer.[8]

Certainly, habit and character render many actions relatively predictable.[9] Still, one who believes in incompatibilist free will must hold that even with people with whom we are familiar there can never be absolute assurance as to how another agent will act.[10] This is especially true when one considers the incalculable effects of divine grace on human freedom. In addition, if our finitude and creaturely variety necessarily renders it possible to fail to consider the proper rule in acting, then it is contradictory to hold that God can assure that free creatures constantly avoid evil. Simply put, if God determines that something will or will not occur, then one is not free to perform (or fail to perform) this action.

V. Evil and Multiple Possible Worlds

While section four makes it clear that God cannot assure that creatures avoid evil without contradicting their freedom, one might suggest that it is

7. See for example John G. Trapani, Jr., "New Genes, Blue Jeans, and Human Beings: Jacques Maritain and the Possibility of Freedom" in *Reading the Cosmos: Nature, Science, and Wisdom*, edited by Giuseppe Butera (Washington, D.C.: American Maritain Association Publications, 2011), 195ff.

8. Ibid., 201.

9. I would suggest that this relative predictability can be explained by St. Thomas's conviction that all desires relate to God as the foundation of being, and hence goodness. Thus, we are inclined to repeat actions that lead to apparently desirable outcomes. However, given Thomas's insight (cited by Maritain—see Trapani, 201, n. 21) that no finite particular good can necessitate a creature oriented to desire God as infinite good, habitual actions may be altered if they cease in time to seem desirable, or are replaced by apparently greater incompatible particular goods.

10. While the Thomistic interplay of primary and secondary causes may not fit well with

still possible for Him to non-contradictorily assure the avoidance of evil, if He can choose to create a world that He foreknows would freely and permanently avoid sin. Even though it is incredibly unlikely that any world will remain evil-free, it is also necessarily logically possible. Where one considers a number of possible worlds even greater than the astronomical odds against any particular world remaining evil-free, some statistical models suggest that it is statistically likely that eventually at least one world would remain evil-free. So, could God choose this world, even if it is only one out of a "googolplex"[11] of worlds, to be the one He creates?

To use previous figures, although there is only roughly a 2 in 100,000 chance that a world where evil is 90% avoidable for each action would remain evil-free for 100 actions, where two such worlds are considered, models that allow for considering cumulative probabilities maintain that the odds of at least one remaining evil-free increases to more than 3 in 100,000. Hence, if God created a sufficiently great number of worlds (say, a number followed by a billion zeroes), the odds that one would defy astronomical odds and remain evil-free might be very close to 100%, without reaching 100% absolutely.[12] Nevertheless, these probabilities do not indicate that God can choose to create a world He foreknows would remain evil-free, as will now be explained.

To the point, the fact that a coin is likely to land heads 100 times in a row if it is tossed $n^{\text{googol plex}}$ times obviously does not mean that one can assure this result by choosing to toss the heads-only series of 100 first. Rather,

---

contemporary discussions of free will and determinism, I use the term "incompatibilist" here merely to convey, in light of the insight noted above, that we cannot be necessitated to pursue finite particular goods, that human freedom is not compatible with any form of necessity.

11. As explained in any sufficiently exhaustive current dictionary, in informal mathematical parlance, a "googolplex" signifies a number with an exponent of "1" followed by a "googol" zeroes, where a "googol" = 10^100 Accordingly, a "googolplex" is commonly denoted as 10^(10^100). I use it here to generically represent any astronomically large number.

12. One way to calculate the probability of a particular outcome occurring at least once over a series of random events is to figure the odds that only alternative outcomes will occur over the entire series, and subtract this number from 1, where 1 denotes 100% of all cases, and the remainder signifies the odds that the event in question will occur at least once. For example, there is a $(1/6)^3$ (i.e. 1/216) chance of rolling three consecutive sixes on a standard die. Hence, there is a 215/216 (roughly 99.5%) chance of a number other than six coming up at least once in three rolls. In my example, as the odds of an object with nine proper uses out of 10 possible uses avoiding an improper use for 100 consecutive situations have been figured as only about 2 in 100,000, this means that there is roughly a 1-.00002 (99,998 out of 100,000) chance of at least one improper use occurring in 100 situations. Even so, a calculator with an exponents function reveals that the odds of 100 consecutive proper uses occurring are about 50% given 35,000 sets of 100 cases, increasing all the way to 99% where 230,240 cases are considered.

the coin-tosser has basically no control over how each toss lands, even if he or she can be almost certain that the coin will eventually land heads 100 times in a row given an astronomically high number of tosses. Nevertheless, one must accept the results of prior tosses before eventually attaining 100 heads in a row.

In the same way, even if God created the number of worlds needed eventually to attain an evil-free world, this evil-free world would simply be a part of a collective world comprised of all individually created worlds in which evil had already occurred. This confirms St. Thomas's conviction that there can be only one world (*ST* I, Q. 47, a.3). God cannot simply skip over these previous worlds and go straight to creating the evil-free world any more than one can make the $n^{\text{googolplex}}$-th numbered toss occur first. (Remember Maritain's contention noted earlier that it is a contradiction even for God to assure that free creatures will act a certain way.) Thus, a creation totally devoid of evil can only result if the first free world God creates happens to remain evil-free. This, of course, is astronomically unlikely.

VI. Conclusion

While demonstrating that moral evil flows from a failure to consider the proper rule for action that is in itself the non-sinful result of natural limitations, Maritain provides a basis for further proving that even though it is logically necessary that evil can be avoided in any free world, it is still nevertheless practically certain to occur. Likewise, the possibilities for sinful actions increase proportionately to greater degrees of creaturely variety. Even so, God cannot be faulted for creating worlds in which He foreknows evil will occur, both because it was genuinely avoidable (though statistically virtually inevitable), and because there is no actual being for whom it would have been better if God had not created this world. In fact, if the rules of probability indicate that it is practically (though not necessarily) certain that moral evil will eventually occur in any free world, the suggestion that God should not create a world in which He foreknows evil will occur actually undermines rather than supports God's omnipotence and goodness, as this would practically restrict Him from creating any free-world. Similarly, the likelihood of an evil-free world arising given a sufficiently great number of worlds does not entail that God can choose to create a world assured of remaining evil-free.

BRYAN R. CROSS

Aquinas on the Original Harmonies and the Problem of Evil

The most common form of the problem of evil today is the evidential or inductive problem of evil. The argument can be summarized as follows. Certain kinds of evils—such as the suffering of animals in forest fires, the suffering of children with cancer, and devastating tsunamis and earthquakes—are such that no good that we are aware of applies to them that would outweigh their evil, and thus justify allowing them to occur. Hence an omnipotent, omniscient and perfectly good being would not allow such evils to occur. Any being that could prevent such evils from happening, but knowingly does not do so, is either not omnipotent or not perfectly good. And yet such evils occur. From these premises the argument concludes that *it is likely* that no omnipotent and perfectly good being exists, and hence that *it is likely* that God does not exist.

The key premise in this sort of argument is the claim that there are some evil events for which, so far as we are aware or have good reason to believe, there are no outweighing goods or justifiable reasons for allowing them to occur. And the key part of that premise, I contend, lies in the phrase "so far as we are aware or have good reason to believe." What gives traction to the evidential problem of evil is a fundamental lack of awareness of the metaphysical context in which evil occurs. That metaphysical context includes as its content the perfection of the order of the world, why that perfection allows evil, and how that evil affects the order.

One reason why the contemporary form of the evidential problem of evil is so influential is that both scientism and skepticism concerning metaphysics situate the problem in a way that excludes the data by which the problem can be effectively addressed. Here we can learn from St. Thomas Aquinas. Aquinas's approach to the problem of evil in *ST* I, q. 2, a. 3 does not accept the problem of evil as the philosophical starting point in reasoning about the existence of God. Instead, Aquinas starts from motion, efficient causation, contingency, gradation, and order. He places the problem of evil in the first objection in Article 3. And that placement is methodologically and philosophically significant. Aquinas treats the problem of evil as an objection to the claim that God exists. But he does not treat the fact of evil in the world as the entirety of the philosophic data from which we may reason concerning the existence of God. If Aquinas were confronted with the typical contemporary formulation of the evidential problem of evil, he would not accept its implicit limitation on philosophic data from which to reason concerning the existence of God.

We can see this by considering how Aquinas responds to the objection that evil in the world is incompatible with God's infinite goodness. Aquinas responds by drawing, at least indirectly, from his fourth way. In his reply to Objection 1 of *ST* I, q. 2, a. 3, Aquinas cites St. Augustine's *Enchiridion*, where St. Augustine writes, "Since God is the highest good, He would not allow any evil to exist in His works, unless His omnipotence and goodness were such as to bring [*faceret*] good even out of evil." Aquinas then adds, "This therefore pertains to the *infinite goodness* of God, that He permits evil to be, and out of it elicits good." Aquinas implicitly draws from his fourth way to argue that since God's goodness is infinite, we should understand the evil we encounter in the world as something that God in His infinite goodness permits to come from created goods and from which He brings good. Aquinas's methodology shows that for him the premises of his five ways are no less fundamental as philosophical starting material than is the fact of evil in the world.

We may even say that, for Aquinas, *goodness* has both metaphysical and epistemic primacy. *What* evil is and *why* evil is are both explained in relation to good. Aquinas explains *what* evil is when, following St. Augustine, he argues that evil is the absence of good [*absentia boni*].[1] He likewise

1. *ST* I, q. 48, a. 1. The absence of positive being is not the same as existing only in the mind, nor does the absence of positive being entail existing only in the mind. We would have no knowledge of a privation such as blindness (given the falsity of any sort of occasionalism and voluntarist divinely predetermined harmony between mind and reality) if that which is missing (e.g., sight) is not still there (in reality) *in some respect*. The privation exists in the substance *as*

explains *why* there is evil, also in relation to good, namely as something allowed by the infinite Good (i.e., God) and from which the infinite Good elicits good. From Aquinas's explanation of evil in terms of good, and his implicit use of one of the five ways in answering the objection from evil, we can see that he would not accept the philosophical skepticism typically implicit in the contemporary discussion of the evidential problem of evil. Attempting to answer the question of God's existence by starting from the problem of evil, apart from the five ways, and apart from the metaphysics of evil as a privation of good, would be an implicit concession to philosophical skepticism. So the first response to the contemporary form of the evidential problem of evil is to re-situate the problem within the broader metaphysical context of the five ways.

The second response to the evidential problem of evil is to show that we do have good reason to believe that the sort of evils referred to in the evidential problem of evil are not gratuitous evils, but are allowed for a good reason that outweighs the magnitude of their evil. This requires providing a still further specified context in which to make sense of the possibility of such evils. Aquinas provides this context in various places in his works. In his question on providence, he raises the following objection:

> A wise provider excludes any defect or evil, as far as he can, from those over whom he has a care. But we see many evils existing. Either, then, God cannot hinder these, and thus is not omnipotent; or else He does not have care for everything.[2]

This is a variant form of the problem of evil, appealing to the existence of evils in the world as evidence that God is either not omnipotent or not perfectly good. Aquinas's reply to this objection explains that God allows certain evils for the sake of the good of the whole universe. He writes:

---

a privation, i.e., a that-which-should-be-there-but-is-not. We can describe the privation as the difference between the telos as formally specified by the nature of the substance and the telos as actualized in the composite. That difference (existing in the actual substance in extra-mental reality) is what the intellect grasps as a privation. That dog should be able to see; it is only because he should be able to see that I can recognize him to be blind. If blindness were merely not having the ability to see, then even the kitchen sink would be blind. But the kitchen sink is not blind, even though it cannot see. So privations are not non-being *simpliciter*, but are rather a certain mode of being, i.e. formally-specified-actualization-but-without-actualization. If we try to analyze privation further, into being or non-being, we lose it. Non-being is necessarily parasitic on being, so privations cannot be analyzed into non-being alone, but only to an irreducible kind of composition of being and non-being. So we should understand evil not simply as the absence of good, but the absence of good where good should be.

2. *ST* I, q. 22, a. 1, obj. 2.

It is otherwise with one who has care of a *particular* thing, and one whose providence is *universal*, because a particular provider excludes all defects from what is subject to his care as far as he can; whereas, one who provides universally allows some little defect to remain, lest the good of the whole be hindered. Hence, corruption and defects in natural things are said to be contrary to some particular nature; yet they are in keeping with the plan of universal nature; inasmuch as the defect in one thing yields to the good of another, or even to the universal good: for the corruption of one is the generation of another, and through this it is that a species is kept in existence. Since God, then, provides universally for all being, it belongs to His providence to permit certain defects in particular effects, that the perfect good of the universe may not be hindered, for if all evil were prevented, much good would be absent from the universe. A lion would cease to live, if there were no slaying of animals; and there would be no patience of martyrs if there were no tyrannical persecution. Thus Augustine says (*Enchiridion* 2): "Almighty God would in no wise permit evil to exist in His works, unless He were so almighty and so good as to produce good even from evil."[3]

Aquinas here explains that the good of the order of the universe requires that there be defects in certain things for the sake of the good of other things, and hence for the perfection of the whole order. Most striking is his statement that "if all evil were prevented, much good would be absent from the universe."

The person advancing the evidential problem of evil will respond to such a claim by insisting that he or she can imagine a world in which these various evils are not present, and which is better off for not having them. So, in responding to the evidential problem of evil, we must show why the perfection of the universe requires the possibility of such evils, and that the goodness of the perfection of the universe is greater than the evils referred to in the problem of evil, such that it is better that there be a perfect universe with the possibility of evils than that there be an imperfect universe.

Making that argument requires explaining in more detail the nature of the perfection of the universe. In *ST* I, q. 47, a.1, Aquinas claims that the perfection of the universe consists of the diversity of things.[4] This diversity of things is a perfection of the universe in (at least) two ways. First, according to Aquinas, goodness is more fully manifested when each grade of goodness is realized. This is why the perfection of the universe requires

3. "It would appear that it was on account of these two arguments, to which we have just replied, that some were persuaded to consider corruptible things—e.g., failing things [*casualia*] and evil things—as removed from the care of divine providence" (*ST* I, q. 22, a. 2 ad 2).

4. *ST* I, q. 47, a. 1.

that there be inequality in created things. It would be an impoverished world if there were beings of only one sort, and if grades of goodness were missing from the universe.[5]

A second way in which the diversity of things is a perfection of the universe is through the order of these diverse things to each other and to God. Order follows directly from diversity of grades of goodness in a unity. On this point Aquinas says, "But order chiefly consists in inequality; for Augustine says (*De Civ. Dei* xix, 13): 'Order disposes things equal and unequal in their proper place.'"[6] Order is not something imposed upon things in some arbitrary way. Nor is it identical to inequality. Rather, unequal things in relation have an ordered disposition to each other proper to their inequality. And since all things that come from a common source have a relation to each other, therefore all the unequal things are related to each other, and hence have a proper order in relation to each other.

What's so good about order? Why does the universe need order to be perfect? According to Aquinas, the order of all things is a kind of unity that reflects in the creation the perfect unity of its Creator. He writes:

> The very order of things created by God shows the unity of the world. For this world is called one by the unity of order, whereby some things are ordered to others. But whatever things come from God have relation of order to each other and to God Himself.[7]

This order of things, according to Aquinas, is a teleological unity in which some created things are ordered to the good of other created things in a hierarchy, all the members of which are ordered to God Himself.[8] For example, we can see order clearly in biology when we study ecosystems, food chains, and life cycles.

For Aquinas, the order of things is observable in nature. In his commentary on Aristotle's *Ethics*, he writes, "There is one sort of order which reason does not produce but only observes; this is the orderly relation of things in nature."[9] This order is not something known to the senses as such,

5. We have some sense of this when an animal species goes extinct; there is a kind of sadness that the unique way in which this kind of creature manifested nobility, beauty, creativity, and other aspects of goodness, is gone forever.

6. *ST* I, q. 96, a. 3.

7. *ST* I, q.47, a. 3.

8. In the opening page of his commentary on Aristotle's *Ethics*, Aquinas notes that there are two kinds of order among things. One of them is the order of parts to a whole, and the other is the order of things toward an end.

9. Aquinas, *Commentary on Aristotle's Ethics*, I, lect. 1, nn. 1–3.

but to reason by way of the senses. For Aquinas, the order of the world is so evident to reason through observation that he argues from the order of the world to the unity of God. He writes that the unity of God

> is shown from the unity of the world. For all things that exist are seen to be ordered to each other since some serve others. But things that are diverse do not harmonize in the same order, unless they are ordered thereto by one.[10]

Here, Aquinas is saying that the order of the world is a unity that integrates into one all the members of that order, and therefore shows itself to have come from a unified Creator. Our knowledge of the order of things in nature is precisely how we are capable of recognizing disorder, as that which is opposed to or lacking the order we already perceive. The fundamental order we perceive must therefore be included within the available evidential resources when responding to the problem of evil.

Both of these ways by which the universe is perfected—that is, fully realizing each *grade of goodness* and manifesting the goodness of the *unity of hierarchical order*—open the possibility for evil in the universe, each in a different way. Aquinas explains how the perfection of fully realizing each grade of goodness opens the door to the possibility of evil when he writes the following:

> Now, one grade of goodness is that of the good which cannot fail. Another grade of goodness is that of the good which can fail in goodness, and this grade is to be found in existence itself; for some things there are which cannot lose their existence as incorruptible things, while some there are which can lose it, as things corruptible. As, therefore, the perfection of the universe requires that there should be not only beings incorruptible, but also corruptible beings; so the perfection of the universe requires that there should be some which can fail in goodness, and thence it follows that sometimes they do fail. Now it is in this that evil consists, namely, in the fact that a thing fails in goodness.[11]

Aquinas is arguing that since the perfection of the universe requires that every grade of goodness be realized, and since at least one grade of goodness is such that it can fail in goodness, therefore the perfection of the universe requires that there be in it things that can fail. And failing with respect to goodness is just what evil is. Hence the perfection of the universe requires that it be susceptible to evil, by having in it creatures capable of failing in goodness.

10. *ST* I, q. 11, a. 3.

11. *ST* I, q. 48, a. 2.

Similarly, the perfection of the universe in its *order* also makes it susceptible to evil in a different way. Recall that for Aquinas things are ordered to each other both as agent to patient, and as proximate end and exemplar to other things within that order.[12] When a being that is capable of failing in goodness exists within a hierarchical order in relation to other beings, then the failing of this being can detract from the teleological fulfillment of the other members of that order, by taking from them or not giving to them good that was due to them from it. This can include material goods, bodily goods, good dispositions, good actions or examples, and the like. This failure on the part of a being within the order does not destroy the order, but it can damage the order in the sense that it can detract from the operational actualization of the order. It can also deprive the other members of the order of the goods they would have enjoyed had this member not failed.[13]

So both aspects of the perfection of the universe make it susceptible in various ways to evil. Having the full panoply of grades of goodness requires including within the universe creatures capable of failing. And the goodness of a unified world requires an ordered world, and hence the possibility of a ripple effect as a result of evil.[14] The susceptibility of a perfect order to evil is a significant part of the metaphysical context by which Aquinas seeks to make the presence of evil in the world intelligible, even while recognizing that the particular justification for particular evil events remains veiled to us. What I am proposing here is that it is ignorance of this metaphysical context that is presently giving so much traction and persuasive power to the evidential problem of evil in many present discussions.

12. "[T]he parts of the universe are ordered to each other, according as one acts on the other, and according as one is the end and exemplar of the other. But, as was said above, this can only happen to evil as joined to some good. Hence evil neither belongs to the perfection of the universe, nor does it come under the order of the same, except accidentally, that is, by reason of some good joined to it" (*ST* I, q. 48, a. 1 ad 5).

13. I say "can" because such failure can also provide the occasion for the greater manifestation of goodness by other members within the order.

14. If it were possible for God to make a world without order, then, in that world the failing of a particular creature would not affect any other creature, because no creature would have any causal relation to any other creature. It would not be one world, but as many worlds as there were creatures. This is why Aquinas can argue from the order of the world to the unity of the world. If there were no order among creatures, there would be as many worlds as there are creatures. (See *ST* I, q. 47, a. 3.)

I. Original Harmonies

Aquinas's account of the order of the world contains four original harmonies within that order. He writes:

> But the very rectitude of the primitive state, wherewith man was endowed by God, seems to require that, as others say, he was created in grace, according to Ecclesiastes 7:30, "God made man right." For this rectitude consisted in his reason being subject to God, the lower powers to reason, and the body to the soul: and the first subjection was the cause of both the second and the third; since while reason was subject to God, the lower powers remained subject to reason.[15]

For Aquinas, man was created in a state of friendship with God, already endowed with the grace by which he was made proportionate to a supernatural end. This friendship with God was the primary harmony on which the other harmonies depended. In addition, man had four preternatural gifts: infused knowledge, immortality, impassibility, and integrity, whereby his lower appetites were perfectly subject to his intellect and will. By the gifts of integrity and impassibility and immortality, man had an internal harmony. His appetites were perfectly subject to reason, he could not suffer any movement against his natural disposition, and his body was perfectly subject to his soul. That internal harmony is the second of the four harmonies.

The third harmony is civic harmony, that is, harmony between human persons. Aquinas holds that in the original condition there was order and harmony between the man and the woman, and that this familial order and harmony would also have become manifested in the larger society, had man not sinned.[16] The fourth harmony is that harmony between man and all other creatures.[17] According to Aquinas, by the dominion God gave to man over all the material world, all corporeal creatures were subject to man.[18]

15. *ST* I, q. 95, a. 1.

16. *ST* I, q. 92, a. 1 ad 2. See also *ST* I, q. 96, a. 4.

17. We see this described in the present *Catechism of the Catholic Church* (*CCC*): "The first man was not only created good, but was also established in friendship with his Creator and in harmony with himself and with the creation around him.... [O]ur first parents ... were constituted in an original 'state of holiness and justice.' This grace of original holiness was 'to share in ... divine life.' By the radiance of this grace all dimensions of man's life were confirmed. As long as he remained in the divine intimacy, man would not have to suffer or die. The inner harmony of the human person, the harmony between man and woman, and finally the harmony between the first couple and all creation, comprised the state called 'original justice'" (*CCC* 373–76).

18. *ST* I, q. 96, a. 1.

Through man's sin, all four harmonies were lost. Man's friendship with God was lost, because his will was turned away from loving God and toward loving things more than he loved God. Man's internal integrity was lost: the lower appetites were no longer perfectly ordered to his reason (hence concupiscence), he became susceptible to suffering, and his body was no longer perfectly subject to his soul (hence physical suffering and death). The harmonious relation between man and woman was disrupted. Finally, man no longer enjoyed perfect, harmonious, dominion over the rest of corporeal creatures.

What is the significance of these original harmonies for the problem of evil? The problem of evil directs its attention to what are called natural evils, more so than to moral evils, because man can be blamed for moral evils, while God alone seems responsible for natural evils. The primary types of evil referred to in the evidential problem of evil are cases of suffering, especially cases of seemingly needless suffering of children and animals.[19] The sort of suffering to which the problem of evil points is related to two of the four harmonies just mentioned: internal harmony, and harmony between man and the rest of material creation.

If there were at present harmony between man and the rest of creation, there would be no devastating tsunamis, or killer tornados, hurricanes, earthquakes, and the like. There would be no diseases caused in man by other creatures (i.e., bacteria, viruses), and no harm done to man by other creatures (snakes, sharks, lions, and the like). And if there were at present internal harmony between man's soul and body and between man's reason and his passions, then there would be no death or suffering.[20]

So, if mankind had those two harmonies (i.e., between man and the rest of the physical world, and internal harmony), that would eliminate the suffering and death that serve as the fundamental data in the problem of evil. Therefore, addressing the problem of evil requires explaining not only that there is a fundamental order, and that this fundamental order must be open to evil, but specifically why it is possible for these two harmonies to be lost, and why they are in fact lost.

19. The present discussions of the problem of evil make much more out of suffering than out of death.

20. Regarding the original state of man's passions, Aquinas writes, "A thing is said to suffer when changed from its natural disposition.... Man was impassible, both in soul and body, as he was likewise immortal; for he could curb his passion" (*ST* I, q. 97, a. 2).

According to Aquinas, these harmonies were not intrinsic to the natures of creatures, but were the result of a superadded gift that could be preserved or lost. Aquinas explains:

Now it is clear that such a subjection of the body to the soul and of the lower powers to reason was not from nature; otherwise it would have remained after sin; since even in the demons the natural gifts remained after sin.... Hence it is clear that also the primitive subjection by virtue of which reason was subject to God was not a merely natural gift, but a supernatural endowment of grace; for it is not possible that the effect should be of greater efficiency than the cause. Hence Augustine says (*De Civ. Dei* xiii, 13) that, "as soon as they disobeyed the Divine command, and forfeited Divine grace, they were ashamed of their nakedness, for they felt the impulse of disobedience in the flesh, as though it were a punishment corresponding to their own disobedience." Hence if the loss of grace dissolved the obedience of the flesh to the soul, we may gather that the inferior powers were subjected to the soul through grace existing therein.[21]

The fundamental order, however, was not lost by sin. All other corporeal creatures remain ordered to man, even though there is much disharmony between creation and man. On account of this disharmony, St. Paul says, "the whole creation groans and suffers the pains of childbirth together until now."[22] And the body remains ordered to the soul, the appetites to reason, and reason still remains ordered to God, even though there is (apart from redemptive grace) disharmony in each relation. Harmony differs from order in that harmony is a correspondence in operation to the underlying order. Disharmony is a lack of correspondence in operation to the underlying order.

II. Sin and the Original Harmonies

And now we can pull together the threads of Aquinas's explanation. It turns out that man is one of those created things capable of failing in goodness by free choice. But man also exists within an observable order, such that the effects of his failure ripple out through the given order in the form of disharmony. The way in which this disharmony ripples out is explained by the underlying order, insofar as man is ordered to other things, and they

21. *ST* I, q. 95, a. 1.

22. Romans 8:22. I am not here making any claim regarding sin's effect, if any, on the relation of animals to each other.

to him. Since man's irascible and concupiscible appetites are ordered to reason, his body to his soul, and the rest of corporeal creation is ordered to man, the effect of sin is a disharmony in each of these relations. What occurred with our first parents' sin was a top-down disharmonization. The original sin was a rebellion in the will that robbed the lower appetites of the proximate good to which they are ordered, thus leaving those appetites like a ship with an obviously inebriated captain such that he cannot command attention or respect. And original sin likewise robbed the body of a rightly ordered soul and robbed creatures of a steward who by his character elicited perfect fealty and devotion. The short of Aquinas's argument is that we lack the harmony of man to creatures, as well as internal harmony, because our first parent acted contrary to the existing order.

This metaphysical context, concerning both the original harmonies and the loss of those harmonies, is typically absent from contemporary formulations of the evidential problem of evil, particularly when one premise in the argument is that there are evil events for which, so far as we are aware or have good reason to believe, there are no outweighing goods or justifiable reasons for allowing them to occur. Providing this metaphysical context regarding the underlying order and harmony in which suffering occurs undermines the plausibility of that premise in the evidential argument from evil.

One primary concern with my claim that the proper response to the evidential problem of evil is to provide the metaphysical context by which to see these purportedly gratuitous evils in an entirely different light is that this is something only accessible via sacred theology. And if we have to appeal to sacred theology to respond to the problem of evil, then it seems we've just begged the question. But I think that objection isn't true. First, even if we did need to appeal to sacred theology, we would still have recourse to the motives of credibility. In that we case, we would still be weighing evidence within one paradigm against the same evidence in another paradigm. And here I think the Catholic position comes out on top. Second, I think Aquinas believed that philosophy could get quite far. Clearly, he thought that natural reason is capable of grasping the order of the world, and the five ways. That alone would transform the problem of evil from an argument against God's existence to an investigation into the reasons God has for allowing evil. Aquinas's arguments that the perfection of the universe requires that it be susceptible to evil are not based directly on sacred revelation. And his arguments concerning the original harmonies are deeply informed by observations of the natures of the things involved in those harmonies. The fundamental problem in making Aquinas's case in response to the evidential problem of evil is not so much a limitation of philosophy, but rather the influence of scientism and its deep suspicion of the truth-discovering possibility within metaphysics.

Part of what stimulated me to write about this was a paradox that occurred to me after reading what Aquinas says about punishment. He writes:

> Now it is evident that all things contained in an order, are, in a manner, one, in relation to the principle of that order. Consequently, whatever rises up against an order, is put down by that order or by the principle thereof. And because sin is an inordinate act, it is evident that whoever sins commits an offense against an order: wherefore he is put down, in consequence, by that same order, which repression is punishment.[23]

For Aquinas, to sin is to act against an order. But when someone rises up against an order, rebelling against it, the order puts down the uprising, to preserve the harmony of the order. This action by an order, against one acting contrary to that order, is precisely what punishment is, according to Aquinas. The purpose of the punishment is not only to preserve the order but to put the disorderly agent back in order. In other words, the disharmony experienced by the disorderly agent, as a result of his disordered actions, is aimed by the order at restoring him to order, insofar as that is possible.

If that is the case, then the purpose of the evils we encounter in this life is to restore us to order, particularly in relation to our supernatural end. Hence there is something very odd and perhaps diabolical about the fact that that which is divinely intended to provoke us to recognize our need for God, our estrangement from God and our intended destiny in God and with God, is precisely that which is used by many as the strongest evidence that there is no God. It may therefore be that the task of the philosopher with respect to the problem of evil is to provide the metaphysical context in which suffering can be sufficiently intelligible to provoke not the denial of God's existence but rather humble self-examination and repentance before a perfectly Good and Just Judge to whom we must all give account.

23. *ST* I-II, q. 87, a. 1. See also Peter Koritansky's *Thomas Aquinas on the Philosophy of Punishment* (Washington, D.C.: Catholic University of America Press, 2011).

JOHN F. MORRIS

Why Must We Not Do Evil?

Avoiding vs. Allowing Evil and the Principle of Double Effect

I. Introduction

One of the many significant contributions that the Catholic tradition has made in the field of ethics is the Principle of Double Effect. It is only through the insight embodied in the Principle of Double Effect that we are able to determine whether or not we are permitted to do certain good actions when we foresee that they will also result in evil side effects. That is, while ethics demands that we avoid evil, the understanding of Double Effect shows that we can allow evil when it is unintended, provided that there is a proportionate reason for doing the good we wish to accomplish. This principle is especially important in contemporary bioethics, where it has gained acceptance among Catholic and non-Catholic health care practitioners and ethicists alike.

However, over the last 40 years, controversy has surrounded the Principle of Double Effect due largely to the influence of certain Catholic moral theologians—primarily those of the proportionalist school. These thinkers in one way or another conclude that all of ethics can be reduced to the Principle of Double Effect and its focus upon the proportion in any action of good to evil. The result has led to a more or less "Catholic" version of utilitarian or consequentialist ethics. Although proportionalists insist their approach does not allow the end to justify the means, most critics conclude that this is precisely what the singular focus on the proportion of good to evil within Double Effect has done—for example, by attempting to justify what have been considered in the Catholic tradition as intrinsic evils, such as direct abortion and contraception. Needless to say, the proportionalists' approach has led to a great deal of confusion.

In this article, I will give a brief overview of the Principle of Double Effect, discuss its use and development within proportionalist thinking, and address some of the prominent arguments against the proportionalist school and its misunderstanding of Double Effect. In the end, I believe that the Principle of Double Effect is primarily a pragmatic tool that helps us judge the prudence of good actions that are intertwined with evil consequences. As such, it is not the primary or sole principle in ethics, but rather the final principle that we should apply before we perform an action in order to insure that we are not going to produce more harm than good. The Principle of Double Effect shows how we can allow actions that are accompanied by evil consequences, but it does not permit or justify directly evil actions. Finally, I will conclude with a reflection on a point that I often find overlooked in contemporary discussions of evil, yet which St. Thomas and Thomists are keen to emphasize—the reasons why we ought to avoid evil in the first place. I fear that in the current age we have become far too complacent about evil and why causing it—or even *allowing* it—is such a serious matter. We must always remember, as Jacques Maritain so aptly describes it, "evil's metaphysical monstrosity"[1] and the damage it does to our character, as well as to our relationships with others in society and ultimately with God.

II. A Brief Explanation of the Principle of Double Effect

It is commonly agreed that the origin of Double Effect reasoning can be found in the *Summa Theologiae, Secunda secundae,* Question 63, Article 7, in St. Thomas's discussion of killing in self-defense.[2] The fact that Double Effect reasoning is introduced by Thomas in the *Secunda secundae,* as op-

1. Jacques Maritain, *St. Thomas and the Problem of Evil* (Milwaukee, Wisconsin: Marquette University Press, 1942), 3.

2. For an excellent treatment of the origins of the Principle of Double Effect, see Christopher Kaczor's *Proportionalism and the Natural Law Tradition* (Washington, D.C.: The Catholic University of America Press, 2002), 24–26.

posed to the *Prima secundae,* in which he laid out the fundamental principles of morality, has led some to conclude that this discussion of killing in self-defense provides a novel introduction of Double Effect reasoning. However, Christopher Kaczor in my opinion correctly argues in his book, *Proportionalism and the Natural Law Tradition,* that "one can read Thomas's analysis of self-defense as an application of principles enunciated in the *Prima secundae,* question 18."[3] Question 18 in the *Prima secundae* addresses good and evil in human action. Thus, after a brief analysis, Kaczor concludes: "... in *Secunda secundae,* question 64, article 7, Thomas applies the principles laid down in the *Prima secundae* to determine whether any human action is good to the case of self-defense."[4]

Kaczor's analysis is a helpful reminder that Double Effect reasoning is not introduced as a distinct form of ethical reasoning, but rather is part of Thomas's principled approach to ethics. This becomes even more important in the later development within the tradition of the actual Principle of Double Effect. The principle does not stand on its own but rather can only be properly understood within the context of other ethical principles.

As for the Principle of Double Effect itself, a number of formulations have been given through the years; but a clear and helpful contemporary statement of Double Effect reasoning can be found in the short work, *Applied Professional Ethics,* by Gregory Beabout and Daryl Wennemann: "Given that the intention and goal of your action is to treat people with respect, make sure that there are no foreseeable bad side effects that are disproportionate with the good of the main effect."[5] The insight behind this principle is simple but important. Most human actions have more than one outcome or effect. For example, if one has surgery for a bad knee, the intention is to heal the knee so that it can again function properly. In addition, this surgery will most likely have other effects as well, such as reducing pain in the knee, increasing mobility, helping one get back to favorite activities like jogging or playing with one's children or grandchildren, and so on. Such effects are generally both foreseen and desired by the agent performing the action. However, there may be other effects that the agent foresees but does not desire, such as the risks and pain involved with the surgery itself,

3. Ibid., 25.

4. Ibid., 26.

5. Gregory Beabout and Daryl Wennemann, *Applied Professional Ethics* (Lanham, Maryland: University Press of America, 1994), 58.

the difficulty of rehabilitating the knee, the possibility of more surgeries if the first does not work, and the expense of both time and money involved in the whole process. Since there are both good/desirable effects as well as bad/undesirable effects involved with such a surgery, the question arises whether or not the agent can choose such an action. We know that we should avoid bad and evil actions, so does the presence of bad side effects make an action like surgery an evil? What is one to do when confronted by both good and bad effects like this? Note, as well, that since the vast majority of human actions have multiple effects (try coming up with an action that has one, single effect—it can be challenging), if we could never do an action that had a bad effect connected with it, there would be a great many human actions that would become immoral.

The Principle of Double Effect, however, provides a principled way to reason through such situations. Double Effect reasoning demonstrates that actions that have foreseeable effects that are both good/desired and bad/undesired can be allowed, but only under certain conditions. First, the intention of the action must itself be good. This is a crucial stipulation of Double Effect reasoning—it only applies when one is considering whether or not to perform an action that is, in itself, already identified as a good action. The problem here is that the good action that the agent is contemplating will also produce foreseeable bad effects. In the case of a bad knee, surgery to heal the knee is generally a good action (if there is informed consent, the doctor is competent, and the like). The second condition of Double Effect reasoning is that one must be able clearly to distinguish the intended good effect of the action under consideration from the foreseeable bad side effects that will accompany the action. With knee surgery, the effect of healing the knee and improving its function is one aspect of the surgery, while the pain and difficulty of rehabilitation is another—the effects are intertwined but rationally distinguishable. The third condition is that none of the foreseeable bad effects can be intended or desired for itself. This condition helps clarify the first by ensuring that an agent is not doing something bad or evil under the guise of doing a good action. For example, suppose someone timed the knee surgery not only to help heal the knee, but also to have the several weeks off from work required by the rehabilitation process in order to get out of doing a big project that will require a lot of time and effort. Here, one of the foreseeable bad side effects is actually desired. The fourth and final condition is that the good of the intended effect must be proportionate to the foreseeable bad effects, in that the action being considered is proportionate to its end. This is the quintessential aspect of Double Effect reasoning. Just because an action is, when considered by itself in general, a good action, does not always justify performing the action. Instead, since we do not live and act in a vacuum, agents must consider the outcomes of their actions to insure that they are not allowing a great deal of evil to occur in the pursuit of some small good effect—to do so would simply not be prudent. And so, in the case of knee surgery, the patient would have to balance the risks and benefits of the procedure, along with other foreseeable concerns related to the cost and overall prognosis involved with the surgery and recovery. The patient would also have to consider all of these factors at both the personal level and the social/family level in making the decision to have surgery. In the end, the overall goal of Double Effect reasoning as developed in the Thomistic tradition is to limit unintended but foreseeable harm in what has otherwise been determined to be a good action.

III. Proportionalism and Double Effect

With this basic understanding of the Principle of Double Effect, we can now consider its use by proportionalists. While there are important differences among proportionalists, one central feature of their approach is the significance of the Principle of Double Effect in ethical decision making. Christopher Kaczor gives an excellent overview of the development of proportionalist thinking in his book, *Proportionalism and the Natural Law Tradition*. Kaczor notes that the contemporary movement began most notably with the work of Peter Knauer, SJ, in the late 1960s:

> In his seminal article "The Hermeneutic Function of the Principle of Double Effect," which began the movement now called "proportionalism," Peter Knauer places double-effect reasoning at the very heart of moral analysis. The article begins: "The principle of double effect leads a marginal existence in the handbooks of moral theology and appears to be useful only in making possible a species of hairsplitting. It is in reality, *the fundamental principle of all morality*."[6]

6. Kaczor, *Proportionalism and the Natural Law Tradition*, 30. The internal quote is from Knauer, "The Hermeneutic Function of the Principle of Double Effect," in *Moral Norms and Catholic Tradition*, edited by Charles E. Curran and Richard A. McCormick (New York: Paulist Press, 1979); emphasis in the original.

Knauer's reasoning for this conclusion goes something like this. Every time a human agent acts, there is a limit on what can be done—we simply cannot do everything. Thus, in acting for one good or goal, other possible goods or goals are abandoned. The loss of these goods and goals becomes an existential or ontic evil. Since every human action will have to leave some of these goods and goals unachieved, then every human action must balance the good to be gained against the goods to be lost—hence, every human action involves an application of Double Effect reasoning.[7]

Following this line of thinking, Knauer went on to reinterpret the four commonly accepted conditions of Double Effect reasoning discussed above. To begin with, Knauer suggests that the first condition, which states that the intention of the action must be good, basically begs the question, because one needs to use Double Effect reasoning to determine if the action is in fact good. That is, since both good and bad effects are involved with every human action, we cannot determine if any action is good or bad as a whole until we apply Double Effect reasoning. So that condition falls away. The second and third conditions also fall away, in that they both require us to understand the intention of the agent. The second holds that the agent must be able to distinguish the intended good effect from the foreseeable bad effect, while the third holds that the agent cannot directly intend the bad effect for itself. However, in Knauer's view, we cannot know if the agent's intention is good or bad without first knowing if the action is good or bad as determined by Double Effect reasoning. The whole point of ethical thinking here is to figure out what is good, what is bad, and which of the two you are trying to do. Thus, everything gets reduced to the final condition of proportionate reason. As Kaczor explains:

> It is Knauer's account of intention that allows him to reduce the second and third conditions to the fourth: proportionate or commensurate reason. Double-effect reasoning has become, for the first time in the tradition, a single principle: "Today the principle of double effect is most briefly formulated as follows: One may permit the evil effect of this act only if this is not intended in itself but is indirect and justified by commensurate reason."[8]

7. For a fuller and more eloquent explanation, see Kaczor, *Proportionalism and the Natural Law Tradition*, "II. How Double-Effect Reasoning Became Proportionalism," 23–44.

8. Ibid., 31. The internal quote is from Knauer, "The Hermeneutic Function of the Principle of Double Effect."

In a relatively short span of time, other thinkers picked up Knauer's train of thought and the focus on commensurate or proportionate reason, which gave rise to the proportionalist school.[9]

Now, it should be noted that not every proportionalist claims that the Principle of Double Effect is the sole principle of ethics. Richard McCormick, SJ, for example, restricts the role of Double Effect to that of a "vehicle for dealing with conflict situations."[10] According to McCormick, these would be situations in which only two courses of action are available, both of which will cause harm. As McCormick explains in his essay, "Ambiguity in Moral Choice":

> Now in situations of this kind, the rule of Christian reason, if we are governed by the *ordo bonorum*, is to choose the lesser evil. This general statement is, it would seem, beyond debate; for the only alternative is that in conflict situations we should choose the greater evil, which is patently absurd. This means that all concrete rules and distinctions are subsidiary to this and hence valid to the extent that they actually convey to us what is factually the lesser evil.... Thus the basic category for conflict situations is the lesser evil, or avoidable/unavoidable evil, or proportionate reason.[11]

For McCormick, in such conflict situations, when an agent chooses to do "the lesser of two evils," the intention is good because the agent is, "making the best of a destructive and tragic situation."[12]

Nevertheless, while there are some differences among proportionalists in terms of methodology and focus, the key concern for this discussion is the primacy given to the Principle of Double Effect in ethical decision making. After all, even for McCormick, Double Effect is the only principle that can help resolve conflict situations, and those are the situations with which we are most interested in ethics. The end result is overall the same—in ethical dilemmas we are required to produce the best state of affairs possible, even when those states of affairs involve doing evil. And so, McCormick concludes:

> If there is a truly proportionate reason for acting, the agent remains properly open and disposed toward the *ordo bonum* whether evil occurs as an indivisible effect or

9. Ibid., especially 30–31.

10. Richard A. McCormick, SJ, "Chapter One: Ambiguity in Moral Choice," in *Doing Evil to Achieve Good: Moral Choice in Conflict Situations*, edited by Richard A. McCormick, SJ, and Paul Ramsey (Chicago, Illinois: Loyola University Press, 1978), 38.

11. Ibid.

12. Ibid., 39.

as a means within the action. However, since evil-as-means and evil-as-effect are different realities, they demand different proportionate reasons. What is sufficient for *allowing* an evil may not in all cases be sufficient for *choosing* it as a means.[13]

While the application of Double Effect may vary between actions that *allow* evil versus those that *choose* it directly, choosing evil itself is required when the only choices available are evil ones to begin with. In his book, *Moral Absolutes: Tradition, Revision, and Truth*, John Finnis summarizes the thinking here in this way:

Though limited in intended scope, the principle and method of these theologians shares in the Enlightenment conception of morality: One's ultimate and immediate responsibility is to bring about good states of affairs in the world and (here they wrongly suppose that this is the same or a consistent, not a competing principle) to prevent the occurrence of bad states of affairs. And if *some* good, then, of course, *more* good. Hence their characteristic moral principle and method: Pursue the course which promises, in itself and its consequences, a net greater proportion of good states of affairs, or (again, too casually supposed to be a coapplicable criterion) a net lesser proportion of bad, overall, in the long run.[14]

Finally, since most proportionalists also connect our moral responsibility to promote the overall best state of affairs possible to the commandment to love God and neighbor, in the end we are left with a more or less Christian utilitarianism. Bruno Schuller, SJ, confirms this notion in his essay, "The Double Effect in Catholic Thought: a Reevaluation." Schuller begins by acknowledging Knauer's view that the Principle of Double Effect ultimately determines the rightness or wrongness of every human action. Schuller goes on to note that many non-Catholic ethicists would be suspicious of such a claim, especially given the origins of Double Effect reasoning within the Catholic tradition. However, Schuller argues that Knauer was not referring to the Catholic understanding of Double Effect, but rather, "to the principle as understood *correctly*."[15] Schuller goes on to add:

If traditional moral theology was mistaken, one is anxious to learn what is the proper understanding of the principle of double effect. To put it briefly, the principle, if interpreted correctly, means consequentialism or a teleological theory of

13. Ibid., 40; emphasis in the original.

14. John Finnis, *Moral Absolutes: Tradition, Revision, and Truth* (Washington, D.C.: The Catholic University of America Press, 1991), 14.

15. Bruno Schuller, SJ, "The Double Effect in Catholic Thought: a Reevaluation," in *Doing Evil to Achieve Good: Moral Choice in Conflict Situations*, 165; emphasis in the original.

> normative ethics. Knauer does not employ these terms. Apparently they were unknown to him when he wrote his articles. Nevertheless, there cannot be the slightest doubt that Knauer's thesis is to be counted among the teleological theories.[16]

Viewing the Principle of Double Effect through a consequentialist or utilitarian lens is significant, because, within that perspective, the concepts of intrinsic evils and moral absolutes dissolve. Prior to the application of Double Effect, one cannot say that any action is impermissible—rather, that is to be determined, according to the proportionalists, by the application of proportionate reason. No small consequence there!

IV. Critical Reflections on Proportionalism

At this point, the critiques against proportionalism have been well established. Many scholars, both philosophers and theologians, have demonstrated its weaknesses and errors. Of the many criticisms raised, three in particular stand out, in my judgment. First is the claim made early on in the development of proportionalist thinking that this approach was not a departure from fundamental Catholic morality, but rather an authentic development of the tradition for the Church in the modern world and a recovery of St. Thomas's own moral thought. Second is the focus upon the Principle of Double Effect as the fundamental principle of moral judgment. Third is the claim that Double Effect reasoning justifies not only allowing evil to occur, but also permits directly causing evil when it is "the lesser of two evils." There are many other important criticisms that have been raised, all of which help illuminate the serious break that proportionalist thinking has made with the Catholic tradition and the internal weaknesses of this approach as an ethical theory in general. However, I believe that the three issues noted above have caused the most confusion in Catholic moral thought over the last several decades, and so deserve special attention.

To begin with, early in its development, even before it was referred to as proportionalism, those who focused on the primacy of Double Effect reasoning within morality presented their work as an authentic development of Catholic moral theology, and indeed argued that their approach was derived from the thought of St. Thomas. As Christopher Kaczor observes:

16. Ibid.

It is not surprising that ethicists turn to the sources of Christian wisdom in their search for answers to difficult contemporary questions. Indeed, both traditionalists and proportionalists characteristically ground their moral theories more or less directly in the work of Thomas Aquinas. He is their lodestar, so the relationship of Aquinas to proportionalism is no mere antiquarian concern.[17]

John Finnis takes this even further, noting that, "Remarkably persistent have been the attempts to gain authoritative support for proportionalism by reading back into the high scholasticism of Bonaventure, Albert, and Thomas the essential proportionalist positions. . . ."[18] For his part, in 1984, McCormick argued that proportionalists, rather than introducing anything new or radical, were simply, "dialoguing with their own tradition on a relatively narrow issue."[19]

Nevertheless, while the issues raised might have appeared narrow at first, the development of proportionalist thought has led to a wide divergence from traditional Catholic morality. This can most easily be seen in the rejection by proportionalists of the concepts of intrinsic evils and moral absolutes. To support this, proportionalists usually turn to St. Thomas, and Question 94, Article 4, of the *Prima secundae,* on natural law. In this well known article, Thomas notes that while norms of the natural law hold true in general, when one descends into matters of detail, these norms may be found to fail and no longer apply to the situation at hand. Thomas's example refers to the norm of returning goods held in trust, which in general holds true for all people. However, proportionalists argue that this is only a general guideline that can change based upon the particular circumstances of a situation. In their view, this is why Thomas goes on to argue that if one is keeping weapons for another who comes to claim those weapons for the purpose of attacking you, the norm no longer holds. And, since all of human life is contingent, intermeshed with all manner of varied and changing circumstances, then no action can ever be determined to be always right or always wrong—hence, there are no moral absolutes. Instead, all moral decisions become matters of proportionate reason.

Based on this reasoning, which they argued was drawn from St. Thomas, proportionalists began to reject various long-standing moral absolutes

17. Kaczor, *Proportionalism and the Natural Law Tradition,* 5.

18. Finnis, *Moral Absolutes: Tradition, Revision, and Truth,* 90.

19. Richard A. McCormick, SJ, *Notes on Moral Theology, 1981 through 1984* (Washington, D.C.: University Press of America, 1984), 114.

within the Catholic tradition, such as the prohibitions against direct abortion and contraception. But this was certainly no small or "narrow" move. As Kaczor explains:

The Catholic Church stands as almost a solitary proponent of the existence of moral absolutes in the modern world. No other church or political body in the West has been as visible in opposition to the prevailing mélange of emotivism, pragmatism, positivism, and intuitionism dominant in the public square. Hence, the attempt to undermine the traditional understandings of moral absolutes from within the Catholic Church itself is significant for the present "culture wars" in Western societies today.[20]

Proportionalism simply does not stand within the Catholic tradition, regardless of the fact that it was developed and maintained almost solely by Catholic thinkers. John Paul II made this explicitly clear in his encyclical letter, *Veritatis Splendor*. In discussing proportionalism, he noted, "Such theories however are not faithful to the Church's teaching, when they believe they can justify, as morally good, deliberate choices of kinds of behavior contrary to the commandments of the divine and natural law. These theories cannot claim to be grounded in the Catholic moral tradition."[21] Although proportionalists have debated the significance of the Pope's words, the claim seems rather definitive.[22]

As for the appeal to Question 94, Article 4, of the *Prima secundae*, many scholars have demonstrated that proportionalists have taken Thomas out of context here (putting it nicely). For example, in his book, *Moral Absolutes*, Finnis points out that the particular article under consideration has nothing to do with the issue of moral absolutes:

Proportionalists who appeal to this text omit to note that the question under discussion in a. 4 has nothing to do with the question of whether there are any exceptionless moral norms. It is, Is the natural law the same for all?, and none of the counter positions which Aquinas articulates in order to refute has any relation to the moral absolutes of the tradition.[23]

20. Kaczor, *Proportionalism and the Natural Law Tradition*, 6.

21. John Paul II, *Veritatis Splendor*, n. 76. John Finnis has also thoroughly demonstrated the incongruity of proportionalism with the Catholic Tradition in his book, *Moral Absolutes: Tradition, Revision, and Truth*. Finnis even notes that one can rightly question whether or not proportionalism is consistent with Christianity itself; see "Chapter 1: Foundations, 4. Rejected when human replaces divine providence," 12–16.

22. For example, see *Veritatis Splendor: American Responses*, edited by Michael E. Allsopp and John J. O'Keefe (Kansas City, Missouri: Sheed and Ward, 1995).

23. Finnis, *Moral Absolutes: Tradition, Revision, and Truth*, 90, n. 10.

That is, the example Thomas gives in this article of returning goods held in trust is not itself a moral absolute. His own discussion shows that this norm is true in general, but the whole point is to show that this is an example of a norm that will change as the contingent circumstances of life change. To hold weapons back from a would-be attacker, or someone who is in a fit of anger, is not stealing. Rather, it now becomes a case either of self-defense, or of prudential judgment in preventing harm or injury to others. The norm is now different because the situation is different. Nor does this make Thomas's view relativistic, as the proportionalists seem to read it. Why? Because Thomas has already demonstrated, in keeping with Aristotle, that there are some moral absolutes. As Finnis explains, "This is made clear many times by Aquinas, when he notes that, although affirmative moral norms, the majority of moral norms, hold *semper sed non ad semper*, there are also negative moral norms, the minority, which hold *semper et ad semper*, always and everywhere without exceptions."[24] Proportionalists may claim to find support for their rejection of moral absolutes in this article from Thomas, but only by extracting it from the thought of Thomas taken as a whole. In the end, Germain Grisez's observation that Peter Knauer was, "carrying through a revolution in principle while pretending only a clarification of traditional ideas" holds true for the proportionalist movement as a whole.[25]

The second area of confusion is related to the first claim just discussed, that proportionalism is a development of the Catholic tradition, and especially the thought of St. Thomas. While positioning their work as an extension of, or for some a recovery of, Thomas, proportionalists also claim that the Principle of Double Effect is the sole, or at least primary, principle of ethical and moral decision making. As noted in the previous section, this is a hallmark of proportionalistic thinking. When the notion of intrinsic evil is removed, one cannot say that any action is good or bad in itself. Rather, every action always involves competing goods, and so the human agent must balance the good to be gained against the goods to be lost. Hence,

24. Ibid., 91.

25. Germain Grisez, *Abortion: The Myths, the Realities, and the Arguments* (Washington, D.C.: Corpus Books, 1970), 331. It is worth noting that, later in the movement, proportionalists slowly began to grant these points. For example, in 1989, Richard McCormick conceded in regards to Grisez, "I do not believe 'revolution' is too strong a word for the developments that have occurred in moral theology in the last 30 years" ("Moral Theology 1940–1989: An Overview," *Theological Studies* 50 [1989], 6–7).

every human action involves an application of Double Effect reasoning—it is, as Knauer said, "*the fundamental principle of all morality.*"[26] The implication here is that this is the view of Thomas and the Catholic tradition as well. We must also recall that, in this reduction of all morality to the Principle of Double Effect, there was also a reduction of all moral reasoning to the sole criterion of proportionate reason. The four commonly accepted conditions of Double Effect developed within the tradition held that the intention of the action must in itself be good, that the good intention must be distinguishable from the foreseeable bad side effect, the bad side effect must not be intended for itself, and the action must be proportionate to its end. As explained above, proportionalists argue that the first three conditions are superfluous. All that matters is the application of proportionate reason, which in their view is basically a weighing of good effects versus bad effects, or in some cases of bad effects versus worse effects.

Anyone familiar with the *Summa Theologiae* will easily recognize that the suggestion that Thomas held the Principle of Double Effect as the sole, or even primary, principle of ethical reasoning is simply false. Double Effect reasoning is not presented early in Thomas's discussion of morality, but rather arises in the middle of his overall treatment of human action. Further, it is introduced as an application of earlier moral concepts addressed by Thomas, such as justice, to the specific question of killing in self-defense. As Christopher Kaczor so carefully explains in his book, *Proportionalism and the Natural Law Tradition*:

> Thomas's treatment of double-effect reasoning comes as the 178th of 304 moral questions treated in the *Secunda pars* of the *Summa*, midway through the *Secunda secundae* at question 64. He has already treated many other "moral" topics not only in the *Secunda secundae* but also in the *Prima secundae*.... Because it presupposes so many principles laid down in the *Prima secundae*, Thomas's analysis of self-defense should be understood as an application of the principles of judging human action given in the *Prima secundae*.[27]

Thus, in neither way is Double Effect reasoning fundamental to moral thinking for Thomas the way proportionalists imply. Thomas does not make primary use of Double Effect reasoning in his own moral discussions. Nor is the Principle primary as a principle, because it is itself an application

26. Peter Knauer, SJ, "The Hermeneutic Function of the Principle of Double Effect," quoted in Kaczor, *Proportionalism and the Natural Law Tradition*, 30; emphasis in the original.

27. Kaczor, *Proportionalism and the Natural Law Tradition*, 36.

of other, more fundamental principles. The same can, of course, be said for the Catholic tradition as well. In its two thousand year history, it is only the proportionalists beginning in the 1960s who gave the Principle fundamental importance. While Double Effect reasoning is certainly important, and one can say its influence has grown in recent years as a tool for handling many specific and difficult problems, it is not the sole, or even primary, principle of moral decision making within the Catholic tradition.

All of this goes back to the importance of the four conditions that relate to the proper application of the Principle of Double Effect. By reducing these four conditions into the last one that relates to proportionate reason, proportionalists obscure the actual thought process that is at work with Double Effect. However, for both Thomas and the Catholic tradition, there are moral absolutes and other moral principles that apply prior to Double Effect reasoning. It is these very principles that help us determine if an action, in and of itself, is good and can be considered as an ethical option when acting. Thus, the four conditions must be retained; for some actions will never require an application of Double Effect, since they are already determined to be wrong in light of other, more fundamental, moral principles. As Joseph Boyle notes in his essay, "Toward Understanding the Principle of Double Effect," there is a certain redundancy in the four conditions that relate to Double Effect reasoning. Nevertheless, Boyle observes that "The redundancy of the traditional formulations of the PDE, however, is understandable if one considers the casuistical purpose for which the PDE was meant to be used and the distinctions the scholastics were accustomed to make."[28] To put this in simpler terms, applying the Principle of Double Effect involves a process. In this process, reason must examine several factors in order to make a final determination that the action under consideration is good and can be performed. The first is to make sure that one does not directly perform an action for an immoral purpose. Thus, the Principle of Double Effect does not allow us to justify any action we may wish to perform—we cannot work the system. The second condition is equally important, for, if one cannot distinguish the good effect from the bad side effect, then the action would be directly causing evil. In such a case, the bad is not really a side effect, but is part of the main effect and so should not

28. Joseph M. Boyle, Jr., "Toward Understanding the Principle of Double Effect," in *The Doctrine of Double Effect: Philosophers Debate a Controversial Moral Principle*, edited by P.A. Woodward (Notre Dame, Indiana: University of Notre Dame Press, 2001), 12.

be performed. The third condition then helps insure that the agent is not choosing an evil means to achieve a good end. Some object that this condition is covered by the first two conditions. That may be true in most cases, but not all. The process of Double Effect reasoning is significant, then, to make sure that nothing slips through the cracks of our moral decision making. Boyle provides a helpful example to illustrate the importance of all of these first three conditions in the application of the Principle of Double Effect:

> … the first condition would exclude, for example, giving someone money in order to get him drunk; the second, making oneself drunk in order to give someone a lesson in the value of sobriety; and the third, giving someone money in order to get him drunk in order to teach him a lesson. In the first case, the "positing of the cause" is permissible and there is no evil means to a good end, but the aim is evil. In the second case, the aim is good but the cause posited—getting oneself drunk—is evil. In the third case, the final end of the action is good, as is the positing of the cause, but an intermediate means is evil—namely, getting the person drunk.[29]

What must be noted here is that, in all three cases Boyle provides, one would not reach the fourth condition and apply proportionate reason to determine if the action was permissible. The first three conditions have already shown each possible action as impermissible. Further, these first three conditions rely upon principles other than Double Effect to make the above determinations.

In sum, the Principle of Double Effect is not appealed to first in the decision making process, nor *should* it be appealed to first once the proper role of the four conditions is understood. To determine if an intention or means is good, one must first have an understanding of what makes something good or bad, which is no small task. (This is probably why Thomas does not get around to Double Effect reasoning until the midpoint of his discussion on morality.) Indeed, how can the proportionalists claim that all of morality comes down to proportionate reason, when such reason requires a prior understanding of good and bad, right and wrong? Where is this moral knowledge coming from in the first place? John Finnis sums up the problem here well when he writes:

> … choices must be guided by moral principles such as exclude unfairness, intention to harm or impede basic human goods, or other immoral motivations.… And

29. Ibid.

these principles must all be satisfied if the action is to be right, morally good. As soon as one can see that an option fails one of the moral tests, one knows that that option is wrong. To go on examining the other aspects of the option is then mere distraction. Indeed, it is merely to torment oneself with temptation. In reality, the injunction to consider all the goods and bads in the totality of the situation, when there is no rational criterion for processing all the information, cannot (for all its authors' good intentions) be other than an invitation to devise rationalizations for doing what one feels like.[30]

A proper understanding of moral decision making shows that the application of Double Effect reasoning comes late in the process, and not first. And so, the four conditions should be retained to avoid the temptations to which Finnis alludes.

Finally, it is important to reflect on the proportionalists' conclusion that the Principle of Double Effect allows us to justify doing evil to achieve good, or that it requires us to do the so-called "lesser" of two evils when we have only evil options from which to choose. As noted above, Richard McCormick observed, "Now in situations of this kind, the rule of Christian reason, if we are governed by the *ordo bonorum*, is to choose the lesser evil. This general statement is, it would seem, beyond debate; for the only alternative is that in conflict situations we should choose the greater evil, which is patently absurd."[31] Most proportionalists, including McCormick, would qualify this statement by making a distinction between ontic evil, which they also refer to as pre-moral, and moral evil. Given their reduction of the whole of morality to Double Effect reasoning, an action is only a moral evil when it lacks proportionate reason. All other bad actions would be ontic or physical evils. The distinction between physical and moral evil does indeed arise within the Catholic tradition, with the exception that in the tradition more than just a lack of proportionate reason can make a physical evil also a moral evil. Proportionalists make a lot out of this distinction. In the end, they conclude that Double Effect reasoning allows one to permit moral evil for a proportionate reason, while also allowing one to directly intend or cause a pre-moral evil, once again, when there is a proportionate reason for choosing the evil. This allows proportionalists to maintain that they do not support causing or doing evil (meaning for them, "moral" evil). Never-

30. Finnis, *Moral Absolutes: Tradition, Revision, and Truth*, 96–97.

31. McCormick, "Chapter One: Ambiguity in Moral Choice," in *Doing Evil to Achieve Good: Moral Choice in Conflict Situations*, 38.

theless, as many scholars have pointed out, this position, whether proportionalists intended so or not, allows for a great amount of evil to be done.

The problem in this case goes back to misunderstanding the proper role of the Principle of Double Effect. As has been noted, the Principle is not the sole, nor even the primary, principle of ethical decision making. Rather, it is an application of other, more basic and fundamental principles. This was clearly the view of St. Thomas. John Finnis emphasizes throughout his book, *Moral Absolutes*, that, "In every context in which a moral issue is to be resolved, Aquinas refuses the invitation to solve the issue by identifying 'the lesser evil'. . . ."[32] Later, Finnis explains more fully that:

> The requirement of "proportionateness" proposed by Aquinas at the origin of the "doctrine" used no concept of greater good or lesser evil and involved no scrutiny of overall net consequences; it merely required that the action which causes the foreseen harm must be no more harmful than is necessary for defending oneself then and there: the act must be *proportionatus fini*, proportioned to its own end.[33]

Yet, the mistake persists. Doing "the lesser of two evils" has become a faddish way to justify one's actions. And so, we must correct this type of thinking. As Frs. Ashley and O'Rourke explain in their book, *Health Care Ethics: A Theological Analysis*:

> Sometimes people try to justify actions as "the lesser evil," but it is contradictory to claim it can ever be ethical to do what is evil or unethical in itself, even under duress. In some situations, however, persons find themselves with a "perplexed conscience"; that is, it seems to them that all their options, even the option of doing nothing at all, are unethical—In such a situation, they must do what seems to be the least evil, not indeed because it is evil, but because it seems to be a good option. In practice, however, given the needed time to think the matter through and to achieve a well-formed conscience, the principle of double effect may permit an objectively good solution to moral dilemmas by providing an option which is not "the lesser evil" but which is simply good.[34]

This means that in some cases one may think he or she is doing "the lesser of two evils" when in reality one is actually performing a good action.

32. Finnis, *Moral Absolutes: Tradition, Revision, and Truth*, 56, n. 48.

33. Ibid., 97.

34. Benedict M. Ashley, OP, and Kevin D. O'Rourke, OP, *Health Care Ethics: A Theological Analysis*, 4th Edition (Washington, D.C.: Georgetown University Press, 1997), 193. For a fuller account of this misunderstanding, see Kaczor, *Proportionalism and the Natural Law Tradition*, "VI. Doing Evil To Achieve Good," 141–70.

It also means that at times persons may be trying to claim they are doing "the lesser of two evils" to justify performing a genuinely bad action as determined by other principles prior to applying the Principle of Double Effect.[35] In the end, we must always remember that the task of ethics is to do good and avoid evil—the amount of evil (i.e., greater or lesser) is simply irrelevant in the decision making process.

So, what is the proper way to understand the Principle of Double Effect? What is its role and function in moral decision making? I believe that the Principle of Double Effect is primarily a pragmatic tool that helps us judge the prudence of good actions that are intertwined with evil consequences, and as such it is not the primary or sole moral principle in ethics. Rather, in the decision making process, Double Effect is the final principle that we should apply before we perform an action in order to insure that we are not going to produce more harm than good. As such, the Principle of Double Effect shows how we can allow actions that are accompanied by evil consequences, but it does not permit or justify directly evil actions.

V. Conclusion: Why must we not do evil?

To conclude, it is worth noting that the discussion of Double Effect and the confusions associated with the proper application of this principle caused by proportionalist thinking is not merely an abstract debate suited for the journals. Rather, the rise of proportionate reason as the sole criterion for ethical decision making has already had a deep impact upon the Catholic faithful, which in turn has had a deep impact upon society as a whole. As we have noted, the Catholic Church is one of the few clear defenders of the notion of moral absolutes. And while it may be the case that few among the laity pay attention to the type of intellectual debate raised by proportionalism, an erosion of traditional Catholic morality has been occurring more subtly within the Church as a result of this thinking, and has given rise to widespread dissent in regard to the Church's teachings. The net result is that many bad actions are done under the guise of doing "the lesser of two evils."

In the literature, a number of diverse and interesting reasons have been

35. For an example of the principled natural law approach as a process in which the Principle of Double Effect comes last, see Gregory Beabout and Daryl Wennemann, *Applied Professional Ethics*, especially Chapters 2 and 4.

given for why all of this has occurred, from the obvious misreadings of St. Thomas to the ever-increasing pressures of life in a secularized world; there are many factors that led to the rise of proportionalism. But what concerns me more is the impact that proportionalism has had, and will continue to have in the future, on the Church and the Catholic faithful. Whereas the philosophical and theological errors and weaknesses of proportionalism have been well demonstrated, including at the very highest levels of the Church, the theory and its rejection of traditional Catholic moral norms continues to be presented as authentic Catholic doctrine. The influence comes mainly from the seminaries and schools of theology. Christopher Kaczor captures this insight well when he observes that proportionalism:

> ... has a tremendous influence, if only implicitly, on the day-to-day lives of millions of people. Unlike many academic moral theories, proportionalism has been translated into practice through the education of priests and other religious educators who serve as teachers on the local and pastoral level. Contemporary training in Catholic moral theology is dominated by one school: proportionalism. No less an authority on the subject than Richard McCormick writes: "So-called proportionalists include some of the best known names in moral theology throughout the world.... My acquaintance with the literature leads me to believe that most theologians share similar perspectives." The sociological influence of this "revised natural law theory" as it is sometimes called should not be underestimated.[36]

I myself have experienced what Kaczor observes here. I went through all four years of a college seminary, and attended a theologate seminary for one year. The professor who taught our course on Fundamental Moral Theology had studied in Rome under Josef Fuchs, SJ, a prominent proportionalist. Our class was nothing but proportionalism. Having received a strong grounding in Thomistic philosophy as an undergraduate, I was skeptical of my professor's approach early on. However, the rest of my classmates seemed to take a less critical eye, mainly focusing on what was needed to pass the class and move on. But the influence was there. I am not surprised, then, when I hear reports of the current relativism found in pastoral counseling on matters such as abortion, contraception, sterilization, in vitro fertilization, divorce and remarriage, and so on. It even appears at times that very little advice or teaching is given: "follow your own conscience" seems to cover it all. But rather than empowering the laity and modernizing the

36. Kaczor, *Proportionalism and the Natural Law Tradition*, 7.

Church, as its supporters sometimes claim, I believe proportionalism and the relativistic attitudes it has engendered have done a great disservice to the faithful. A moral fiction has replaced the truth, and many have been led astray by the very people they turned to for help. It is at this point that I believe we need to pause and reflect upon the basic question of, "Why must we not do evil?"

To begin an answer to this question, we must start by recalling what evil is in the first place. Evil is a privation—a lack of goodness that a thing should have, an absence of proper being. But, as Jacques Maritain reminds us in *St. Thomas and the Problem of Evil*:

> That does not mean that evil does not exist, or is merely an illusion, or that we need only deny its existence, as do the Christian Scientists, to make it disappear. Evil does exist in things, it is terribly present in them. Evil is real, it actually exists like a wound or mutilation of the being; evil is there in all reality, whenever a thing—which, insofar as it is, and has being, is good—is deprived of some being or of some good it should have.[37]

One might conclude today, however, just the opposite: that evil is just an illusion, or an archaic notion left over from the Middle Ages. Indeed, people do not like even to speak of evil. They will refer to things as "bad," but the term "evil" seems too strong for the contemporary ear. After all, when we are supposedly doing "the lesser of two evils," the action is not really "evil" is it? Unfortunately, pretending that we are not doing an evil action or trying to justify doing an evil action as the "lesser choice" does not work. Evil always leaves its mark. Sometimes, the mark is physical—someone is hurt, something gets damaged, or someone dies as a result of our action. The physical lack is usually noticeable. But sometimes there is no apparent physical damage left behind after a bad action. Nevertheless, evil always leaves a metaphysical mark. Maritain puts it this way: "That that which has no being in itself, nor essence nor form, nor order, nor determination, and cannot have,—in other words, that evil exists, is real and efficacious,—it is in this that appears to us evil's metaphysical monstrosity."[38] Even when no bad consequences arise as a result of bad action in the physical world that we can measure and weigh, evil leaves its mark as a gaping hole in reality.

The case is even more serious with moral evil—the evil that results from

37. Maritain, *St. Thomas and the Problem of Evil*, 2.
38. Ibid., 3.

human action. Sometimes physical evil is beyond our control. But moral evil flows out of our free choice. That is why moral evil rips the very fabric of our humanity. It cannot exist of its own, and so it exists off of physical things and moral agents. For human agents, our actions give life, in a sense, to evil, and we do so at a terrible cost—our very self. As Maritain observes, "Evil is therefore efficacious not by itself but through the good it wounds and preys upon as a parasite, efficacious through a good that is wanting or deflected, and whose action is to that extent vitiated. What is the power of evil? It is the very power of the good that evil wounds and preys upon."[39] And so, when we choose evil, we willingly allow this parasite to destroy us. And, just like a parasite, evil eats away at us quietly—the damage is often not seen until it is too late to stop.

Of course, one of the major problems in understanding the nature of evil and why we must not do it is that it usually does not feel like we are destroying ourselves when we do bad actions. In fact, many bad actions do not feel bad at all, which is why it is easy to try to justify them. This is because our will is drawn to goodness, and we can choose any good presented to the will even when there are other higher goods at stake. That is, we can focus on and choose what Aristotle calls the apparent good instead of the true good.[40] But the apparent good is lacking, and thus often is evil. Unfortunately, as we do evil actions, our view of the true good becomes corrupted. Herein lies one of the great dangers of evil—as its power in us grows, it becomes harder for us to recognize it as evil. Aristotle often compared this to the way illness corrupts the body and alters what appears good to us.[41] For example, our favorite foods lose their appeal when we have the flu, and normal volumes of noise seem too loud when we have a headache. Evil has a similar affect on our understanding of good and bad. This also relates back to Aristotle's view of habituation.[42] While doing good actions helps make us virtuous, doing bad actions conversely makes us vicious. Aristotle is clear to point out that this does not happen after only one or two actions—this process takes time. But, if one continues to do bad actions, one will become a vicious person. Our actions mold our character. Once again, because the process is slow and takes time, we are often

39. Ibid., 2.
40. See Aristotle, *Nicomachean Ethics*, Book III, Chapter 4, 1113a15–1113b.
41. Ibid.
42. See Aristotle, *Nicomachean Ethics*, Book II, as well as Book III, Chapter 5, 1113b5–1115a5.

unaware of our own moral development—whether good or bad. And so we need to be constantly mindful of the "soul-making significance of moral action," to use the words of John Finnis.[43] As he goes on to explain later in his book, *Moral Absolutes:*

> ... every choice, once made, lasts in one's character. As behavior, performance, cause, one's choice and action may be frustrated and utterly fail. But unless and until one repents of it—that is, reverses it by some contrary, incompatible choice—one retains the character which one specified and created for oneself by intelligently shaping and freely adopting the object of that choice.[44]

I believe that this is why Aquinas does not merely say that the first precept of natural law is to do good and choose "the lesser evil." Aquinas does not even say we must do good, but we can "allow evil." Certainly, Aquinas does recognize that we can permit or allow evil at times, based on an understanding of the way God allows both physical and moral evil. But I do not believe that Aquinas ever intends us to take situations in which we might have to allow evil lightly. That is why the first precept of the natural law is to *avoid* evil. Think on that for a moment. Not only should we not cause evil directly—but we should *avoid* it, stay away from it, and not be party to evil actions. Why? Because, as Aquinas knew all too well, evil is a parasite. Once it takes hold, it begins to do damage. It is difficult to shake because its influence is subtle. Given time it will corrupt our whole being. God's grace is, of course, more powerful than evil. But when we are not aware that we are sick, we do not go to the doctor. The same is true for one in evil's subtle grasp. We think we are fine, we think we are being ethical, we think we are pursuing the true good—all because of the deadly influence of evil. Even to be near evil is to take a great risk! That is why we ought to avoid it. And if that is true of allowing evil, then it is certainly even clearer in the case of causing evil. When the proportionalists then say that it is acceptable for someone to cause an evil in order either to achieve a greater good or as "the lesser of two evils," they have given us a bad prescription.

So why must we not do evil? Because it wounds and damages us. And as evil wounds and damages us, it also wounds and damages our relationships: our relationship with self, our relationship with others, and most of all our relationship with God. God's grace can certainly heal the wound of

43. Finnis, *Moral Absolutes: Tradition, Revision, and Truth*, 23.
44. Ibid., 73.

evil. But will we recognize our need for grace while under the influence of evil? To openly advise anyone to take such a risk, by telling someone it is acceptable to do evil, is itself a great evil!

In the end, the Principle of Double Effect is an important principle in contemporary ethics, and its influence is growing. It is primarily a pragmatic tool that helps us judge the prudence of good actions that are intertwined with evil consequences. As such, it is not the primary or sole principle in ethics, but rather the final principle that we should apply before we perform an action in order to insure that we are not going to produce more harm than good. Why take this caution? Because we must not take evil and its subtle power for granted. Instead, we must avoid evil at all costs. The Principle of Double Effect shows how we can allow actions that are accompanied by evil consequences, but it does not permit or justify directly evil actions. The errors of proportionalism do not reduce the importance of the Principle of Double Effect, and it should not be rejected because of the way it has been misused by some thinkers. Rather, those who work in the natural law tradition must strive to explain and defend the proper understanding of Double Effect and the important role it plays in ethical decision-making as the final principle we apply before acting, to insure that we are being prudent.

DENIS A. SCRANDIS

How Maritainian Choice of Evil Forms the Moral Object

Recent Thomistic scholarship has produced several significant treatments of St. Thomas Aquinas's theory of action. One of these is Denis Bradley's *Aquinas on the Twofold Human Good.*[1] Although this textual analysis is admirable, Jacques Maritain would take serious issue with its account regarding both the choice of evil and the formation of the moral object. What does Bradley report and conclude? Overall, his analysis assigns responsibility for moral evil to defective psychological powers and habits of action.[2]

What is there in Bradley's treatment that would be unacceptable to Maritain? If a defect were in the very nature of the will (rather than in its exercise), then the choice of evil would not be free but rather from nature. In addition, if an evil choice were attributable to a prior evil, then we would have an indefinite regress and no true explanation. Moreover, the Creator of our being and nature would be at fault. In his own exploration of these issues, Maritain looked for a cause of evil that is free, that is not itself evil, and that is certainly not God. Let us begin with a sketch of the psychological principles of the voluntary moral action.

I. The Complete Voluntary Action

Aristotle and St. Thomas Aquinas contributed elements to a theory of action in their explorations of moral issues. Both analyzed human action in

1. Denis Bradley, *Aquinas on the Twofold Human Good* (Washington, D.C.: Catholic University of America Press, 1997); hereafter cited as *Bradley.*

2. Ibid., 278–79.

terms of a series of operations performed by interactive, alternating powers that proceeds like a dialogue between intellect and will and that builds a complete human or voluntary action. The theory consists of 12 steps with six contributed by intellect and six by will. The first four steps establish an end for an action, the second four steps discover or design a means by which to achieve the end, and the last four execute the means and monitor the attainment of the end.

The first four steps are as follows. The intellect initiates the process when it apprehends some object as a good and proposes it to the will as an end. The will, responding to the object's goodness, may wish it as an end. The intellect then considers the attainability of the end. (Is it a true good? Is it consistent with the trajectory of my life? Is it something that *I* want?) The will may then intend to attain this end. The second four steps design or develop the means to the end. The intellect deliberates about the means. The deliberated means can vary in complexity from simple, direct, action to a complex train of steps. It can involve the cooperation of others and can extend over years. The will may or may not consent to proposals offered by the intellect. Eventually a practical judgment of choice selects one definite means terminating the deliberation and specifying the deliberated means to the will. The will may or may not choose this means to the end at this time. The final four steps execute the means and monitor the attainment of the end.

II. Maritain on Choice of Evil

In his book *God and the Permission of Evil*,[3] Jacques Maritain examines the cause of moral evil. Maritain works within the Thomistic worldview in which God creates and sustains in being free and fallible creatures. As the First Cause of motion, God activates created natures throughout the life of the world. Maritain distinguishes moral or blamable evil (or sin) from physical evil. Although God is innocent of moral evil, God is not uninvolved in physical evil. As the transcendent First Cause of the universe, God wills and causes the good of the universe and of the things therein. Thus the good achieved in nourishing the lion is willed by God, while the losses or evil suffered by the gazelle in nourishing the lion are indirectly and accidentally

3. Jacques Maritain, *God and the Permission of Evil* (Milwaukee, Wisconsin: The Bruce Publishing Co., 1966); hereafter cited as *Maritain*.

linked by nature to the goods and gains willed by God. On the other hand, moral evil is caused by fallible creatures and permitted (sometimes) by God without being willed or caused by God. With God so intimately involved in the lives of His free creatures, Maritain seeks to defend the moral innocence of God, even as God not only sustains the agent in being but even may sustain the agent's motion in the performance of an evil action.

III. The Guiding Principles of Maritain's Position

Maritain begins *God and the Permission of Evil* by setting forth the principles that command his entire discussion of human acts from action theory to salvation. Maritain says: "The fundamental certitude, the rock to which we must cling in this question of moral evil, is the *absolute innocence of God*."[4] He cites two texts in the *Summa Theologiae* of St. Thomas Aquinas. The first asserts that God is absolutely not the cause of moral evil, neither directly nor indirectly.[5] Even the shadow of indirect causality, such as hypothesizing defective psychological powers, must be excluded. The second principle is that "The first cause of the absence of grace comes from us."[6] The first cause of moral evil is to be found in us. Sin is an invention of the free creature. Note well: Thomas's moral theology assigns the first cause of the loss of grace to men, and Maritain's moral thinking assigns to us the first cause of moral evil because we render ourselves without grace at a critical point in the formation of what the act is about, namely, in the formation of the moral object of the action.

IV. The Line of Good and the Line of Evil

Maritain believes that the language and concepts of the discussion of evil must be redesigned to meet the special needs of describing evil. The good is being, i.e., the plenitude or completion of being. Evil, on the contrary, is the absence of being; it is nothingness. When we reason in the line of evil, we must reason in the line of non-being, because evil is in nowise being. Thus, there must be a dissymmetry between, on the one hand, our accustomed and familiar manner of examining and explaining moral acts

4. Ibid., 3.
5. St. Thomas Aquinas, *Summa Theologiae* (hereafter cited as *ST*) I-II, q. 79, a. 1.
6. Ibid., I-II, q. 112, a. 3 ad 2.

from the perspective of being and good and, on the other hand, our newly designed and disciplined manner of looking at and explaining immoral acts from the perspective of non-being and evil. Maritain sees a "fundamental, irreducible dissymmetry, between the line of good and the line of evil."[7] He regards this methodological invention as "a principle which is like a beacon illuminating the whole debate."[8]

Maritain interprets a passage in the *Gospel of John*, "Without Me, you can do nothing" (Jn 15, 5), as a point of departure for the doctrine of the dissymmetry between the line of good and the line of evil; his interpretation illustrates the two lines. As read in the line of being, where God has the first initiative, it says, "Without Me, you can do nothing good." As read in the line of evil, where created liberty has the first initiative, it says, "Without Me you can do nothingness, without me you can introduce into being that nothingness or that *non-being of the due good*, that *privation*, which is *evil*."[9]

Maritain's discussion of the cause of moral evil focuses very sharply, within Thomistic ethics, on the acts of conscience, election, and choice. Conscience is a judgment by the intellect regarding a proposed action that measures the action against the natural law. Election is a judgment of intellect that defines a voluntary action in accordance with the judgment of conscience and proposes it to the will. And choice is an act of the will that projects into the world the concrete action that may, or may not, have been validated by the natural law in the preceding judgments of conscience and election.

Let us examine some moral reasoning which may be attributable to the Good Samaritan (Lk 10, 25–37). The most general moral principle is, "Do good and avoid doing evil." A less general moral principle is "It is good to help people in distress," which, in the context of the Good Samaritan, can be represented by "This injured man *should be helped.*" The judgment of conscience of the Good Samaritan then is "I *should help* this injured man." The judgment of election of the Good Samaritan is "I *will help* this man now," and the following choice of the will produces the celebrated act of mercy. The Samaritan chose as he did in consideration of this rule. Had he not considered the rule, his choice would not have been measured by the natural law (and thus would have been "rule-less"), and his action would have been without the obligation to help as were the actions of those in the parable who walked by.

7. Maritain, *God and the Permission of Evil*, 9. 8. Ibid.

9. Ibid., 33.

V. The Notion of the Non-Consideration of the Rule

Maritain, following the rigors of discourse in the line of non-being, writes that the "non-consideration of the rule" is not an "act of non-consideration," such as when I ignore a distracting noise, but a "non-act of consideration," as when I, while attending to one matter, attend to another, while losing sight of the first. Maritain writes: "This *defectus,* this free failure which is the *cause* of moral evil without being itself an evil, is the *non-consideration of the rule—which* is not, note well, an *act* of non-consideration, but a *non-act* of consideration."[10] This non-act of consideration of the rule is something that is done freely. And a non-act of consideration, though not evil itself, is a non-evil cause of evil.

In the context of a concrete whole action, Maritain distinguishes two features or "instants of nature" in the structure of the non-act.

> *First instant of nature:* not to consider the rule, which is a mere withdrawal from being ... a mere absence of a good that is *not due.* And, *second instant of nature:* to act with this absence, which, from the sole fact that one acts [without the rule], becomes a privation, the absence of a *due* good, and causes the operation to deviate.[11]

The agent's non-act of consideration is not the absence of a due good on the agent's part. On the other hand, consideration of the rule is a due good for the formation of the action. The agent's non-act of consideration removes the rule's measure of the action and causes the absence of a due good on the part of the action. When an action's measure is removed, the object's formation is defective, and a non-evil cause causes an evil action. The moral object that informs choice here is not measured against the rule of the natural law and may be neither ordered to a good end nor without an evil means.

VI. Maritain's "Motions" and the Graces

Maritain describes a "motion" to consider the natural law that is operative psychologically in the judgment of election. He has described it as "shatterable." If the agent cooperates with the motion, a good, natural law-measured action results. And, if the agent does not consider the rule, he shatters the motion to consider the rule and a defective action (one not subjected to the

10. Ibid., 35.
11. Ibid., 36.

first principle of practical reason, i.e., one not consistent with doing good and avoiding evil) results.[12]

Maritain also describes a change that can come over the fragile motion. If the agent accepts the motion to consider the rule, the motion changes into an "unshatterable motion" under which the creature will produce the good act.[13] Maritain identifies his notion of a shatterable motion with the theological notion of sufficient grace and his unshatterable motion with efficacious grace. These identifications were foreshadowed in St. Thomas's observation that the first cause of the absence of grace comes from us.

VII. Bradley on Choosing Evil

Bradley assigns responsibility for moral evil to mistaken judgments influenced by passion, vice, and a disordered will. His discussion of the cause of moral evil begins with the observation that ontological and moral good are different.[14] Ontological goodness is the perfection of a form or nature, while moral goodness is goodness in the order of reason. Thus, to be morally good, an action must be in accord with reason, while an agent must act according to reason. Hence, ontological evil is the privation of a good that duly belongs to a nature. And, moral evil is a characteristic of an action that arises from the will choosing a good that is contrary to the good that reason requires. Thus, morally good actions and morally evil actions constitute different species of actions.[15]

Bradley's discussion of the cause of moral evil continues with the distinction between real moral goods and merely apparent, but actually evil, moral goods. A real moral good is an end or means to an end that is in agreement with the agent's form. An apparent moral good is an evil that has been erroneously judged to be in agreement with the agent's form. More exactly, since the form of man is the rational soul, the moral good of man is found in those ends that are in accordance with the rational soul. Real moral goods (which are in accord with the rational soul) can be ordered to man's ultimate good, which Bradley identifies with the vision of God, whereas apparent moral goods lead one away from the ultimate good.[16] Thus, the judgment of moral good and moral evil falls properly within the

12. Ibid., 39.
13. Ibid.
14. Bradley, *Thomas on the Twofold Human Good*, 275.
15. Ibid., 277.
16. Ibid., 278.

sphere of practical reason. Bradley observes that real moral goods can satisfy desire and are known to be really morally good from their being concordant with the ends of the rational soul and right reason. The end's criterion of moral goodness is being in accord with reason. The deliberated action's criteria for true moral goodness are that the action's moral object and circumstances as well as the agent's end are all in conformity with reason.[17]

This having been said, Bradley then identifies the cause or causes of moral evil. He says first that ends or means that are really morally bad can seem to be morally good because our judgments are "inculpably mistaken."[18] This is puzzling. What does he mean by "inculpably mistaken?" Now, various ends and means to ends appeal to us individually in so far as they appeal to our appetitive habits of virtue and vice. Thus, Bradley possibly means that our judgments about goods that appeal to us can be drawn casually, unreflectively, or innocently (hence "inculpably") if our moral character, which can function as a basis of our judgment, is not taken to be a matter of our personal responsibility. Bradley next says that our judgments "more frequently" about particular actions (or means) are "culpably irrational," because they are made under the sway of the passions, especially that of concupiscence or the intemperate desire for bodily pleasures. Bradley possibly means by "culpably irrational" that yielding behavioral control to intemperate habitual principles establishes a regime of vices. Such a habitual regime, formed by repeated choices of intemperate extremes of pleasure rather than by choices of reason-moderated pleasures, can be called "irrational." And, since one is responsible for one's character formation, those judgments that derive from this self-imposed regime of vices can thus be called "culpably irrational." Now, does Bradley's terminology create a contradiction? First, our judgments were said to be "*inculpably* mistaken;" second, our judgments were said to be "*culpably* irrational," meaning culpably contrary to reason or culpably mistaken. Are our judgments thus both "inculpably mistaken" and "culpably mistaken?" Although Bradley is correct to recognize that passion and habit do influence moral choice, he does not decisively identify the issue of personal responsibility in causing moral evil. Finally, although he does assign to a "disordered will" a role for false judgments about apparent goods, he does not (as we shall see) explore the operations of the will in the choice of evil.

17. Ibid., 281.
18. Ibid., 279.

VIII. Bradley and Maritain on the Cause of Moral Evil in Human Choice

What are we to make of Bradley's account of false ends? If one situates Bradley's account of evil choice into the structure of the 12-stage voluntary act, the will and appetitive habits, when confronted by false but apparent goods, may respond with desire for such goods. And the intellect may mistakenly judge that the enticing but false goods are goods that we should intend. So it seems that Bradley's account of false ends is consistent with the 12-step theory. Yet, is the deliberative process, the steps that design means to ends, accounted for in his claim that a disordered will originates evil? Now, the judgment of conscience is an integral function of deliberation. Thus, in the judgment of conscience, the intellect applies the natural law and either validates a good deliberated means or rejects an evil one. Thereafter, a judgment of election at the conclusion of the deliberative process proposes a good means (not a bad one) to the will. Now, if the will is disordered as Bradley suggests, such a will can reject a good means. But where do the bad means (i.e., those means that are contrary to what reason requires or that are contrary to the agent's rational soul) come from? We know that Bradley says that his will chooses them. And Bradley faults neither the intellect's judgment of conscience nor grace rejected (i.e., the shattered shatterable motion to consider the rule) for means contrary to reason's requirement. How can a non-deliberative power (namely, Bradley's disordered will) deliberate or construe actions? He does not say how such objects come to be available for the will's choice. Bradley's disordered will does not seem to be able to design or deliberate the evil actions it chooses. (Can it then be held accountable for evil choices?)

Certainly, Maritain's moral agent is also subject to all the influences of wounded human nature. Yet Maritain's account of a shatterable motion to consider the rule (natural law) in the judgment of conscience is consistent with the 12-step complete action theory, whether the agent accepts or rejects the motion. The moral object that the judgment of conscience refers to the will's choice does some good or avoids some evil. And the moral object yielded up by "nihilation" has neither been screened for evil nor confirmed in good. It can bear the ill fruits of an evil end and a proportionate and evil means. Thus, Maritain's explanation of the cause of moral evil finds a non-evil cause in the non-act of non-consideration of the rule. Thus, evil is not natural, man is responsible, and God is innocent. Although Bradley's analysis assigns the responsibility for moral evil to defective but undefined psychological principles, his assignment is unsatisfactory, as noted above. Maritain's analysis assigns responsibility for moral evil to the human agent in the exercise of his freedom. Maritain successfully identifies a source of human moral evil that is free, that is not itself evil, and that is not God.

V

TRUTH, FALSEHOOD, AND THE FUTURE OF MAN

ANDREW JASPERS

The Evil of Lying

A Case in Thomistic Realism

In his Commentary on the Gospel of John, William of Alton, a Dominican contemporary of Thomas Aquinas, provides an intriguing interpretation of the "unforgiveable sin" of Matthew 12:31.[1] This is usually interpreted as a sin that fundamentally rejects God's mercy. But Alton gives another example of the unforgiveable sin in Pilate's question, "What is truth?" of John 18:38. Alton points out that the question is asked in the presence of the One who is Truth. Hence, Pilate's question represents a rank and complete denial of the truth itself.

This type of rejection of the truth is familiar to one who has shown another that his position is absurd or contradictory, and yet he still maintains it. Though it may be forgivable, the ultimacy of this rejection is significant. Such a complete rejection would be apt to make a teacher despair of his task, if it were not fairly common. For the rejection indicates an unwillingness to learn, and a refusal to grow in truth and goodness. It is also the antithesis of wonder at reality. The intersection of the good, the true, and reality is a touchstone of St. Thomas's thought. Sin and evil are the consequences of departure from the transcendentals and the order established by God. Through reference to Jacques Maritain's *St. Thomas and the Problem of Evil,* I will treat St. Thomas's thought on the metaphysical origin of ethics and the problem of evil, and show how these doctrines contribute to the understanding of why lying is understood to be a *per se* evil.

1. My thanks to Timothy Bellamah, OP, for providing this reference from an unpublished manuscript.

I. First moment of evil

In *St. Thomas and the Problem of Evil,* Maritain elaborates on an important but relatively undeveloped doctrine of Aquinas on the origin of moral evil. In this doctrine, Aquinas makes an important advance on Augustine's thought on the problem. In *On Free Choice of the Will,* Augustine raises the problem that God would seem to be the cause of sins, since God created the souls from which they come.[2] Augustine locates the cause of moral evil solely in the human will. His notion that moral evil consists in a disorder of loves corresponds to Aquinas's later development. But Augustine does not specify sin's precise origin in the human will.

Aquinas's doctrine describes a metaphysical moment of the will that ontologically precedes an act of choice. In this metaphysical moment, the will adheres to its proper rule or declines to do so. Aquinas specifies what the will declines: "... the will in failing to apply the rule of reason or of the Divine law, is the cause of sin."[3] Before the will proceeds to act, it adverts to God's guidance in revelation or right reason and determines to act in accord with that order or not.

Aquinas describes this moment as "pre-existing" in the moral agent: "... evil never follows in the effect, unless some other evil pre-exists in the agent or in the matter...."[4] This pre-existing defect in the agent is a negation and deficiency in the will, and not yet a privation of a due good in an act. The will's negation is that of an interruption of the order that governs the person's good and the role of the appetible good in it. Here, the will has not yet committed to intending an end through a chosen moral object. Between mere willing (*simplex voluntas*) and the choice (*electio*) of means to one's end, there is a profoundly complex ontological process involving interplay between the will and intellect. And yet the aspects of this unified process can be investigated, provided the parts are not mistaken for discrete acts.

In any moral act, the intellect is presented with an appetible good. At-

2. Augustine of Hippo, *On Free Choice of the Will,* translated by Thomas Williams (Indianapolis: Hackett Publishing Company, 1993), 3.

3. "... voluntas sine adhibitione regulae rationis vel legis divinae, est causa peccati" (*Summa Theologiae* I-II, q. 75, a. 1 ad 3—hereafter refered to as *ST*—translated by the Friars of the English Dominican Province [Westminster, Maryland: Christian Classics, 1948, 1981]; vol. 2, 928).

4. "... nunquam sequitur malum in effectu, nisi praeexistat aliquod aliud malum in agente vel materia ..." (*ST* I, q. 49, a. 1 ad 3; vol. 1, 254).

taining that intended good and the means to it require the intellect's reasoning and the will's movement. The first ontological, and not chronological, moment is for Aquinas the openness or closedness to supra-personal guidance. Maritain rightly takes this moment to be a condition of metaphysical freedom.[5] Why is this moment metaphysically required? When one proceeds to a choice of means, one needs to be guided by something. Maritain points out that Aquinas holds that God has the first initiative of any good act.[6] This guidance is either the order of reality as established and revealed by God or it is not. Maritain argues that "This moment of non-consideration of the rule is so to speak the spiritual element of sin."[7]

It is not supposed that the moral agent consciously brings to mind this rule in every act. Maritain observes that "the faultiness of the will does not consist in not paying attention in act to the rule of reason or of divine law, but in this: —that without taking heed of the rule it proceeds to the act of choice."[8] Thus, the habitual sinner would presumably have a virtual intention of having once refused to obey its rule and continuing so to neglect it, without being conscious of this neglect in subsequent acts.[9] At the same time, studied ignorance or culpable negligence of a particular moral rule would be conscious departures of the will from its ultimate rule.

Although the will is ultimately responsible for turning away from divine wisdom and right reason, it may be occasioned by other internal causes, or by external causes through internal causes. Aquinas states: "hence it follows that nothing external can be a cause of sin, except by moving the reason, as a man or devil by enticing to sin; or by moving the sensitive appetite, as certain external sensibles move it."[10] Thus, St. Thomas maintains that the will is fundamental to us sinning. But he maintains that the good desired in sinning may be occasioned by ignorance of the intellect, or a disordered passion or weakness of the appetites.

5. Jacques Maritain, *St. Thomas and the Problem of Evil* (Milwaukee, Wisconsin: Marquette University Press, 1942), 27.

6. Ibid., 37.

7. Ibid., 32.

8. Ibid., 28.

9. Austin Fagothey, SJ, describes the virtual intention as one that was "once made and continues to influence the act now being done, but is not present to the person's consciousness at the moment of performing the act:" *Right and Reason,* 2nd edition (Rockford, Illinois: Tan Books, 1959, 2000), 99.

10. "Unde relinquitur quod nihil exterius potest esse causa peccati, nisi vel inquantum movet rationem, sicut homo vel daemon persuadens peccatum; vel sicut movens appetitum sensitivum, sicut aliqua sensibilia exterior movent appetitum sensitivum" (*ST* I-II, q. 75, a. 3; vol. 2, 928).

II. The *Ens Reale/Ens Rationis* Distinction

While elaborating Aquinas's explanation for the origin of moral evil, Maritain makes a telling statement that moves the ethical discussion into the metaphysical. He notes that in introducing the non-consideration of its rule, the will "has introduced the condition which will cause the texture of being to give way … such an act will bear in itself the teeth-marks of nothingness."[11] This remark about damage to the texture of being recalls Maritain's concern with the empirical sciences of his day, and his desire to renew the study of the philosophy of nature. Maritain believed that idealistic tendencies in science disoriented scientific inquiry, and that the philosophy of nature could correct this. He develops these ideas in *Science and Wisdom* and *Philosophy of Nature*.[12]

The decision to forego reference to the philosophy of nature, and hence of the empirically real, is analogous to the will's departure from its proper rule before it proceeds to act. Both movements neglect the real order in which a truth or being is situated. There is nothing yet sinful in such a scientific abstraction, cf. mathematical abstractions, provided one does not proceed to act as though the abstraction suffices for reality itself. For instance, mathematical abstraction cannot distinguish between living and non-living beings. And any civil engineer would admit that not all that can be modeled can be constructed. Considering something solely as an *ens rationis* is not yet metaphysically culpable, but it is defective. Idealist physical science is not then on this analogy akin to nihilism, but it is critically lacking the fuller truth of real being.

Maritain discusses the real relation and distinction between a thought and its object. He points out that adequation in Thomistic epistemology has nothing to do "with a copy or material transfer." Adequation is between the being of a thing and the "being affirmed by the mind" in the act of judgment.[13] Maritain holds that Descartes's mistake was taking the object to be in thought, and "not as an intelligible entity rendered present to the mind through an immaterial form."[14] In reality, the object retains its integral na-

11. Jacques Maritain, *St. Thomas and the Problem of Evil*, 33.

12. Cf. Giuseppe Butera, *Reading the Cosmos: Nature, Science, and Wisdom* (Washington, D.C.: American Maritain Association, 2011).

13. Jacques Maritain, *The Degrees of Knowledge*, translated by Gerald B. Phelan (New York: Charles Scribner's Sons, 1959), 88.

14. Ibid., 128.

ture in the world, while the knower may have a concept that has a real relation to it. The Cartesian mistake of subsuming the real object by the object known eviscerates the object's nature. Beings of reason in the mind need to be referred to real objects to be conceived adequately. Without such a reference, real beings are made beings of reason when one divorces the relation of reason (*ratio*) from the object's integral nature.

III. The Relation of Word-*Ratio*-Thing

Having surveyed St. Thomas's thought on the origin of moral evil and an analogous idealistic flight from the rule of nature, we can detect its implications in language by looking at the metaphysical elements of an assertion. Aquinas makes this connection in his "Treatise on the Angels" in the *Summa Theologiae*. In reply to the objection that demons are perverse because of falsehood in the intellect, St. Thomas replies that their perversity is instead in not being subject to Divine wisdom.[15] Analogously, the human intellect errs in falling short of the truth that is presented to it. But, because our nature is more complex than the angels', we have more occasions to err.

Ordinarily, an assertion is represented by a combination of signs or words that refer to *rationes*/concepts, through which a thing (*res*) or state of affairs is known.[16] The judgment of a thing's real existence and what it is presents the condition for error. That is, we may misidentify an object. The use of speech adds another occasion for error in that an assertion may refer more or less to a concept in its linguistic context. But, again, an assertion need have some relation to a concept, else mistaken terms for concepts, e.g., seen particularly when one errs in speaking a foreign language, would be impossible. The relation of a being and its thought has an ontological basis, while thoughts and speech have only a conventional relation.

Applied to truth-telling, one can distinguish a verbal construal of the state of affairs, the intellectual grasp of the state of affairs being verbally construed, and the state of affairs itself. The state of affairs itself has its being in reality and is the ultimate reference for the verbal and intellectual

15. "Nam protervitas daemonum est secundum quod non subduntur divinae sapientiae" (*ST* I, q. 58, a. 5; vol. 1, 291).

16. John P. O'Callaghan points out that "mere" beings of reason, like unicorns, have no real referent. *Thomist Realism and the Linguistic Turn: Toward a More Perfect Form of Existence* (Notre Dame: University of Notre Dame, 2003), 192. Prepositions and other purely linguistic terms also have no apparent conceptual referent.

construals. And it is clear that the latter two admit of "inadequation," deliberate or not, depending upon the agent's intellectual and linguistic abilities.[17] That is, one can choose to characterize a state of affairs in a multitude of ways, as one conceives specific aspects of a relevant *ratio*/concept in contrast to others and asserts that selected aspect.

The derangement of a verbal construal of the *ratio,* or concept relevant to a state of affairs, is difficult to assess. Besides the many *rationes* relevant to states of affairs, the relation of an assertion to its *rationes* involves manifold contextual elements, including the assertion's meaning in the language itself, in its present circumstances, and its asymmetrical sense in the mind of the speaker versus the hearer. But, again, some common reference must be possible, else successful communication would not be possible. And, although the linguistic order is only conventionally related to the *rationes* through which things are known, this order becomes normative when one proceeds to speak. That is, the social nature of language establishes inter-subjective norms of vocabulary, syntax, and grammar, respective of places, times, and cultures.

IV. *Contra Mentum* as the Lie's Definition

Having seen the ontological elements of an assertion, the grounds for Augustine's and Aquinas's notion that the lie is an intentional speaking of something *contra mentum* are evident. The lie begins in the intellect's presentation of a difficult good to the will. Intending this good and deliberating about means to it, the intellect discovers an insuperable or at least significant obstacle to attaining it through truthful communication.[18] In lying, the truthful order of reality is itself the obstacle to the will's end. The appetible good, known through a phantasm, is typically known by complementary aspects. The context of communication delimits the relevant aspects of *rationes* involved. A lie assumes a false *ratio,* or aspect thereof, that presents itself as *contra mentum,* namely of the truthful mental *ratio.* The lie

17. Rev. Julius A. Dorszynski, *Catholic Teaching about the Morality of Falsehood* (Washington, D.C.: Catholic University of America Press, 1948), 73. Dorszynski denies that the faculty of speech is only for communicating ideas and judgments of the speaker's mind. He says adequation is normally a good, but sometimes it is inappropriate, e.g., when a secret needs to be concealed.

18. The jocose lie seems less to fit this description of a typical deceptive lie, unless perhaps the good sought is esteem or friendship, which only seems possible through a jocose lie.

begins in the false judgment of the thing and a *ratio*. When one knowingly proceeds to assert this false judgment in pursuit of a difficult good, one lies.[19] It is the choice of a false assertion and proceeding to assert it that satisfies the definition of the lie. The reason for its essential evil involves something more.

A lie is typified by its compositeness and its analogous, hylomorphic, structure. It is composite because it is used as a means to another end, except in the case of the pathological liar.[20] Its hylomorphic structure is seen in St. Thomas's relation of an instrumental act to an intrinsic end. He writes that "one sin is also the formal cause of another: because in the act of fornication committed for the purpose of theft, the former is material while the latter is formal."[21] In this way, we can see how the lie is related to the difficult good sought. At the same time, the lie itself must have a form/matter structure, as the agent's intention is formal to the matter of the assertion chosen. He writes in the same article of the *Summa*: "A sin has matter, not of which but about which it is, and it has its form from its end."[22] From this, we can see that the lie has an intelligible form/matter structure, and may be *per se* evil even if the end sought is otherwise good.

Aquinas elaborates on this as follows: "Now a lie is evil in respect of its genus, since it is an action bearing on undue matter. For, as words are naturally signs of intellectual acts, it is unnatural and undue for anyone to signify by words something that is not in his mind."[23] From the doctrine of the origin of moral evil described above, we can see that choosing the unnatural and undue assertion is preceded by the choice of a *ratio* or aspect of it that is inadequate to the context. The undue assertion must presuppose a deranged *ratio*, deranged from the true order of reality, else the assertion would be rejected as incompatible with the lying intention. A lie is thus

19. This condition distinguishes actors from liars: the actor neither asserts nor subverts the truthful order for the sake of a difficult good.

20. The "pathological liar" may be a euphemism for a malicious liar, who wills lying for its own sake.

21. ". . . unum peccatum sit formalis causa alterius: in actu enim fornicationis quae propter furtum committitur, est quidem fornicatio sicut material, furtum vero sicut formale" (*ST* I-II, q. 75, a. 4; vol. 2, 930).

22. "Materiam autem habet peccatum non ex qua, sed circa quam" (*ST* I-II, q. 75, a. 4 ad 1; vol. 2, 930).

23. "Mendacium autem est malum ex genere. Est enim actus cadens super indebitam materiam: cum enim voces sint signa naturaliter intellectuum, innaturale est et indebitum quod aliquis voce significet id quod non habet in mente" (*ST* II-II, q. 110, a. 3; vol. 3, 1660).

contra mentum, and its evil derives from having departed from the ontological norm. The evil is in choosing a false *ratio* against the true one held in mind for the purpose of assertion, and this presumes that the reality of the true *ratio* has been negated.

Joseph Boyle says that for Aquinas what is undue is an assertion's voluntary falsity, and the matter is the mere assertion.[24] But, for Aquinas, the assertion itself has a *ratio* and a form/matter structure. The matter of the assertion is its propositional content and its form is its *ratio*, or intelligible structure, which specifies its ends. That is, each intelligible assertion is choiceworthy on the basis of which ends it is apt to be directed to by the will. Thus, the matter of the moral object (*finis operis*) cannot simply be assimilated into the agent's intention (*finis operantis*). The agent's intention references the intentions of the act, and their correspondence determines the fittingness of the particular act. Falling on undue matter is willing a false *ratio* that has been dislodged from its proper order so as to deceive. The will's departure from its rule is formal to the matter of the deranged concept. Intending the difficult good, the will then intends that good through the matter of the concept.

Apart from this, the assertion itself is ordered or not to a plan to attain that good within its context. When the person intent on lying unwittingly speaks a true statement, the intent alone deranges the matter. In this case, the assertion involves both an intentional and unintentional derangement from the order of reality. The speaker intends to derange the known *ratio* from its true place in the order of reality, but then, through a misapprehension of that reality, unintentionally asserts something in accord with it. And such a true statement, coinciding with ontological and linguistic orders, will be less likely to have deleterious consequences. But the agent has still intended to lie, even though he has not successfully chosen a lying assertion.

This case of a lie with no adverse consequences explains why Aquinas states that "neither does any effect belong to the species of its cause."[25] The evil of the lie is found in an analysis of the moral object, and not essentially

24. Joseph Boyle, "The Absolute Prohibition of Lying and the Origins of the Casuistry of Mental Reservation: Augustinian Arguments and Thomistic Developments," *American Journal of Jurisprudence* 44 (1999): 61.

25. ". . . sicut nec aliquis effectus pertinent ad speciem suae causae" (*ST* I-II, q. 110, a. 1 ad 3; vol. 3, 1658).

in its effects. For this reason, the new natural lawyer account of the lie's evil consisting in its direct opposition to the basic goods of self-integration, authenticity and solidarity in the community misses the mark.[26] A lie's effect on basic goods is inessential to the evil of the lie. This is not to say that more ultimate evil intentions of the agent and accidents like scandal may not increase the gravity of a lie's evil.[27] The definition of a lie is that it is essentially speaking an assertion *contra mentum*, but its evil is found in the will's intentional departure from the normative order of reality in pursuit of a difficult good, fashioning creation according to the agent's own lights.

Within this context, one can see what deliberately concealed speech like euphemisms involve. In euphemistic assertion, one chooses an assertion related to a *ratio* that adequately conveys the relevant concept, though without the potentially problematic associations that another assertion might carry. This is different from equivocal communication, where one chooses an assertion that does not adequately convey the sense of the relevant concept as it is determined by context and usage. In this, I will argue that the continued controversy over the moral permissibility of craniotomy involves an unacceptable equivocation on the part of the new natural lawyers.

Craniotomy is an emergency operation performed when a Caesarian section is impossible. It involves a mother who is delivering a child feet-first, and the child's head is too big to be delivered successfully. The child's head is surgically collapsed and removed so as to save the mother's life. This is admittedly a difficult moral problem. However, describing the operation as "resizing the cranium," as the new natural lawyers do,[28] is not an acceptable euphemism, since the nature of a cranium is such that it cannot be resized, much less crushed, without directly killing the person. "Resizing the cranium," is instead an unacceptable equivocation.

26. Germain Grisez, *Living a Christian Life*, Vol. 2, of *The Way of the Lord Jesus* (Quincy, Illinois: Franciscan Press, 1993), 405.

27. Aquinas notes that if a lie is intentionally opposed to God, religion or neighbor, it will be a mortal sin. In addition, a lie that is otherwise a venial sin can become mortal if it is done in scandalous circumstances: *ST* II-II, q. 110, a. 4.

28. John Finnis, Germain Grisez, and Joseph Boyle, "'Direct'" and 'Indirect': A Reply to Critics of Our Action Theory," *The Thomist* 65 (2001): 28. Christopher Tollefsen also does not give adequate attention to the *finis operis* of such an act, exaggerating the similarity between squeezing and crushing the cranium in "Is a Purely First-Person Account of Human Action Defensible?" *Ethical Theory and Moral Practice* 9 (2006): 449–50.

V. Conclusion

In this essay, I have considered Aquinas's doctrine on the origin of moral evil. Aquinas sees a metaphysical moment of the will's departure from its proper rule as the first condition for a morally evil act. The will's movement away from the order of being is analogous to a confusion in metaphysics between beings of reason and real beings, one that Maritain and Simon challenged in their renewal of the philosophy of nature. Further, it was shown that assertoric speech involves the triadic structure of word-*ratio-res,* which is normative for truth-telling. The intentional dimensions of Aquinas's and Augustine's definition of a lie as essentially speaking an assertion *contra mentum* were shown. And it was shown that the lie's evil is found in the will's departure from the normative order of reality so as to obtain a difficult good, fashioning creation in one's own image. And, although we can surely trust in God's mercy and forgiveness after we confess when we lie, and are called to extend that mercy to those who lie to us, a precise notion of the evil of the lie helps prevent presumption of that mercy and enables us to better live in the truth.

ROBERT VIGLIOTTI

The Anti-Humanism of Technological Humanism

The technologies of altering human genetics, once the domain of speculative fiction, are at last here. Human beings are already able to intervene and modify the genetic code in ways unimaginable even a few years ago, and our power over the human genome grows at an ever increasing rate. The rapid pace of these developments demands that we pause now to consider both the benefits such technologies offer and the harms they can inflict. The immediate question of the safety of genetic engineering will always challenge our judgment, even in instances where we deem the benefit of cures for genetic disorders to be worth the risk of the procedures. Beyond the immediate and constant questions of safety, we must also ask the long-term question of what such technology can do to our human nature itself, and we must determine how this power over our own physical being will be morally employed. Many commentators on the state of contemporary science see the development of our scientific knowledge and the application of that knowledge through technology as the fruit of our centuries-old humanistic tradition of thought, which has great faith in the rationality and the decency of human beings and which directs the use of those human faculties to the ongoing project of improving our lives by education, medicine, and social progress. Many of the applications of our current technology are extensions of the human struggle against suffering as we learn to manipulate the matter both of the world and of our own bodies at deeper levels and with ever greater efficacy. The potent new tool of genetic engineering gives hope to a great many people that our lives, or at least the lives of our children, will be freed from the numerous diseases that still afflict humanity, especially the genetic disorders that have thus far resisted our control. Our technology offers the further hope that these victories will extend indefinitely into the future, as we overcome still more obstacles and improve the lot of humanity in undreamed of ways. This hope in its most general form may be called technological humanism, the hope that new scientific knowledge and powerful technologies promise indefinite improvement to the human condition.

Yet, even while scientists and bioethicists debate the appropriate use and limits of our present ability to perform genetic modifications on human beings, some enthusiastic advocates of biotechnology champion its use not just for medical therapies, but also for enhancing human faculties and for overcoming natural human limitations. These advocates claim that rapid advances in a crucial and interrelated group of technologies—genetics, robotics, information, and nanotechnology, or the GRIN technologies for short[1]—will open up possibilities for us far beyond those hoped for by the typical technological humanist. Not only will these technologies be able to fight disease, assist the disabled, and let us live longer; they will also, according to these advocates, completely overcome our bodies' vulnerabilities and enhance our mental and physical capacities. Humanity will eventually surpass the limitations by which human nature or the human condition has, in their view, historically been defined. The most ardent of these advocates call themselves "transhumanists," claiming that science and technology have at last placed control of human evolution in our own hands, allowing us to determine for ourselves what the future of human nature will be. The anticipated goal of this technological transcendence is to usher in a new type of "posthuman" being, the nature of which even they can presently only guess at.

While the adherents of transhumanism believe that their vision of humanity's future is new, made possible only by the recent rapid and unsettling growth in technology, the underlying principles of their brand of technological humanism is not at all new. Transhumanism rests on the same promethean principles as the philosophical position that Jacques Maritain called anthropocentric humanism, which, he argues, is the culmination of major trends in modern philosophy and which inevitably results in a pernicious form of humanism combined with atheism. This type of promethean

1. Joel Garreau, *Radical Evolution: The Promise and Peril of Enhancing Our Minds, Our Bodies —and What It Means to Be Human*, 1st edition (New York: Doubleday, 2005), 419.

atheism is epitomized, according to Maritain, in the philosophical theory of Marx and was instantiated in the political reality of Soviet communism. Maritain's analyses of these philosophical and historical phenomena provide a philosophical framework for understanding the metaphysical foundations of technological humanism and transhumanism, and his work in ethics permits an evaluation of the psychological and moral roots of this controversial application of science and technology. Together, Maritain's analyses form a Christian humanist contribution to the contemporary debate over technology and the future of human nature.

I. From Technological Humanism to Transhumanism

In the last decade alone, our understanding of the human genome and our ability to change it have advanced at a startling rate, and continued advances in genetics will force difficult questions about the future of humanity upon us. The decoding of the human genome was originally expected to be completed in the year 2020; however, with steady advances in computing power, this work was completed years ahead of schedule, in 2003. Our ability to map genes and to understand their complex interactions continues to grow at an ever-increasing rate as advances in information technology also continue apace. With advances in the other related GRIN technologies, our ability to alter the genomic sequence of living beings will enable us to make profound changes to human biology, not only curing genetic diseases incurable just a few years ago, but also controlling many of our genes as we wish. Currently, we are able to fight a small number of genetic disorders that involve the action of single gene. One way these disorders can be addressed is by retroviral gene therapy, which involves manipulating the genetic codes of viruses by replacing the virus's genes with genes chosen by researchers. When a virus normally enters the body, it attacks healthy cells and deposits its own genetic material into the cells to reproduce itself. By changing the genetic payload that such a virus delivers, we can introduce new gene sequences into the cells that replace or alter the activity of the malfunctioning genes. This therapy has been performed successfully on a few patients with X-linked severe combined immunodeficiency disease, better known as "bubble baby syndrome."[2] These proce-

2. Genomics.Energy.Gov, "Gene Therapy," http://www.ornl.gov/sci/techresources/ Human _Genome/medicine/genetherapy.shtml.

dures still remain risky, and their failure can sometimes result in the death of the patient. In addition, our understanding of genetic disorders caused by the interaction of multiple genes is at a very early point and currently prevents us from intervening therapeutically. Yet there is good reason to be optimistic about our ability to decode these interactions. As computing power continues to grow, it is reasonable to expect that before long we will also be able to map out the complex interactions between genes. This advance will not only bring still more genetic disorders under our therapeutic powers, but it will also reveal to us the underlying genetic basis for a wide variety of mental and physical qualities such as memory, intelligence, emotional responses, physical strength, endurance, speed, longevity, disease resistance, and healing processes. Therapies developed for treating physical disorders will at the same time lead to technologies that can enhance these mental and physical qualities. For example, studies on the treatment of rats genetically modified with Huntington's Chorea, a debilitating neurological condition, have shown that changes in their environment, pharmacological treatments, and neural stem cell treatments have all proven effective in combating the disorder. Each of these treatments when used on a healthy or normal brain could be conceivably used "to increase the neural complement of normal brains and increase cognitive performance in normal individuals."[3] Thus, the door that opens the way to future therapies will also open the door to future biological enhancements.

Such advances, especially when coupled with advances in neuropharmacology and stem cell research, give hope to those who suffer or to those whose children suffer debilitating and fatal diseases. Yet there is much support for developing these therapies without much thought about the implications of their use. Such hope for continued medical progress is grounded in a long-standing and deeply embedded set of cultural values that directs the employment of science and technology toward the overcoming of all obstacles in the pursuit of a good human life. In Western societies in particular, we tend to see science and technology as the collective efforts of human intelligence, ingenuity, and labor in our struggle with nature to provide each human being the conditions for living a fruitful, satisfying, and an as-comfortable-as-possible life. The roots of this will to power over na-

3. Julian Savulescu, "Genetic Interventions and the Ethics of Enhancement of Human Beings," in *Readings in the Philosophy of Technology*, edited by David M. Kaplan (New York: Rowman and Littlefield, 2009), 420.

ture can be traced back through the history of humanism, which began in the Renaissance and developed through the modern era into the Enlightenment, leaving a profound imprint upon Western culture. Renaissance humanism began as the idea that human beings contain within themselves the dignity and the power to direct their own lives toward the good. Although not necessarily opposed to religious belief, humanism celebrated the powers of the human mind and the beauty of the human form. The period saw renewed interest in classical authors who were believed to provide all that was needed to live a good human life through their works of philosophy, rhetoric, history, and the other humanities. Renaissance humanism also believed that human beings were active and creative beings meant to engage the world. Therefore, human learning in all its forms serves a purpose other than the still contemplation of the cosmos or of God; the sciences and their fruits are for the never-ending business of improving human life. Indeed, Francis Bacon reinterpreted the book of Genesis as saying that human beings are the *imago Dei* by virtue of their powers of creation and that God has commanded humanity to use technology to carry out a divine mission of love by steadily improving the human condition.[4] By the time the eighteenth century dawned in Europe, humanism had incorporated the newly established scientific method and had given rise to the Enlightenment conviction that the power of the unaided human reason would accomplish the utopian task of transforming self, society, and nature through the application of rational and scientific principles. Education would produce rational minds and moral behavior, bureaucratic organization would reorder society into efficient and rational forms, and science and technology would allow us to become lords and masters of nature, remaking it to serve human needs. Already, the rapid advancements brought about by the scientific method were inspiring utopian visions, such as Bacon's New Atlantis, of a world transformed and a humanity transcendent.

Technological humanism may be described as the belief that the purpose of science and technology is to improve continually the quality of human life and as the faith that additional breakthroughs in technology will extend our grasp ever deeper into human biology to further this goal. What distinguishes technological humanism from earlier incarnations of

4. Carl Mitcham, "Three Ways of Being-with Technology," in *Philosophy of Technology: The Technological Condition: An Anthology*, edited by Robert C. Scharff and Val Dusek (Malden, Massachusetts: Blackwell Publishers, 2003).

humanism is that we have come to place our hopes almost solely in science and technology to solve the problems of the world and of our lives. Renaissance humanism celebrated the natural nobility of the human spirit, and it turned therefore to the classical writers who encouraged the growth of the virtues and who taught us how to maintain a dignified countenance in the face of the natural constraints of human life. Technological humanism, however, turns only to technological interventions to alleviate, modify, and eliminate the sources of, or the struggles with, those natural constraints. The spirit need no longer struggle to master the flesh. We all share in these hopes to some degree; a cure for cancer, or at least a treatment that reduces it to a managed illness, and advances in stem cell therapies or robotics that enable accident victims and wounded veterans to regain mobility, are recognized by most people as unqualified blessings. But technological humanism takes those hopes further and grounds its understanding of a good human life upon the benefits that can be bestowed by technology. It is the attitude of Nietzsche's Last Man, if we can imagine this feeble and self-satisfied creature blinking amidst the shining chrome and electronic beeps of its small technological world. Perhaps this attitude is best summed up in the beliefs expressed by Aldous Huxley's World Controller, Mustapha Mond, from *Brave New World*, when he states that "Anybody can be virtuous now. You can carry at least half your morality about in a bottle. Christianity without tears—that's what [the all-purpose euphoric pharmaceutical] soma is."[5] Technological humanism seeks solutions without personal learning or growth, quality of life without quality of spirit or character.

Technological humanism as described above is still a fairly moderate point of view, since it is primarily concerned with therapeutic uses of these technologies. There are, however, those who enthusiastically embrace the full possibilities of these new biotechnologies and who wish to alter human beings so radically that our normal biological capabilities are enhanced and our natural limitations are overcome. Advances in genetic engineering, robotics, human-computer interfacing, psychopharmacology, and neurology are already affecting our human embodiment. Gene therapies can enhance the function of our immune system or of the production of red blood cells as well as ease the natural restrictions on muscle growth; robotic prosthetics are not only stronger than the limbs they replace but are now also able

5. Aldous Huxley, *Brave New World & Brave New World Revisited* (New York: Harper & Row, 1965), 183.

to provide rudimentary sensation; and the deaf can hear with cochlear implants and the blind can see with cameras wired to their visual cortex.[6] Embryos are already being screened for genetic diseases or to determine their sex before implantation, and now this screening has extended to cosmetic features like hair color and eye color.[7] The supporters of human enhancement believe that continued developments in these areas will open up a whole new range of possible ways of being for humans in the future. Once we have therapeutic uses of biotechnology, the door will be opened to new kinds of enhancements that will supplement our existing capabilities and perhaps add new capabilities to the human mind and body. For example, once we understand the complex interaction of genes that influence our mental faculties, we might be able to increase capacities like intelligence and memory. We may find ways to extend our perceptual faculties by integrating the input from electronic equipment such as infrared and ultraviolet cameras into our sensorium. The boundary between humans and computers will become blurry, and it will soon be difficult to determine where the human ends and the machine begins. One of the chief goals of this far-reaching biological enhancement is to make our bodies disease proof and to extend the human life span not merely to one hundred or one hundred-fifty years but indefinitely, perhaps as much as a thousand years. In the far-flung future, some of these thinkers hope that it may even be possible to construct computer simulations of our minds so that our minds will be free from our bodies altogether.

These radical supporters of enhancement technologies call themselves transhumanists for several reasons. First, these technologies have already begun seriously to challenge our understanding of human nature. The term "transhuman" is used to indicate the transitional stage of human existence that we are now entering. Humans have been slowly changing the facts of their existence for thousands of years, and the twentieth century has already seen a tremendous burst of technological changes that have dramat-

6. See, for example, Rebecca Boyle, "New Neural Interfaces Can Bring True Feeling to Artificial Limbs," *Popular Science*, last modified Jan. 27, 2012, http://www.popsci.com/technology/article/2012–02/new-neural-interfaces-can-bring-electric-feel-artifical-limbs/; Jennifer Hicks, "First Bionic Eye For US Market Awaits Approval From FDA," last modified Jan. 27, 2013, http://www.forbes.com/sites/jenniferhicks/2013/01/29/first-bionic-eye-for-us-market-awaits-approval-from-fda/.

7. See "Designer Baby Row over US Clinic," last modified March 2, 2009, http://news.bbc.co.uk/2/hi/7918296.stm.

ically altered the human condition. For example, just within the last century, global average human life expectancy has increased by approximately thirty years to sixty-seven years, which is itself "three times longer than our Pleistocene Predecessors." The belief that the human condition is "static" and will remain so despite the anticipated growth in technology this century is, they argue, simply "implausible."[8]

Second, transhumanism is a rallying cry for a project to which we should commit our lives and resources because overcoming human nature is the most desirable goal for the human species. Some within the transhumanist camp see this transformation of human nature not simply as an inevitable consequence of technological advance, but also as a goal to be embraced and worked toward. Some transhumanists define the nature of human beings almost solely in terms of our limitations. Our corporeal nature hinders our intellectual and expressive capacities, holding us back from becoming what we wish to become and from experiencing all that we wish to experience. Worse, our bodies are traitors to our minds. We age, we grow weak and sick, and we die, bringing our adventure in existence to an end. This attitude toward the human is most forcefully expressed by Simon Young in his transhumanist manifesto:

> Humanity—a species so weak it defines its own existence as tragic! How long must we endure such a pitiful condition? … "Human"—the very word is synonymous with suffering and failure … humanity is a disease state from which to be cured!… What is "the human condition" but an affliction? What is a human being? A weak mind in a decaying body, a bundle of primitive emotions, and a brief life in the knowledge of inevitable death—extinction for the rest of eternity![9]

Young's contempt for and wish to escape the limitations of human nature may be rhetorically overstated, but the theme of leaving behind the natural limits of human nature is common to all the transhumanists. The more sober Nick Bostrom argues that biotechnology will someday permit the existence of "posthuman" beings, that is, "possible future beings whose basic capacities exceed those of present humans as to be no longer unambiguously human by our current standards."[10]

8. Nick Bostrom, "The Future of Humanity," in *A Companion to the Philosophy of Technology*, edited by Jan-Kyrre Berg Olsen, Stig Andur Pedersen, and Vincent F. Hendricks (Chichester, United Kingdom; Malden, Massachusetts: Wiley-Blackwell, 2009), 553.

9. Simon Young, *Designer Evolution: A Transhumanist Manifesto* (Amherst, New York: Prometheus Books, 2006), 32.

10. Nick Bostrom, "The Transhumanist Faq," in *Readings in the Philosophy of Technology*, 346–47.

Third, transhumanists explicitly link their philosophical perspective to the humanist tradition and see it as a logical extension of the optimistic goals of the Enlightenment into the biological nature of human beings. Bostrom harkens back to the Renaissance humanist ideal of "the well-rounded person, one who is highly developed scientifically, morally, culturally, and spiritually" and one whose dignity lies in his or her capacity for self-creation. Bostrom quotes Giovanni Pico della Mirandola's 1486 *Oration on the Dignity of Man* approvingly when describing the unique power of human beings to choose their own form of existence. Mirandola writes:

> We have given you, O Adam, no visage proper to yourself, nor endowment properly your own, in order that whatever place, whatever form, whatever gifts you may, with premeditation, select, these same you may have and possess through your own judgment and decision. The nature of all other creatures is defined and restricted within laws which We have laid down; you, by contrast, impeded by no such restrictions, may, by your own free will, to whose custody We have assigned you, trace for yourself the lineaments of your own nature.... We have made you a creature neither of heaven nor of earth, neither mortal nor immortal, in order that you may, as the free and proud shaper of your own being, fashion yourself in the form you may prefer. It will be in your power to descend to the lower, brutish forms of life; you will be able, through your own decision, to rise again to the superior orders whose life is divine.[11]

For Bostrom, human dignity is located in our "aspirations, and ideals, our experiences, and the kinds of lives we lead." Human "autonomy" is the utmost value and that autonomy must be extended until we are freed of the constraints of human biology and even of matter itself.[12] Transhumanism therefore carries on the tradition of earlier forms of humanism, yet its access to new powers allows its ambition to supersede the older forms. According to Bostrom, "We are not limited to traditional humanistic methods, such as education and cultural development. We can also use technological means that will eventually enable us to move beyond what some would think of as 'human.'"[13] This view is echoed by Young, who states that "essentially, transhumanism is an extension of humanism into the biological realm. Where humanism is the belief in the progress of

11. Mirandola, quoted in Bostrom, "Dignity and Enhancement," in *Human Dignity and Bioethics : Essays Commissioned by the President's Council on Bioethics*, edited by Adam Schulman and the President's Council on Bioethics (Washington, D.C.: President's Council on Bioethics, 2008), 183–84.

12. Bostrom, "Transhumanist Faq," 345.

13. Ibid.

humanity into the present biological state, transhumanism is the belief in the ability of the species to transcend the limitations of its biological conditions through technology."[14]

The transhumanists rightly see humanity at a momentous crossroads; for the first time in history, human beings are now on the verge of controlling their own evolution. Rather than having reached the end of human evolutionary history, we have only begun a new chapter. In the view of the transhumanists, evolution itself is leading us to a state of being that transcends our current nature. Evolution, they argue, moves towards ever more complex and powerful forms, and, if our evolving is not yet done, we can expect humans to gain new and more sophisticated forms of perception, cognition, communication, and social interaction. Evolution has an almost mystical meaning in this worldview. The natural processes that have shaped our existence thus far have given rise to a brain that can comprehend and employ for itself these self-same processes. The human mind is nature become self-aware and deliberate. According to Young, "evolution is the unfolding of potential—a continual increase in the complexity of structures, forms, and processes in nature. Human beings are a conscious aspect of the process of evolutionary complexification. *Humankind is the mind of evolution become conscious of itself*.... Humanity is imbued with an instinctive Will to Evolve."[15] Futurist Ray Kurzweil adds that "evolution moves toward greater complexity, greater elegance, greater knowledge, greater intelligence, greater beauty, greater creativity, and more of other abstract and subtle attributes, such as love.... And God has been called all these things, only without any limitation...."[16] Thus, the idea of evolution provides for some transhumanists a sense of teleological meaning for humanity as a whole and can play the role of a religion. Beliefs usually associated with religious faith, such as immortality and resurrection, are redeemed through technology. We will live in the age of "spiritual machines," according to Kurzweil, where whatever it is that makes us unique beings will live indefinitely within computer networks and virtual realities.[17] However, it seems to go unnoticed by these authors that this view of evolution is far closer to Spencer's Social Darwinism than to any scientific form of Darwinian evolution.

14. Young, *Designer Evolution*, 58.

15. Ibid., 39; emphasis in the original.

16. Kurzweil, quoted in Garreau, *Radical Evolution*, 262.

17. Ray Kurzweil, *The Age of Spiritual Machines: When Computers Exceed Human Intelligence* (New York: Viking, 1999).

Those who are wary of such change, to whom the transhumanists refer as bio-conservatives—or less charitably, bio-Luddites—argue that even if we have the power to alter our basic biological nature to such a degree that we no longer recognize enhanced beings as human, such power is undesirable, dangerous, or immoral.[18] The transhumanists reply that enhancing ourselves has been part of our nature since our first appearance on the planet. We have used technology to overcome diseases, to inhabit every inhospitable corner of the globe, to repair and replace organs, to let the infertile procreate, to transform the structure of the brain through cultural and chemical interventions, and so on. The enhancements that await us are different in degree, not kind. Bio-conservatives must choose either to accept the future of modification or reject all modifications and interventions, including those we presently use. Against concerns that such enhancements would threaten the fabric of democratic societies by exacerbating existing social inequalities and creating new ones, the transhumanists reply that the principles of a liberal democracy will remain unchanged and that its rules and rights will remain applicable to both the enhanced and unenhanced. In fact, these technologies will be such a potent source of happiness that many of society's ills will be cured. Some transhumanists would further argue that the genetic modification of children is morally obligatory for parents.[19]

II. Transhumanism or Christian Humanism?

While the advances in technology that are without doubt occurring around us occasion the optimism of the moderate technological humanism and the utopian visions of the transhumanists, the principles underlying these positions have been seen before in the history of philosophy. Jacques Maritain has traced the historical development of humanism and analyzed its particular manifestations in the nineteenth and twentieth centuries. Maritain has seen how humanism has detached itself from its original impulse to celebrate the excellences of the human being and has taken a promethean turn by asserting human independence and self-sufficiency. The foundation of humanism, according to Maritain, is the essential ten-

18. See, for example, Francis Fukuyama, "Transhumanism," *Foreign Policy*, no. 144 (2004); Micheal Sandel, "The Case against Perfection: What's Wrong with Designer Children, Bionic Athletes, and Genetic Engineering," in *Human Enhancement*, edited by Julian Savulescu and Nick Bostrom (Oxford and New York: Oxford University Press, 2009).

19. Savulescu, "Genetic Interventions and the Ethics of Enhancement of Human Beings," 425.

dency to render man more truly human and to manifest his original greatness by enabling him to partake of everything in nature and in history capable of enriching him. Such greatness requires both that man develop his latent tendencies, especially those involving his creative powers and the life of reason, and that he work to transform into instruments of his liberty the forces of the physical universe.[20]

Thus, what humanism fundamentally affirms and honors is not the problem. But Maritain describes two basic forms that humanism may take, a theocentric and an anthropocentric form. The theocentric humanism, which is the core of Maritain's call for a renewed Christian humanism for the contemporary era, celebrates the natural human while still affirming the human being's supernatural calling. The difference between Maritain's theocentric humanism and all forms of anthropocentric humanism is the recognition that the nature of humanity transcends the purely human frame. We must be understood to possess an "open human nature" and an "open reason" that allows us to transcend beyond the immanent realm of our minds and of the natural world toward supra-rational truths and supernatural grace.[21] In theocentric humanism, "God is the center of man," and human existence is ordered toward spiritual values higher than anything found in the natural world.[22] We have been warned since the time of the ancient Greeks not to define our humanity in a way that separates us from these transcendent possibilities.

Despite ancient and Christian wisdom, modern humanism has taken the other course and adopted instead a strictly naturalistic perspective. Human being has consequently been defined as "closed in upon itself" and "absolutely self-sufficient" without transcendent reason, truth, or grace.[23] This is no mere error, according to Maritain; it is a denial of the transcendent.[24] This choice places human beings at the center of the cosmos. The historical process of the secularizing of the image of humanity occurred in gradual stages beginning in the Renaissance, and it continued into the Enlightenment, when all that is "consecrated and elevated above nature by God" is

20. Jacques Maritain, *The Twilight of Civilization*, translated by Lionel Landry (New York: Sheed & Ward, 1943), 3.

21. Ibid., 5.

22. Maritain, *Integral Humanism; Temporal and Spiritual Problems of a New Christendom* (New York: Scribner, 1968), 27–28.

23. Maritain, *The Twilight of Civilization*, 4.

24. Maritain, *Integral Humanism*, 2.

brought back down to the profane world and made a natural attribute of human nature.[25] Natural human reason and natural human goodness would suffice to redeem humanity and to rework creation, to build with human hands what had been promised by God. All the goods guaranteed by God and Gospel, such as liberty, peace, dignity, fraternity, justice, and love, would be seized by human beings as their own birthright. The alliance of naturalistic humanism and scientific positivism ultimately reduced the conception of human nature to a product of nature itself, without any metaphysical distinction. Yet the conquest of nature must continue unabated, for only by transforming the matter of this world can humans reform the difficult conditions of life. As Maritain writes

> Modern man constantly progressed toward good and toward the possession of the earth—without having to face evil on earth, for he did not believe in the existence of evil; evil is only an imperfect stage in evolution, which a further stage was naturally and necessarily to transcend.... Modern man placed his hope in machines, in technique, and in mechanical or industrial civilization.... And how can one who does not possess the standards of human life, which are metaphysical, apply them to our use of the machine? The law of the machine, which is the law of matter, will apply itself to him, and enslave him.[26]

Maritain thus argues that conquest and reworking of nature without a transcendent source of meaning and values can only have dire consequences for human nature.

For Maritain, it is a great tragedy that humanism took the anthropocentric and naturalistic, rather than the theocentric, path. To sever human nature from its transcendent nature, from the "something which breathes above time" and from the "personality whose most profound needs surpass the whole order of the universe," is already to have committed violence towards humanity.[27] This rejection of the transcendent nature of humanity is ultimately a kind of anti-humanism.[28] Anthropocentric humanism leaves human beings adrift and puts upon them the responsibility for truth, values, and meaning without providing an eternal and transcendent source for them. What follows is a human being's deliberate basic choice to face the difficulties and evils of life without guidance from above or any rule that is not the product of humanity's own devising. The result is what Maritain

25. Jacques Maritain, *The Range of Reason* (New York: Scribner, 1952), 186.
26. Ibid., 187.
27. Maritain, *Integral Humanism*, 2.
28. Ibid.

calls absolute atheism.[29] This kind of atheism is more than a simple lack of belief. It is, according to Maritain, "rather a refusal of God, a fight against God, a challenge to God."[30] The dialectic of anthropocentric humanism leads inevitably to absolute atheism, and, furthermore, without centering human existence upon God, anthropocentric humanism must inevitably strive to elevate humanity to God's position. Maritain shows how this condition has been made manifest in the twentieth century through Marxist theory and in the political reality of Soviet communism.

Traditional concepts of a human nature that endures throughout history are, according to Marx, actually reflections of the particular socio-economic situation in which humanity finds itself at any given moment. These concepts of humanity are necessarily flawed and ideological, and their purpose is to justify the social and political bonds placed upon the majority of human beings, that is, the working class. Furthermore, Marx adopts from Feuerbach the belief that traditional religious conceptions of the divine are but an expression of the multifaceted alienation imposed upon the proletariat by socio-economic forces. God is merely the projection of all the human powers that have been opposed by a recalcitrant nature and that have been wrested away by systematic injustices. Thus, the interpretations of human existence and of its relation to the divine derived from all traditional philosophies and theologies have long imposed limitations on human nature. Such religious conceptions must be jettisoned from society as a species of false consciousness that causes humanity to acquiesce meekly to those limitations. With the awakening of true class consciousness, humanity shakes off those bonds and rejects the limits unjustly forced upon it; and the image of collective humanity will be transformed into a promethean titan astride the earth. The image of humanity as self-creator will replace the belief in humanity as a created being; in Maritain's analysis, the "notion of human nature gives way to that of process of self-creation of man by man."[31] This transformation of the concept of human nature does not simply banish God from human thought and affairs; this transformation is the apotheosis of a collective humanity that arrogates to human beings the attributes formerly belonging to God. Marx wrote

29. Maritain, *Range of Reason*, 106.

30. Ibid., 98.

31. Jacques Maritain, *Moral Philosophy: an Historical and Critical Survey of the Great Systems* (New York: Scribner, 1964), 457.

early in his career that "man is the supreme being for man," meaning that all the alienated qualities properly belonging to humanity but projected upon God will be reclaimed for humanity.[32] A promethean humanity claims for itself not only the power of creating or recreating the world in its own image, but also the power of self-creation and of total self-sufficiency or *aseity* that only the divine may possess. The new deified humanity will not have any "supratemporal attributes," but will instead be completely merged with nature and submerged in history.[33] And the price human beings will pay for divinity will be to become de-individualized into collective humanity and to sacrifice the personal, the spiritual, the more than human part of human beings. Maritain notes that "a total rejection of Transcendence logically entails a total adherence to Immanence," and the human being can only give him or herself over to the great flux of history, abandoning belief in any truth above history and despairing of any life beyond the flux.[34]

According to Maritain, anthropocentric humanism and absolute atheism originate not from a theory or philosophical arguments but from a place much more personal and intimate. Belief and unbelief spring instead from an original movement of the will that results in a basic moral choice about how one will confront the difficulties inherent in the human condition. Maritain describes the human condition as

> that of the spirit united in substance with flesh and engaged in the universe of matter. It is an unhappy condition. In itself it is such a miserable condition that man has always dreamed of a golden age when he was more or less freed of it, and so miserable that on the plane of revelation, the Christian religion teaches that mankind was created, with the grace of Adam, in a superior condition in which it was free of sin, of pain, of servitude and of death, and from which it fell through its own fault. The Judeo-Christian tradition also teaches that after the end of history and in a new world the human condition will be supernaturally transfigured.... Indeed, the tragic perplexity in which we are placed consists in the fact that we can neither refuse the human condition nor accept it purely and simply.[35]

Our condition demands that we acknowledge both that suffering and great moral evils are inescapable in this life and that part of our humanity transcends this world. We are in the world, but we are not of it. This awareness allows us to see that this world is not equal to what is best in human nature, and it allows us to make a radical break with the world precisely in order to

32. Marx, quoted in Ibid., 219.

33. Maritain, *Integral Humanism*, 61.

34. Maritain, *Range of Reason*, 107.

35. Maritain, *Moral Philosophy*, 452–53.

work toward its improvement and to serve our fellow human beings. We neither reject our condition nor accept it purely and simply. Thus, we are confronted with an initial existential choice. By virtue of human freedom, each must make an act of faith whether to transcend the human condition with the gifts of grace or "to confront good and evil in a totally and absolutely free experience, in which any ultimate good and any rule coming from above are cast aside forever." For Maritain, the latter is just as much an act of faith as the former, but it is "an act of faith in reverse gear."[36] The atheist at the same moment rejects the human condition, refusing to acknowledge the suffering inherent in our current state yet also refusing to appeal to any source outside of nature or humanity itself. Maritain remarks that to refuse the human condition in this way is "to dream of leaving our limits and to wish to enjoy a total liberty in which our nature would expand through its own powers. . . ."[37] The anthropocentric humanist chooses to fight against the human condition, to reject the state of suffering that is part of human existence, and to work towards an utter transformation of all of nature. "Those who believe neither in the state of innocence nor in original sin put the golden age at the end of history, not at the beginning, and fancy that man will attain it in the last stage of his terrestrial adventure, through his own liberating effort, thanks to science and to radical social transformations."[38]

From Maritain's perspective, there is little that is new to be found in the latest versions of humanism. Whether speaking of the moderate and commonplace form of technological humanism or the more radical transhumanism, there are many similarities between these new forms and the atheistic anthropocentric humanism that Maritain has analyzed. While the more general technological humanism is held by many who would consider themselves religious and who see no incompatibility with faith, the day-to-day existence within this perspective is rather a kind of practical atheism. Maritain describes practical atheists as those "who believe that they believe in God who in actual fact deny His existence by their deeds and the testimony of their behavior."[39] Such persons have faith in God but do not truly accept the human condition as it is, and they rely on God as a stop-gap only until science can deliver on its promises. Transhumanism, on the other hand, has a much more aggressive view towards religion. According

36. Maritain, *Range of Reason*, 107.

37. Maritain, *Moral Philosophy*, 454.

38. Ibid., 452.

39. Maritain, *Range of Reason*, 103.

to Bostrom, transhumanism is necessarily a naturalistic perspective relying chiefly on the scientific method for its understanding of the world. While preferring to call it a worldview rather than a religion, he acknowledges that transhumanism may take the place of religion for some people, because "it offers a sense of direction and purpose and suggests a vision that humans can achieve something greater than our present condition." So long as the demands of faith do not contradict the principles of transhumanism, Bostrom grants that "certain forms of religiosity ... may well be compatible with transhumanism."[40] More extreme views such as Young's see the very idea of God as nothing more than the alienated and reified power over life and death. Young asks how one could accept the idea of a compassionate God who is responsible for disease and disasters and who also "would wish us to suffer from limitations we are able to overcome by our own hands." He wonders why such a divinity would "be deemed worthy of authority over our lives."[41] Young does, however, find good things to say about Teilhard de Chardin.[42] Young's questioning of God expresses what Maritain sees as "a resentment against God and a revenge against God ... because [the atheist] will not forgive Him the world and evil."[43]

Transhumanism is what Maritain describes as "a state of interior revolt against the fact that one is a man." This form of anthropocentric humanism refuses to recognize the complexity and ambivalence of the human condition and to find the source of human worth in an ambition to rise qualitatively and metaphysically above that condition. But the transhumanists, having already dismissed the spiritual dimension of humanity, set about remaking the biological dimension. Maritain could find in the transhumanist's impulse to heal and to cure a noble and compassionate perspective, much as he found Marx's intuitions about the suffering, alienation, and injustice of the capitalist society in the industrial revolution to be suffused with Judeo-Christian values.[44] But the errors of these two worldviews spring from the same root, a refusal to ground human dignity in a supernatural sustaining source. Instead, the transhumanist turns not to God, not even toward a stable concept of human nature, but only toward one's own self as the source of truth, value, and dignity. This turn toward the individual alone seems more extreme than Marx's turn toward a collective human-

40. Bostrom, "Transhumanist Faq," 359.

41. Young, *Designer Evolution*, 320, 50.

42. Ibid., 358.

43. Maritain, *Integral Humanism*, 63.

44. Ibid., 46.

ity. But having denied the transcendence of the self by reducing it entirely to the material realm, the transhumanist must now desperately seek ways to make the self eternal; yet he can only do so on the material plane. The only kind of transcendence left within the temporal realm is to endure endlessly through time. Thus, the mortal self must be made immortal by the indefinite extension of material life, whether in a biological or a cybernetic form.

Even if we grant the transhumanists success in this endeavor of life-extension, it seems unlikely they will truly succeed in the goal of a meaningful life of value and dignity. If the true source of value and meaning for life rests in a spiritually transcendent realm, all the transhumanist can accomplish is an indefinite span of perhaps pleasurable but ultimately pointless experiences. We may be able to live indefinitely long lives, with many new abilities, but what the transhumanist fails to answer is the most basic question of existence—what is its purpose? For what purpose would we want endless experiences and what will we do with our new abilities? Human mortality means that our time on earth is limited and therefore infinitely valuable. Each choice has profound meaning precisely because we have a limit, and by choosing we commit ourselves to certain ways of being to the exclusion of others. In an unlimited life, choices have no meaning, for we can be all things and try all possibilities, so choices express no real values and require no real commitment. What could such a life mean? For all the talk of progress and transcendence, transhumanists are actually only interested in escape. Clearly, from Maritain's or any Christian's perspective, so long as the transhumanists reject actual transcendence of the material realm, no matter how we may manipulate our biology, there will be no escape and no purpose or meaning in the attempt at escape.

CONTRIBUTORS

JOHN J. CONLEY, SJ, holds the Knott Chair in Philosophy and Theology at Loyola University Maryland. He is the author of *The Suspicion of Virtue: Women Philosophers in Neoclassical France* (Cornell University Press, 2002) and *Adoration and Annihilation: The Convent Philosophy of Port-Royal* (University of Notre Dame Press, 2009). Research interests include ethics, aesthetics, and modern French philosophy.

BRYAN CROSS received a B.S. in Cellular & Molecular Biology from the University of Michigan, an M.Div. from Covenant Theological Seminary, and in December of 2012 successfully defended his Philosophy Ph.D. dissertation titled "Alasdair MacIntyre on the Practice of Philosophy" at Saint Louis University. His dissertation investigates the implications of MacIntyre's philosophy regarding our understanding of both the pedagogy and practice of philosophy. He has taught philosophy at Saint Louis University, Lindenwood University, and Kenrick-Glennon Seminary. He presently lives in Saint Louis, Missouri, with his wife Carol and two daughters.

LAURA L. GARCIA is Scholar in Residence in the philosophy department at Boston College philosophy department. Her research focuses on philosophy of religion and metaphysics. Recent publications include "Preserving Persons" in *The Contribution of John Paul II to Bioethics* and "Authentic Freedom and Equality in Difference" in *Women, Sex, and the Church: A Case for Catholic Teaching,* and "A Feminist Defense of Male/Female Complementarity," forthcoming in a series of lectures presented to Xavier University's Center for Faith and Culture.

JAMES G. HANINK is Professor of Philosophy at Loyola Marymount University (Los Angeles). His interests center on metaphysics, epistemology, ethics, and political philosophy. He has contributed regularly to publications of the American Maritain Association, most recently "Does the Philosophy of Nature Need the Intuition of Being? If So, What Is It?" in *Reading the Cosmos: Nature, Science, and Wisdom*, edited by Giuseppe Butera (2011), 99–110. For a recent contribution to the Canadian Jacques Maritain Association, see his "The Metaphysics of Moral Evil: Context, Truth and Character," in *Études Maritainiennes/Maritain Studies*, XXVI: 99–109. Hanink is active in University Faculty for Life. See, for example, his "Jacques Maritain and the Embryo: A Master's Muddle," in the UFL Proceedings, *Life and Learning* XV: 249–62. He and his wife Elizabeth, long active in pro-life advocacy, have five children and four grandchildren.

REV. ANDREW JASPERS is a priest of the Archdiocese of Saint Paul and Minneapolis. He is a recent lecturer and resident instructor in philosophy and theology at Creighton University in Omaha, Nebraska. He studied philosophy and theology at Marquette University and Fordham University, and he specialized in Thomistic ethics with Fr. Joseph Koterski, SJ. He recently completed his seminary studies at the Saint Paul Seminary of the University of St. Thomas in St. Paul, Minnesota. He was ordained a priest for the Archdiocese of Saint Paul and Minneapolis in May, 2013, and currently serves as an Associate Pastor there. He is the 2012 recipient of the American Maritain Association Graduate Student Award. He is also a review editor for the *Linacre Quarterly*. He has contributed articles to the *New Catholic Encyclopedia*, the *Linacre Quarterly*, and to volumes sponsored by the American Catholic Philosophical Association, the University Faculty for Life, and the American Maritain Association.

JOHN F. X. KNASAS is a professor at the Center for Thomistic Studies, University of St. Thomas, Houston, Texas. He has published many books and articles devoted to contemporary Thomistic concerns.

STEVEN A. LONG is a Professor of Theology in the graduate theology program at Ave Maria University and a correspondent member of the Pontifical Acadamy of St. Thomas Aquinas in Rome. He has previously taught at the University of St. Thomas, St. Joseph's College, Christendom College, and the Catholic University of America. His research interests include Thomistic metaphysics and natural law; the theology of grace in relation to human freedom; the philosophy and theology of law; the nature of the object of the moral act; and particular moral issues such as the death penalty.

He has published many articles in such journals as *Communio*, *The National Catholic Bioethics Quarterly*, *Nova et Vetera*, *Revue Thomiste*, and *The Thomist*, as well as book chapters on such topics as divine providence, the death penalty and *Evangelium Vitae*, the doctrine of just war, and religious freedom. His book *The Teleological Grammar of the Moral Act* was published in 2007 by Sapientia Press. His work *Natura Pura: On the Recovery of Nature in the Doctrine of Grace* was published by Fordham University Press in 2010. He is also the author of *Analogia Entis: On the Analogy of Being, Metaphysics and the Act of Faith*, published by the University of Notre Dame Press in 2011. With the Academic Dean of the St. Paul Seminary School of Divinity at the University of St. Thomas, Dr. Christopher Thompson, he is the co-editor of a collection of essays derived from the Lilly sponsored Habits of Mind seminars, titled *Reason and the Rule of Faith* published in November 2012 by University Press of America.

ERIC MANCHESTER is a professor and chairperson for the department of Theology and Philosophy at Caldwell College in New Jersey, where he has taught since 2004. A 1989 graduate in social science and philosophy from Northwest Nazarene University, he completed a PhD in philosophy at Marquette University in 1999, focusing on early modern philosophy, while completing a dissertation on the role of free will in John Locke's philosophy of religion. He has served as president of the Wesleyan Philosophical Society, while participating regularly in the University Faculty for Life and other academic organizations. Several of his publications explore the relation of early modern thinkers, and Locke in particular, to the theology of John Wesley, as well as the relation of modern conceptions of personhood to political and economic philosophy. Select publications include "Modern Philosophy and the Economic Subversion of Natural and Ecclesial Personhood" in *Gift and Economy: Ethics, Hospitality, and the Market* (Cambridge Scholars Publishing, 2012), "Locke on Bodily Rights and the Immorality of Abortion" (*Select Proceedings for the University Faculty for Life*, 2006), and "Trinitarian Stewardship and the Limits of Capitalism and Socialism" (*Analytic Teaching: A Community Journal of Inquiry*, 2005), along with articles and reviews in *Conversations in Religion and Theology* (Wiley-Blackwell Publishers), the *Wesleyan Theological Journal*, the *International Quarterly* and *Philosophy of Religion: Introductory Essays* (Beacon Hill Press, 2003). He and his wife Paula currently reside in Lansdale, Pennsylvania.

JOHN F. MORRIS is a Professor of Philosophy in the Department of Philosophy at Rockhurst University in Kansas City, Missouri. His specialties include medieval philosophy and St. Thomas Aquinas, as well as contemporary ethics and medical/bioethics, especially natural law ethics. He has published articles on these topics in a number of journals, including *Ethics & Medics, The Modern Schoolman, Kansas Journal of Law and Public Policy, OT Practice,* and *the ASHA Leader*. He has also published essays in a variety of philosophy anthologies. Further, Morris edited his own anthology on medical ethics titled *Medicine, Health Care & Ethics: Catholic Voices* (The Catholic University Press of America, 2007), in which he also authored a chapter on stem cell research. He has given more than 100 workshops and presentations on issues related to professional ethics, medical ethics, and most specifically on the science and ethics of stem cell research. Dr. Morris's professional background includes serving on the American Occupational Therapy Association's *Commission on Standards and Ethics* (1998–2004), as well as the *Ethics & Human Values Committee* of Carondelet Health in Kansas City, Missouri (1997–2002; and 2009–2012, including being Chair of the Committee from 2011–2012). Morris also serves as an advisor to the local Bishops in the Kansas City area on the issues of stem cell research, cloning, and human embryos.

SIOBHAN NASH-MARSHALL is a Professor of Philosophy and the Mary T. Clark Chair of Christian Philosophy at Manhattanville College, where she is also chair of the philosophy department. She received her Ph.D.s from Fordham University (1998) and the Università Cattolica di Milano (1997). Her specializations are metaphysics and medieval philosophy. Her most recent publications include "Boethius's Influence on Theology and Metaphysics to the XVI c." in *Brill Companion to Boethius in the Middle Ages* (2012) and "Bugie, maledette bugie e genocidio" in *Vita e Pensiero* (2012). She is currently writing a book concerning the problem of evil, a problem on which she has published several articles in recent years, including the forthcoming, "Saint Anselm and the Problem of Evil, or on Freeing Evil from the Problem of Evil," *International Philosophical Quarterly*. She has taught a wide range of courses in philosophy, including an advanced seminar on *Boredom.*

BERNADETTE E. O'CONNOR is a professor of philosophy at the University of the Incarnate Word in San Antonio, Texas. Her research interests are in Thomistic metaphysics and Heideggerian *Seinsdenken*. She has several essays in forthcoming volumes from the American Maritain Association.

JONATHAN J. SANFORD is a Professor of Philosophy and the Assistant Vice President of Academic Affairs at Franciscan University of Steubenville. He is the editor, with Michael Gorman, of *Categories: Historical and Systematic Essays* (CUAP, 2004), and a book in Wiley-Blackwell's Philosophy and Popular Culture series, *Spider-Man and Philosophy: The Web of Inquiry* (2012). He has published on significant figures in the history of philosophy, including Aristotle, Anselm, and Scheler, and is especially interested in addressing metaphysical and ethical questions from an Aristotelian-Thomistic perspective. His research in the last five years has focused on virtue theory, and his latest manuscript, *Before Virtue: A Critical Reflection on the Contemporary Virtue Ethics Movement,* is currently under press review.

JAMES V. SCHALL, SJ, is a Professor Emeritus of Georgetown University. His books include *The Mind That Is Catholic, The Regensburg Lecture, The Modern Age, At the Limits of Political Philosophy,* and *On the Unseriousness of Human Affairs.* His *Political Philosophy and Revelation: A Catholic Reading* will be published by the Catholic University Press in 2013.

DENIS A. SCRANDIS teaches philosophy at St. John's University, Jamaica, New York. His career in academic philosophy began with a BS in Philosophy at The College of the City of New York in 1966 and a MA in philosophy from Marquette University in 1972. He was a founding member of the American Maritain Association (AMA) at Niagara University in May 1977 and is a frequent AMA presenter. Along the way he was a missile combat crew commander in the USAF and a senior financial analyst for the City of New York. While teaching health care ethics, he developed and published "A Demonstration of the Personhood of the Human Embryo," *National Catholic Bioethics Quarterly* (Winter, 2009), which received the Catholic Press Association's 2nd place prize for "Best Essay, Scholarly Magazine," 2010. His current research interests include human action theory, the foundations of ethical judgment, and the metaphysics of freedom.

MARY CATHERINE SOMMERS is Professor of Philosophy and Director of the Center for Thomistic Studies at the University of St. Thomas (Houston). She has a BA from Whitman College (1971), an MSL from the Pontifical Institute of Mediaeval Studies (1976) and an MA (1972) and PhD (1982) from the University of Toronto. Her work includes an edition of Walter Burley's *Quaestiones super librum Posteriorum* (Toronto: PIMS, 2000); articles on Burley and on Aquinas's concept of religion and religious life, e.g., "Defense and Discovery: Brother Thomas' *Contra Impugnantes*" in *Laudemus viros gloriosos: Essays in Honor of Armand Maurer CSB* (Center for Thomistic Studies Series, University of Notre Dame Press, 2007); "Marriage Vows and 'Taking up a New State'" (*Nova et Vetera,* English Edition, Vol. 7, No. 3 [2009]: 679–95); and "*Fides* and *Fidelitas* in Thomas Aquinas," to be published in the proceedings of the colloquium *Confiance, bonne foi, fidélité: la notion de "fides" dans la vie des sociétés médiévales 9 vie-xvie* (at the Institut Catholique d'Études Supérieures, October 11th, 2012). She is currently working on two articles on contemplation in Aquinas: "The 'Life' Christ Chose: Contemplation and Action in the *Summa Theologiae*" and "'Out of the Fullness of Contemplation': The Fate of Aquinas' Innovations to the Concepts of the *Vita Contemplativa* and the *Vita Activa.*" Sommers is a member of the Fellowship of Catholic Scholars, the South Central Renaissance Conference, and American Catholic Philosophical Association, where she is serving her third term on the Executive Council (1994–96; 2005–07; 2012–).

FEDERICO TEDESCO is in the PhD program in the philosophy department at the University of Verona. His research is on the Peripatetic-Thomistic philosophy of logic. He has published several reviews in *Notes et Documents* and articles concerning both epistemology and the peculiar paradoxes raised by the theory of person. He is a member of the *Institut International Jacques Maritain* of Rome.

MICHAEL D. TORRE is the recently elected President of the American Maritain Association (October, 2012). He had previously served as a Vice President of the *Institut International Jacques Maritain.* He is currently a professor of philosophy at the University of San Francisco. His book *Do Not Resist the Spirit's Call: Francisco Marín-Sola on Sufficient Grace* has just been published (in July 2013) by the Catholic University of America Press. He previously edited the American Maritain Association volume *Freedom in the Modern World: Jacques Maritain, Yves R. Simon, Mortimer J. Adler* (1989, second printing: 1990), and has contributed numerous articles to its series, of which he has been the General Editor since 2009. This book marks the eighth and final volume under his General Editorship. 2009 also saw the publication of his *God's Permission of Sin: Negative or Conditioned Decree?* by Fribourg University Press.

ROBERT VIGLIOTTI is Associate Professor of Philosophy at Rockhurst University in Kansas City, Missouri. He works primarily in the areas of phenomenology and the philosophy of technology. He has written on the early work of Martin Heidegger and his relation to neo-Scholasticism, on moral issues in the philosophy of technology, particularly concerning human genetic modification and transhumanism, and on the philosophy of film.

NIKOLAJ ZUNIC is Associate Professor of Philosophy at St. Jerome's University in Waterloo, Ontario, Canada. He earned his BA at the University of Toronto and MA and PhD at the Institute of Philosophy of the Catholic University of Leuven, Belgium. His research focuses primarily on issues in philosophical anthropology in the tradition of theistic personalism. He has published articles in the *American Catholic Philosophical Quarterly*, *The Heythrop Journal*, and *Maritain Studies/Études maritainiennes*. He is the editor of *Distinctions of Being: Philosophical Approaches to Reality*, a volume of the American Maritain Association book series just published, in June 2013. He currently serves as the Vice-President of the Canadian Jacques Maritain Association. He lives in Kitchener, Ontario, with his wife, Erin, and their six children.

INDEX OF NAMES

PUBLICATIONS OF THE AMERICAN MARITAIN ASSOCIATION

GENERAL EDITORS

Anthony O. Simon (1990–2004)

Michael D. Torre (2009–2013)

Jacques Maritain: The Man and His Metaphysics

Edited by John F. X. Knasas, 1988

ISBN 978-0-268-01205-2, (out of print)

Distributed by the University of Notre Dame Press

Freedom in the Modern World: Jacques Maritain, Yves R. Simon, Mortimer J. Adler

Edited by Michael D. Torre, 1989, Second Printing, 1990

ISBN 978-0-268-00978-6

Distributed by the University of Notre Dame Press

From Twilight to Dawn: The Cultural Vision of Jacques Maritain

Edited by Peter A. Redpath, 1990

ISBN 978-0-268-00979-3

Distributed by the University of Notre Dame Press

The Future of Thomism

Edited by Deal W. Hudson and Dennis Wm. Moran, 1992

ISBN 978-0-268-00986-1

Distributed by the University of Notre Dame Press

Jacques Maritain and the Jews
Edited by Robert Royal, 1994
ISBN 978-0-268-01193-2
Distributed by the University of Notre Dame Press

Freedom, Virtue, and the Common Good
Edited by Curtis L. Hancock and Anthony O. Simon, 1995
ISBN 978-0-268-00991-0
Distributed by the University of Notre Dame Press

Postmodernism and Christian Philosophy
Edited by Roman T. Ciapolo, 1997
ISBN 978-0-8132-0881-7
Distributed by the Catholic University of America Press

The Common Things: Essays on Thomism and Education
Edited by Daniel McInerny, 1999
ISBN 978-0-9669226-0-8
Distributed by the Catholic University of America Press

The Failure of Modernism:
The Cartesian Legacy and Contemporary Pluralism
Edited by Brendan Sweetman, 1999
ISBN 978-0-9669226-1-5
Distributed by the Catholic University of America Press

Beauty, Art, and the Polis
Edited by Alice Ramos, 2000
ISBN 978-0-9669226-2-2
Distributed by the Catholic University of America Press

Reassessing the Liberal State:
Reading Maritain's Man and the State
Edited by Timothy Fuller and John P. Hittinger, 2001
ISBN 978-0-9669226-3-9
Distributed by the Catholic University of America Press

Faith, Scholarship, and Culture in the 21st Century
Edited by Alice Ramos, and Marie I. George, 2002
ISBN 978-0-9669226-5-3
Distributed by the Catholic University of America Press

Jacques Maritain and the Many Ways of Knowing
Edited by Douglas A. Ollivant, 2002
ISBN 978-0-9669226-4-6
Distributed by the Catholic University of America Press

Truth Matters: Essays in Honor of Jacques Maritain
Edited by John G. Trapani, Jr., 2004
ISBN 978-0-9669226-6-0
Distributed by the Catholic University of America Press

The Human Person and a Culture of Freedom
Edited by Peter A. Pagan Aguiar and Terese Auer, O.P., 2009
ISBN 978-0-9669226-7-7
Distributed by the Catholic University of America Press

Maritain and America
Edited by Christopher M. Cullen, S.J. and
Joseph Allan Clair, 2009
ISBN 978-0-9669226-8-4
Distributed by the Catholic University of America Press

The Renewal of Civilization:
Essays in Honor of Jacques Maritain
Edited by Gavin T. Colvert, 2010
ISBN 978-0-9669226-9-1
Distributed by the Catholic University of America Press

The Vocation of the Catholic Philosopher:
From Maritain to John Paul II
Edited by John P. Hittinger, 2010
ISBN 978-0-9827119-0-3
Distributed by the Catholic University of America Press

Reading the Cosmos: Nature, Science, and Wisdom
Edited by Giuseppe Butera, 2011
ISBN 978-0-9827119-1-0
Distributed by the Catholic University of America Press

Distinctions of Being: Philosophical Approaches to Reality
Edited by Nikolaj Zunic, 2013
ISBN 978-0-9827119-2-7
Distributed by the Catholic University of America Press

Love and Friendship: Maritain and the Tradition
Edited by Montague Brown, 2013
ISBN 978-0-9827119-3-4
Distributed by the Catholic University of America Press

Aquinas and Maritain on Evil: Mystery and Metaphysics
Edited by James G. Hanink, 2013
ISBN 978-0-9827119-4-1
Distributed by the Catholic University of America Press

CPSIA information can be obtained at www.ICGtesting.com
Printed in the USA
BVOW08s2044130314

347631BV00004B/7/P

9 780982 711941